Using the Law

Using the Law
Practical Decision Making in Mental Health

ANDREW B. ISRAEL

New Mexico Highlands University

LYCEUM
BOOKS, INC.
Chicago, Illinois

© 2011 by Lyceum Books, Inc.

Published by
LYCEUM BOOKS, INC.
5758 S. Blackstone Avenue
Chicago, Illinois 60637
773-643-1903 fax
773-643-1902 phone
lyceum@lyceumbooks.com
www.lyceumbooks.com

6   5   4   3   2   1   10   11   12   13   14

ISBN 978-1-933478-47-0

Ethical principles of psychologists and code of conduct. © 2002 American Psychological Association. Adapted and used with permission.

Code of ethics (1996 & Supp. 2008). © 2009 National Association of Social Workers. Adapted and used with permission.

2006 code of ethics. © 2005 National Board for Certified Counselors. Adapted and used with permission.

Printed in the United States of America.

Library of Congress Cataloging-in-Publication Data

Israel, Andrew B., 1958–
Using the law : practical decision making in mental health / Andrew B. Israel.
p. cm.
Includes bibliographical references and index.
ISBN 978-1-933478-47-0 (pbk. : alk. paper)
1. Mental health personnel—Legal status, laws, etc.—United States. 2. Mental health laws—United States—Decision making. 3. Law and ethics. I. Title.
KF2910.P75I8484 2011
344.7303′22—dc22
2010020514

For Brian M. Israel

Contents

CHAPTER 1

Introduction to Law-Based Decision Making in the Mental Health Professions

The Groundwork for Making Professional Choices

The mental health professions are more alike than they are different. Although jargon, knowledge bases, and historical traditions distinguish them, they are united in their aim of assisting clients and patients with problems that often cannot be categorized within the confines of one professional discipline. The comparatively recent tendency to treat clients through multidisciplinary team approaches is one reflection of this fact.

These points notwithstanding, professional textbooks and treatises tend to be discipline specific. Moreover, practitioners searching through such tracts often have a hard time finding practical legal and ethical guidance that helps them resolve practice dilemmas involving clients and coworkers. When works do offer such guidance, they often present it in the context of standards unique to one profession. As a result, common practice dilemmas that social workers, counselors, psychologists, physicians, and nurses may share often appear to have different answers, depending on which professional code of ethics or law treatise one consults. This approach is archaic and inefficient.

In response to a significant problem, this book approaches professional choices from a unified perspective that views decision making as an orderly process that shares essential characteristics with all the mental health disciplines. More than that, it invites readers to interpret professional issues from a communitarian, rather than an individualistic, perspective. With these issues in mind, the system for addressing professional dilemmas is useful for practitioners and students in mental health settings. The book is intended as a textbook for law and ethics courses in multiple disciplines and as a reference manual for practicing social workers, counselors, and psychologists; the vignettes and case examples included use scenarios culled from those professions. In addition, ethical standards cited in the book emphasize the National Association of Social Workers Code of Ethics (the NASW Code), the National Board for Certified Counselors Code of Ethics (the NBCC Code), and the American Psychological Association's Ethical Principles of Psychologists and Code of Conduct (the APA Code). Provisions from the aforementioned professional codes are reprinted with the permission of each respective board.

An additional note is in order concerning the author's choice to reference the NBCC Code of Ethics rather than the American Counseling Association (ACA) Code. The NBCC confers advanced certification on counselors in the areas of school counseling, clinical mental health counseling, and addictions counseling. According to the NBCC, professional counselors, rather than legislators, have formulated the practice standards adopted for these certification areas; therefore, they are intended to hold counselors with advanced certification to the highest levels of professional accountability. Therefore, for the purposes of this book, all case examples featuring professional counselors assume that each counselor involved has advanced NBCC certification. Although the NBCC and ACA codes are similar in many areas, counselors are encouraged to review the ACA Code for further guidance concerning the ethical standards established for professional counselors.

Using Law and Professional Ethics in Decision Making: Advantages and Challenges

Despite the inclusion in this book of much discussion addressing ethical principles and cultural and regional factors that guide professional decision making, at its heart, this book is a legal reference. This is to say that the book introduces a law-based system for analyzing mental health practice dilemmas in a pragmatic way. The rationale for this approach, as later chapters detail, is the contention that applying elements of essential legal reasoning to common practice situations is both advisable and feasible on a routine basis for mental health providers who lack formal training in the law.

Most decision-making models in mental health and in the business world regard law as outside the scope of the ethical decision-making process (Christensen, 2008). In fact, Christensen (2008) suggests that the law is most often regarded in ethical decision-making models as external to the process of making decisions in ethics-based approaches. Indeed, textbooks abound with the introduction of ethics-based decision-making models, rarely including a legal analysis in the framework of the model. This exclusion is unfortunate given the interdependence of law and ethical codes, a point expounded on later in this book. Indeed, it is clear that many ethical decision-making models rely on cognitive moral development theory, a hypothesis that suggests that law itself is the compass most individuals rely on in developing their own sense of moral and intellectual development. This development is essential to the formulation of an overview of moral precepts that are vital to the success of any decision-making approach (Christensen, 2008). Law is an integral aspect of any decision-making model because it forms at least part of the basis of the moral, experiential, and social learning that individuals engage in during their lifetimes to form a set of values or a personal, moral center. It is that moral center that lies at the heart of professional ethical codes, and the development of ethical standards in the codes can be clearly linked to a shared set of moral values developed in each profession. It is interesting to note, therefore, that law is often an unidentified but vital ingredient in the creation of professional ethical codes.

Another indication of the interrelationship between law and ethics is natural law theory (Stanford University, 2010). An integral part of the precepts forming the foundation for the U.S. Constitution, this theory views natural law as consisting of the principle of practical rationality. Thus, according to natural law theory, all persons tend to possess an "intrinsic directedness toward the various good that the natural law enjoins us to pursue" (Stanford University, 2010, n.p.), and this includes in some but not all interpretations the recognition that natural law is a product of divine providence. Just as important, natural law assumes that its precepts are knowable to human beings. For those natural law theorists who look to practical, rational discourse and human behavioral tendencies to understand the development of moral precepts, there is a clear line of connection between natural law and the development of ethics and ethical codes.

Having examined the interrelationship between law and ethics, the author must note that the system for decision making presented in this book introduces several basic, key, common law principles into the framework proposed. The aim of doing this is to acknowledge the teachings of the scholarly references and arguments cited previously; it is important and necessary to include legal analysis in the assessment of mental health practice dilemmas, and indeed, the introduction of this analysis can make practice decision making more effective, efficient, and complete.

In the course of introducing legal concepts to develop a framework for professional decision making, the author has selected and identified several key common law—or court-created—concepts that judges have considered, analyzed, and developed over the course of hundreds of years in the Anglo-American legal system. Thus, the concepts presented have the benefit of having been tested before courts in the context of innumerable, changing factual patterns over the years. Thus tested, one of the essential values of these concepts is their flexibility and adaptability to unique practice dilemmas. However, although the framework presented in this book plainly identifies the interdependence of legal and ethical principles in the assessment of mental health dilemmas, and further presents the case for a law-based strategy for decision making, it is important to note that no argument is made here that a legal analysis alone will adequately address all of the permutations and combinations of the myriad practice dilemmas that exist. Stated differently, the author does not suggest that a law-based decision-making framework will function fully and effectively without consideration of ethical, cultural, and pragmatic considerations. Moreover, it is not argued here that, by noting the interrelationship of law and ethics, the two concepts mean exactly the same thing. This important point requires particular attention.

As Santa Clara University's (2010) Mark Kula Center for Applied Ethics aptly and straightforwardly describes the difference between ethics and law:

> Ethics is not following the law. A good system of law does incorporate many ethical standards, but law can deviate from what is ethical. Law can become ethically corrupt, as some totalitarian regimes have made it. Law can be a function of power alone and designed to serve the interests of narrow groups. Law may have a difficult time designing or enforcing standards in some important areas, and may be slow to address new problems. (n.p.)

The law-based decision making proposed in this book seeks to protect against the dangers outlined in the foregoing quote by avoiding the mistake of espousing adherence to law in all its countless forms. Rather, the approach introduced here urges practitioners to identify those essential and helpful legal principles that enjoy broad support in our society and guide the basic professional relationship between mental health providers and their clients.

In contrast to law, ethics can be roughly characterized as a set of behavioral benchmarks that tell members of a society how to behave in various life situations. Although a complete review of ethical principles and decision-making approaches based on ethical analysis is plainly beyond the scope of this book, it is possible to identify the sources from which ethics derive. From the standpoint of professional ethics, ethics are most often culled from the values espoused in a particular profession. Those values stem from many key philosophical perspectives and objectives in a given profession, including, on occasion and as earlier stated, legal precepts. In the mental health field, beneficence, or the goal of promoting a client's best interests, is a key inspiration for many ethical standards. Utilitarianism, or the aim of doing the most good and least harm for clients, is another theoretical paradigm that guides the creation of ethical principles. Especially in the health and mental health professions, individual liberty, privacy, and the importance of maintaining the freedom of the client's choice are central values that, in certain measure, reach as far back as the teachings of Hippocrates more than two thousand years ago. Another ancient value voiced in modern professional codes is virtue—the concept that practitioners should behave in a manner that reflects professional honesty, competence, fairness, and integrity.

If one studies the professional codes of ethics outlined in the appendix of this book, it will be apparent that there is much similarity and overlap in the values and ethical standards voiced in the social work, counseling, and psychology professions. This is hardly surprising, as each of these professions can be regarded as a historical outgrowth of even older professions, such as medicine and law. For that reason, professional codes of ethics address comparable situations that occur in the various fields of mental health practice. It is also interesting to note that professional codes of ethics do not ordinarily rank-order the importance of the values and ethical standards contained in them. It is fair to say that this tendency stems from an understandable reluctance on the part of the drafters of professional ethical codes to single out any particular value as more important than others addressed in the codes. Indeed, one would be hard pressed to conclude that any particular value, such as beneficence toward clients, is more or less vital than any other value, such as professional virtue or utilitarianism. It can certainly be said that it is futile to apply a measure to any of these philosophical paradigms to assess its relative "importance."

At the same time, however, it is also fair to conclude that the failure of professional ethical codes to impose a rank-order on individual principles may be historically understandable but also renders the codes difficult for users to employ as references in the pursuit of ordinary decision making. Some ethicists have responded to this assessment by noting that the whole concept of depending on ethical codes for decision making creates an overreliance on codes, which are usually expressed as prescriptions, proscriptions, and outright injunctions against certain types of behavior. As McGrath (1994) has expressed it, "Much of our society's concept of ethics is a variant on the idea of obedience to authority" (p. 27). The reason for this dependence on rigid codes of ethics, as McGrath sees it, is that decision makers "are so anxious to have closure and certainty that [they] will gladly accept any ideas, no matter how convoluted or narrow, to settle . . . questions" (p. 46).

In contrast to seeking out a commitment to a set of prescriptions or proscriptions defined in an ethical code, McGrath (1994) suggests that decision makers can and must undergo a process of ethical maturation during which time they learn to incorporate sources of reference for decision making into a personal system for addressing practice dilemmas that recognizes the strengths and weaknesses of all ethical codes and treatises. McGrath suggests that, through this process, decision makers can become aware of and educated in the rules that govern professional practice, but they can also accept responsibility for their own decision making. As McGrath puts it, "the monumental step is for all active or aspiring participants in the process to freely discuss possibilities and to consider, in a strictly nonjudgmental manner, the implications of axioms and logical rules" (p. 47).

The most important point that McGrath's comments underscore is that there is no such thing as a foolproof decision-making system, whether it is founded on the law, on a series of ethical standards, or on both. Every analytic framework sets forth important criteria against which practice dilemmas can be evaluated, but in the final analysis, the job of the decision maker is to apply appropriate principles to the problem at hand, a task that requires a least a modicum of subjective interpretation and thought.

With the foregoing discussion in mind, the author's aim is to create a decision-making framework based on a consideration of essential legal principles. The most important aspect of the proposed framework outlined in this book is the flexibility built into a system based first and foremost on a review of several key common law principles. The author's contention is that this flexibility provides an opportunity for decision makers to assess their own practice dilemmas on the basis of a review of the most fundamental of these common law doctrines, with a further invitation to mental health practitioners to supplement this review with relevant ethical, regional, cultural, and pragmatic considerations. Again, this book's focus is on identifying common law principles and highlighting their application in mental health practice. It is the author's goal to provide a useful system for the everyday analysis of practice dilemmas, but it is also his intent that this system serve as a helpful complement to the ethics-based models on which many decision-making systems are founded.

Note about Terminology

The phrase "mental health professions" is meant to convey occupations whose primary aim is to enhance the mental health and social functioning of clients and patients through direct services; these professions include social work, counseling, and psychology, among others. Professionals trained in these disciplines often provide additional support services to their clients and to the public in general that advance basic survival needs. These services include, among others, welfare and public assistance; child welfare investigations; probation services; community organizing; and social program research, development, and administration. As listed here, these forms of support are referred to cumulatively as human services.

Note about Vignettes and Case Examples

This book includes three brief vignettes and twenty-seven case examples that demonstrate the application of a decision-making system for mental health professionals. Although actual events have inspired several of the scenarios, the characters and interventions described in the scenarios are entirely fictitious and not intended to portray any real person, alive or deceased. Nevertheless, every effort has been made to ensure factual accuracy in the book's depiction of current national and regional social issues, the characteristics of geographical regions, and the actual problems that diverse ethnic and racial groups experience in the United States.

Tools Necessary for Effective Decision Making

Why present a book on applied law and decision making? Mental health professionals and students alike understand that making practice decisions involves consideration of the legal, ethical, moral, regional, cultural, and personal factors that affect practice. The decision maker who consults these various reference sources for guidance faces the problem of choosing an appropriate legal or ethical principle, or perhaps a more subjective consideration, on the basis of its apparent applicability to the problem at hand. Even worse, the decision maker consulting law treatises is likely to find broad, technical surveys of legislation and court decisions that offer little help in resolving everyday practice problems.

Applied law is law that is usable and applicable to the solving of daily problems in the mental health professions. Decision makers are more likely to use law that is simply explained and practical to apply as a primary source of reference in addressing common practice dilemmas.

Consider, for example, the case of a child protective social worker investigating the possibility of medical neglect in a Hispanic family in northern New Mexico. The professional fears that a child is being denied appropriate conventional medical treatment for asthma in favor of a faith-based remedy that employs the use of *curanderos* (traditional healers) and herbal therapy (Applewhite, 1995; Harris, 1998; Keegan, 1996; Luna, 2003; Turner, 1996). Is this a ground for removing the child from the home? To address this question, the professional may consider legal principles (including the law governing the professional's responsibility to protect vulnerable children), ethical standards (the right of the family to make its own choices concerning health care), regional and cultural standards (the long-standing acceptability of traditional forms of medical treatment in some communities), and personal standards (e.g., how the professional's own ideology views the treatment provided to this child).

The decision maker considering the preceding problem may look to a number of reference sources, including law and ethics textbooks, professional ethical codes, and public agency policies, to make a choice about what action to take. The professional is likely to discover quickly that a variety of scholarly textbooks and manuals exist on the market today, and each tends to focus singularly on the subjects of law and ethics as separate disciplines. Moreover, the professional may find a significant amount of overlap or even contradiction among each of the principles that the reference sources present. At this point, both the contradictory answers suggested in these textbooks and their failure to address the big picture—what is the best resolution to this problem for all parties involved?—may overwhelm the professional.

In reality, making a decision concerning the foregoing dilemma depends on the professional's ability to integrate and apply legal, ethical, cultural, and regional considerations in a specific order that maximizes the likelihood that both the professional's and the client's obligations and interests are addressed fully and simultaneously. This book presents a strategy for doing just that.

Organization of This Book

This book surveys basic legal principles governing practice decisions in the mental health professions. More than that, however, it presents the subjects of law and ethics not as separate disciplines but as related and interdependent, with each one having a role in guiding professionals to make effective and sensitive practice decisions. Toward that end, this book invites practitioners and students to consider the legal and ethical aspects of professional practice in a ranked order, and it introduces a decision-making framework whose primary aim is to assist in addressing practice dilemmas in a structured and unified way.

In addition to surveying legal principles that affect practice, the decision-making framework and supporting materials teach a law-based strategy for reaching informed practice decisions in a regional and cultural context. This diversity model uses illustrative practice examples that emphasize multicultural clients, communities, and practice situations throughout the United States. The reason for this emphasis is the emerging importance of diversity as a major factor in the interplay among law, ethics, and cultural context. A few words are warranted here concerning the centrality of this point in this book. The old-fashioned notion of the United States as a melting pot does a disservice to the impact on our society of countless cultural traditions that stem from centuries-old Hispanic, African American, Native American, Asian, and other ethnic practices and beliefs. These influences not only play a major role in shaping and contributing to contemporary civilization but also directly bear on the role of those factors in the successful design and delivery of health, mental health, and social services in the United States.

A compelling demographic factor illustrates the primacy of the preceding point: The number of states in the United States that are described as minority-majority—meaning that the number of minority persons (i.e., self-described on U.S. Census questionnaires as Hispanic, African American, Native American, Asian and/or Pacific Islander, or other nonwhite classification) exceeds 50 percent of the state's overall population—is plainly on the rise (Gutiérrez, 2007). Hawaii plainly has met this criterion since its statehood in 1959. More recently, with its burgeoning Hispanic population, New Mexico became a minority-majority state in approximately 2000, when the Hispanic population reached about 42 percent of the total, and the combined minority population, including Hispanic, Native American, and African American groups, exceeded 50 percent (Bureau of the Census Staff, 2001). California and Texas have followed suit as minority-majority states, and the U.S. Census now indicates that in at least three additional states— Nevada, Georgia, and Maryland—the overall percent of non-Hispanic white residents has fallen below 60 percent (Gutiérrez, 2007). New Mexico stands perhaps as the best example of how changing demographics internally represent a harbinger for the United States as a whole: with cultural traditions predating Columbus, the state's 1912 constitution included protections, primarily to Spanish speakers, that have encouraged the preservation of some of those traditions. Indeed, New Mexico presently leads the nation with the greatest percentage—more than 30 percent—of Spanish speakers (Gutiérrez, 2007). All of the states cited previously provide examples of how rural and urban population areas have developed thriving, diverse populations that increasingly represent a microcosm of the United States in the twenty-first century.

With the preceding points in mind, the decision-making framework presented here is applicable for use in a variety of practice contexts and with a diversity of client populations. In addition, although the readings emphasize social work, counseling, and psychology practice, the framework is easily adaptable for use in practice in any of the mental health professions. For this reason, appropriate provisions of the codes of ethics of several such professions are presented.

The materials and case examples included in this book are intended to assist practitioners and students in accomplishing four goals.

Goal 1: Develop a Strategy for Making Effective Professional Practice Decisions

As noted, this book introduces a decision-making framework that invites practitioners and students to make practice decisions based on an ordered consideration of both legal and ethical standards. Chapter 2 describes the construction of the framework, and the appendix provides a summary of the framework itself. The terms *law* and *ethics* are defined and their inter-relationship explained in more detail later. In the meantime, to make the most effective use of the framework, it is important for practitioners and students to realize from the outset that both legal principles (e.g., informed consent, confidentiality) and ethical standards (e.g., the social worker's responsibility to seek social justice, the counselor's duty to be aware of client stereotyping and more direct forms of discrimination) may affect the resolution of a practice dilemma. In addition, it is important to note that the order in which one considers these principles will influence the decision. Various practice dilemmas to which the framework will be applied illustrate this concept.

Goal 2: Gain Knowledge of Basic Legal Principles Associated with Common Mental Health Practice Areas

As a primary step in making practice decisions, mental health professionals must have a sense of the more overarching legal standards governing the rights and obligations conferred on members of our society. These principles, such as those bestowed by the U.S. Constitution (e.g., the right to due process and equal protection) and by the legislative and common law of our states (e.g., informed consent, confidentiality), govern professional practice and impose specific responsibilities on all providers that offer services to the public. Developing an understanding of these principles is perhaps the single most important step in constructing an overall strategy for addressing everyday practice dilemmas, as will be demonstrated when the decision-making framework is introduced and applied to specific problems. Furthermore, an understanding of basic legal principles governing practice serves to make the mental health professional more effective as a fully informed agent for social change.

The overarching legal principles that are discussed in chapters 3–8 include the following:

- Duty to practice reasonably competently
- Informed consent
- Identification of the primary client
- Specific legal responsibilities of public agency professionals
- Constitutional principles influencing practice
- Confidentiality
- Completion of a legal inventory
- Ability to stay abreast of state, local, and agency responsibilities governing practice

Goal 3: Understand the Purposes and Limitations of Professional Codes of Ethics

Professional codes of ethics have both their purposes and limitations, as will be more fully explored later. The interrelationship between law and ethics is an area of confusion for practitioners and students alike, and this differentiation will be described as well. One of the commonest pitfalls for decision makers facing practice dilemmas is the tendency to attempt to apply professional codes of ethics without considering the impact of legal standards governing the same dilemmas. The result may be that a decision maker makes an ethically "correct" decision that violates the law. The decision-making framework introduced here presents a system for avoiding this problem. The appropriate use of professional codes of ethics and subjective considerations in decision making is more thoroughly addressed later in this book. Although primary emphasis is placed on the NASW, NBCC, and

APA codes, the strategy the framework suggests applies for mental health professionals bound by alternate codes.

Goal 4: Make Decisions in a Cultural and Regional Context

Legal principles are important but not exclusive sources of information in making professional decisions. Sometimes their explanation requires consideration of regional and cultural norms used to interpret these standards. For example, taking the *curandero* example again, the law may permit the use of alternative healing methods if practiced according to recognized religious practices in a jurisdiction. Furthermore, there are occasions—perhaps many of them—when neither the law nor any professional code of ethics addresses a specific practice dilemma. In such instances, cultural and regional norms may attain a dominant role in guiding the decision maker to the most effective practice decision. This book includes numerous examples of the use of cultural and regional context in decision making to demonstrate the manner in which the framework treats the consideration of cultural and regional issues. For the reasons previously addressed, the diverse communities throughout the United States offer rich practice examples illustrating the framework's use. Although the practice scenarios selected focus on situations experienced in a particular region or by an individual ethnic group, the essential strategy of this diversity-inspired approach is almost universally applicable.

CHAPTER 2

Constructing a Law-Based Framework for Professional Decision Making

Sources of Information for Making Professional Decisions

What sources of information do mental health practitioners ordinarily rely on to make practice decisions? To answer this question, consider the situation of a mental health provider in private practice offering counseling services to a variety of walk-in clients. Suppose further that one particular client has come to seek the therapist's assistance in treating his depression. During a counseling session, the client tells the therapist that he feels guilty over his commission of a bank robbery some fifteen years earlier, which the police have never solved. How should this client's revelation guide the therapist's clinical conduct with the client? What decisions are to be made from a professional standpoint relative to this client's treatment? The therapist's personal sense of morality, professional ideology, or religious conviction may suggest instinctively that the client is to be condemned and that the therapist is morally obliged to take some action to ensure his prosecution. Clinical training, however, may compel the therapist to continue to counsel the individual to ascertain what mental health issues, if any, may be driving this person's revelation. Moreover, pragmatic considerations may lead the therapist to believe that there is little the therapist can do realistically in the way of informing any civic authority without the client's additional cooperation; for example, the savvy therapist may reasonably fear that the client will deny having ever told the story as soon as the therapist reveals it to the authorities.

Finding that personal feelings regarding this client are somewhat conflicting, the therapist might then seek guidance from a more formal authority. Specifically, a natural step would be to seek out the professional code of ethics governing the therapist's mental health field. In the case of a social worker, this would mean the National Association of Social Workers Code; a certified counselor, including a marriage and family therapist or other licensed mental health therapist, would likely examine the National Board for Certified Counselors Code; a clinical psychologist would consult the American Psychological Association's Ethical Principles of Psychologists and Code of Conduct.

Reviewing any of the previously mentioned codes for guidance in addressing this dilemma, one might reasonably reach the conclusion that the therapist should maintain confidentiality of all the client's statements unless there are "compelling professional reasons" (NASW Code, ethical standard 1.07c), a need to prevent "clear and imminent danger to the client or others" (NBCC Code, section B4), or it is necessary to "protect the client/patient, [professional], or others from harm" (APA Code, ethical standard 4.05b), thus making it appropriate to reveal them. Perhaps the present situation might constitute such a "compelling" reason, but this conclusion would rely at least in part on the therapist's subjective interpretation of the rather broad language used in the standard. Delving further into any of these codes, one might discover the professional obligation to help clients set their own personal goals and identify their own paths in life (NASW Code, ethical standard 1.02, governing self-determination), the professional's burden to respect the integrity and promote the welfare of the client (NBCC Code, section B1), or the requirement that the professional take reasonable steps to avoid harming clients and/or patients and others with whom the professional works (APA Code, ethical standard 3.04). Perhaps the therapist might justifiably observe that any of these duties would conflict with some of the other choices the therapist has already considered.

Delving still further into an appropriate code, the therapist might uncover more ethical standards that admonish the professional to promote even broader societal aims, such as the commitment to seek social justice (NASW Code, ethical standard 6.01), the prevention of exploitation of individuals and groups (NASW Code, ethical standard 6.04d), the protection of public confidence in professional practice (NBCC Code, section A13), and the minimization of harm where it is foreseeable and unavoidable (APA Code, ethical standard 3.04). All these responsibilities certainly might have some application in the present scenario.

How can the therapist resolve all these seemingly inconsistent obligations? A review of any of the aforementioned codes quickly reveals that the ethical responsibilities they outline are not rank ordered, so they do not provide much guidance in the way of establishing which standards take precedence. Therefore, it may be perplexing to try to get clear direction from an ethical code on the issue of what precisely to do in this scenario.

Bewildered by the array of possible issues to consider, the therapist in this example might decide to contact a personal or agency attorney to learn more about the applicable legal responsibilities in the state in which the therapist practices. The therapist might learn from the attorney that a relevant licensing law requires professionals, including psychotherapists, social workers, counselors, psychologists, and other mental health providers, to keep all their clients' communications confidential, except when they represent a threat of future violence or criminal activity. The attorney could reasonably suggest that, on the basis of this law, the therapist's client is entitled to keep his past conduct a secret in the context of his psychotherapy and to hold the therapist to a bond of confidentiality. In other words, the attorney might advise that the therapist is legally obligated to take no formal action concerning the client's statements.

This may be the technically correct legal answer, but is it also the right practice decision? Put differently, is the answer consistent with the therapist's clinical and therapeutic goals? The therapist's attorney might suggest that it is, because if one violates the law, jail is the outcome. Not swayed by this pragmatic argument, the therapist might express a sense of idealistic frustration to the attorney. The attorney is likely to respond that the law is based on good public policy, which suggests that this client, like all clients who seek out the help of mental health professionals, would be far less likely to have done so without the implicit understanding that what he tells to the professional is private and must not go beyond the consultation room. Thus, the attorney might suggest that the therapist be thankful that the client has felt secure enough to seek consultation, as now at least the opportunity exists to help him work on all the issues that have driven him to seek assistance. Without this law, in all probability, the unfortunate story the client has revealed would never have been brought to the surface in the first place. Perhaps, the attorney might counsel, continued clinical work is possible with this client in a manner that upholds the law but that also fulfills some of the objectives of applicable professional standards.

Does the "right" legal answer inevitably point the way toward the best clinical practice decision in all professional dilemmas? As the preceding scenario suggests, and for reasons that the next section more fully explores, assessing the legal impact of a professional dilemma at the very least leads to a more effective and efficient consideration of the range of practice options available to the decision maker. Therefore, the legal assessment is an inseparable part of thorough professional decision making.

A Law-Based Strategy

Defining the Law

As noted, the foregoing scenario suggests that seeking out the "right" legal answer to a clinical practice dilemma eliminates some of the confusing alternatives one may face in attempting to resolve a frustrating professional problem. This is not an accident. Much law, including law governing practice in the mental health professions, such as the requirement to maintain client confidentiality, is based on at least some sound, rational basis and presumptively reflects the most basic, shared values of society. For this reason, the operating definition of *law* applied here is a binding set of shared values in a community, the community being a city, state, nation, or other politically organized jurisdiction that unites people by language, culture, religion, tribal affiliation, or custom.

Defining law as a set of shared values emphasizes the communitarian function—and not simply the binding nature—of law and lawmaking (Etzioni, 1998; Tam, 1998; van Seters, 2006; Watson, 1999). *Communitarianism* in the present context is intended to convey the idea that the most effective and socially just practices are the result of cooperative inquiry, a search for common values, and the recognition that all people in a community share some mutual responsibility for their collective good (Tam, 1998; van Seters, 2006; Watson, 1999). Viewed in this light, no practice choice can be truly personal, because each decision inevitably has consequences that affect others. Unlike the values represented by individual preferences and political ideologies, or articulated in particular codes of ethics, most members of a community, not merely one individual or profession, share the values the law advances. Understood in this way, the law can be regarded as a means to attain the greatest good for the most members of a community. In addition, this *utilitarian* interpretation of law, when incorporated into an overall decision-making process, requires that all practice decisions be made, at least to some extent, from a communitywide, regional, or even global perspective, not simply from a personal or professional one (Conry & Beck-Dudley, 1996; Murphy, 2001; Roberts & Reich, 2002; Shaw, 1998).

What about law that does not reflect shared community values? A prime example of this problem may exist today in the Indian territory of the United States, where tribes that have traditionally defined their communal values through an unwritten religious and social tradition are increasingly finding this customary law displaced by federal and state legislation (see, e.g., the Indian Civil Rights Act [ICRA] of 1968). The assimilationist aim of this lawmaking may be a symptom of the overall trend toward the increasing definition and codification of new laws by Congress and state legislatures (Callan, 2005). This tendency may well reflect legislators' growing willingness to use lawmaking as a means of social control in a society that seems ever more out of control. Under the definition of law used in this book, a credible argument can be made that at least some of this law is invalid, unconstitutional, or both.

What, then, can be done about law that fails to reflect the shared values of a community? Mental health professionals keenly interested in the pursuit of social justice are well aware of the myriad examples of oppressive, racist, sexist, ageist, and homophobic law that has existed historically. Often these examples are cited in support of the premise that all law is invalid, to be mistrusted, and inherently antithetical to the values associated with social change. This almost-nihilistic political ideology is not pragmatic because it tends to ignore the vast body of law that is both useful in ordinary life and professional practice and representative of the shared values of a community. (For a more detailed assessment of the impact of ambivalence toward the law and the effect of this ambivalence on society, see Stauffer, 2007.) Much of this law is very helpful in the daily resolution of professional practice dilemmas. The legal principle governing confidentiality in mental health settings, as already cited, is just one example of this type of law. The decision-making framework presented in this book summarizes this principle and other basic legal doctrines in a usable format.

As to laws that are unjust and oppressive, the framework offers a strategy to identify and correct them in a way that enforces the ideal that law should be presumed valid—a presumption that is necessary to promote full citizen participation in a collective society. It also underscores the point that, as far as decision making in the mental health professions is concerned, individual choices should be considered in the context of the shared values of a community.

Step 1: Law in Decision Making

As suggested by the bank-robber dilemma discussed earlier, basic legal standards such as the principle of confidentiality are helpful in resolving mental health practice problems. At what stage in the decision-making process should decision makers consider and apply these standards? The answer becomes apparent if the definition and purposes of law are borne in mind. These can be summarized in a way that offers three basic arguments for the proposition that a thorough review of applicable law should be the first step in making any practice decision in the mental health professions. Each is considered individually.

Communitarian and/or Utilitarian

The "right" legal answer to a problem, when sought and considered first, best leads the professional to consider possible answers to a practice dilemma in a manner that ensures consideration of those values most important to the professional's community. This strategy maximizes the likelihood that the decision maker makes a choice that seems "right" while increasing the benefit and limiting the likelihood of risk to all those whom the problem immediately affects.

Effectiveness and/or Efficiency

The "right" legal answer to a problem, when considered first, best ensures that the decision maker consider a range of options in a more expeditious manner. When a professional dilemma has a specific legal impact, application of the appropriate legal principle minimizes the need to investigate and rank other sources of information and narrows the gamut of practice choices facing the decision maker.

Practical

Following the law first is the best strategy to stay out of trouble. This may seem merely a banal consideration to anyone who has not had to contemplate the consequences of a professional decision while sitting in a jail cell. Nevertheless, for law to be binding, as that word is used in the definition of *law* presented here, there must be consequences for its infraction. These consequences, including civil litigation and criminal prosecution, are the focus of later discussion.

Additional support for the idea that mental health professionals should first consider the applicability of legal principles in evaluating practice dilemmas comes from professional ethical codes themselves. All such codes admonish professionals about the primacy of the law, although they sometimes do so in an oblique manner. For example, the NASW Code, in ethical standard 1.01 ("Commitment to Clients"), advises social workers that "specific legal obligations may on limited occasions supersede the loyalty owed clients." The APA Code, ethical standard 1.02, rather fancifully and vaguely advises psychologists to resolve conflicts with the law by "mak[ing] known their commitment to the Ethics Code and tak[ing] steps to resolve the conflict." In a 2010 revision to the same ethical standard, the APA removed a provision appearing in earlier versions of the standard that had advised psychologists, "If the conflict is irresolvable via such means, psychologists may adhere to the requirements of the law, regulations, or other governing legal authority." This revision now seems to leave psychologists without any specific guidance as to when to adhere to the law. The APA Code does, however, direct use of the law for guidance with respect to the issues of confidentiality (ethical standard 4.01). Section A13 of the NBCC Code urges professional counselors to "avoid behavior that is clearly in violation of accepted moral and legal standards"; it expresses no additional concern that there might not be any such thing as "accepted moral standards." The indirect language used in these codes may reflect mainly each profession's explicit emphasis on defining a unique set of core values; carving out some professional turf for each discipline may be an implicit objective, as well. In any event, all professional licensing organizations, including those governing the major mental health disciplines, regard their members as owing an obligation to their communities that supersedes any profession-specific consideration.

Promotion of Diversity

Among the essential legal principles that are the focus of this book are due process and equal protection, both emanating from the U.S. Constitution and each having a specific impact on the way mental health professionals make practice decisions. These principles protect the right of diverse people to be treated fairly despite their racial, gender, or religious differences. By elevating the examination of these constitutional protections to a place of first importance in decision making, professionals ensure that they raise diversity considerations to a preeminent role in the resolution of practice dilemmas instead of keeping them merely as an aspirational ideal to review along with other ethical and ideological factors.

In light of the preceding arguments, the decision-making framework requires the user to first consider the applicability of some basic legal principles governing mental health professionals and their clients in any practice decision. Toward that end, the book outlines a series of essential principles, including the duty to practice reasonably competently (chapter 3), the duty to seek informed consent (chapter 4), the duty to identify the primary client (chapter 5), the duty to treat clients and coworkers with due process and equal protection (chapter 6), the duty to maintain confidentiality (chapter 7), and the legal inventory (chapter 8), all of which summarize the most important legal standards affecting mental health professionals in practice. Note that the six essential principles describe the basic elements of all professional relationships and are virtually universal in their application in the United States. For this reason, this book uses court decisions and legislation from a number of jurisdictions to explain the scope of these principles. Readers, though, are discouraged from allowing the book to serve as a substitute for the seeking of legal advice concerning applicable standards in the state and community in which they practice.

Step 2: Using Professional Codes of Ethics

As the bank-robber example suggests, the law is an appropriate starting point for making practice decisions. It is not, however, the end of the story. In many practice dilemmas, one may find after reviewing applicable law that there simply is no clearly defined legal principle governing the outcome. In such situations, mental health professionals need to look to more discipline-specific sources for guidance and assistance in making practice decisions. Of these, they most often use professional codes of ethics, such as the NASW Code, the NBCC Code, and the APA Code. Indeed, codes of ethics are often the first sources of enlightenment sought out by decision makers concerned with resolving problems consistently with the ethical principles advanced in their own profession. Why is this not the most effective strategy for making professional decisions? To answer this question, it is necessary to explore the nature and uses of ethical codes.

Codes of ethics present sets of practice standards that direct the professional as to what is the "correct" thing to do in an area of practice. Here, the concept of professional ethics must be distinguished from the term *ethics* as it is used both in common parlance and in scholarly discussion: *Ethics* frequently is used in a general sense to describe moral values or ideals that individual members of society subscribe to in their personal lives. In comparison to this terminology, *professional ethics* describes a set of enforceable practice standards that support the values and aspirations existing in a profession. Just as the law binds the members of an entire community and enforces the shared values of its members, ethical codes intend to promote the ideals of a single professional discipline. The law is enforceable against members of a community through civil or criminal remedies, and similarly, ethical standards are enforceable through disciplinary action against the professional who has violated them.

To demonstrate the relationship between professional ethics and values, consider the APA Code's principle C, "Professional and Scientific Responsibility." Among other things, this provision asserts the value that psychologists should "uphold professional standards of conduct." This aspirational ideal is enforced through a variety of binding rules and expectations, including ethical standard 1.04, which requires psychologists to practice "only within the boundaries of their competence." Similarly, promoting the "dignity and worth of the person" is an oft-stated social work value expressed in the preamble to the NASW Code. Among a number of rules that support this ideal in the NASW Code, ethical standards 1.09 and 2.07 sustain this goal by mandating that social workers refrain from sexual relationships with clients and employees under their supervision.

In contrast to legal standards, ethical principles vary from profession to profession because different disciplines advance differing internal goals. As an example, all attorneys, under the American Bar Association's (2004) *Model Rules of Professional Conduct*, share the professional value that encourages them to take "whatever lawful and ethical measures are required to vindicate a client's cause" and to act "with zeal in advocacy upon the client's behalf" (rule 1.3, comment 1). This value is enforced by an ethical standard mandating lawyers to represent their clients "with reasonable diligence and promptness" (rule 1.3). Correspondingly, social work values as expressed in the NASW Code, ethical standard 6.01, articulate the somewhat-broader aspiration that social workers have a duty to represent not only their clients' interests but also the "general welfare of society." Does this difference in the expression of professional values by two distinct disciplines mean, for example, that a public defender who defends a murder suspect vigorously and aggressively—knowing that the client is guilty—might be upholding legal values while contravening the values of social workers? Can the practice decision to advocate strenuously for a client be the "right" practice decision for the lawyer but the "wrong" one for a social worker?

The answer to both of those questions is possibly yes, which underscores one of the reasons codes of ethics are not always helpful as the first step in a decision-making strategy. Codes of ethics advance the interests of a particular profession without necessarily promoting all the shared values of a community as expressed in its public laws. Moreover, professional codes of ethics ordinarily are enforceable through disciplinary action only by an individual licensing body against one of its own members. In an age in which multidisciplinary practice strategies have been adopted for the delivery of mental health and human services by medical, psychological, child welfare, and even legal agencies, approaching a practice decision by primary reference to a professional code of ethics may work contrary to the interests both of the client and the professional.

A general weakness of ethical codes is that they often are better at articulating overarching and general, aspirational ideals (i.e., values) than they are at setting standards that prescribe or proscribe particular behavior (i.e., ethics). Thus, the NASW Code broadly espouses the promotion of client well-being (ethical standard 1.01); the development of people, communities, and environments (ethical standard 6.01); and the advancement of client self-determination (ethical standard 1.02) as social work aspirations but offers only a handful of enforceable standards in the pursuit of those ideals.

ample, as already noted, the NASW Code clearly proscribes conduct specifically in the case of social worker–client sexual relationships. Interestingly, in the very portion of the NASW Code in which ethical standards are set forth ("Introduction to Ethical Standards"), the code warns readers that only "some of the standards that follow are enforceable guidelines for professional conduct, and some are aspirational." The introduction goes on to explain that "the extent to which each standard is enforceable is a matter of professional judgment to be exercised by those responsible for reviewing alleged violations of ethical standards." This extraordinary lack of certainty by NASW itself as to the binding quality of its own "standards" raises serious questions about whether any relied on in disciplinary proceedings against social workers would be enforceable in subsequent litigation by the subjects of such proceedings.

The reason for the cautionary stance by NASW regarding enforceable standards may be that the framers of the NASW Code have remained somewhat ambivalent about how they envision the code's purpose (Woodcock, 2008); when drafting the present code, the NASW may have regarded the imposition of stricter standards as an undesirable substitute for allowing flexibility. In the NASW Code, ethical standards 1.06 and 3.01, respectively, caution social workers to avoid social relationships and conflicts of interest with clients and colleagues, but only where there is a "risk of harm or exploitation." The ambiguity inherent in this standard may serve the purpose of ensuring flexibility in the standards' interpretation, but it also unfortunately makes them virtually meaningless in the absence of a situational, regional, cultural, or some other subjective context unique to every practice situation.

Another weakness of ethical codes in the analysis of practice choices is that they often fail to rank order the standards contained in them. In other words, they identify specific duties, such as, in the case of the APA Code, guidelines relating to professional competence (ethical standards 2.01–2.06), informed consent (ethical standard 3.10), and confidentiality (ethical standards 4.01–4.07), and then offer little or no guidance as to which responsibility takes precedence. This tends to render codes of ethics problematic when practitioners use them initially in the assessment of practice dilemmas. Instead, their usefulness is more evident as interpretive devices that supplement and help explain applicable legal standards. Specifically, they tend to enrich the professional context in which practice scenarios take place.

A final general weakness of ethical codes is that they tend to emphasize practice goals all too often from a national, urban perspective, with precious little attention paid to regional variations and cultural issues in practice. For example, the NBCC Code, section A2, cautions professional counselors that, when they accept employment with an agency or other employer, their acceptance implies agreement with institutional policies and procedures. To highlight the overrigidity of this provision, note that, in the case of a counselor's employment with a national network of mental health providers, the provision appears to encourage allegiance to professional practices that might not represent the best interests of persons in a particular community. One could certainly argue that, for clients who live in a rural setting, speak a language other than English, or whose cultural affiliation demands flexibility in the delivery of treatment modalities, the NBCC Code would do well to encourage counselors to impart culturally competent strategies with such clients. Unfortunately, the only reference to diversity in the NBCC Code, contained in section A12, advises counselors rather imprecisely to have "awareness of the impact of stereotyping and unwarranted discrimination."

In light of the foregoing, what role should codes of ethics play in mental health professionals' decision making? To answer this question, it is appropriate to consider the relationship between the law and ethical codes in some greater detail. As already noted, the law is a strategy for enforcing the shared values of a community. Law governing the rights and responsibilities of mental health professionals often relies on standards enunciated in professional ethical codes to describe the parameters of practice. Thus, legislatures enacting licensing statutes and courts interpreting the legal duties to be imposed on social workers, counselors, and psychologists, among other professionals, often rely on ethical codes in performing these functions. Specifically, many licensing laws explicitly require the professionals subject to the legislation to practice according to an identified ethical code. In addition, principles described in ethical codes occasionally themselves become law when the general public embraces them. Consider, for example, the ethical prohibition against sexual relationships between psychotherapists and their clients. In several states, this practice has been criminalized through the adoption of statutory law.

The preceding discussion should make it evident that law and ethics are interrelated, with each having a role in the interpretation of the other. Therefore, ethics treatises that address ethics as a discipline discrete from the law do a disservice to the reader. This is especially true when textbooks identify practice exemplars as ethical "dilemmas" and provide an accompanying analysis based solely on generally relevant ethical standards. In reality, most practice dilemmas have both legal and ethical aspects, and both must be evaluated to address these practice scenarios competently.

To reiterate, ethical codes are useful in evaluating practice decisions in the context of overriding legal responsibilities that the decision maker should first seek to satisfy. They offer guidance by articulating values and imparting ethical standards relevant to professionals in a particular practice discipline. Moreover, they are enforceable in the sense that professionals subject to them face disciplinary sanctions for their violation. For all the reasons discussed in this section, they are most appropriately considered only after one has completed a consideration of applicable law. For that reason, the decision-making framework introduced in this book sets forth the rule that ethical principles be applied only as a second step in the analysis of any practice decision. Two brief vignettes follow; the scenarios demonstrate typical ways in which practitioners can conduct an ordered consideration of law and ethics in decision making.

VIGNETTE 1: THE ANGRY CLIENT

Paula Mackey is a clinical social worker providing mental health services at a public clinic in a largely Hispanic-serving community center in Lansing, Michigan. At the beginning of the counseling session, Abe, a Hispanic client, makes disparaging remarks about Anglo clients and suggests that he believes they receive preferential treatment at the clinic and that this fact has influenced the quality of his progress with Paula, an Anglo therapist. Abe complains to Paula, "We're in the capital of Michigan and the guys in charge give all kind of good citizen awards for big-shot Mexicans, but the service doesn't trickle down to us in the community; the whites have the governor in their pocket and they get everything—even at this community center—including the only good counselors." Upset about the tenor of the discussion, an agitated Paula elects to review it with her supervisor, who suggests that Paula discuss it openly with her client at the following session; attempt to correct her client's mistaken impressions; address directly his racially charged opinions; and if all else fails, consider transferring the client to another therapist, matched by ethnicity. The practice decisions Paula must make in this scenario include the manner in which she discusses this issue with her client and her course of action at the following therapy session.

Consulting her NASW Code of Ethics, Paula ascertains that social workers have a responsibility to promote social justice (ethical standard 6.01), a guideline that might inspire Paula to take the stance that racism in all its forms must here, as everywhere, be confronted as it arises. In addition, Paula uncovers ethical standard 1.02, which suggests that social workers have a responsibility to honor their clients' right to self-determination, which suggests that Paula should carefully evaluate the client's expectations concerning therapy and then attempt to honor them. In light of that standard, further discussion of Abe's beliefs, Paula is inspired to believe, would probably be futile and in any event inappropriate.

Consulting relevant law, Paula believes that constitutional principles, including equal protection and due process, may have application in this dilemma, insofar as they suggest that a public employee—the community center is sponsored by the city—should not use either Abe's ethnicity or the content of his speech as the basis for any official action involving clients. In other words, Paula concludes, transferring Abe's case might not be in compliance with basic constitutional principles.

Following the decision-making framework, Paula elects to apply general legal principles first, which leads her to choose not to modify the general course of her work with the client and to avoid, at least for the present, the transfer of Abe's case. Instead of confronting Abe directly with his race-based beliefs, Paula elects to continue exploring the mental health aspects of the client's statements, consistent with those legal and ethical standards that may offer additional guidance in this area. As she sees it, perhaps she needs to examine alternative cross-cultural practice techniques with Abe. As Paula's supervisor also counsels, however, "I'm not for racially matching clients and therapists, but don't ignore the possibility that Abe's comments might have more truth in them than we're ready to admit."

Vignette 2: The Coffee Shop

A licensed, certified professional counselor, Robert Wu, observes an elderly client, Harry Driscoll, in a local coffee shop in Smith River, California, a small, rural town in which both the counselor and the client live and work. Harry invites Robert to have a cup of coffee with him at a local coffee shop, which serves as the watering hole for the town's population. What should Robert do?

Following the decision-making framework, Robert recognizes no law that specifically forbids this type of socializing. Persuaded that a review of applicable ethical standards would supplement his legal analysis, Robert uncovers NBCC Code sections A8, A9, and B9, which warn licensees to avoid dual relationships that may harm or impair professional judgment. Whether there is actually such a risk in this scenario may depend in some measure on the cultural and regional traditions of the people in Smith River, where Robert and Harry both live and work. Therefore, in this scenario, Robert would be wise to consider the application of these ethical standards in the cultural context of the community. If the type of social encounter Robert and Harry are sharing is the norm, as it might be in many small towns, then the risk of harm or exploitation would seem to be low or nonexistent. In fact, refusing to engage in a reasonably innocuous social encounter would appear to do little to protect the clinical relationship Robert and Harry have experienced and might actually do more to harm the positive results obtained during the pair's counseling sessions. It is interesting to note that a version of this practice scenario seems frequently to appear in ethics treatises, often with an author's suggested resolution supporting the notion that professionals and clients should strictly keep their social distance in the interest of avoiding the creation of a dual relationship and blurring the professional boundary. This conclusion seems to be based on an overly rigid, formal, and urban slant that some treatises appear to adopt. The discerning professional more appropriately should engage in the type of analysis applied in this vignette, which explores the possibility that professional choices must be based on, among other things, a consideration of regional and social context. In this scenario, the fact that Robert could find no direct law affecting his decision to have a brief social encounter with Harry probably provides an important clue that one ought not to assume that any such encounter necessarily violates the best interests of the client; the absence of law here signals the need for contextual analysis rather than a search for consistency among hazy ethical standards.

Step 3: Investigating Regional and Cultural Context and Personal and Ideological Beliefs

Vignette 2 suggests plainly that some legal and ethical standards are sufficiently general as to require some degree of subjective interpretation. Thus, a review of contextual issues, including regional and cultural factors, personal ideological considerations, and other subjective factors that assist in the interpretation of ethical standards, needs to be included during the consideration of practice dilemmas. This third step in decision making is an important component of the framework presented here. Another vignette underscores the importance of this step.

VIGNETTE 3: THE DREAM CATCHER

Fred Darrow, an Anglo clinical psychologist and a provider affiliated with a state mental health agency, is engaged in therapy with a Navajo client, Selena House, in Farmington, New Mexico. Upon the completion of services, Selena offers Fred a dream catcher made of bird feathers as a symbol of the mutual shared association that the two have enjoyed. The gift is intended as a personal token commemorating the professional relationship between Selena and Fred and has no ostensible monetary value. She makes an additional gift to Fred of artwork she has completed that arguably has at least some monetary value. Fred's practice decisions in this scenario involve his handling of the gifts and his communications to the client regarding the gifts.

Following the framework, Fred explores the law applicable to this scenario, thoughtfully examining whether regional variations might influence his application of law to the present scenario. As in vignette 2, Fred finds no applicable law that would rule out acceptance of the dream catcher, but he does find state law that forbids the acceptance of gifts with an appreciable monetary value. Fred decides fairly quickly that the law is not an impediment to his acceptance of the dream catcher and that, in view of the relevant cultural traditions of his client, acceptance of the gift would be both appropriate and in Selena's best therapeutic interests. In contrast, Fred is satisfied that acceptance of the artwork would violate law forbidding the acceptance of gifts by state employees.

Fred is next inspired to review the APA Code to evaluate whether its principles support his initial legal analysis. Reviewing applicable ethical standards, Fred is particularly interested in determining whether it is ethical in any circumstance to accept gifts from a client. Because gift giving by clients runs the hazard of creating a social relationship with a client, Fred seeks out APA ethical standard 3.05a, which sets forth guidelines concerning multiple relationships. Specifically, the standard suggests that psychologists avoid relationships that could reasonably be expected to impair the psychologist's objectivity or competence or to risk exploitation or harm to the person with whom the professional relationship exists. Interestingly, the same standard acknowledges that some multiple relationships simply may not be harmful. As the standard puts it, "Multiple relationships that would not reasonably be expected to cause impairment or risk exploitation or harm are not unethical." Fred finds APA ethical standard 3.08, governing exploitation of clients, to be equally applicable. It admonishes simply that "psychologists do not exploit . . . clients/patients."

As was the situation in vignette 2, these ethical standards' overt ambiguity seems to offer some leeway to psychologists to evaluate the cultural and regional context of their social relationship with a client. As was also the case with vignette 2, the ethical standards' ambiguity renders them virtually meaningless without a thorough review of community and cultural norms governing the scenario. This point is further supported by the APA Code's ethical standard 2.01b, which suggests that, among other competencies, psychologists should display cultural awareness of their clients.

Consistent with the framework, Fred proceeds to review the cultural context of the gifts the client conferred, with a specific emphasis on evaluating the risk of harm or exploitation inherent in this transaction. Such a review naturally requires that Fred be versed in the cultural meaning of the exchange and, if conducted fully, is likely to acquaint Fred with the cultural and spiritual meanings of gift giving and sharing in general in American

Indian communities. It might further suggest to him that it could be more harmful to the client to reject the gifts than to accept them (Brucker & Perry, 1998; Smolar, 2002). The framework's cultural component therefore assists in the interpretation of legal and ethical standards that affect the dilemma. The result this approach suggests, namely that the psychologist acts appropriately if he accepts the dream catcher, is consistent both with cultural competence and with clinically advisable practice (Brucker & Perry, 1998; Smolar, 2002). Moreover, the legal restriction placed on Fred's acceptance of the artwork arguably requires Fred to engage all his clinical knowledge and sensitivity in explaining his stance to Selena.

In addition to considering cultural and regional norms, Fred might be likely to integrate his own clinical training and ideological perspectives in his resolution of the practice dilemma. Consistent with the communitarian stance, this consideration is most usefully undertaken only after the decision maker has objectively explored the cultural context of the client's gifts. This strategy is appropriate in the resolution of other practice dilemmas that require the decision maker to interpret legal and ethical standards.

Step 4: Doing What Is Possible to Do

A final concept incorporated in the decision-making framework is the issue of practicality, or pragmatism. To demonstrate how this principle applies in the resolution of practice dilemmas, reconsider vignette 2, "The Coffee Shop." As already noted, applicable legal and ethical standards require at least some subjective assessment of whether there is a risk of harm or exploitation to Harry, the client, or the further danger that the professional's judgment will be impaired if Robert, the professional, has coffee with Harry. As previously discussed, this assessment requires some consideration of cultural expectations.

Missing from this analysis is the point that, especially in a small town, it may simply be impractical to avoid patronizing a business establishment (including, for example, a coffee shop that almost all the town's residents frequent) when the price of such avoidance is the forgoing of one's morning coffee. Aside from this arguably frivolous example of pragmatism in decision making, the consideration of practicality is of more pressing importance to mental health and human service administrators acutely concerned with the daily economic, social, and administrative exigencies that affect their decisions. In other words, the "right" decision in practice may realistically hinge on how much money there is in an agency's budget.

In the final analysis, the "correct" professional practice decision may rest not just on the legal, ethical, cultural, regional, and personal considerations specifically present in a situation but also on a consideration of what is doable or attainable in the real world. Unfortunately for decision makers looking for practical guidance, professional codes of ethics do not ordinarily address pragmatism as an ideal. Nor, for that matter, do professions such as social work that concern themselves expressly with the pursuit of social justice generally embrace pragmatism. This is true even though pragmatism's unspoken role in the everyday consideration of practice dilemmas is undeniable.

Is pragmatism consistent with the ideals of the mental health professions? Does it comply with the framework's consideration of cultural context? The answer to both questions is yes (Baert, 2005; Joas, 1993; Shalin, 1986; Tamanaha, 1999; Topper, 2000). First, pragmatism aids in the evaluation of legal and ethical standards that require some subjective interpretation; it also assists in the identification of laws and ethical standards that are overreaching or unfair. Second, pragmatism and the promotion of cultural diversity are interrelated in the sense that it is eminently practical to serve clients and design mental health and human services that meet the needs and expectations of most members of a community. For those reasons, a consideration of pragmatic concerns is a specific part of the framework presented here. Indeed, that consideration of pragmatism represents the fourth and final component of the framework.

The Decision-Making Framework Summarized

The decision-making framework can be summarized in four essential steps:

1. All mental health and human service practice dilemmas should be presumed to have potential legal and ethical implications. Attempt to address a practice dilemma by considering—with the assistance of agency or personal counsel, if possible—the potential legal implications first. If there is a clear answer based on an applicable legal principle, apply the principle.
2. If no clear legal answer is generated or if multiple answers emerge, apply an appropriate professional code of ethics governing the mental health practice discipline with which the decision maker is affiliated.
3. If the ethical code suggests several possible answers, attempt to resolve the dilemma by applying cultural, regional, and personal, ideological considerations.
4. If all preceding steps fail to identify a clear answer, apply pragmatic considerations.

These four steps represent an overall strategy for making practice decisions in the mental health professions. Because this framework relies on a review of essential legal principles as the first and most important step, these principles will be discussed here individually. The complete framework, together with a summary of legal principles, ethical standards, and interpretive notes, is included in the appendix.

CHAPTER 3

The Duty to Practice
Reasonably Competently

Overview of the Duty

Several essential legal principles govern the mental health professions. The duty to practice reasonably competently is discussed first. As with all the legal principles discussed herein, the duty to practice reasonably competently states a responsibility that lies at the heart of the relationship between all professionals and their clients. As the case examples show, understanding the nature and scope of this duty assists the decision maker in resolving numerous professional dilemmas. Consistent with the strategy presented in the framework, the ability to identify instances in which this legal principle applies guides the professional to recognize the big picture in practice and diverts the alert decision maker from the often-confusing application of conflicting subsidiary considerations, including broad ethical aspirations and more subjective issues.

With regard to the duty to practice reasonably competently, there is much common ground among social work, counseling, psychology, and other allied health and human service professions. In terms of the essential duty of care owed to the client, professionals in each of these fields face a comparable standard because most of the disciplines offer analogous or at least similar services, and their members often practice together in interdisciplinary teams in the areas of psychotherapy, school counseling, alcohol and substance abuse treatment, marriage and family therapy, child welfare, forensic assessment, educational testing, probation services, and many others.

The duty to practice reasonably competently is the most fundamental of the legal principles discussed here. To understand this concept, however, it is necessary to appreciate the nature and scope of the major mental health

professions. This task is more imposing than one might expect. In fact, legislatures often have a difficult time defining them, and their elements as recognized in licensing laws vary significantly from state to state. The reason
for this is largely that legislatures differ in the strategy that they adopt in
defining a particular profession: some regard a narrow legislative authorization of a profession's scope of practice as essential to the protection of public
safety, whereas others apply the strategy that a broad definition enhances
the public understanding of each of the types of treatment strategies the
particular profession employs. For this reason, these laws do not necessarily
provide a good and consistent overall definition of *competent practice* in a
mental health discipline. Nevertheless, they offer an enlightening introduction to the problems associated with defining the skills necessary to attain
competence in practice.

Legislative Definitions of Social Work

Of the mental health disciplines, social work has been the most notoriously difficult to define. As an example, the New Mexico legislature defines
the practice of social work expansively as "a professional service [that] emphasizes the use of specialized knowledge of social resources, social systems
and human capabilities to effect change in human behavior, emotional responses and social conditions" (N.M. Stat. Ann., § 61-31-6[B], 2008).

The foregoing definition of social work is broad enough to include almost
every professional service known to humankind and is therefore not terribly helpful in assessing the basic nature of the duties that social workers
owe to all clients. Compare the previous definition with the more limited,
clinically based one adopted by the California legislature: "The practice of
clinical social work is defined as a service in which a special knowledge of
social resources, human capabilities, and the part that unconscious motivation plays in determining behavior, is directed at helping people to achieve
more adequate, satisfying, and productive social adjustments" (Cal. Bus. &
Prof. Code § 4996.9, 2008).

Unlike the New Mexico definition, which includes elements of counseling, community organizing, administration, and research, the California
definition suggests that the most essentially definable aspect of social work,
from the public perspective, is the practice of psychotherapy, or clinical social work. This definition paints social work as a profession similar to psychology or psychiatric nursing. Given these wide variations in the public's
perception of social work practice, not much can be gleaned from legislative
definitions that explain the fundamental nature of the legal relationship
between social worker and client.

Legislative Definitions of Psychology and Counseling

Psychology and professional counseling are more concrete in their defined scope of practice and therefore easier for legislatures to define. In a definition typical of many states, Illinois describes clinical psychology as "the independent evaluation, classification and treatment of mental, emotional, behavioral or nervous disorders or conditions, developmental disabilities, alcoholism and substance abuse, disorders of habit or conduct, [and] the psychological aspects of physical illness" (225 Ill. Comp. Stat. 15/2, 2009).

Similar to Illinois's definition of psychology, Texas's legislature defines professional counseling as "the application of mental health, psychotherapeutic, and human development principles to facilitate human development and life; (2) prevent, assess, evaluate, and treat mental, emotional, or behavioral disorders and associated distresses that interfere with mental health" (Tex. Occ. Code Ann. § 503.003, 2007).

Unlike many other states that identify and differentiate among a number of mental health-related disciplines, New Mexico subsumes a number of professional disciplines under its definition of *counseling*. Under New Mexico's definition, counseling includes such diverse areas as the practice of professional mental health counseling, marriage and family therapy, professional art therapy, and alcohol and substance abuse counseling (N.M. Stat. Ann. § 61-9A-4, 2008).

Despite the more limited range of psychology and counseling, state legislatures' statutory definitions still do not offer much in the way of guidance as to how to carry out these professional activities and what expectations to place on practitioners. To better understand these standards, it is useful to examine the courts' responses to this question. Indeed, courts grappling with the problem of identifying the nature of the duty professionals owe to their clients have often looked to common law for guidance (*Am. Home Assurance Co. v. Pope*, 2007; *Karen L. v. Dep't of Health & Soc. Servs.*, 1998). Common law is a body of judicial opinions that cumulatively explain the rights and obligations of all members of society (*Hamdan v. Rumsfeld*, 2006; *Smothers v. Gresham Transfer, Inc.*, 2001). Under the common law system, the law evolves as individual judges examine and apply prior court decisions in the consideration of new and ever-changing factual situations. This process relies on the rule of stare decisis, which requires judges to treat prior court decisions, or precedents, as entitled to respect. By examining common law, it is possible to ascertain first whether there is any definable duty imposed on individuals in a given profession and, second, how that duty contrasts with similar responsibilities imposed on all other mental health disciplines.

In examining the duties required of professionals to their clients, the common law ordinarily looks to statutory standards explaining specifically the expectations placed on the professional (*Dunn v. Catholic Home Bureau for Dependent Children*, 1989). As pointed out previously, this presents a difficult problem for judges when the statutory definitions of some professions—most notably social work—can be so vague and variable from state to state (*Horak v. Biris*, 1985; *Martino v. Family Serv. Agency*, 1982; *Terrell C. v. Dep't of Soc. & Health Servs.*, 2004). Consequently, courts examining the coverage of social work responsibilities have tended to apply a commonsense standard derived from the expectations imposed on other professionals and, in particular, psychologists. In general, a social worker, as any other professional, must engage in reasonable conduct (*Franet v. County of Alameda Soc. Servs. Agency*, 2008; *Roe v. Catholic Charities*, 1992). What precisely is reasonable conduct? Simply put, it is an objective standard that includes engaging in behavior that is considered acceptable to the "reasonable" social worker (*Heinmiller v. Dep't of Health*, 1995; *Rogers v. County of San Joaquin Human Servs. Agency*, 2007). Similarly, psychologists and counselors are supposed to practice consistently with the expectations placed on a reasonable member of each respective profession (*F. G. v. MacDonell*, 1997—pastoral counselor; *Figueiredo-Torres v. Nickel*, 1991—psychologist; *Hart v. Bennet*, 2003—unlicensed but practicing psychologist; *Jarzynka v. St. Thomas Univ. Sch. of Law*, 2004—law school counselor; *Jones v. Lurie*, 2000—psychologist; *Miller v. Ratner*, 1997—psychologist; *Sain v. Cedar Rapids Cmty. Sch. Dist.*, 2001—school guidance counselor).

Reasonableness can also be understood as a fiduciary responsibility imposed on social workers, counselors, psychologists, and physicians, among others. This means that, when a trusting client voluntarily seeks the professional's services, and the professional agrees to provide them, the provider undertakes a duty to render the services honestly and faithfully (*Aufrichtig v. Lowell*, 1995; *Doe v. Harbor Schs., Inc.*, 2006; *Eckhardt v. Charter Hosp.*, 1997; *F. G. v. MacDonell*, 1997; *Horak v. Biris*, 1985; *Petrillo v. Syntex Labs, Inc.*, 1986; *State ex rel. Dean v. Cunningham*, 2006). State licensing laws may create specific fiduciary responsibilities, by, for example, imposing particular standards on clinical practitioners. Responsibilities can also arise when unlicensed persons provide services to clients, which typically occurs when a client seeks specific advice, information, psychotherapy, or other assistance from a person who represents himself or herself to the public as a counselor or therapist.

How does one best ensure that one is behaving in a manner that mirrors the conduct of the reasonable professional? The following list summarizes this range of conduct as evinced from a number of court decisions that have defined on a case-by-case basis the reasonable-practice standard as it has been imposed on various mental health professionals:

- Practicing with reasonable competence; this includes practicing with the skill and care expected of a prudent practitioner engaged in the same kind of professional practice, with the same degree of training, in a similar community, and under similar circumstances (*Alejo v. City of Alhambra*, 1999—social worker; *Figueiredo-Torres v. Nickel*, 1991—psychologist; *Heinmiller v. Dep't of Health*, 1995—social worker; *Hertzel v. Palmyra Sch. Dist.*, 2007—school counselor; *Naidu v. Laird*, 1988—psychiatrist; *Roe v. Catholic Charities*, 1992—social worker; *Roska v. Sneddon*, 2006—protective service social worker; *Sain v. Cedar Rapids Cmty. Sch. Dist.*, 2001—school guidance counselor; *Vernon v. Rollins-Threats*, 2005—social worker–marriage and family therapist).

Among other things, reasonably competent professional practice has been noted to include the following general aspects:

- Being licensed, which includes practice within the definition of the mental health service being offered and according to the licensing law of the state in which one practices (*Corgan v. Muehling*, 1991; *Dunn v. Catholic Home Bureau for Dependent Children*, 1989; *Horak v. Biris*, 1985)
- Having certification in the area of specialization in which one is practicing (*Corgan v. Muehling*, 1991; *State v. Louis*, 1994)
- Engaging in conduct reasonably calculated to help the client (*Roe v. Catholic Charities*, 1992)
- Engaging in appropriate personal conduct that supports the purposes of the professional relationship (*Figueiredo-Torres v. Nickel*, 1991)
- Avoiding conduct that might harm the client in a way that is foreseeable to the professional, which requires the professional to take into account the likelihood of injury to the client and the burden to the professional—financial and otherwise—of guarding against it (*Hertzel v. Palmyra Sch. Dist.*, 2007; *Roe v. Catholic Charities*, 1992)
- Avoiding conduct that may cause foreseeable harm to a member of the public other than the client (e.g., as when the professional does not address a client's threat to commit a violent act against a third party) (*Hertog v. City of Seattle*, 1999—probation counselor; *Hertzel v. Palmyra Sch. Dist.*, 2007—school counselor; *Naidu v. Laird*,

1988—psychiatrist; *Perreira v. State*, 1989—psychiatrist; *Tarasoff v. Regents of Univ. of Cal.*, 1976—psychiatrist and psychologist)

More specific aspects of reasonably competent practice include the following:

- Keeping abreast of professional developments and research in one's area of practice (*White v. N.C. Bd. of Exam'rs of Practicing Psychologists*, 1990)
- Practicing according to the public rules and regulations in existence in the state in which the professional practices (*Karen L. v. Dep't of Health & Soc. Servs.*, 1998)
- Practicing within ethical standards (in most situations, this includes practice in conformance with the NASW, NBCC, or APA codes, as relevant) (*Deatherage v. Examining Bd. of Psychology*, 1997; *Doe v. Finch*, 1997)
- Making appropriate documentation to keep track of the client's progress and other continuing issues related to the services provided (*Jacqueline T. v. Alameda County Child Protective Servs.*, 2007; *Ortega v. Sacramento County Dep't of Health & Human Servs.*, 2008; *Valcin v. Pub. Health Trust*, 1984—hospital)
- Honoring the policies and procedures of one's agency (*Jacqueline T. v. Alameda County Child Protective Servs.*, 2007; *Karen L. v. Dep't of Health & Soc. Servs.*, 1998; *Ortega v. Sacramento County Dep't of Health & Human Servs.*, 2008)
- Obeying the principle of informed consent (see chapter 4) (*Modi v. W. Va. Bd. of Med.*, 1995)
- Obeying the principle of confidentiality (see chapter 7) (*Figueiredo-Torres v. Nickel*, 1991; *Jaffee v. Redmond*, 1996)
- Adequately assessing the client and investigating the factual substance of representations made to the professional (*Weaver v. Dep't of Soc. & Health Servs.*, 2001)
- Competently managing client privacy issues (see chapter 7) (*Eckhardt v. Charter Hosp.*, 1997; *Jaffee v. Redmond*, 1996)
- Competently managing the duty to report and investigate child and elder abuse, and other legal responsibilities imposed on mental health professionals by law (*Hertzel v. Palmyra Sch. Dist.*, 2007; *Jacqueline T. v. Alameda County Child Protective Servs.*, 2007; *Ortega v. Sacramento County Dep't of Health & Human Servs.*, 2008; *T. M. v. Executive Risk Indem., Inc.*, 2002; *Tarasoff v. Regents of Univ. of Cal.*, 1976; *Williams v. Coleman*, 1992)

- Cooperating and communicating with other professionals involved in the treatment process—a responsibility that would appear to mandate competence in multidisciplinary planning and coordination of services (*Alejo v. City of Alhambra*, 1999; *Bielaska v. Orley*, 2001; In re *Rebekah R.*, 1994)
- Maintaining appropriate professional boundaries with clients and avoiding inappropriate social or sexual relationships with clients (see chapter 5) (*Adams v. Bd. of Clinical Soc. Workers*, 2005; *Corgan v. Muehling*, 1991; *Doe v. Harbor Schs., Inc.*, 2006; *Heinmiller v. Dep't of Health*, 1995; *Simmons v. United States*, 1986)
- Designing programs and services using suitable research and investigation (In re *McKnight*, 1990—developmental disability treatment program)
- Administering programs and supervising employees with due attention paid to agency needs and the client population (*Duran v. Apodaca*, 1980; *Joseph A. v. N.M. Dep't of Human Servs.*, 1983)

These obligations can be summarized as the reasonable-competence standard, a doctrine that is encapsulated in the framework as principle 1. Observe that the reasonable-competence standard does not require perfection in the delivery of mental health services, nor does it imply that a practitioner must obtain a satisfactory clinical result in all practice situations. Rather, practicing reasonably competently, as the courts have noted, means delivering services with a regard for consequences that are foreseeable to the professional. This concept suggests that reasonable professionals must recognize their limits as persons and professionals. They must also make practice decisions in the context of their standing as members of the professional community of allied mental health providers. In other words, mental health practitioners must be able to view practice from a multidisciplinary perspective and not be limited by the philosophies and traditions of their own, individual fields. Conformance with this standard invariably is evaluated according to the practice expectations imposed on mental health professionals in one community or region. Providing mental health and human services inevitably requires a mutual interaction between professional and client whose success depends on the cooperation and effort of both parties. Note also that the courts' interpretation of reasonable competence evolves over time as new judges consider this same standard in the context of changing factual scenarios.

As developments in technology identify new practice techniques and fresh ways—such as the Internet—to disseminate information, expectations imposed on the reasonable mental health professional will change as well, especially because the World Wide Web may tend to remove or lessen former regional boundaries. Considering the growing body of research that suggests the importance of incorporating diversity considerations into the practice repertoires of mental health professionals, it is inevitable that cultural competence will increasingly be considered a part of the reasonable-competence standard.

In light of the foregoing discussion, one should not spend as much time attempting to memorize the preceding practice standards as to understand their intent and spirit. This is especially true when one considers the overlap among the mental health professions and the tendency of courts to evaluate practice standards on a case-by-case basis according to community standards. Despite the increasing willingness of mental health agencies to use professionals from different disciplines interchangeably to provide basic mental health services, courts occasionally recognize differences among the professions based on variances in training and responsibilities (*Briscoe v. Prince George's County Health Dep't*, 1991). It is therefore useful to survey some of the unique elements of practice in each of the mental health professions—social work, counseling, and psychology—that supplement the reasonable-competence standard outlined previously.

Elements of Reasonably Competent Social Work Practice

Courts note that social work is a profession by reason of the foundation of specialized knowledge and skills that are the result of classroom education and field training (*Jaffee v. Redmond*, 1996; *State v. Louis*, 1994). This being said, one is not a social worker merely by reason of providing services that social work may comprise, such as performing psychosocial assessments, data collection, and research (*State v. Louis*, 1994). Consequently, one should describe one's self as a social worker only to the extent that such a description is consistent with the specialized training one has received (*State v. Louis*, 1994).

What do courts regard as the skills within the specific range of competencies expected of social work? Among other things, these include the gathering, reporting, and assessment of psychosocial information, the investigation of suspected child abuse and neglect, and the protection of children affected by such conduct (*Alejo v. City of Alhambra*, 1999; *Jacqueline T. v. Alameda County Child Protective Servs.*, 2007; *Ortega v. Sacramento County Dep't of Health & Human Servs.*, 2008); and individual, marriage, and family counseling (*Horak v. Biris*, 1985). Thus, social work and professional counseling have elements in common. In the recent past, courts generally were reluctant to recognize social workers as competent to diagnose and treat mental illness or to perform clinical psychological examinations, diagnostic assessments, and evaluations to gauge the dangerousness of criminal defendants for forensic purposes (*State v. Louis*, 1994). Recently, this trend has changed, as it is acknowledged that advanced clinical social work practice may consist of additional specialized training and certification in these areas (*People v. R. R.*, 2005—holding that the evaluation, making, and rendering of diagnoses and prognoses, formulation of treatment plans, and treatment of mental disorders are all in the scope of practice of clinical social workers; *United States v. Brown*, 2006—outlining the scope of practice of forensic social work and analogizing this field to the work of criminal mitigation specialists or psychologists).

In their use of an expansive definition of social work, some state legislatures may authorize social workers to practice in areas for which professional standards simply have not been defined. Thus, some states specifically certify social workers to engage in health and human service agency administration, to practice community organizing, and to teach social work courses at the university level, even though courts encountering these practice specialties have noted the difficulty of ascertaining exactly what professional expectations should be imposed on social workers practicing in these areas (*Horak v. Biris*, 1985). Even though few courts have yet identified practice standards in some of these social work specialties, it is possible for the prudent social worker to make an intelligent estimate of the range of practice expectations, given the reasonable-competence standard. Indeed, at least one court, in *Roe v. Catholic Charities* (1992), has suggested that one can identify variances from the reasonable-competence standard simply by applying the definition of *malpractice* offered in *Black's Law Dictionary* (rev. 4th ed., 1968): "[Malpractice means] any professional misconduct, unreasonable lack of skill or fidelity in professional or fiduciary duties, evil practice, or illegal or immoral conduct." According to the *Roe* court, "the elements necessary to establish a malpractice action are the same elements required of any negligence case." That being said, to identify the reasonable-competence standard, one can invert the *Roe* court's definition and describe the standard as including conduct representing the expected application of skills, fidelity to the client, and professionalism anticipated of social workers in particular practice settings.

Understanding and applying the reasonable-competence standard in assessing one's duties as a social worker is the most helpful first step in evaluating professional responsibilities to the client, regardless of one's specialty area. For example, licensed social workers employed as program designers and agency administrators should estimate their duties to clients and supervisees by evaluating the skills, training, and care normally expected of prudent program administrators—regardless of the administrator's specific mental health discipline—in a community or region.

Elements of Reasonably Competent Counseling

The responsibilities of counselors are both similar to and distinguishable from psychologists and social workers. Courts have been willing to impose on marriage and family therapists, drug and alcohol rehabilitation specialists, school guidance counselors, probation officers, and even unlicensed treatment providers a duty to practice reasonably competently within the scope of their training and according to community standards (*F. G. v. Mac-Donell*, 1997; *Hertzel v. Palmyra Sch. Dist.*, 2007; *Jarzynka v. St. Thomas Univ. Sch. of Law*, 2004; *Sain v. Cedar Rapids Cmty. Sch. Dist.*, 2001).

Because counselors offer a wide variety of services, both informational and psychotherapeutic, the key to understanding the extent of any counselor's duty to a client is identifying how the parties define the terms of their professional relationship at the commencement of services. If counselor and client mutually agree that the client should receive information or therapy, then the professional has the duty to provide it responsibly. Thus, pastoral and school guidance counselors both form fiduciary relationships with their clients, even though the subject matter of their counseling may be starkly different (*F. G. v. MacDonell*, 1997; *Hertzel v. Palmyra Sch. Dist.*, 2007; *Jarzynka v. St. Thomas Univ. Sch. of Law*, 2004; *Sain v. Cedar Rapids Cmty. Sch. Dist.*, 2001).

Counselors assume a fiduciary role in a manner that is often similar to psychologists and clinical social workers. In such circumstances, their obligation to practice reasonably competently is comparable to the duty those mental health professionals owe. In other situations, however, the role of the counselor is more informational. Such is the case with school guidance counselors, for example. With respect to counselors who disseminate information, the duty to practice reasonably competently extends to the accurate communication of the information that the client has sought. In this sense, the counselor's responsibilities most resemble those of an attorney. Thus, a high school guidance counselor has been held to practice incompetently by giving a college-bound student inaccurate information concerning the course requirements necessary to compete in intercollegiate sports (*Sain v. Cedar Rapids Cmty. Sch. Dist.*, 2001).

With the advent of the Internet, a new market for the offering of clinical counseling services has opened widely, and thus far, professional counselors seem to have tapped the Internet most extensively. With this point in mind, the NBCC has adopted professional standards for Web-based counseling. Unfortunately, these standards do little to answer the questions that this new technology raises about the ability of Internet-based counselors to practice reasonably competently as that standard is defined here. One of the more pressing of these questions is, By what community standards should a counselor's practice be judged when thousands of miles may separate the counselor and client? Although as yet unanswered by courts, the likely response to this question is that counselors are to be expected, as any other professionals would be, to conform their practice to those standards imposed within both the client's and the professional's home communities. In other words, the quality of counseling services is likely to be assessed according to regional expectations existing in the communities in which both parties are physically situated.

Elements of Reasonably Competent Psychology Practice

Psychologists and other mental health providers bring special responsibilities to their professional relationships with clients. At the very least, reasonably competent practice means that psychologists must diagnose mental illness properly and apply appropriate treatment (*Zagaros v. Erickson*, 1997). In addition, courts have noted that the psychotherapy relationship is inherently different from all other professional associations. Because of the intensity and closeness of the professional bond between psychologist and client, the capacity for harm to the client is great if the professional mishandles the relationship. For example, a psychologist's failure to identify sexual abuse or other external threats to the client and additional failure to protect the client from such threats is at variance with the reasonable-competence standard (*T. M. v. Executive Risk Indem., Inc.*, 2002). Furthermore, a psychologist's personal conduct outside of the professional relationship is relevant in the assessment of professional responsibility to the extent that it may affect the client's clinical progress. As examples, sexual and inappropriate social relationships with clients are considered malpractice. In addition, the maintenance of a harmful dual relationship with a client that involves a business transaction, for example, in the case of a client hired to work in a psychologist's office, is also improper (*Overton v. Bd. of Exam'rs in Psychology*, 1996).

In addition to the responsibilities noted previously, psychologists administer tests, perform psychological evaluations, conduct forensic assessments, and make recommendations in connection with involuntary commitment hearings. Unlike social workers and counselors, licensed psychologists

practicing in hospital settings in some areas have attained the right to receive clinical and staff privileges identical to those of psychiatrists (*Reiff v.
Ne. Fla. State Hosp.*, 1998). Moreover, psychologists have gained the legal
authority in some states and one federal territory—New Mexico, Louisiana,
and Guam—to prescribe medications (N.M. Stat. Ann. § 61-9-17, 2008; La.
Rev. Stat. Ann. § 37-2372, 2008; 10 Guam Code Ann. § 12827, 2008), with
additional proposals to extend this right pending in several states. Leaders
of the psychology profession have been successful in arguing that allowing
psychologists to prescribe psychotropic medication increases the access of
clients in rural and inner-city areas to psychopharmacological treatment. It
is plain, however, that extending the pharmacology option to psychologists
will also change the boundaries of reasonably competent practice for those
professionals. Given the additional risk of harm to clients that results from
misdiagnosis and inappropriate prescription of medications, the responsibility of prescribing psychologists to protect their clients from foreseeable
harm would appear to be greater.

Consequences for Breach of the Duty
to Practice Reasonably Competently

There are several consequences that may arise from a mental health professional's failure to practice within the parameters that the reasonable-
competence standard mandates. These consequences include, among others,
civil liability, criminal prosecution, and disciplinary action by the licensee's
professional board. The nature of each of these remedies is discussed individually here.

Civil Liability

Many of the cases cited earlier began as civil lawsuits seeking monetary
damages against a professional accused of violating the duty to practice
reasonably competently. As has already been noted, the duty itself is the
result of common law principles developed over the course of time, in large
measure the cumulative outcome of individual court decisions. When a victimized client brings a court action alleging that a professional has breached
the duty to practice reasonably competently, the resultant lawsuit often
claims professional malpractice, a tort, or civil wrong, for which the victim is compensated through the award of financial relief. Tortious conduct
is answerable ordinarily by rewarding the victim with compensatory, and
occasionally punitive damages, intended to offset the impact of the harm

caused by the misconduct—and in the case of punitive damages, to punish the wrongdoer and deliver a message to the public regarding the nature of the wrongdoing. The category and amount of damages awarded the victim ordinarily depend on whether the malpractice was negligent (i.e., accidental); reckless; or on occasion, intentional.

Liability, or legal responsibility for malpractice, may be imposed on the professional and others directly or indirectly contributing to the professional misconduct. Thus, the professional responsible for malpractice may face direct liability for the behavior, which means that the cost of the misconduct is imposed directly on the responsible professional. Alternatively, the professional's employer or agency may face vicarious liability, a concept predicated on the principle that an employer stands responsible for the misconduct that employees commit during the course of their employment. Finally, a professional's direct supervisor may be liable for negligent supervision when the supervisor has failed to oversee the professional in a manner consistent with the standards that the duty to practice reasonably competently suggests.

Of the mental health professions, psychologists and professional counselors most often have been the target of court-imposed liability. This willingness by courts to impose legal responsibility on members of the two professions can be attributed mainly to the rather concrete manner in which licensing legislation defines their professional responsibilities and, perhaps, because large agencies or hospitals that carry liability insurance often employ these professionals. Interestingly, and perhaps questionably, courts have cited the existence of financial resources to pay a malpractice judgment as a ground for the imposition of liability (*Tarasoff v. Regents of Univ. of Cal.*, 1976).

In the case of social workers, courts have come to different conclusions about whether they should face malpractice liability. Because social workers have until recently worked mainly for public agencies, courts generally have been reluctant to impose liability on professionals performing important governmental social work functions, such as child protective services. A dominant position such courts have voiced is that the imposition of liability on government social workers would interfere with their very important public responsibilities. Therefore, courts often readily enforce the blanket of immunity from civil lawsuits placed on public-sector social workers by state legislation (*DeShaney v. Winnebago County Dep't of Soc. Servs.*, 1989). With the entry of social workers into the provision of psychotherapy and related services, however, courts have begun to examine social worker misconduct in a new light, with due regard for public safety issues caused by the increasing demand for clinical social work services.

Although a number of courts have recognized the tort of social worker malpractice (see, e.g., *Horak v. Biris*, 1985; *Roe v. Catholic Charities*, 1992), judges have been hesitant to apply the doctrine except in cases in which, first, the duty of the social worker has been clearly or intentionally violated and, second, important public policy demands the assessment of liability. For example, courts have been willing to impose civil liability in a number of cases involving social workers engaged in psychotherapy or counseling. The reason for this willingness, as courts have noted, is that judges have been satisfied with the relatively clear statutory, licensing, and ethical standards governing those areas of social work practice. Often, courts have analogized clinical social worker misconduct to psychologist or psychiatrist malpractice (*Horak v. Biris*, 1985). Furthermore, these cases have often involved a willful or deliberate commission of malpractice, such as sexual misconduct with a client, an impropriety so severe, with long-term harm so plainly foreseeable, as to leave the court with no doubt as to whether any practice standard has been violated.

In other cases involving social workers in child welfare, courts remain disinclined to assess civil liability for negligence. Courts have offered several reasons for this. First, courts have noted the difficulty inherent in identifying the boundaries of the professional relationship between the client and the social worker offering child welfare services. Second, courts have offered compelling public policy arguments militating against the imposition of civil damages on child welfare social workers and their protective service agencies. For example, courts examining cases involving social workers participating in child abuse investigations and foster care placements have noted that imposing civil liability for reasonable mistakes made during the course of such investigations and placements would greatly burden already-scant social work resources and would force social workers to adopt a more defensive practice stance; this fear-of-lawsuit mentality could be expected to divert child protective social workers from their primary emphasis on protecting the safety and best interests of children (*Jacqueline T. v. Alameda County Child Protective Servs.*, 2007; *Karen L. v. Dep't of Health & Soc. Servs.*, 1998; *Ortega v. Sacramento County Dep't of Health & Human Servs.*, 2008). Courts in such circumstances have tended to resist assigning civil liability in situations in which clear moral blameworthiness has not been demonstrated (*Karen L. v. Dep't of Health & Soc. Servs.*, 1998).

In addition to lawsuits alleging civil liability for breach of the duty to practice reasonably competently, civil rights litigation is an available tool when a claim arises that a professional has violated the constitutional rights of a client. Under section 1983 of the federal Civil Rights Act of 1871, money damages and other forms of relief are available to the victims of such misconduct. Unlike damage claims founded on the professional's breach of a common law practice standard, the object of civil rights litigation is to seek compensation, and often to secure other forms of corrective relief, from actions taken by government agencies, officers, and employees. Thus, state and federal government professionals employed in mental health, child and adult protective services, forensic psychology, veterans affairs, and other areas of public-sector practice must be aware not only of the basic duty to practice reasonably competently but also of their responsibilities under the U.S. Constitution.

Mental health professionals frequently provide services to clients in the context of a contractual relationship entered into by the professional either with an agency and/or employer or directly with the client. In these instances, the professional not only has the duty to practice reasonably competently but also has the additional responsibility to honor the terms of the contract. In situations in which this duty has been violated, civil litigation alleging breach of contract offers a remedy for the injured client or agency and/or employer (*Chew v. Meyer*, 1987; *King v. Conant*, 2005). Although a comprehensive discussion of contract law is beyond the scope of this book, it will suffice here to note that lawsuits alleging breach of contract must demonstrate that a contract has existed between the professional and the agency and/or employer or client, that the professional has violated one or more terms of the contract, and that damages have resulted as a consequence of that breach (*Roe v. Catholic Charities*, 1992).

Criminal Responsibility

Violations of practice standards that vitally affect the public interest are punishable through the criminal justice system. Unlike tortious conduct, which most often involves negligent or reckless behavior with unintended but foreseeable consequences, criminal conduct almost always involves intentional violations of practice standards. Note, however, that some intentional conduct, such as sexual behavior involving a client, may be simultaneously tortious and criminal. Unlike tortious behavior, much of which is defined in the common law, all criminal conduct must be specifically created by a legislative body and enacted as statutory law for it to be enforceable. Criminal prosecution is intended to serve as a deterrent strategy, first by punishing the wrongdoer for the violation of a public standard and second by alerting the public to the consequences resulting from the offense (*Grey v. Allstate Ins. Co.*, 2001).

Professional licensing legislation ordinarily contains provisions that encompass criminal sanctions for its violation; thus, breach of statutory provisions such as the duty to maintain confidentiality may have criminal consequences. It is therefore imperative for mental health professionals to be familiar with licensing laws pertaining to them and the responsibilities those laws impose on them in the state where they practice.

In addition to criminal sanctions for the violation of licensing requirements, some states have criminalized other forms of professional misconduct that contravene important public standards. With respect to clinical social workers, counselors, and psychologists, the most important example is sexual misconduct. Some states define sexual contact between psychotherapists and their clients—even if it is consensual and performed after the formal termination of therapy—as criminal sexual penetration or a similarly characterized felony (see, e.g., Wis. Stat. Ann. § 940.22, 2008; Mich. Comp. Laws Serv. § 750.520a–b, 2009; Minn. Stat. Ann. § 609.341-342, 2008; N.M. Stat. Ann. § 30-9-10, 2008). In explaining society's intolerance for sexual relations between psychotherapists and clients, courts have noted that an important aspect of the therapist-client alliance distinguishes it from virtually all other professional relationships: it is inherently more damaging to the client if the relationship is exploited (*Elliott v. N.C. Psychology Bd.*, 1997; *Horak v. Biris*, 1985; *Simmons v. United States*, 1986). Specifically, psychotherapy often involves the client's transference of feelings to the therapist in a way that allows the therapist to assist the client in addressing them. Sexual relationships between the therapist and client distort this process and therefore render extraordinary—perhaps permanent—harm to the client (*Horak v. Biris*, 1985; *Simmons v. United States*, 1986). Considered in this light, the states noted earlier, among others, have regarded criminalization of this conduct as an appropriate deterrent strategy.

The duty to report suspected child abuse has traditionally been imposed on medical personnel, teachers, and social workers, among other health and human service professionals. In recent years, some states have expanded this duty to impose the same responsibility on all members of the public, with criminal sanctions for its violation (see, e.g., N.M. Stat. Ann. § 32A-4-3, 2008). Despite the good intentions of this legislation, it may be the cause in some areas of an increase in anonymous reports of child abuse, a factor that may already be responsible for artificially inflated statistics identifying the number of reported child abuse cases. Specifically, these statistics may reflect that more reports of alleged child abuse are being made, not that the actual rate of confirmed child abuse cases is on the rise. Enforcement against members of the public seems questionable in light of the burden it places on untrained individuals to recognize the incidence of child abuse and neglect in all their myriad forms. Regardless of its enforceability against the general public, mental health professionals who violate the duty to report remain subject to criminal prosecution as well as civil actions by victims (*Williams v. Coleman*, 1992).

The use of a deterrent strategy through criminal prosecution has also been attempted in at least one case involving child-protective-service social workers. In 1996, two New Mexico social workers were indicted on felony charges that they had negligently permitted physical and sexual abuse of a child to occur by mishandling the foster care placement of a three-year-old toddler in the state's custody (Daniels, 1996). The theoretical basis for this prosecution was that the social workers had violated clear and unequivocal practice standards by not adequately monitoring the child's foster care placement, thus allowing child abuse in the foster family to occur unabated. In this instance, the severity of the resultant harm to the client was extreme enough in the eyes of prosecutors to warrant criminal prosecution. Ultimately, however, the dismissal, refiling, and final dismissal of the criminal charges played out extensively in regional and national media (Daniels, 1997), with the result that the usefulness of the prosecution in deterring future social work misconduct has been called into question, if not dismissed entirely. In light of the extensive burden already imposed on social work resources nationally, it is questionable whether the imposition of criminal liability for practice mistakes ultimately serves the purposes intended. The failure of prosecutors in other jurisdictions to adopt the same approach used in the New Mexico case perhaps stands as testament to the near futility of this law enforcement strategy. Based on the New Mexico experience, a compelling argument can be made that the deterrent strategy advanced by criminal prosecution in all cases is best reserved for more willful, deliberate, and malicious conduct.

Disciplinary Action

Protection of the public is the most significant reason for requiring licensure of social workers, counselors, psychologists, and other mental health professionals (*Heinmiller v. Dep't of Health*, 1995). The laws of each state grant professional licensing boards authority to regulate each mental health discipline, to certify professionals admitted to practice, and to impose disciplinary measures for violations of licensing standards. Licensing boards ordinarily have broad legislative authority to establish practice standards consistent with the public interest. In each professional discipline, these standards generally include requirements that the professional

- Practice consistently with the ethical code established in the discipline

- Be mentally fit to practice
- Practice reasonably competently
- Practice appropriately within the areas authorized by the license class

Both the extent of available disciplinary measures and the manner in which enforcement procedures are carried out vary extensively depending on the state and the profession. It is generally true, however, that licensing boards may revoke a professional license or impose extreme forms of discipline on a licensee, such as license suspension and revocation, to the extent that it is necessary to protect the public from substandard practice.

Licensing suspension and revocation often occur when a licensing board can demonstrate a threat to the public by way of the professional's demonstrable violation of one or more of the practice standards already mentioned. Clear negligence, criminal behavior, persistent substance abuse that renders the practitioner unfit to practice, and sexual misconduct involving clients or supervisees are all examples of violations deemed important enough to warrant severe discipline.

Disciplinary proceedings that licensing boards institute must follow administrative procedures governed by state law. The essential elements that must be demonstrated in a disciplinary proceeding are, first, the violation of a practice standard and, second, the threat of harm to the public resulting from the violation. Often, licensing boards procure the assistance of professionals familiar with practice standards to offer expert testimony during disciplinary proceedings to help explain the meaning of the professional standard in question and the significance of its violation. Such testimony is most useful when the expert is able to describe the link between the licensee's misconduct and the basic duty to practice reasonably competently. Affording this insight ordinarily requires that the expert have familiarity with specific guidelines governing the licensee's area of practice and knowledge of practice standards in effect in the geographical community in which the licensee practices.

Using Reasonable Competence to Make Professional Decisions: Case Examples

The elements of reasonable competence constitute the first in a series of fundamental legal principles useful in the resolution of a variety of practice dilemmas that mental health professionals experience. To the extent that one can identify a dilemma as implicating the duty to practice reasonably competently, one has a useful tool for identifying the practice choices available and applying them in an effective manner. Several practice dilemmas follow in which the duty to practice reasonably competently is identified and applied according to the decision-making framework.

Case Example 1: Individual Therapy in Lanai, Hawaii

Donald Strom has been a licensed clinical psychologist in Newark, New Jersey, for the past fifteen years. Fascinated with Hawaiian culture, Donald has accepted a position with a family service agency in Lanai, Hawaii, a rural island community whose dominant Native Hawaiian population has been experiencing a socioeconomic transition from a traditional farming community to an increasingly tourist- and casino-driven society. Reports have suggested that the transition has had a critical impact on community mental health, with the result being an erosion of family stability and cohesion (Matsuoka & Benson, 1996). An additional effect has been a fairly rapid shift in values and cultural beliefs as a result of the in-migration of non-Native groups. As a result, families appear to be dissolving in greater numbers, there are more identified problems in marital relationships, and there has been a measurable increase in child abuse and neglect rates (Matsuoka & Benson, 1996).

Donald has chosen to practice in Lanai partly on the basis of his review of national professional journals, some of which have suggested that rural community mental health agencies have a spotty record nationally in the design and implementation of outpatient services for individuals and families in crisis. Donald fervently believes that his practice will cater to the needs of such persons. His mode of therapy, honed over the course of his professional career, emphasizes the use of individual counseling and psychodynamic techniques that promote self-awareness, personal growth, and enhancement of self-esteem. Donald is aware of his newness to the community, and he believes that what he lacks in regional experience, he more than makes up for by filling a critical gap in mental health services. His attitude is inspired by the APA Code's principle D ("Justice"), which suggests that psychologists have a duty to make known to underserved communities the benefits of psychological services, including therapeutic knowledge and skills.

Donald enthusiastically embraces other ethical standards and professional values of clinical psychology, specifically with regard to the need to promote client well-being and self-determination (APA Code principle E, "Respect for People's Rights and Dignity," and principle A, "Beneficence and Nonmaleficence"), and he believes that his practice methods are consistent with those standards. He is also aware, however, that the APA Code advises psychologists to receive the training and experience necessary to ensure the cultural competence of their services (ethical standard 2.01a–c, "Boundaries of Competence"). Donald hopes to acquire this cultural competence as he engages in practice, but he also believes that, in light of the demand for services, he has much to offer right away as an experienced therapist.

Shortly after the opening of his office in Lanai, Donald meets Mrs. Kanahele, a sixty-two-year-old retired schoolteacher who complains of sadness and "nerves," symptoms she attributes to her husband's alcoholism and her "family history" of depression. In addition, she is upset about her teenage grandson, who lives with her and her husband and has become increasingly angry and "out of control" in recent weeks. Mrs. Kanahele desperately wants help to deal with her situation. What decisions should Donald make about his intervention?

This case example suggests that Donald, despite his best intentions, may not yet be in a position to practice reasonably competently. Clearly, he has adopted a practice methodology during his years in Newark that he has applied successfully for some time. However, despite his superficial acknowledgment of the APA Code's areas of guidance, Donald now seems prepared to apply his practice technique in a new and culturally distinct community. Moreover, he may be ready to do so without a significant understanding of regional norms and the cultural viability of his technique—a mistake that would seem to be directly at odds with the standard of care mandated by the duty to practice reasonably competently. Donald frames his position largely on the basis of his years of experience and a basic confidence in the value of his own professional experience. As noted, Donald means well; he has sought ethical guidance from the APA Code and has examined the standards previously outlined. Indeed, Donald may even feel conflicted when he attempts to apply the blizzard of ethical directives outlined earlier. As a result, he may offer his psychotherapeutic services to Mrs. Kanahele with the expectation that the exchange between client and therapist serve as a cultural learning experience for both. Unfortunately, Mrs. Kanahele probably has no personal need to be sought after as an educational opportunity for her therapist.

In this case, the duty to practice reasonably competently directs specifically that Donald assume the responsibility to practice as a fully informed clinical psychologist would in Lanai, Hawaii. This principle outlines a number of burdens that Donald has to meet before implementing a practice strategy, and Donald must understand that the legally defined burdens supersede the broad ethical considerations outlined previously. First, to competently assess Mrs. Kanahele and determine the appropriateness of a practice intervention, Donald must be familiar with his client's family background, cultural worldview, and the nature and quality of her relationships with her family and community (Chandler & Bell, 1995; Matsuoka & Benson, 1996; Olson & Anders, 2000; Takeuchi, Kuo, Kim, & Leaf, 1989; Walker & Irvine, 1997). Second, Donald has the obligation to be familiar with literature and research outlining practice strategies appropriate for populations living in rural Hawaii. In performing this research, Donald is likely to learn that socioeconomic change in the area has a direct relationship with family and marital dissolution and may be a critical predictor of client well-being (Matsuoka & Benson, 1996). Moreover, Donald is likely to learn that individual psychotherapy—Donald's practice modality throughout his career—is likely to be less successful with regional populations than family counseling (Chandler & Bell, 1995; Matsuoka & Benson, 1996; Walker & Irvine, 1997), a practice approach that Donald may be uncomfortable with and unprepared to provide. Nonetheless, the literature indicates that a psychodynamic approach, the treatment modality Donald has been most familiar with, may simply be wrong for this client. Walker and Irvine (1997) have underscored the importance of incorporating traditional Hawaiian culture into mental health programs. They note that unlike the Western, psychodynamic structure of the human psyche, traditional Hawaiian custom views wellness as dependent on personal *mana* (spirit) and regards illness as a loss of *mana* resulting from a lack of *pono* (balance or harmony). Therefore, the Hawaiian perspective emphasizes that, when one become ill, treatment must be applied to restore balance with emotional cleansing—*Ho 'opono pono* (to correct or set things right, to remove mental obstacles to healing). Olson and Anders (2000) supplemented this model by suggesting that, in view of the link between socioeconomic change and community mental health, psychotherapists must work to combine social advocacy with clinical expertise to ensure a continuity of care.

If Donald applies the duty to practice reasonably competently first in his evaluation of practice choices, he must be prepared to offer culturally and regionally appropriate practice techniques at the commencement of therapy. Even if a pressing need for services exists, regardless of whether Donald's intentions are ethical and sincere, reasonably competent practice suggests that a practitioner who has not yet acquired the ability to provide appropriate services should not offer any, nor should the practitioner provide a client with services from which he or she is not reasonably likely to benefit. With this in mind, Donald must seek alternatives to his initial plan of action consistent both with the reasonable-competence standard and with the ethical guidelines cited earlier. This may even mean declining to treat Mrs. Kanahele and instead referring her for services that include culturally competent, family-based therapy.

Is the practice choice this discussion suggests overly harsh? Should no avenue be left open for Donald to acquire the skills necessary for him to grow competent in his use of culturally competent treatment strategies? How does the reasonable-competence standard help Mrs. Kanahele immediately? The answer to all these questions depends on whether the professional believes Mrs. Kanahele is better off being exposed to individual psychotherapy—even if it is not ideal for her needs—than having no assistance at all. In this scenario, the duty to practice reasonably competently promotes the principle that the professional should first do no harm. This canon is one of many that find more protection in the law than in ethical codes. (Were Donald to review more thoroughly the APA Code, he would in fact uncover a provision addressing this issue, ethical standard 3.04, "Avoiding Harm"; its place alongside competing standards, however, together with its broad scope, makes it difficult to identify and apply as a first step in this scenario.)

With this case example in mind, the reader is invited to reevaluate vignettes 1 ("The Angry Client)," 2 ("The Coffee Shop"), and 3 ("The Dream Catcher") in terms of the duty to practice reasonably competently.

Case Example 2: Addressing Attrition among Native American College Students

Mary Vazquez, a certified, master's-level counselor, provides guidance and counseling services at a public community college near Marysville, Washington, adjacent to the Tulalip Indian Reservation. Marysville's population of about twenty-five thousand is in excess of 88 percent white/Anglo, but as noted, it lies adjacent to an Indian reservation with approximately ten thousand residents. Mary is in the process of designing a program intervention that will focus on the problem of high attrition rates among nontraditional students at her college. She is particularly interested in addressing the needs of Native American students, who make up 25 percent of the total student body, a substantial increase over previous years. She is well aware that many of these students are the first in their families to attend college and may require additional support services to assist in their adjustment to college life. Aware of her duty to practice as a reasonably competent counselor would in her community, Mary proceeds to study the problems that Native Americans experience on college campuses. She locates research concerning the Spirit Lake Reservation in North Dakota that suggests that, first, intensive family support should be provided and that, second, basic college courses should be offered to the greatest extent possible on the reservation (Rousey & Longie, 2001). Mary decides to incorporate the results of her research in the design of a culturally appropriate program. She is uncertain, however, whether the college's administration will support any suggestion to offer additional college courses on an Indian reservation in the college's catchment area. What steps must she be prepared to take before completing her program design and presenting it to the college's dean of students?

Both this case example and the previous one highlight the duty to practice reasonably competently; each focuses on the need to stay abreast of current scholarly literature and research, and to incorporate that information in the design and implementation of programs. In contrast to the situation in the previous case example, in this scenario, Mary has researched attrition issues concerning Native students and has come to certain conclusions that she has incorporated into her proposed program. What, then, has Mary omitted? If she understands fully the duty to practice reasonably competently, then she also understands that keeping aware of national research is one good step in program design. It is, however, only the first step. By incorporating the results of research concerning the Spirit Lake Reservation into her program design, Mary may have overextended the limits of this research in terms of its applicability to her client group. Without undertaking a local needs assessment to ascertain the accuracy of the data, she runs the risk both of stereotyping her clients and of designing her program incompetently. Indeed, reasonably competent practice means practice that is appropriate based on community standards. Therefore, conducting a community needs assessment in this context is no less necessary than conducting a psychosocial assessment of a client about to receive psychotherapy. In the case of program design, it means remaining familiar with scholarly research in the relevant field but at the same time taking appropriate steps to determine the relevance of the research to the community in which one practices. In this instance, making an assumption about Native Americans in general, without testing the assumption on the basis of a community needs assessment, violates the duty to practice reasonably competently. In this case example, competent practice may be regarded not simply as a legal standard but also as a useful practice tool that mandates the appropriate consideration of diversity issues in professional decision making.

Case Example 3: The Licensee

Jade Melman, a recent graduate of a master's-level program in social work, is anxious to put her newly acquired clinical skills to the test. As part of her graduate program, Jade has completed basic course work in clinical social work practice, psychopharmacology, human behavior in the social environment, and group work. Now licensed in New York as a master social worker, but lacking any advanced training or certification as a clinical social worker, she accepts a position as a psychotherapist at a community mental health center in a rural town in upstate New York in a county that is large geographically but fairly sparsely populated. The mental health center has been desperate to hire a therapist for some time to adequately address the service needs of the community. Jade will practice under the supervision of the licensed psychologist who oversees outpatient services at the center.

Having reviewed the law in New York governing social work practice, Jade knows that, in general, clinical social workers certified in that specialty have the legal authority to diagnose and treat mental illness. She is uncertain, however, about the specific practice expectations associated with her area of specialization.

The duty to practice reasonably competently suggests several responsibilities that Jade and her supervisor have with respect to Jade's rendering of clinical services. First, Jade arguably does not meet the threshold amount of posteducational field experience necessary to practice clinical social work competently, at least in the absence of ongoing supervision. If she proceeds to see clients without informing them of her training limitations, lack of field experience, and the fact that she must practice under close clinical supervision, then clients are likely to assume that Jade has a level of qualification reasonably expected from a trained, experienced clinical social worker.

In light of the duty to practice reasonably competently, what options do Jade and her supervisor have with respect to any representations they convey to clients about Jade's qualifications? Moreover, exactly what should be the extent of Jade's participation in the delivery of client services? For one thing, Jade can assist in the provision of services to her supervisor's clients, a most reasonable arrangement in terms of providing needed services to clients while allowing Jade to receive training necessary for an apprentice clinical social worker. Put differently, Jade should refrain from treating clients independently of her supervisor (i.e., from accepting her own clients) until she has satisfied her training regimen. This arrangement reflects the manner in which a reasonable therapist practicing in a rural, service-deprived community should offer care: both Jade's supervisor and Jade can ensure the competence of the services offered and provide needed treatment in an underserved area. At the same time, this arrangement must be explained to clients at the commencement of services so that they have a realistic appreciation of the professional duties that Jade and her supervisor, respectively, owe to them and can intelligently consent to receive services.

What exactly should Jade and her supervisor explain to clients? First, they should make clear that services will be provided to each client under the direct supervision of Jade's supervisor; second, the extent of Jade's credentials, along with their limitations, should be explained to clients; third, the supervisor's credentials should be discussed with clients; finally, clients should be advised as to the nature of the supervisory relationship between Jade and her supervisor. If this explanation is provided, then clients will have a more reasonable and fully informed understanding of the services they are receiving and the preparedness of the professionals providing them. In this scenario, offering a clear explanation serves to identify the professional relationships between the client and each provider and the responsibilities that Jade and her supervisor are to assume. In the manner just described, Jade can enjoy a professional relationship with her supervisor's clients, but from a legal perspective, her duty to practice reasonably competently requires that she practice at least initially under supervision and that she acknowledge and convey her limited training to prospective clients. This approach should be employed at least until Jade has attained the practice experience sufficient to allow her to offer care with the reasonable competence expected of mental health providers in the community.

What additional responsibilities does Jade's supervisor have? Most important, with Jade's limited practice experience explained to clients, the supervisor must be prepared to assume primary authority for the responsible provision of clinical care to each client. Consistent with this responsibility, the supervisor must provide services that match those reasonably expected from a provider with advanced clinical training. If this is to be accomplished, during the period allotted for Jade's training, the supervisor must ensure that Jade's treatment of each client conforms to the skill level expected of a clinician with Jade's education and degree of training. This responsibility makes the provision of appropriate supervision to Jade a vital duty.

Given the large geographical size of this rural community, the limited number of available services, and the multiple responsibilities of Jade's supervisor, it may be reasonable for the supervisor to extend considerable latitude to Jade in the performance of her job functions, including intake and assessment of clients and direct clinical dialogue with them, provided that Jade's supervisor does not cede responsibility for the essential therapeutic environment until Jade is reasonably competent to manage it independently.

The professional apprenticeship not only serves the needs of Jade and her supervisor but also is a fairly typical way that clinicians can achieve advanced training while honoring the duty to provide reasonably competent mental health care. It is an essential process in the field preparation of virtually all clinical mental health providers.

How does application of the duty to practice reasonably competently promote the quality of psychotherapeutic services rendered in a community?

Most important, it offers a baseline level of protection to the client. The degree of protection may be lacking in some communities where the stark absence of mental health resources may interfere with enforcement of the quality and competence of services. As an example, in the Navajo Nation, which lies in the Four Corners region of Arizona, Colorado, Utah, and New Mexico, as many as five hundred social workers may be offering basic mental health services to clients in a geographical area of approximately twenty-six thousand square miles. Of the five hundred service providers, only a handful have advanced clinical social work training and certification. Navajo leaders have become aware of this public health crisis and are forging relationships with university-level mental health programs to offer advanced clinical training sufficient to meet this critical need.

When providers understand the boundaries of their own professional competence and are able to communicate this information to clients, they open a more effective clinical dialogue. That openness leads to more competent assessment, more effective treatment, and clearer expectations for clients. Indeed, defining these expectations appropriately may represent the single most important ingredient in any clinical intervention. The responsibility of a professional to communicate effectively concerning the potential benefits and hazards presented to the prospective client describes yet another fundamental legal principle whose understanding and application can assist the decision maker in assessing and resolving everyday practice dilemmas. This duty to seek informed consent is related to and interconnected with the duty to practice reasonably competently; it is discussed in more detail next.

CHAPTER 4

The Duty to Seek
Informed Consent

THE DUTY TO PRACTICE REASONABLY competently describes the essential responsibility of mental health professionals to render services consistently with the expectations imposed on them in a community. As already noted, a significant part of that duty includes communicating with the client in a manner that facilitates the assessment of the presenting problem, together with the professional's consideration and design of services that address the problem. The duty to seek informed consent explains the professional's responsibility to communicate enough information concerning the risks and benefits of the services the professional offers to allow the client to make a reasoned decision to choose those services. The duty applies to all health and human service professionals, including social workers, counselors, psychologists, physicians, and attorneys.

As with the duty to practice reasonably competently, the duty to seek informed consent actually takes effect even before the client makes the conscious decision to accept professional services. In this sense, informed consent is a prerequisite to the legitimate acceptance of any health service. Indeed, without obtaining it, the professional cannot provide services lawfully. In some circumstances—most notably surgery and other medical and psychiatric procedures performed on involuntary patients—it may even be criminal for the professional to provide services to the client in the absence of informed consent (*Bee v. Greaves*, 1984; *Laskowitz v. Ciba Vision Corp.*, 1995; Sacks, 2008; Stephens, 2007). For this reason, state legislation sometimes defines responsibilities associated with the provision of informed consent. With this in mind, mental health professionals should be familiar not only with the common law principles governing informed consent but also with health and licensing codes in effect where they practice.

The doctrine of informed consent derives from a time-honored common law principle that emphasizes a client's or patient's right to determine the nature and scope of the professional services required, whether those services are in the area of medical treatment, legal assistance, psychological care, counseling, or social work. When a patient or client approaches the professional with a presenting problem, the duty to seek informed consent mandates that the professional assist the client in preserving his or her own right to choose voluntarily the type and extent of the responsive intervention. Specifically, this means that professionals are obliged not only to describe the services they have to offer but also to outline alternative means of treating the same problem, together with the risks and benefits of each approach. Some professionals may feel awkward doing this when they have confidence in a particular treatment modality or practice perspective. Even so, it is imperative from the standpoint of protecting the client's basic right to make informed choices about professional services.

The requirement that professionals seek informed consent has been incorporated into numerous professional codes of ethics, including the NASW Code (ethical standard 1.03), NBCC Code (section B8), and APA Code (ethical standard 3.10). However, especially in the NBCC provision, more stress is placed on the requirement that the professional inform the client than on the need to obtain the client's consent. Therefore, given the rather general coverage of informed consent in ethical codes, it is important to emphasize that this duty is at first a legal principle, the application of which extends to relationships between all professionals and their clients, and whose coverage may be broader than some ethical codes would imply. Consequently, informed consent is one of several basic legal standards whose application professionals in any practice dilemma should identify first before considering the ethical guidelines unique to one profession. Adopting this strategy will greatly help the decision maker address numerous practice dilemmas. Furthermore, it will help the practitioner make better practice decisions that advance important societal goals rather than focus on the often conflicting professional aspirations advocated in each mental health discipline.

Origins and Elements of the Common Law Duty to Seek Informed Consent

As a legal doctrine, courts initially recognized informed consent in the context of relationships between physicians and their patients. At the heart of informed consent is the idea that the patient seeking medical services alone has the right to weigh the risks associated with a particular treatment and then make an individual decision to accept or reject them (*Bee v. Greaves*, 1984; *Rasmussen v. Fleming*, 1987; *Schreiber v. Physicians Ins. Co. of Wis.*, 1999; *Wicks v. Vanderbilt Univ.*, 2007). In formulating the doctrine, courts have been primarily concerned with two different but related freedoms: the first of these is the patient's right to choose services freely. This right can be secured only by patients' demanding of full and accurate information from professionals (*Hull v. So. Ill. Hosp. Servs.*, 2005; *Laskowitz v. Ciba Vision Corp.*, 1995; *Mohr v. Commonwealth*, 1995). Second is the right to be free to forgo treatment, a privilege that is often associated with the individual's right of privacy (*Bee v. Greaves*, 1984; *Dep't of Health & Mental Hygiene v. Kelly*, 2007; *Rasmussen v. Fleming*, 1987). Courts have often described this right in terms of a person's sense of bodily integrity and liberty to control and care for physical, health-related needs. This right is best preserved when the individual is solely responsible for making choices concerning his or her medical treatment (*Bee v. Greaves*, 1984; *Dep't of Health & Mental Hygiene v. Kelly*, 2007; *Rasmussen v. Fleming*, 1987).

The first freedom associated with informed consent—the right to choose services—has long been recognized in the case of individuals who freely seek out professional assistance. The second freedom—the right to decline services—has been acknowledged in the case of persons for whom the government or treating caregivers seek involuntary treatment. This freedom has often been recognized in cases involving the right of nondangerous psychiatric patients and prison inmates to decline psychosurgery and forced administration of psychoactive medication (*Bee v. Greaves*, 1984; *Dep't of Health & Mental Hygiene v. Kelly*, 2007; *Riggins v. Nevada*, 1992).

Mental health professionals concerned with the application of informed consent need to understand each freedom that the doctrine enforces, because they will provide services both to clients who seek them out voluntarily and to clients for whom services have been mandated, most often by a court (Regehr & Antle, 1997). Note, however, that these freedoms are actually related. An individual's choice concerning health services can never be truly voluntary unless the individual has information concerning the risks of treatment and the existence of alternative strategies to address the problem (*Goldberg v. Boone*, 2006; *Laskowitz v. Ciba Vision Corp.*, 1995).

Courts have expanded the scope of informed consent to include the services rendered by a number of mental health professions, including social workers, counselors, psychologists, nurses, and others for whom state law has imposed the requirement of licensure (*Andrews v. Bd. of Soc. Worker Licensure*, 2005; *Laskowitz v. Ciba Vision Corp.*, 1995; *Sakler v. Anesthesiologist Assoc.*, 2001). As courts have noted, the justification for this broadening of

informed consent is that it is an integral part of the duty to practice reasonably competently, a responsibility that applies to all health professionals
(*Laskowitz v. Ciba Vision Corp.*, 1995).

The scope of informed consent extends not only to those who traditionally would be considered as having the legal status of client but also to
other persons, such as human research subjects, whose health and personal
privacy may reasonably be expected to be affected by the experimental
treatment or research undertaken (*Abdullahi v. Pfizer, Inc.*, 2009; *Modi v.
W. Va. Bd. of Med.*, 1995; *Stanley v. Swinson*, 1995). Federal law recognizes
extensive protections that require the obtaining of informed consent before
human-subjects research (U.S. Department of Health and Human Services
Rules Governing the Protection of Human Subjects, 2009) and under the
health and mental health codes of numerous states. When human research
subjects receive or are offered the opportunity to receive services from the
researcher, even more difficult informed consent issues arise. These issues
are addressed subsequently and are the particular subject of case example 8,
"The Research Study."

Informed consent has three essential components. First, the professional
must assist the client seeking services in having a reasonable understanding of the risks and benefits of the proposed service; second, the client must
make a decision concerning treatment that is fully voluntary; third, the client must have the capacity to choose (*Logan v. Greenwich Hosp. Assoc.*, 1983;
Rasmussen v. Fleming, 1987). Every mental health decision maker must be
thoroughly familiar with the components of informed consent, and a detailed discussion of each follows.

Understanding the Risks and Benefits

Each professional has a duty to provide, in a form that the client can reasonably understand, the following minimum information:

- The professional's assessment of the client's presenting problem
- The services the professional proposes to address the problem
- The professional's opinion as to the benefits or risks to the client
  that might result if the client accepts or rejects services
- The nature and availability of alternative services to address the
  problem

How much information is a "reasonable" amount? The courts have variously answered this question by evaluating the following: what a reasonable
professional in a particular community should be expected to disclose on

the basis of the professional's training and experience, or in some jurisdictions, the amount of information that a reasonable person of the client's background could be expected to require to choose whether to receive services (i.e., the objective standard) (*Ashe v. Radiation Oncology Assocs.*,1999; *Haupt v. Kumar*, 2008; *Laskowitz v. Ciba Vision Corp.*, 1995).

Consistent with a community-sensitive definition of *reasonableness*, the cautious decision maker should base the disclosure of information not only on professional training and experience but also on a consideration of the factors that characterize both the client and the client's community, including age and cultural demographics; these issues are relatively certain to have a role in the client's choice regarding services.

As an example of the burden that informed consent places on a psychotherapist, consider the case of a clinical social worker, counselor, or psychologist specializing in the treatment of mood disorders and substance abuse in an Oneida Indian Nation community in central New York State. The therapist must assume that a reasonable client with signs of clinical depression would want to be aware of all treatment modalities available to address the depression before making a decision to choose the approach this particular therapist offers. Therefore, the professional must be prepared to discuss alternative therapeutic options, including pharmacological, cognitive-behavioral, and culture-specific treatments that the client would likely want information about before committing to one particular therapy. This is the case even if the professional is strongly ideologically opposed to any one of these approaches. It would be a mistake if the therapist overemphasized, for example, the use of culture-specific remedies or, conversely, underemphasized them. Stereotyping the client threatens the sufficiency of informed consent as much as the therapist's imposition of his or her own treatment approach does.

In addition to the types of disclosures mentioned previously, the professional's lack of experience in, or personal predisposition against, a particular form of service should be revealed, because it may additionally affect the client's willingness to grant informed consent to a particular service. Therefore, the client has the right to consider the professional's position regarding a treatment approach before making a decision about services. Case example 5, "The Forest Fire," explores this point in more detail.

In view of the broad duties outlined earlier, informed consent imposes a burden on all psychotherapists to have knowledge that extends beyond the bounds of their individual professional disciplines. This may be a troubling thought to some therapists who believe that their training and licensing credentials insulate them from this responsibility. However, from the client's perspective, it is entirely reasonable and necessary. A mentally ill client does not feel troubled in a social work way but feels only a generalized sense of affliction. The protection informed consent provides maximizes the chance of recovery by enhancing the client's knowledge about alternative routes to improvement.

One of the additional risks mental health professionals should be prepared to discuss with their clients is the existence of any conflict of interest the therapist might have in providing a particular service (*Duttry v. Patterson*, 2001; *Horak v. Biris*, 1985; In re *Disciplinary Proceeding against Marshall*, 2007); *Moore v. Regents of Univ. of Cal.*, 1990; *Petrillo v. Syntex Labs, Inc.*, 1986). Such a conflict is a risk to any client in the sense that it may compromise the quality of the service and the professional's ability to deliver care independent of an outside influence; the client ought to reasonably expect that the professional's independent commitment to the client is unequivocal. Conflicts of interest may include economic interests the professional has in a particular service, consulting contracts connected with the service, involvement in research projects related to the service, or external business or social relationships with the client. Professionals are also required to disclose personal attributes, interests, and experiences that may also threaten to interfere with the provider's ability to offer independent commitment and competent services to the client, such as the professional's physical impairment or lack of experience in a particular practice area (*Faya v. Almaraz*, 1993—holding that a doctor was required to reveal the fact that he had AIDS before performing surgery on the patient, because the patient should have considered the risk of infection with AIDS in making a decision as to whether to have the operation; *Johnson v. Kokemoor*, 1996). Some associations, including sexual and inappropriate social or business relationships, may be so innately threatening to the client's best interests that, even with full disclosure, they destroy the client's very capacity to grant informed consent.

The duty to seek informed consent applies to all mental health professionals, sometimes in ways that are not immediately recognizable. For example, in the case of a protective service social worker seeking to place a child for adoption, the duty requires the social worker to advise potential adoptive parents regarding the child's medical and psychological history (*Jackson v. State*, 1998; *Mohr v. Commonwealth*, 1995; *Roe v. Jewish Children's Bureau of Chicago*, 2003). In this instance, imposing the responsibility to advise is based on the presumption that the adoptive parents' decision to adopt may be based at least in part on whether they are able to cope financially and emotionally with children who may have special needs (*Jackson v. State*, 1998; *Mohr v. Commonwealth*, 1995; *Roe v. Jewish Children's Bureau of Chicago*, 2003). Reasonable disclosure, in this context, may extend to the conveyance of information pertaining to the birth mother's medical, psychological, and genetic background, because adoptive parents are likely to require such information to make an informed decision about whether to adopt a child (*Jackson v. State*, 1998; *Mohr v. Commonwealth*, 1995; *Roe v. Jewish Children's Bureau of Chicago*, 2003).

In all professional relationships, the informed consent dialogue must include a discussion pertaining to confidentiality and its limits, because the client's expectation of privacy may be an important motivating factor in the decision to seek services. At the same time, the client must be made aware of circumstances, such as suicidal ideation or threats of violence, that will require the professional to disclose this information to a third party. Limitations on the rule of confidentiality therefore represent a risk to the client that may also influence his or her decision to choose services. The professional's duty to disclose the limits of confidentiality is problematic; the very discussion of exceptions to confidentiality may discourage an already-hesitant client from seeking services. Handling of this discussion is therefore best accomplished in a humanistic manner that avoids legalistic jargon lifted verbatim from agency policies, statutes, or well-known lawsuits.

At the heart of informed consent is reasonable disclosure. Note that this means disclosure not only to the professional's primary client (i.e., the child to be adopted, in the case of the protective service social worker) but also to those legally empowered to make decisions on the client's behalf (i.e., the potential adoptive parents, in the case cited here) and other persons who potentially are at risk of suffering harm as a result of a failure to disclose (*Jackson v. State*, 1998; *Mohr v. Commonwealth*, 1995; *Roe v. Jewish Children's Bureau of Chicago*, 2003).

As noted earlier, advancements in technology—including, specifically, access to information resulting from Internet access—may be changing the practice expectations associated with informed consent, especially with respect to rural practitioners, and decreasing the extent to which professional standards vary among communities. Thus, if a counselor in Whiteville, North Carolina (site of President Bill Clinton's 1999 speech "Bridging the Digital Divide"), is able to electronically access essentially the same databases of practice knowledge that are available to a comparable professional in New York City, then the rural practitioner will likely be held to a higher standard of familiarity with alternative practice approaches and expected to pass this information on to the client. Moreover, as health maintenance organizations (HMOs) and other health-care providers continue to collect extensive treatment data via computer, they may come under increasing pressure to do a better job of informing potential patients and clients as to the safety of certain health-care procedures and the performance records of their providers (Hellwage, 2000). The impact of this pressure may well extend to social workers, counselors, psychologists, and all those health professionals who provide HMO-associated services.

Internet-based services raise even more serious questions about the ability of participants to achieve full disclosure of the risks and benefits pertaining to Web counseling. As already noted, the NBCC has embraced Internet-based counseling for professional counselors, within certain broadly defined limits. Section B12 of the NBCC Code imposes only minimal requirements governing informed consent on counselors intending to use the Web. Specifically, it requires them to advise potential Internet clients of the availability of "local sources of care" before instituting any long-distance professional relationship. This provision fails, however, to address the overriding problem concerning Internet counseling. More specifically, it may interfere with the heart of any professional relationship by diminishing the provider's ability to convey complete information about the services offered and by thwarting the client's opportunity to pose questions concerning those services. Moreover, electronic counseling simply does not provide a comparable substitute for in-person assessment.

Voluntariness

As noted previously, mental health professionals most frequently work with clients who seek their services voluntarily. At other times, they may work with clients who have come to treatment involuntarily, typically as the result of a court order. Each category of client is addressed separately here.

VOLUNTARY CLIENTS

With respect to clients who freely seek the professional's services, the best way to preserve their voluntary pursuit of treatment is to obey the duty to provide reasonably complete disclosure of the risks and benefits associated with services. Failure to provide this information in essence removes from the client the ability to select the professional's services consciously and ultimately interferes with the client's freewill choice regarding treatment. In this sense, providing reasonable disclosure fosters informed consent. As noted, such disclosure must include a practical review of alternative approaches to the client's presenting problem, in addition to a full discussion of the services the professional offers.

The solicitation of potential clients through advertising and in-person appeals raises important questions concerning the ability of such persons to agree voluntarily to the services promoted. This problem most obviously arises in the context of mental health providers who advertise. It also presents itself in the case of professionals who lecture publicly on clinical or other subjects related to mental health at academic conferences or through mass media. In both instances, those who have attended a workshop or watched an advertisement may seek out the services of the presenter or advertiser. All too commonly, the indiscreet presenter may be tempted to serve the needs of the often-enthusiastic listener and prospective client without explaining the benefits of alternative approaches or drawbacks of the service being promoted.

The significance of this problem may be lost on a generation of mental health professionals who regard advertising generally as legal and, within limits, ethical and therefore promote their services avidly. They are correct in the sense that courts have upheld the right of professionals to solicit clients on the ground that it protects the First Amendment right to free communication and that it promotes the public interest in aiding the dissemination of accurate information about the availability of services (*Bates v. State Bar*, 1977; In re *R. M. J.*, 1982).

Codes of ethics, including the NASW Code (ethical standard 4.07), the APA Code (ethical standards 5.01–5.06), and the NBCC Code (section F1), generally permit advertising. Moreover, they have adopted the spirit of the court decisions mentioned previously by imposing the requirement on solicitation that it not subject clients, especially vulnerable persons, to undue influence. Undue influence is ordinarily presumed to take place when solicitation of clients is done in person, where the solicitor has the opportunity to use personal authority to suggest the need for services directly. Interestingly, none of the ethical codes cited here absolutely bans in-person solicitation. The APA Code (ethical standard 5.06) seems to permit it to the extent that it is "invited," a provision apparently intended to cover public lectures and demonstrations, which unfortunately may actually offer the most dangerous opportunity for the kind of self-promotion by solicitors that sometimes renders impossible the conveyance of informed consent.

Ethical codes aside, advertising does raise informed consent problems. Civil malpractice suits based on the violation of informed consent have been brought against health professionals making overtly misleading claims to the public. For example, in *Karlin v. IVF America, Inc.* (1999) a medical clinic's excessively optimistic reports in its advertising and promotional literature concerning its human fertilization program led to disappointed patients filing multiple informed-consent-based claims. In this case, as in others, the mass-market approach of the clinic's promotion plainly drove the enthusiasm of potential patients, who then sought the services of the advertiser (see also *Feldman v. Tenn. Bd. of Med. Exam'rs*, 2003—a physician acted unlawfully by mailing eight thousand postcards to past and present patients offering a 50 percent discount on office visits if they brought in a new patient; *Desnick v. Dep't of Prof'l Regulation*, 1996—an ophthalmologist used a telemarketing firm to offer free eye exams and free transportation to the elderly in the hope that, once they arrived at the office, they would consent to more extensive eye surgery). Considered in this light, the most potentially dangerous impact of client solicitation on the client's ability to give informed consent is the interference that it may cause with the client's conscious process of deliberation. When solicitation is carried out through mass media, as has been done in the recent past with health and mental health services, its greatest impact may well be on the rural, poor, and under-educated people most vulnerable to the effects of this information (Albee, 1999; Long, 2003; McMichael & Beaglehole, 2000; Quigley, 2001). Given this fact, client solicitation clearly has the potential to interfere with potential clients' open-minded consideration of treatment alternatives (*Dezen v. Bureau of Prof'l & Occupational Affairs*, 1999—a social worker believed erroneously that he could list himself as a psychologist in the Yellow Pages because he was a "practitioner of the healing arts," p. 1135; *Tex. Bd. of Med. Exam'rs v. Burzynski*, 1996).

The impact of advertising on the voluntary choice of mental health services raises interesting questions about the meaning of *voluntariness* in the context of informed consent. The U.S. Supreme Court has suggested that voluntary choice is compromised when a person's "will has been overborne and . . . capacity for self-determination critically impaired" (*Schneckloth v. Bustamonte*, 1973, p. 225). One health-care ethicist has proposed a definition of *voluntariness* that is even more stringent than that of the Supreme Court: voluntariness exists when there is an "absence of controlling influences" exerted by others and the client retains "the ability to choose either one of at least two options" (Hewlett, 1996, p. 233). To satisfy this definition, the client must be free of manipulation or the selective conveyance of information to influence a decision. Under either definition of voluntariness, substantial questions can be raised concerning the impact that direct client solicitation, including advertising, may have on the ability to provide informed consent ("Alabama to investigate," 2008—revealing the astonishing Alabama investigation of more than one hundred uncertified agencies falsely advertising themselves as substance abuse treatment providers; D. Johnson, 1979—offering an interesting historical impression of the blizzard of health-care advertising by mental health agencies and alcoholism treatment centers, among other providers, following the removal of restrictions on advertising in a series of court decisions in the 1970s; Pestello & Davis-Berman, 2008—reporting on the direct marketing of psychiatric medications via the Internet and the implications of this trend on mental health nationally).

Undue influence may present significant problems not only when clients are solicited but also when therapists seek their participation in research studies (Hewlett, 1996). Medical ethicists have noted that, despite the legal restrictions placed on researchers with respect to the obtaining of informed consent, participants in clinical research are unlikely to be free from subtle influences. Specifically, patients rely on the position of trust that their physicians retain to gain assistance in decision making regarding health-care choices. Patients often perceive physicians as powerful figures whose future care may diminish in quality if the patient declines to take part in the testing of new medical procedures or drugs. This problem is present as well in the mental health professions. Despite the emphasis these professions place on egalitarian service delivery and the client's right to self-determination, there is nonetheless an inherent power differential between professionals and their clients; this is especially true with respect to the relationship between psychotherapists and their clients. For clinical social workers, counselors, and psychologists who seek to involve their clients in the research of new treatment modalities, this lesson is an important one; it may persuade such researchers to exercise more care in the solicitation of participants and rely more on independent, trained personnel, such as client advocates, to explain the risks and benefits of participation (Hewlett, 1996).

INVOLUNTARY CLIENTS

Mental health professionals often provide services to clients who have not sought them voluntarily. This situation arises regularly in the case of clients who lack capacity, either legal or mental, to make life choices that involve mental health services, among other issues. Clients in this category do not have the ability to provide informed consent in a voluntary and knowing way. Included in this group, among others, are persons who have been involuntarily committed for institutional mental health services and individuals for whom life-sustaining treatment is sought against their will. As to the rights of members of the latter group, they are the focus of later discussion.

Other persons present themselves to mental health professionals for services because they have been court mandated to do so, because of child abuse proceedings, criminal prosecutions, divorce proceedings, domestic-violence-related civil and criminal cases, adult protection cases, or legal guardianship cases. Still other instances arise, such as in the area of adult or juvenile probation services, in which a client must submit to drug testing and other conditions of parole, probation, or delinquency adjudication. In all such circumstances, how can the duty to seek informed consent be honored without violating the client's fundamental privacy right?

In reality, the duty of mental health providers to seek the voluntary participation of clients is modified in the case of those who are court ordered
to receive services. In these instances, the satisfaction of informed consent
should be understood in terms of the transfer of formal decision-making authority to another legal entity, most often a court. In the case of individuals
under court order, an important state interest—most often related to public
protection—usually authorizes a court to assume responsibility for seeking corrective treatment on the recipient's behalf. Often, the state's concern
involves the protection of a vulnerable person, such as a child caught in an
abusive relationship or a victim of criminal conduct. Much like a guardian
protecting a ward, the court may approve services that can address the root
causes of the aberrant behavior.

Whenever possible, courts ordering services do so with the recipients'
willing consent. On such occasions, the individual's agreement to seek services may provide a means of avoiding imprisonment or ending litigation
that the person is more than happy to endorse. In such circumstances, clients literally consent to treatment as a means, for example, to avoid a jail
sentence or to recover custody of their children. Given the situational pressure, however, clients cannot really be thought of as approving services in a
completely voluntary manner. This is especially true considering the routine
requirement that a client's progress in a court-ordered treatment program
be reported to the court. Sometimes, court-ordered treatment may be more
coercive, with the court mandating a particular mental health or substance
abuse treatment plan or other course of behavioral therapy. In all these instances, whether the client has given nominal consent or has been ordered
to treatment outright, the professional should regard the court as the ultimate decision maker in terms of the services that are provided; in effect, the
court provides informed consent in the client's name.

As an example of substituted informed consent, a court may order a re-
spondent in a child abuse proceeding to receive individual anger management therapy, parent effectiveness training, or even substance abuse and
mental health treatment (Rittner & Dozier, 2000). A criminal defendant
convicted of drug possession may be ordered to rehabilitation. Similarly,
an individual convicted of stalking may be ordered to receive both jail time
and court-ordered psychological treatment (see, e.g., Georgia's stalking and
harassment law, Ga. Code Ann. § 16-5-90[d], 2009, which provides that a
judge may consider this remedy in sentencing a convicted stalker). A mo-
torist who has pleaded guilty to driving under the influence of alcohol (i.e.,
a DUI) may be ordered to attend victim-impact panel sessions and physical handicap educational programming administered by Mothers Against
Drunk Driving (MADD) (*State v. Lattimer*, 2001).

In any of the foregoing scenarios, courts usually are under a clear legislative mandate to tailor their orders to address the conduct that has invoked the state interest that each court is empowered to protect. If courts exceed that mandate by placing excessive requirements or restrictions on a client, they may violate fundamental constitutional freedoms, including the client's right to privacy (see chapter 6). For example, a court that orders an unruly but mentally competent criminal defendant to receive antipsychotic medication during pretrial detention impermissibly invades the detainee's freedom to reject such treatment (*Bee v. Greaves*, 1984; *Dep't of Health & Mental Hygiene v. Kelly*, 2007; *Riggins v. Nevada*, 1992). Similarly, the increasing tendency of family courts in some areas to impose the requirement of marriage counseling before the consideration of divorce may run afoul of the constitutional right to privacy. In both instances, the forced treatment of the client may violate the voluntariness component of informed consent and thereby unacceptably invade the client's personal privacy. This constitutional doctrine helps explain why legislatures historically have avoided enacting mental health treatment components in their criminal legislation, even though compelling research suggests that they are so vitally important in the long-term prevention of some types of criminal behavior (Peebles, 1999).

Clearly, there has been a general trend in judicial opinions opposing involuntary inpatient commitment and especially forced medication of persons without a clear demonstration that these persons represent a threat of harm to themselves and others (Werth, 2001). However, a public event in 1999 had a prominent role in directing public opinion in favor of the enhanced used of forced treatment and administering of psychoactive medication to treat mentally ill persons, with a corresponding impact on state legislation. Specifically, a young woman named Kendra Webdale was murdered by a man suffering from chronic schizophrenia. He pushed Kendra in the path of an oncoming New York City subway train (Appelbaum, 2005). The resultant public outcry led the New York legislature to enact legislation—known as Kendra's Law—giving courts the authority to force mentally ill persons who are not presently demonstrated to pose an immediate risk of harm or violence but have had a record of past violence and are demonstrably at risk to engage in future violence to receive mandatory outpatient treatment, including forced medication. The criteria for granting courts this authority include a finding that these persons have failed to respond to past treatment, thus resulting in multiple hospitalizations and past violence to themselves or others (Appelbaum, 2005). The statute authorizing forced outpatient care, known as assisted outpatient treatment (AOT) is intended to prevent future acts of violence in the case of a person who has shown past violence with a likelihood of relapse. It also permits courts to reinstitutionalize offenders if they do not follow the outpatient treatment regimen. New York's AOT statute (N.Y. Mental Hyg. § 9.60, 2009) requires that the offender is at least eighteen years of age, is mentally ill, is unlikely to survive in a community without supervision, has a history of noncompliance with mental health treatment (at least two hospitalizations in the previous thirty-six months or an act or threat of violence to self or others within the past forty-eight months), is unlikely to voluntarily participate in treatment, and needs further treatment—including, if necessary, forced medication—to prevent relapse or deterioration likely to lead to new episodes of violence.

Such AOT statutes have been enacted in more than forty states, and all display the same proactive intent demonstrated in New York's statute to attempt to prevent tragedies before they happen. Nevertheless, these statutes have not been adopted without continuing, intense criticism both of the constitutionality of the approach and of the observation that AOT statutes have had a severely disproportionate impact on nonwhite offenders, especially African Americans (Appelbaum, 2005). This outcry notwithstanding, the state's highest appellate court found New York's statute constitutional (In re *K. L.*, 2004). At the same time, there is at least one instance of a court decision outside of New York finding fault constitutionally with the statutory approach adopted in AOTs (see, e.g., *Protection & Advocacy Sys. v. City of Albuquerque*, 2008).

How can the mental health professional honor both the letter and spirit of informed consent when working with an involuntary client? First, the professional must clearly convey information to the client at the commencement of services and explain the professional's obligations to the court that has requested the service. This may involve explaining the limits on confidentiality that the treatment situation imposes. Second, the professional must seek the client's voluntary participation in all aspects of treatment to the extent possible. Third, the professional should honor the client's right to receive an explanation of the risks and benefits of the services ordered. The fact that the client's treatment may not be entirely voluntary does not eliminate this important component of informed consent.

Capacity

Mental Capacity

Capacity is an important component of informed consent because, without it, a client is unable to make an educated decision regarding services. It is related to the voluntariness component in that, lacking capacity, a client for whom services are provided is essentially receiving them involuntarily. Mental capacity can be defined as the ability to participate in a reasoned decision-making process regarding the risks and benefits of treatment (*Bee v. Greaves*, 1984). To be regarded as having mental capacity, one seeking treatment must have a reasonable understanding of one's own physical and mental condition, the risks and benefits of the services proposed to address the condition, and the consequences of receiving no services at all (*Rasmussen v. Fleming*, 1987). Consistent with constitutional guarantees that all adult citizens enjoy, persons who have attained adulthood are presumed to have the mental capacity to provide informed consent. This means simply that all treatment decisions made by a person with capacity must ordinarily be honored, even if they defy common sense or the ideological perspective of the professional provider (*Bee v. Greaves*, 1984). Note that in the case of gravely ill or terminal patients who otherwise satisfy the definition of mental capacity, they have the right to refuse medical treatment. Clients who are aged, depressed, forgetful, or whose thinking may be mildly compromised have the same right. It is an unfortunate reality, however, that these persons are sometimes treated as if they lacked mental capacity.

Under certain circumstances, a family member, guardian, or a representative of the state may seek to demonstrate that an individual lacks the mental capacity to consent to medical, mental health, or human services. Frequently, this situation arises in the case of the severely mentally ill, the frail elderly, or those with substance abuse–induced psychosis. Less frequently, it arises in the case of persons declining medical services whose conditions are reasonably amenable to conservative treatment approaches. With respect to these individuals, an interested advocate concerned with the patient's welfare, typically a close family member or mental health agency, may seek appointment as a legal guardian (see, e.g., Uniform Probate Code §§ 5-301 to 5-318, 2004/2006; enacted in eighteen states).

The purpose of guardianship is to convey to a concerned individual the legal right to grant informed consent for appropriate medical or psychiatric services on behalf of a vulnerable person. Although the legislative standards for the granting of guardianship vary from state to state, a patient's inability to provide informed consent is a critical component. Consistent with the spirit of informed consent, even when a patient fails to meet the legal standards governing mental capacity, it is appropriate that a guardian reasonably consult with the patient where possible to ascertain the patient's wishes concerning treatment and living arrangements. In some situations, the granting court may expressly limit guardianship in such a way as to narrow the guardian's authority to specific medical conditions or areas of decision making or to impose clear responsibility on the limited guardian to consult with the patient on important matters pertaining to care and living arrangements. In some states, legislation may provide for the appointment of a treatment guardian whose responsibility extends solely to mental health care issues.

Guardianship is conferred at the conclusion of a court proceeding in which a person's lack of mental capacity is demonstrated. It is often granted in conjunction with conservatorship, in which an individual or organization—the conservator—is granted the legal authority to manage the person's financial assets. State statutes governing guardianship and conservatorship typically require that a person's mental capacity be demonstrated on the basis of, among other things, a review of the person's psychosocial functioning. Mental health professionals acting in the capacity of visitors appointed by the court often undertake such a review. In conjunction with expert medical witnesses, visitors assist the court in the consideration of the person's capacity for informed consent regarding both health-care decisions and financial estate management.

Alternatives to guardianship exist that avoid the extreme measure of removing from an individual all right to decision making. A more satisfactory approach involves personal life planning before a person's incapacity, including the identification of surrogate decision makers capable of making important life choices on a person's behalf in the event of incapacity. Without this prior planning, surrogate decision makers not previously chosen by an incapacitated person may be forced to consider various health-care options on behalf of the person, including end-of-life decisions and the termination of artificially maintained medical treatment. In support of individual life planning, all states have legislation allowing a mentally competent person to designate advance directives (Nakashima, 2004). Under the Uniform Health-Care Decisions Act (1993), presently in effect in Alabama, Delaware, Hawaii, Maine, Mississippi, and New Mexico—and its adoption being considered in other states—the process for appointing surrogate decision makers has been liberalized, allowing an individual to designate his or her surrogate health-care decision maker via a power of attorney. The act even contains a provision entitling a close family member or friend to make health-care decisions even in the event the patient has failed to complete a written power of attorney in advance of the incapacity (see, e.g., Wyoming's version of the act, the Wyoming Health Care Decisions Act, at Wyo. Stat. Ann. § 35-22-406[c], 2008).

Persons who lack mental capacity often are sufficiently ill to warrant more invasive treatment. In such instances, the mental health codes of all states provide a mechanism through commitment proceedings in which to mandate treatment for these patients. In these cases, the heightened procedural standards of most states require not simply that patients lack the capacity to consent to treatment but also that they be demonstrated harmful to themselves or others. This elevated standard is the culmination of a series of court decisions (see, e.g., *Commonwealth v. Bruno*, 2000; *Kansas v. Hendricks*, 1997) recognizing that the state's interest in institutionalizing a person for mental health treatment does not arise unless a specific threat to health and safety—either the person's or the public's—is demonstrated. However, as already noted, state legislatures have expanded the use of assisted outpatient treatment with persons who are both mentally ill and have a history of violence and noncompliance with mental health services (Appelbaum, 2005). State legislatures also have expanded the use of civil commitment proceedings as a means of providing alternative mechanisms for the institutionalization of criminal sexual predators (*Commonwealth v. Bruno*, 2000; *Kansas v. Hendricks*, 1997).

Various constitutional protections, including the Fourteenth Amendment's due process clause, govern the extent to which a person can be involuntarily confined for mental health treatment (*Commonwealth v. Bruno*, 2000; *Kansas v. Hendricks*, 1997). One doctrine, the *least-restrictive-means principle*, holds that a person's right to personal privacy supersedes a state's power to confine involuntarily unless it can be demonstrated that this measure is the most minimally invasive way to provide appropriate treatment. Even then, constitutional doctrine mandates that commitment be avoided unless the state can illustrate that the patient is likely to benefit from treatment (In re *Mental Illness of Thomas*, 1996). Consistent with these constitutional protections, federal and state mental health statutes and administrative regulations provide a series of protections to institutionalized patients, including, for example, the right to freedom from excessive medication, the right to an appropriate diet, the right to adequate medical attention, the right to a humane physical and psychological environment, and the right not to participate in experimentation without informed consent (see, e.g., N.M. Stat. Ann § 43-1-6, 2008; Restatement of Bill of Rights of Mental Health Patients, 2008).

LEGAL CAPACITY

The requirement of legal capacity can be understood as a means of protecting vulnerable members of society from seeking services for which they lack the ability to choose in an informed way. Imposing the condition of legal capacity on the right to grant informed consent supports the presumption that minors ordinarily lack the reasoning sophistication to consider the risks and benefits of alternative mental health services. Therefore, in many circumstances, only an adult or legal guardian of a child younger than eighteen years can provide informed consent on behalf of that child. Legal capacity additionally supports the doctrine of family privacy, which guarantees the solitude of the parent-child relationship and the principal authority of parents to raise their children and consider their best interests without interference either by the state or by outside professionals (*Gruenke v. Seip*, 2000; *M. L. B. v. S. L. J.*, 1996).

A recent trend in the law has chipped away at the grant of exclusive authority to parents to make health, mental health, and other medical choices on behalf of their children. Indeed, a growing number of state legislatures have created statutory rights for minors that allow them to consent to health and mental health care; counseling related to substance abuse, alcoholism, and sexual activity; and abortion, without the requirement of parental approval (Alan Guttmacher Institute, 2009; Albright, 2006; Watts, 2005). States granting minors the right to consent to mental health services and counseling include Alabama (health and mental health treatment connected with pregnancy, venereal disease, drug dependency, alcohol toxicity, or any reportable disease; Ala. Code Ann. § 22-8-6, 2009), California (minor twelve years or older may consent to mental health treatment; Cal. Fam. Code § 6924, 2008), Illinois (minor older than twelve years can consent to outpatient psychotherapy or counseling, with parental approval required for more than five sessions; 405 Ill. Comp. Stat. Ann. § 5/3-501, 2009), New Mexico (minor fourteen years or older may consent to psychotherapy and to receive psychotropic medication; minors younger than fourteen can consent to initial mental health assessment; N.M. Stat. Ann., § 32A-6A-14, 2008), New York (minors can consent to mental health services and minors sixteen years or older can consent to receive psychotropic medication; N.Y. Mental Hyg. § 33.21, 2009), and Texas (minors can consent to counseling for suicide prevention, chemical addiction, or dependency and for sexual, physical, or emotional abuse; Tex. Fam. Code Ann. § 32.004, 2009), to name a few. In many cases, these rights have been tempered by statutes authorizing or permitting treating providers to notify parents in the event their children are being treated or, in certain cases, by limiting the right of minors to receive psychotropic medication without parental notification and/or consent.

A trickier question is whether the grant to minors of the right to give informed consent to make decisions about health and mental health care also conveys to minors the right to refuse health or mental health care, including medication (Albright, 2006; Watts, 2005). The vast amount of legislation in this area simply avoids the question. It is to be noted, however, that courts in some states have adopted a principle known as the mature-minor rule, which gives a minor the common law right to consent to and to refuse health and mental health treatment in cases in which the minor is demonstrably intelligent, mature enough, and otherwise mentally competent to understand the risks and benefits associated with potential treatments; where this maturity and cognitive ability exist, the minor is granted the right to be solely responsible for treatment decisions without parental consultation or permission (Albright, 2006; Watts, 2005). Although the mature-minor rule seems only to have been adopted in a handful of states, including Illinois and Tennessee (In re *E. G.*, 1989; *Cardwell v. Bechtol*, 1987), it is based on an extension of the right of personal privacy to children and adolescents to the same degree their parents enjoy this privilege constitutionally. As the Illinois Supreme Court has explained: "If the evidence is clear and convincing that the minor is mature enough to appreciate the consequences of her actions, and that the minor is mature enough to exercise the judgment of an adult, then the mature-minor rule affords her the common law right to consent to or refuse medical treatment" (*In re E. G.*, 1989, pp. 327–328).

It is therefore important for mental health providers to be fully apprised as to the law regarding the right of minors to consent to services in the state where treatment is to be offered. It has also been suggested that additional states are likely to adopt the mature-minor rule. Therefore, providers are well advised to assess the cognitive ability and maturity level of all of their child and adolescent clients in the interest of preserving the right of mature minors to consent to and decline services. Indeed, this approach is consistent with the emerging legal trend that recognizes the importance of honoring the right to privacy of minors with respect to the selection of mental health services (Vukadinovich, 2004).

Only in a few states does public policy comprehensively grant the right of informed consent by minors to a variety of health and human services, most notably when important public health concerns mandate it and children are deemed sufficiently mature to choose multiple services. California probably offers the most widespread recognition of the legal rights of minors in a variety of contexts, though unlike New York's statute, California law does not yet include a right of access by minors to psychotropic drugs. This limitation notwithstanding, California's legislative scheme offers a hint as to the likely future trend of minor consent law in other states. In addition to the rights granted to minors in California cited earlier, the state offers the following statutory protections:

- The freedom to consent to an abortion (*Am. Acad. of Pediatrics v. Lundgren*, 1997)
- The receipt by minors twelve years or older of medical care and counseling related to alcoholism and substance abuse (Cal. Fam. Code § 6929[b], 2008)

- The right to family-planning services, including contraception (Cal. Fam. Code § 6925, 2008)
- The right to medical care related to infectious, contagious, or communicable diseases (Cal. Fam. Code § 6926[a], 2008)
- The receipt of medical care associated with the prevention or treatment of pregnancy (Cal. Fam. Code § 6925, 2008)
- The right of access to HIV/AIDS testing and treatment by minors twelve years or older (Cal. Health & Safety Code § 121020, 2008; Cal. Fam. Code § 6926[a], 2008).

In addition to the circumstances already noted, some states recognize several more controversial situations in which minors can grant informed consent for general health-care services. Most notable of these are the receipt of abortions and the obtaining of contraceptive information. More than half of states entitle minors to consent to receive pregnancy-related services and abortions, either with or without parental notification (Alan Guttmacher Institute, 2009). The right to receive prenatal care and delivery services is guaranteed to minors in some states, as is the right to seek medical treatment in an emergency when parental consent is impossible to obtain. In at least two states, Alabama and South Carolina, minors over the age of fourteen and sixteen, respectively, currently can grant informed consent to most types of medical care (Ala. Code § 22-8-4, 2009; S.C. Code Ann. § 20-7-280, 2007) (in South Carolina, legal capacity to consent is restricted to nonsurgical health care). Given this diversity in regional interpretation of the legal capacity principle, the reader is encouraged to consult appropriate state legislation to identify specific situations in which minors may obtain services independently.

Note that an individual who lacks legal capacity but fits one of the state-defined exceptions outlined in the previous discussion may still lack the mental capacity to voluntarily consent to services. In such circumstances, treatment guardianship together with parental cooperation may be necessary to ensure safe and appropriate care.

As a general rule, the exceptions to legal capacity allowing minors to gain access to health and human services enforce a growing nationwide public policy supporting early intervention in the treatment of emotional and mental conditions, substance abuse, and teenage pregnancy. An area of pressing national concern involves the right of a minor to consent to an abortion. States that predicate a juvenile's right to obtain an abortion on a parent's informed consent or judicial waiver are, in the opinion of at least some courts, interfering with the right of a woman to control her own body and destiny (*Am. Acad. of Pediatrics v. Lundgren*, 1997; *Planned Parenthood v. Farmer,* 2000). Thus, even when state legislatures decline to recognize statutory exceptions to the requirement of legal capacity, courts may be willing to create them in limited circumstances; this is particularly true when it comes to the promotion of public health.

Exceptions to legal capacity may occasionally present challenging issues for mental health professionals who work with families (i.e., children and parents together). In these instances, the rights of children and parents alike must be thoroughly considered with regard to the respective rights of children and their parents to consent to and refuse services. These rights have a specific impact on the fundamental legal duties owed to clients, including the duty to practice reasonably competently, the duty to seek informed consent, the duty to identify the primary client (see chapter 5), and the duty to preserve confidentiality (see chapter 7). A review of the case examples presented later demonstrates this point. In addition, mental health professionals who reside in states in which the rule of legal capacity is strictly upheld and who also understand the public policy behind the creation of exceptions to legal capacity, are in a unique position to lobby for legislative changes that improve the well-being of young clients who presently lack the legal standing to seek health and mental health services.

As with the rule of mental capacity, legal capacity is intended to support clients' voluntary choice of services. Specifically, the doctrine advances the concept that the provision of services to a child unable to appreciate the consequences of a choice really amounts to the involuntary imposition of services on that child. The legal-capacity doctrine also promotes the idea that, except in the circumstances outlined previously, a parent's surrogate decisions are thought to be more likely to preserve a child's best interests. As noted, the recognized exceptions to the requirement of legal capacity give voice to the idea that competent minors also have the right to participate in decision making regarding their own physical and mental health.

Legal capacity also helps to explain how court-ordered services can be provided to clients consistent with the letter and spirit of informed consent. As the discussion concerning voluntariness disclosed, courts can attain the right to make decisions on a person's behalf when important public policy demands that the community be protected from the consequences of the person's behavior. This concept may be understood equally well in the context of capacity: a person who commits a crime or engages in conduct that may threaten the welfare of others may sometimes be understood in a legal sense to lose the right to decline treatment options that may protect the interests of those endangered by the person's conduct.

Just as they must understand effective strategies to present services to involuntary clients, mental health professionals should adopt decision-making

strategies with mentally and legally incapacitated clients that honor the philosophy underlying informed consent. As with involuntary clients, incapacitated clients often have at least some ability to understand and participate
in the services they are receiving. Mental health professionals must seek to
engage them in aspects of decision making in a manner that both recognizes
the policy behind vicarious consent and respects human dignity. How is
this objective best accomplished with incapacitated clients? In the case of
children and adults with disabilities, it is appropriate to seek consent from
the client in addition to the parent or guardian. Although the mental health
professional may have to respect the ultimate authority of the parent or
guardian to make treatment decisions, it is consistent with competent clinical practice to seek the voluntary participation of the protected client. Thus,
psychotherapists, child welfare workers, and other mental health professionals should, where appropriate, seek consent from underage clients, mentally
incapacitated adults, and medically fragile clients with the aim of allowing
the client to choose or reject the services.

Informed Consent and the Fear of Liability

There appears to be widespread fear in the medical and mental health professions concerning potential liability for violation of the duty to seek informed consent. Most of this fear seems to have arisen from the reputed
increase in civil lawsuits alleging informed consent and other malpractice
issues. This fear has resulted in a focus on documentation and a corresponding emphasis that professionals place on the preparation and completion
of informed-consent forms by clients before the initiation of services. Indeed, some professionals seem to equate the duty to seek informed consent
with documentation, yet they do not have identical meanings. Although
the informed-consent form may be intended to memorialize the client's understanding of services and, further, to limit liability for claims that the
professional has violated informed consent, it does not always accurately
demonstrate that informed consent truly has been obtained. When a boiler-
plate form is placed in front of a client before any substantive discussion
between professional and client, then by definition it cannot substantiate
informed consent. In such an instance, the form serves simply as documentation of the client's request for treatment and does not demonstrate that an
informed-consent dialogue actually has occurred.

The best strategy for avoiding informed-consent-based malpractice
claims is to follow the guidelines discussed here. Once attained, informed
consent should be documented with the client's approval in a format both

parties—professional and client—are willing to review, reconsider, and modify as both client and professional design and redesign services (*Kovacs v. Freeman*, 1997).

Consequences for Breach of the Duty to Seek Informed Consent

As noted, professionals have a duty to seek informed consent both from their clients and from those, such as research subjects, whom their conduct may affect. As with the duty to practice reasonably competently, the duty to seek informed consent may be enforced not only by clients but also by persons who may suffer foreseeable harm as the result of the professional's failure to honor it. In fact, violation of the duty to seek informed consent is itself a breach of the duty to practice reasonably competently. This point is not purely academic. In some states, courts recognize violation of the duty to seek informed consent as an independent ground to impose civil liability on a mental health professional if a client or research participant suffers damages as a result of the violation.

Many civil lawsuits have been brought on behalf of mentally ill individuals from whom informed consent was not sought in medical or psychiatric research or during the provision of new or experimental psychiatric services (*Abdullahi v. Pfizer*, 2009; *T. D. v. N.Y. State Office of Mental Health*, 1995). Other cases have involved the failure of human service agencies to provide complete and appropriate information to adoptive parents concerning the birth family's medical and psychological history (*Gibbs v. Ernst*, 1994; *Jackson v. State*, 1998; *Roe v. Jewish Children's Bureau of Chicago*, 2003). Damages claimed in these cases have covered such diverse areas as physical injury; psychological trauma; and in the case of adopting parents, the cost of raising a child whose poor health resulted in extensive medical bills (*Gibbs v. Ernst*, 1994; *Jackson v. State*, 1998; *Roe v. Jewish Children's Bureau of Chicago*, 2003). In certain instances, courts have even held that some research is so inherently dangerous that the participant's informed consent cannot render the research lawful or acceptable (*Grimes v. Kennedy Krieger Inst., Inc.*, 2001—children developed elevated levels of lead dust in their blood while participating in nontherapeutic research on lead paint abatement).

Remedies sought in medical or psychological research cases have included not only the award of money damages but also, on occasion, court orders enjoining the offending clinician, researcher, or mental health agency from engaging in the conduct that is the subject of the complaint (*Kus v. Sherman Hosp.*, 1995; *T. D. v. N.Y. State Office of Mental Health*, 1995).

Periodically, courts have faced large-scale informed-consent violations committed by state-sponsored institutions against particularly vulnerable adults
and children (*T. D. v. N.Y. State Office of Mental Health*, 1995). Such cases
have often involved the involuntary medication of psychiatric patients or
prisoners in penal institutions. Invariably, state officials defending these
cases have sought unsuccessfully to explain such violations in terms of the
need to "control" patients, the public policy favoring the undertaking of
important medical research, or the logistical burden of seeking guardianship or other substituted consent from an individual patient's guardian or
representative.

All of the practices noted here have been recognized as violating victims'
fundamental right to privacy. On occasion, they have mandated wholesale
changes in state regulations governing institutional mental health services
and research. Indeed, informed consent is considered such a basic human
right that one court has recognized the standing of a medical researcher at a
major university to contest his firing after whistle-blowing the questionable
practices of experimenters studying the relationship between exposure to
secondhand cigarette smoke and contact with radioactive materials (*Stebbings v. Univ. of Chicago*, 2000).

Excessive zeal in conducting forensic research lies at the bottom of the
apparent mistakes made in the criminal investigation of suspected child
sexual abuse in the now-notorious *McMartin Pre-School* case in California.
In 1983, a social worker spurred on by a single allegation of sexual abuse
against caregivers at the preschool proceeded to interview hundreds of children in an effort to uncover additional instances of abuse (*Buckey v. County
of Los Angeles*, 1992). The social work investigator, apparently convinced
that the abuse had taken place, asked persistent, leading questions, even
after children had denied that any abuse had occurred. The investigator's
heartfelt ideological view that child abuse is deeply rooted in American society was allowed to drive her forensic research to the extent that it took precedence over the direct, factual information the children offered. Considered
in the context of informed consent, children were subjected to questioning
that was plainly coercive, and it rendered their participation essentially involuntary. As an example, children were told that they needed to be "good"
and help tell about the "bad" things that had happened. Moreover, the investigation led ultimately to the dismissal of a number of indictments in the
criminal case against the *McMartin* defendants and to extensive revisions
in the management of child abuse investigations and especially practices
connected with the questioning of children.

Violation of informed consent represents the breach of a practice standard essential in all mental health professions. Consequently, violating the

standard can have licensing consequences (see, e.g., *Modi v. W. Va. Bd. of Med.*, 1995), or even criminal ramifications (*People v. Watkins*, 2003).

Psychotherapists in Colorado have been convicted of reckless child abuse and sentenced to jail time in connection with the death of a ten-year-old girl subjected to so-called rebirthing therapy (Haugaard & Hazan, 2004; Mercer, 2001; Nicholson, 2001; *People v. Watkins*, 2003; Rouse, 2001). The "therapy," which involves simulation of the birth process by bundling the child in blankets as a purported therapy for childhood attachment disorder, is intended to allow the child to rebond with his or her mother through the simulated experience of birthing (Haugaard & Hazan, 2004; Mercer, 2001). Instead, in the Colorado case, it resulted in the child's smothering. The therapists reportedly failed to respond to the child's screams for help, apparently convinced that this expression of anxiety was a critical component of the therapy. Insofar as the therapy became involuntary, the therapists' approach represents not simply criminally negligent practice but also the utter repudiation of the doctrine of informed consent.

Using Informed Consent to Make Professional Decisions: Case Examples

Informed consent is one of the most useful legal principles for mental health professionals to understand and apply in everyday decision making. Because it sets so many of the basic ground rules for the professional-client relationship, identification of informed-consent dilemmas can greatly assist the decision maker in getting to the heart of an otherwise-perplexing practice problem. In this respect, informed consent addresses the essential tasks of the professional relationship, including client assessment, establishment of rapport, discussion of the client's expectations regarding the services to be provided, engagement of the client in the design of services to be provided, and other important areas that often determine the success of an intervention.

Many of the issues associated with informed consent also promote important professional ethical principles, such as the advancement of client self-determination and well-being. As the decision-making framework suggests, however, understanding informed consent as an enforceable legal responsibility underscores the mental health professional's duty to identify and apply it—along with the other primary legal principles identified in this book—first when important practice decisions are to be considered.

The subsequent case examples not only demonstrate the usefulness of informed consent in evaluating complex practice situations but also highlight its application in cross-cultural practice. This should not be surprising, because diversity has such a significant impact on the quality of the professional relationship between providers and clients. Illustrative examples highlighting diverse populations follow.

Case Example 4: The Welfare Office

Lu Chen, a fifty-three-year-old, recently widowed housewife living in East Oakland, California, has applied for income support, including Temporary Aid to Needy Families (TANF), food stamps, and other public assistance programs. Lu, an immigrant, relied exclusively on her husband before his death for her financial support. She has several adult children, each of whom lives close to his or her mother. East Oakland is an ethnically diverse city of about eighty-eight thousand people with an African American population of approximately 51 percent of the total. Its Asian residents, representing about 4 percent of the overall population, are also diverse and include Chinese, Vietnamese, Laotian, and other Southeast Asian persons residing mainly in East Oakland's downtown area. East Oakland's Latino population is the fastest growing, with a rate of increase exceeding 100 percent since 2000.

Lu is primarily a monolingual Chinese speaker but does understand some common English phrases. At the time of her application for benefits, Lu received informational materials relevant to her case that explain in general her rights and obligations under each program. Some of the materials are in comic-book form and all are translated into Mandarin Chinese. A posted sign on one of the walls of the welfare office outlines the rights of the applicant, such as the right to appeal a denial of benefits. The sign's information is translated into several languages, including Chinese. Detailed administrative rules and regulations describing income and other program conditions are not provided, but they are made available through the Internet, also translated into a number of languages, and are available at the welfare office in print form by request. The applications Lu has to complete require, among other things, her verification of income and attestation as to the amount of property she owns. These applications are translated as well into Chinese. A caseworker who speaks some Chinese is on staff at the welfare office, but he is the only staff member who does so; all Chinese clients who enter the office for services are referred to him.

This case example represents a nontraditional application of the informed-consent doctrine in the sense that it involves the delivery of human services rather than health or mental health care. Nevertheless, informed consent governs the professional relationship here every bit as much as it does the affiliation between a clinical provider and a client. The decision maker who recognizes the application of informed consent in this case example will obtain useful assistance in identifying responsibilities that apply to health and human service professionals, including all of the administrative tasks of practice, including client intake, assessment, and claims processing.

In this scenario, language barriers that may seriously impede Lu's understanding of her rights and obligations under government programs challenge the requirements of informed consent. Can dissemination of general information about Lu's rights and obligations be presented to Lu in a form that reasonably ensures her comprehension of what she is receiving and what her responsibilities are for receiving it? The answer depends in large measure not only on the clarity of the paperwork Lu is required to sign but also on the quality of the dialogue between Lu and her caseworker before, during, and after her application for benefits. If a fully bilingual professional is not provided to Lu at the time of her intake, then her informed consent to receive services cannot reasonably be obtained. The time-limited, bureaucratic atmosphere of a typical welfare office does not justify the avoidance of this responsibility. If it is provided, then informed consent must continue throughout Lu's involvement with the government programs and cannot cease with the application process. It must even include competent advice to Lu concerning possible alternatives to some of the public assistance programs that Lu is to consider. Considering the demographics of the community in which Lu lives, a culturally conscious welfare worker should be reasonably familiar with the role of extended family involvement in Chinese American tradition, especially the custom of adult children's financial support of older parents (Ishii-Kuntz, 1997). The welfare worker may appropriately use such information to help Lu to contemplate her reliance on family assistance in preference to one or more of the government programs to which she may apply.

The program rules and regulations the agency posted on the Internet are also likely to have an impact on Lu's expectations and ability to conform to the requirements of the welfare programs. Lu cannot, however, be reasonably expected to access this information without ongoing assistance from the agency worker. Nor can Lu be expected to request a copy of program rules and regulations on her own initiative; she certainly is not likely to understand any part of this material without additional, personalized aid from the worker. Therefore, the agency's promotion of Internet use as a means of conveying program information may be high tech and inexpensive, but it is not an appropriate way, either culturally or realistically, to seek informed consent from clients.

Courts have demonstrated that government employees' failure to honor informed consent can be legally enforced. Indeed, government agencies and their employees have suffered civil sanctions for professional misconduct in connection with their failure to provide sufficient assistance to clients during the welfare application process (*Reynolds v. Giuliani*, 1999). In 1999, New York City welfare workers—evidently pressed by new state legislation imposing financial cutbacks—acknowledged turning away applicants for assistance and failing to provide prompt access to food stamps and Medicaid; in response, a federal judge ordered the city to retrain workers, revise benefit applications, and increase the visibility of posted signs outlining applicant rights (*Reynolds v. Giuliani*, 1999).

Case Example 5: The Forest Fire

Noel Patrick practices individual and family psychotherapy in Los Alamos, New Mexico. A licensed independent social worker, Noel has ten years of experience in the treatment of anxiety disorders. In his practice, Noel emphasizes cognitive and behavioral techniques that are intended to increase the ability of the client to identify and address specific life stressors that precipitate anxiety attacks. Noel's new client, Peter Baca, is one of many San Ildefonso Pueblo members employed at the nearby Los Alamos National Laboratory. An engineering technician, Peter has sought Noel's assistance in dealing with his "nervousness." Evacuated from Los Alamos along with thousands of others during the Cerro Grande forest fire of 2000, Peter suffered no immediate, overt mental health symptoms following the fire. However, approximately three years after the catastrophe, Peter began to experience recurrent, vivid dreams in which he was finding himself trapped at the end of a long evacuation line of cars unable to leave the town site to return to the pueblo. Together with the dreams, Peter has suffered occasional migraine headaches and bouts of anxiety for three years following the original emergence of symptoms. The most recent appearance of these symptoms seems to have coincided with a recent work conflict involving Peter's supervisor. His stress has started to interfere with his employment, and Peter has found that he is unable to concentrate. Peter also reports that he is drinking heavily and fears it may be getting out of control. Peter is upset with himself that he cannot get the experience of his evacuation out of his mind. Early in 2006, Peter decided to seek assistance.

Noel assesses Peter's symptoms using the *Diagnostic and Statistical Manual of Mental Disorders* (*DSM-IV-TR*) (American Psychiatric Association, 2000). Initially inclined to regard Peter's symptoms as evidence of post-traumatic stress disorder (PTSD), Noel is also a committed and culturally sensitive therapist. He therefore seeks more information about the personal significance of Peter's symptoms. During comprehensive interviews with

Peter and additional research into the assessment of stress in American Indian clients, Noel has also evaluated the degree of Peter's cultural affiliation with the pueblo. After briefly exploring a number of treatment options with Peter, Noel notices Peter's favorable reaction to a traditional approach involving consultation with a tribal healer (Villa, 2001). This approach is not familiar or even comfortable to Noel, and he does not personally share the opinion that it is a fully sufficient approach to addressing Peter's symptoms. Nevertheless, he regards it as in Peter's best interests to follow his client's wishes and therefore accompanies Peter on a consultation visit with a tribal medicine man. The parties agree that Noel will assist the tribal healer in the delivery of therapy.

In this case example, Noel's assessment raises questions about the therapist's unintentional stereotyping of a client in a manner that may influence the client's informed choice of a treatment approach. In his zeal to be culturally responsive, Noel may have overreacted to his client's favorable response to a suggested course of therapy and understated his own preference for a treatment strategy with which he is more familiar. Furthermore, in the course of pursuing cultural relevance, Noel risks engaging Peter in an approach with which Noel has neither personal nor professional experience. Apart from the more obvious questions that Noel's lack of knowledge raises about his ability to comply with the duty to practice reasonably competently, specific informed-consent questions are raised as well. Specifically, in contrast to case example 2, "Addressing Attrition among Native American College Students," the present scenario involves a kind of misrepresentation by the professional to the client. If Noel proceeds to attempt to collaborate with the tribal healer and engages in this joint therapy without genuinely adhering to the belief system that lies at its heart, professional dishonesty compromises the relationship between client and professional. What happens, for example, if the treatment is ineffective and Peter seeks an explanation for its failure?

Noel's situation may be comparable to that of a psychiatrist in West Virginia who applied "depossession therapy" in the treatment of a patient who allegedly believed spirits had possessed him (*Modi v. W. Va. Bd. of Med.*, 1995). Not actually believing in the client's possession, the therapist nevertheless hypnotized the client while chanting incantations in an effort to rid the patient of his destructive beliefs. The West Virginia Medical Board regarded this conduct as inconsistent with the duty to seek informed consent. Specifically, the board noted that a therapist has a responsibility to help the patient make choices from among all available practice alternatives. Thus, remaining silent as to one's own professional orientation out of the concern that it might interfere with the client's personal belief system is patronizing, deceptive, and countertherapeutic. In Peter's case, Noel's actions represent nothing more than playacting based on the belief that the client's ethnic heritage demands this approach. Here, Noel seems to have made the unfortunate assumption that Peter would forgo treatment unless it were provided through a close approximation of the client's traditional cultural beliefs.

What should Noel have been prepared to do in this case example? First, he might have disclosed fully the existence of multiple treatment approaches, including the DSM-IV-TR-inspired approach that is consistent with Noel's own professional orientation. Rather than jump to the conclusion that Peter's situation warranted a culturally based treatment, Noel should have also shared his own predisposition toward the Western medical approach. This choice might seem distasteful to a clinical social worker concerned with avoiding the imposition of an external belief system on the client. Nevertheless, in this instance, Noel's thorough discussion of his own treatment approach was a required element of seeking informed consent.

The lesson for the culturally sensitive clinician is that any client should expect to receive the therapist's own opinion regarding services, and the therapist should be prepared to offer that opinion in a nonpatronizing manner. If on full disclosure of alternative approaches, Peter had knowledgably selected a traditional Native American approach, Noel might simply have referred Peter to the healer, who could then have assumed responsibility for a culturally based treatment approach. Noel's adoption of a collaborative strategy in which he visited the tribal healer along with Peter probably did not benefit Peter and unnecessarily insinuated himself into Peter's treatment in a manner violative of informed-consent principles. Had Noel remained faithful to the duty to seek informed consent, he would have avoided imposing a particular service on Peter at the same time that he limited his practice modality to one he was competent to provide.

Case Example 6: The Guidance Counselor

Isaac Depuis is a middle school guidance counselor in Carbondale, Illinois. He has a master's degree in guidance and counseling and is licensed in Illinois. Clayton Cradle, a fourteen-year-old eighth grader of African American heritage is referred to Isaac after his homeroom teacher reports persistent "acting out" in class. The behavior consists of cutting classes, schoolyard fights, and clownish conduct in class. During a series of three forty-five-minute counseling sessions, Isaac learns that Clayton has little contact with his father, who is divorced from his mother. In addition, Clayton's mother has remarried, and Clayton does not get along with his stepfather. Isaac

suspects that Clayton suffers from mild depression and low self-esteem, and
he schedules Clayton for twice-weekly counseling sessions.

The rules of informed consent suggest that, in some states, as noted earlier, children Clayton's age have the legal capacity to grant informed consent in connection with verbal counseling and psychotherapy. As also noted,
adolescents in Illinois are protected under the mature-minor principle, and
under certain circumstances, they can refuse mental health treatment. According to Illinois legislation, minors twelve years or older also have the
statutory right to grant informed consent to receive counseling or psychotherapy (405 Ill. Comp. Stat. Ann. § 5/3-501, 2009). In this case example, the
clinical relationship between Clayton and Isaac must be based on the same
precepts that govern any association between client and therapist. Here,
however, the administrative authority that Isaac has over Clayton may lead
him to diagnose and prescribe treatment in essentially the same manner
that a teacher assigns homework. As with any adult client, Clayton has the
right to a full and competent assessment of his problem, including its potential cultural and familial aspects, together with the freedom either to accept
or forgo services. This fact imposes a particular burden on Isaac to ensure
the voluntariness of the services proposed. However, it may be especially
difficult for Isaac to deliver these services in a school setting; Isaac's role as
a guidance counselor generally is regarded as more disciplinary than clinical. Indeed, even the notion that a school guidance counselor might have
the responsibilities associated with informed consent—the very idea that
children could have legal rights in this setting—could be unsettling to those
used to the routine operating procedure of many schools.

When a child consciously seeks services for a self-identified mental health
problem, the therapist is required to provide full disclosure of alternative
treatment approaches. Even if the therapist practices in a state in which the
minor's legal right to consent is not clearly established, the therapist must at
least provide this information to the parent or guardian. The same rule applies to a child for whom treatment is initiated at the suggestion of the professional. Assuming, then, that Isaac can obtain Clayton's informed consent
to counseling, Clayton is still entitled to an explanation of his problem and
a discussion of all appropriate treatment options. This may open the door
to additional informed-consent problems because Clayton is also entitled to
know that he may benefit from at least one additional treatment option—a
referral to a physician for medication that may be appropriate for him if
he is in fact clinically depressed. In this event, under Illinois statutory law,
Clayton would appear to need his mother's consent to receive psychoactive
drugs, although Illinois courts recognize the right of a mature minor to seek

medical treatment, so Clayton might still be able to consent himself to further treatment options without his mother's approval. Conferring this right on Clayton would be more likely in the event Clayton's mother has abandoned, neglected, or abused him, thus placing him in the position of needing treatment without the availability of parental oversight. Clayton may be more than willing to consent to confidential, individual counseling with Isaac but unwilling to explore options that may require the active involvement of his mother. Informed consent additionally suggests that Clayton must be advised of his right to confidentiality, limitations on that right, and Isaac's duty to report certain kinds of conduct (e.g., suspected child abuse) that may be revealed in the course of counseling.

Precisely what are the rights of Clayton's mother regarding informed consent in this scenario? If Clayton has behavioral problems that affect his performance in school, then plainly, Clayton's mother has the right to disclosure of this information, consistent with her caretaking duties as Clayton's guardian. It does not mean, however, that she has the right to know the substance of any clinical discussions between Isaac and Clayton, at least to the extent that such disclosure is not necessary for the continuation of Clayton's treatment. This subject area is private, as appropriate clinical practice standards demand. Clayton's mother does, however, have the statutory right in Illinois to grant permission for additional therapy if Clayton is to receive more than five sessions (405 Ill. Comp. Stat. Ann. § 5/3-501, 2009). Given the application of the common law's mature-minor principle in Illinois, Clayton arguably also enjoys the privilege to seek or deny services. Suppose that, in the course of Clayton's counseling, Isaac determines that Clayton's condition may warrant family therapy. At this stage, Isaac is obliged to advise Clayton and to seek both Clayton's and his mother's consent to the referral for services.

In this case example, the application of informed-consent standards, including the rules relating to legal capacity, work to protect Clayton's right not to have services imposed on him. The idea that Clayton enjoys this right of personal privacy may surprise anyone who has attended middle school. Nevertheless, it exists, within boundaries, at least with respect to the student's freedom to decline more invasive interventions, such as prescribed therapy. As the court in *Gruenke v. Seip* (2000) observed, students have the right not to be forced to disclose personal matters, given the fact that "school-sponsored counseling and psychological testing that pry into private family activities can overstep the boundaries of school authority" (p. 307).

It may seem that the doctrine of informed consent imposes an extraordinary burden on the unsuspecting school guidance counselor in this case example. In reality, it spells out a strategy for effective mental health practice that enhances the best interests of the client. The public school has long served as an institution in which socialization and conformity have been accomplished, usually by being imposed on students. Forced acculturation unfortunately has been true with respect to minority, and particularly African American, children on whom clinical diagnoses and behavioral disorders sometimes have been stamped more frequently than on other children (Davis & Stevenson, 2006; Green, McIntosh, Cook-Morales, & Robinson-Zañarto, 2005). Given this fact, strict interpretation of the rules of informed consent serves to guarantee the student's right to a sense of personal integrity that is conducive to mental health and academic success. Therefore, the ability of a mental health professional to identify informed-consent issues in all areas of practice is essential. As with each of the basic legal principles discussed in this book, some regional variations exist, and the competent professional must become familiar with local differences.

Case Example 7: The Faith-Based Service

A church-administered counseling program in Baltimore, Maryland, offers mental health and support services to young women who have become pregnant. The program's mission statement emphasizes the reinforcement of spiritual values, education, financial responsibility, and the enhancement of self-esteem in girls experiencing the consequences of teenage pregnancy (Corcoran, 2001). The counseling program has a clientele that consists largely of young African American women. Consistent with the strong family and church ties that are an important part of the cultural heritage of African Americans (Rubin, Billingsley, & Caldwell, 1994), a vital community in this city, counseling often includes the extended families of young women who have sought services from the program. The average age of young pregnant women seeking services is fifteen and a half years, and for this reason, the program's emphasis on family solidarity is particularly important. The program advocates for the family's continuing involvement in support for the mother. Birth control and abortion violate the religious ethics the church advances, and the clinical director therefore advises program counselors to stress the moral and spiritual concerns favoring childbirth.

Melissa Zak recently has started her new job as a counselor with the program. A clinical social worker with several years of experience offering comparable services to clients in a secular program in Boston, she is aware of the church program's mission statement but also believes in the importance of helping her young clients help themselves. Melissa believes that the only way to advance this ideology is to maximize the amount of information that clients receive. In view of the program's treatment philosophy, she is prepared to adopt a low profile during her initial months in her position and then plans to seek a healthy dialogue with the clinical director about suggested changes in the program's framework.

Minors in Maryland generally can consent to mental health treatment and counseling services (Md. Code Ann., Health-Gen. § 20-102, 2008); therefore, the program's restrictions also interfere with Melissa's duty to seek informed consent from prospective clients. In addition, young women in Maryland (Md. Code Ann., Health-Gen. § 20-103, 2008) and some other states have the legal capacity to provide informed consent for abortion-related services in certain circumstances, even if they are still minors. By discouraging Melissa from discussing abortion as an alternative treatment approach available by law, clients are not able to make a fully informed decision to accept the counseling services offered by the church. Melissa herself may already recognize this point, and perhaps has understood even before assuming her new job that the program's restrictions might present an obstacle that she would have to surmount to provide reasonably competent services to clients. In the meantime, however, she seems resigned to avoiding the problem and enforcing her employer's policies. This approach may be a conservative choice intended to extend her professional life at the agency, or it may reflect the respect she is willing to pay to the program and the clinical director. Because the program has some effective elements that bring families together, are regionally and culturally appropriate, and that Melissa enthusiastically endorses, it may simply be hard for her to criticize it. Regardless of Melissa's motives, however, her strategy does not address the informed-consent problem that presently exists.

Melissa is obliged to seek this consent by describing all treatment strategies reasonably available to her clients. She cannot evade this responsibility by honoring the church's restrictive policy. Unless she resolves this point with the clinical director, her professional relationships with potential clients are undermined before they begin. She may wish to discuss this issue with the clinical director in a manner that honors the spirit of the program's founders but also respects the minimum standards the duty to seek informed consent imposes. Melissa may recommend, for example, that the church amend its informed-consent policy to explain all options available to the client, along with an explanation of the program's own religious orientation. She may recommend additionally that an appropriate referral system be implemented to place clients in communication with alternate service providers. Consistent with the requirements of informed consent, it is perfectly appropriate to discuss one's faith-based perspective, provided that the professional also discusses different available approaches with the client. It might be noted that a counselor working at an abortion clinic should have an equivalent, informed-consent-based burden to advise prospective patients of alternatives to abortion.

Case Example 8: The Research Study

Patricio Ortega, an adjunct research professor at a university school of psychology, is undertaking a scientific study to survey the presence of anxiety spectrum disorders in a population of elderly persons representing various demographic groups in a multicultural community in Miami, Florida. As part of the study, Patricio will conduct interviews with community members and distribute several assessment instruments that mental health professionals commonly use to identify anxiety disorders. Following completion of the research, treatment is to be offered as necessary to study participants at the university's mental health clinic. Consistent with federal policy (U.S. Department of Health and Human Services Rules Governing the Protection of Human Subjects, 2009), Patricio has prepared an informed-consent form in English and Spanish that outlines the benefits and risks expected from the research. He has obtained informed-consent forms from a self-identified population of seventy-five Cuban American immigrant participants (of whom thirty-five are monolingual Spanish speakers), twenty non-Hispanic Whites, and five Native Americans.

Undertaking human-subjects research is a potential minefield for mental health professionals not entirely familiar with the boundaries of informed consent. As already noted, federal policy has been developed to extend informed-consent protections to human research participants, and it requires that research institutions, such as universities and medical facilities, establish institutional review boards (IRBs) to monitor the satisfaction of informed consent. It is important for the researcher to know and apply the rules of informed consent discussed here in addition to relying on the IRB process to confirm the researcher's compliance with these principles. Understanding the broad dictates of informed consent generally provides better overall guidance for the researcher than do the confusing and sometimes contradictory internal standards that state and private institutions adopt for the review of research proposals. Often, this review is undertaken by an insular group—the IRB membership—that lacks the time to give research proposals significantly more than a minimal examination for compliance with the federal regulations cited previously. Indeed, psychological testing proposed at even renowned research institutions is occasionally prone to insufficient review (Emanuel, Wood, Fleischman, & Bowen, 2004; Lehrman & Sharay, 1997; Redman & Caplan, 2005).

One of the most prolific dangers connected with institutional research concerns the failure to fully advise already mentally ill participants of the risks the research poses (Lehrman & Sharay, 1997; Lunstroth, 2007). For example, in some research, the testing of mentally ill subjects may exacerbate symptoms; in other instances, the questioning of those who have had mental disorders in the past may promote a relapse of the earlier symptoms (Lehrman & Sharay, 1997). Moreover, an inadequate research design, including the use of instruments whose cross-cultural application has not been demonstrated, may lead to the over- or underreporting of mental health symptoms by subjects who simply do not understand the questions posed. If clinical services are then offered to test-study participants, some may ultimately agree to an unnecessary intervention. In other words, the satisfaction of informed consent depends on a culturally competent research design.

What do these issues reveal about how Patricio should undertake his research study? In this case example, the university's IRB must evaluate Patricio's research proposal to assess the anticipated risks of the research, the expected benefits, and the quality of the informed consent that has been sought. However, even if the IRB approves Patricio's research design, he still must take reasonable steps to verify the cultural and regional appropriateness of his methodology. In addition, he should implement such procedures as are necessary to ensure that participants truly understand the risks and benefits of participation. This may present a significant problem when subjects are frail or vulnerable, when language or literacy barriers exist, or when cross-cultural communication may influence the expectations of the participants. At the very least, Patricio must be mindful of the presence of anxiety, PTSD, and related disorders among immigrant populations and understand that his research format must account for the risk of retraumatizing participants. This is especially true in the light of evidence suggesting the experience of cognitive and memory difficulties that may be present in PTSD sufferers (Moore, 2009).

In this scenario, to ensure that study participants actually understand the risks and benefits the research presents, Patricio and his staff must be willing to engage in dialogue with study participants before, during, and after the undertaking of the research. This multistep process promotes issue clarification and absolute support of the participants during the stress of the testing. Should Patricio and his staff choose instead to rely simply on the dissemination of an informed-consent document at the commencement of the testing, this will almost certainly violate both the letter and spirit of informed consent, especially when the form may be nearly unintelligible to participants who are elderly and/or lack significant formal education (Lehrman & Sharay, 1997; Lunstroth, 2007). Even if participants cannot understand the form, the avoidance of *vergüenza* and *deshonra* (shame and dishonor, respectively) (Echevarria-Doan & Marquez, 2006; Lorenzo, 2005) may well lead those reading the form to claim they understand it even when they do not. For these reasons, Patricio should consider the use of trained, multilingual clinical assistants who are available to provide ongoing support and psychological reinforcement to study participants and who can facilitate the discussion of questions that study participants may have throughout the undertaking of the research.

Patricio must also be prepared to ensure the voluntariness of his participants' involvement. Where Patricio has advised prospective study participants that he is prepared to offer clinical aftercare services to them, both their voluntary consent to the research and the integrity of their responses to test questions are questionable; stated simply, the possibility of aftercare may unduly influence participants to take part in the study.

An additional informed-consent problem arises if study participants ultimately accept Patricio's offer to provide clinical services to them; specifically, the link between the research and the services raises a question as to whether the services have actually been sought voluntarily rather than driven solely by participation in the research. Furthermore, Patricio's own involvement in the research may limit his ability to obtain informed consent for his clinical work with participants. The reason is that his willingness to provide treatment is at least partly grounded in his professional interest in the research study, including the scholarly publications and potential financial remuneration that may result. The effect is to create a conflict of interest that may influence the treatment stance he takes with his future clients; at the very least, it threatens the independence and reliability of the clinical services and therefore compromises his clients' best interests (*Moore v. Regents of Univ. of Cal.*, 1990). This type of conflict is a risk that all research participants—and prospective clients—need to understand.

For the foregoing reasons, Patricio best obeys the principles of informed consent if he refrains from offering any clinical services to research participants and instead seeks an alternative means of providing care. In addition, his conflict of interest should be explained to all participants in the research study at the commencement of the research. As a safe approach that honors the letter and spirit of informed consent, Patricio may wish to dissociate himself entirely from the aftercare program, leaving the provision of clinical services to a therapist not directly involved in the research.

CHAPTER 5

The Duty to Identify
the Primary Client

SOME OF THE BASIC LEGAL RESPONSIBILITIES that underlie the professional relationship between mental health providers and their clients have already been the focus of much discussion here. Specifically, reasonable competence in the delivery of services and the pursuit of informed consent in professional relationships are two fundamental duties that promote the best interests of clients. Recognizing the importance of satisfying these duties may therefore help the professional make practice decisions more effectively and expeditiously.

Where a mental health provider offers services to a single client, the duties a professional relationship imposes may be identified in a fairly straightforward manner. Often, however, professionals work not with individual clients but with client groups that include marital couples, families, civic associations, and sometimes entire communities. Sometimes the professional provides services to one family member, such as a child, though other family members, such as parents, have important peripheral interests in the quality of the services provided. Public-sector professionals are often called on to provide services simultaneously to a government agency and to individuals who come into contact with that agency. In all these instances, it may sometimes become difficult for the conscientious professional to identify the client(s) to whom he or she primarily owes professional duties.

Identifying the primary client may also be critical when multiple parties are involved in the referral of a client for services or in the payment for those services. For example, when a client is court ordered to receive treatment or referred to a mental health provider by another professional (e.g., an attorney of a primary care physician), or when a client seeks reimbursement for services through an insurance company or other third-party payor, professional or business obligations to those third parties may influence the provider's judgment. In such circumstances, understanding how to identify the primary client may be of critical importance in evaluating how the professional must exercise his or her responsibilities. Identifying the primary client may also be a helpful way to resolve practice dilemmas in which multiple parties are involved and seemingly conflicting interests are at hand.

The duty to identify the primary client requires that the decision maker take the following steps:

1. Identify the person(s)—the primary client—with whom the provider has agreed to establish a professional relationship. The primary client may be an individual, family, or vulnerable population to whom the professional has agreed to provide relevant services or whose interests the professional is legally bound to protect.
2. Identify the professional duties owed to the client (e.g., the duty to practice reasonably competently, the duty to seek informed consent, and the duty to maintain confidentiality) (see chapter 7).
3. Perform the duties owed to the client.

As with each of the basic common law principles discussed in this book, following the steps mandated by the duty to identify the primary client will support clients' best interests and maximize the likelihood of advancing important societal goals enforced by the duty. As the decision-making framework suggests, the duty to identify the primary client should be considered, along with the other basic legal principles, a first step in the decision-making process. As the subsequent case examples demonstrate, a decision maker who can sort through a practice dilemma to identify the primary client in each scenario has an important aid for determining the duties owed to that client and the best way to resolve the client's situation.

The duty to identify the primary client often is inadequately explained—or even worse, confused—by professional ethical codes. For example, the NASW Code, the NBCC Code, and the APA Code all express important but often broad, aspirational ideals governing practice, including the advancement of human welfare and social justice, but they pay little attention to identifying specifically to whom professionals primarily owe these obligations. None of these professional codes actually defines the term *client*, which is essentially a legal concept. Most confusingly, the NASW Code's preamble describes *client* not in its strict, legal sense but as a term "used inclusively to refer to individuals, families, groups, organizations, and communities." This interpretation omits any discussion as to the manner in which the professional relationship is created and seems to suggest instead that the provider owes duties to several elements of society simultaneously, whether or not people voluntarily seek services. This important failing sometimes leads code users to categorize certain practice situations involving multiple parties as ethical conflicts of interest in which the law actually may suggest instead that the decision maker owes a legal duty to only one of these parties. In light of this fact, the decision maker who recognizes and applies the duty to identify the primary client before undertaking a review of any of the ethical codes will likely avoid this unnecessary confusion.

Establishing Professional Relationships with Clients

Professional relationships between mental health providers and their clients are instituted in a variety of ways. Some are initiated when a person voluntarily seeks out the services of a professional to assist with the person's own problem, such as a mental health issue. Others start when a family member vicariously engages the professional's services, as when parents seek a provider's assistance on behalf of a minor child. On other occasions, another professional seeks out the social worker's, counselor's, or psychologist's services, as when an attorney refers a client for a mental health consultation. Sometimes courts order clients to seek services, as when criminal defendants or respondents in child abuse proceedings are directed to receive counseling. A professional relationship between a government service agency and a client is created when legislation directs the agency to protect the interests of certain vulnerable members of a community, such as the victims of abuse and neglect. When the agency hires mental health providers, such as child and adult protective social workers or forensic psychologists, their professional relationships with the endangered clients commence the moment that they accept public employment.

Regardless of the diverse ways in which mental health providers begin affiliations with clients, the end result is the establishment of a professional relationship. A professional relationship with a client is created when the provider voluntarily agrees to provide services to an identified individual or group—or voluntarily agrees to represent the interests of a legally protected class of vulnerable persons—and the client (or the client's surrogate, if the client lacks capacity) voluntarily agrees to accept them (*Bienz v. Cent. Suffolk Hosp.*, 1990—physician-patient relationship; *Gillespie v. Univ. of Chicago Hosps.*, 2008—physician-patient relationship; In re *Investigation of Underwager*, 1997—psychologist-client relationship; In re *Marie H.*, 2006— an emergency psychiatric team does not establish a physician-patient relationship with an incapacitated person whom the team is committing involuntarily until the patient later accepts services and thereby creates a contract with the physician; *People v. Simms*, 2000—attorney-client relationship; *Ward v. Most Health Servs., Inc.*, 2008—physician-patient relationship created on patient's behalf by patient's employer, who hired physician to perform patient's physical examination; *Zinermon v. Burch*, 1990—civilly committed mental patients and hospital). The individual, group, or class that is the chief beneficiary of the professional services is the primary client. The professional relationship is sometimes memorialized by a contractual agreement, expressed either verbally or in writing, in which the parties mutually agree on the services to be provided, including the cost, if applicable, of the services. This relationship imposes a number of burdens on the professional, including, most notably, basic legal responsibilities.

Note that the legal definitions of *professional relationship* and *client* serve an important purpose consistent with communitarian principles. First, they emphasize the point that the fundamental responsibilities that all mental health professionals owe to their clients—each of the legal principles outlined in this book—apply to all professional relationships regardless of the specific discipline each provider represents. This fact is often confused by technical variations in the ethical standards and aspirational ideals expressed in individual professions. It is important for the mental health and human service provider to understand that the professional relationship imposes standards of care that transcend the individual values of particular professions and unite all providers in their commitment to the protection of client welfare. This commitment is essentially the same whether the professional service is medical care, legal representation, psychological assistance, counseling, or social work. Therefore, contrary to the myriad desirable values that ethical codes identify, the law recognizes that mental health professionals have their limits. Awareness of this fact can inspire a measure of comfort in the realization that the law does not expect omnipotence from mental health professionals, and it can also impress the individual provider with a healthy sense of personal and professional humility.

Informed Consent and the Professional Relationship

Creation of a valid professional relationship with a client depends on the receipt of informed consent from the client or surrogate representing the client's best interests. Honoring the duty to seek informed consent protects the client's privacy and self-determination, and it is consistent with reasonably competent practice. A person, guardian, or other representative often seeks mental health and human services on behalf of underaged, infirm, or incapacitated people. In these circumstances, the legal capacity to provide informed consent is vested in a party best able to protect the vulnerable person's interests. Although the incapacitated individual does not directly provide informed consent, he or she is the primary client to whom the provider owes central legal responsibilities. For example, in the case of a mother who brings her young child to a family physician for a medical consultation relating to the child's hyperactivity, the mother provides informed consent; the primary client, however, is the child. The physician owes specific legal duties to that child, including the duty to practice reasonably competently. If the physician does not discuss with the mother important risks and disclosures pertaining to the treatment of hyperactivity, then the mother cannot provide informed consent. In this instance, the professional's failure to seek informed consent violates practice duties owed to the primary client (i.e., the child).

Professionals often owe independent duties to a person who provides informed consent on behalf of a vulnerable client. For example, a parent or guardian may contract with a therapist to offer clinical services to a child. Failure to provide the services may represent a breach of contract with the parent that warrants legal relief.

Guardians, surrogates, and other individuals who have the responsibility to make informed decisions on a vulnerable person's behalf themselves have a legal duty to the client to act with reasonable care in making such decisions. This fiduciary duty means that the law imposes a commitment to prudence and trustworthiness that obliges the fiduciary to make reasonably competent decisions that protect the health and property of the vulnerable person. For example, if a guardian were to consent to a course of rebirthing-therapy treatments for a minor ward (see chapter 4), he or she may well violate the fiduciary duty.

Identifying the Primary Client in Practice with Families and Groups

Mental health professionals who practice with families and groups often provide services to a number of clients simultaneously in counseling, psychotherapy, community organizing, and other areas. The fact that family or group forums are used to provide services does not detract from the fact that each and every member of a client group enjoys the status of a primary client. Each individual is therefore entitled to the rights and protections afforded to primary clients. This entitlement may prove troublesome for the professional who regards the family, group, or community singularly as the client. Indeed, it could prompt an otherwise-cautious professional to broaden the scope of services in a way that appropriate attention is not paid to the right of each individual to such legal protections as informed consent and confidentiality. In group settings involving vulnerable individuals who are particularly susceptible to group influences, the ability of such individuals to communicate effectively with the facilitator may be compromised. The careful provider therefore needs to prepare for group practice in such a way that respects the basic rights of all members. Precautions may include holding individual informed-consent dialogues with all group members before their admission to the group. Consistent with the requirements of informed consent, these dialogues should address the risks and benefits unique to group treatment.

Group practice presents unique challenges for the mental health professional concerned with honoring the legal rights of each individual group member. Upholding confidentiality, for example, may be burdensome where the group facilitator has no control over the activities of members outside of the group session and where the facilitator may interact with individual group members away from the group setting. In either event, it is a risk of group practice that the maintenance of confidentiality depends on the willing cooperation of all group members.

Identifying the primary client presents special considerations for those mental health professionals involved in practice with large groups, such as social workers involved in community organizing, political advocacy, and regional economic development. In fact, the concept of identifying a primary client may seem unnatural to a professional used to practicing in informal organizational settings with spontaneously created coalitions of community members or civic associations. Nevertheless, the duty to identify one's primary client is as necessary a task with large client groups as it is with individual clients, and for all the same reasons. The duty means literally that every member of a community for whom services are provided voluntarily is a primary client of the professional who undertakes such services. Moreover, it implies a responsibility on the part of the organizer to seek informed consent from potential clients. This concept should give pause to any organizer who believes that professional responsibilities do not apply in this area of mezzo practice (services provided to groups, agencies and organizations) and macro practice (services provided in the larger societal environment, including the political sphere).

The difficulty of defining reasonably competent practice in mezzo- and macro-level human services, such as community and political organizing, has bedeviled judges, some of whom have been unable to ascertain exactly what practice standards should be expected of such professionals (see, e.g., *Horak v. Biris*, 1985). This fact notwithstanding, in considering case examples 2, "Addressing Attrition among Native American College Students," and 12, "Yucca Mountain" (later in this chapter), one will note that each

addresses program development and organizing issues in minority communities, and each demonstrates the vital safeguarding role that identifying
the primary client plays in the promotion of individual well-being and community diversity. Indeed, if the community developers in each case example
fail to undertake a community assessment that tests the applicability of
their research to the local population, then they truly are disregarding their
duty to identify the primary clients. Appreciating this point in community
development, political organizing, and agency administration places these
areas of mental health and human service specialization squarely in the
same legal context as more traditional, micro-level practice modalities (i.e.,
direct practice with individual clients). Specifically, it demands adherence to
minimal legal responsibilities as surely as in the case of more conventional
practice with individual clients and family groups.

Identifying the Client in Public Agency Practice

Identifying the client in public agency practice is a task required of every
professional who accepts employment with the government. In contrast
to the relationship between private-sector professionals and their clients,
the association between government servants and their clients is expressly
defined by legislation that advances special societal goals. The aspiration
government agencies most often voice in the design and implementation of
health and human services is best described by the legal and philosophical
doctrine known as parens patriae, which means literally "'the parent of his
or her country' and refers to the role of the state as sovereign and guardian
of persons under legal disability" (*Kelm v. Kelm*, 2001, p. 301, n. 1) (quoting
Garner and Black's [1999] *Black's Law Dictionary*, p. 1137). According to parens patriae, the government has a moral obligation to protect the interests
of those vulnerable citizens who are unable to protect themselves (In re
Kendall J., 2000; *Kelm v. Kelm*, 2001; *Steele v. Hamilton County Cmty. Mental
Health Bd.*, 2000; *New Hampshire v. City of Dover*, 2006).

Over the past hundred or more years, state legislatures have cited parens
patriae in the creation of extensive child welfare, adult protective services,
mental health, and other government bureaus charged with the administrative responsibility of protecting the public interest in each of these respective areas. These departments are sometimes described as executive agencies because typically they are placed under the ultimate administrative
authority of the chief executive of a jurisdiction, such as a governor, at the
state level, or the president, at the federal level. The additional, synonymous
terms *public agency* and *government agency* are used interchangeably here
as well to describe these service bureaus.

As an example of the legal responsibilities of government agencies, state legislation creating human service departments has given such bureaus broad authority to administer public welfare, food stamp, and medical assistance programs for needy persons (*State* ex rel. *Taylor v. Johnson*, 1998). Similarly, many state legislatures have addressed the needs of mentally ill citizens by establishing community mental health boards empowered with the authority to house incapacitated persons and provide both voluntary and involuntary treatment (*Steele v. Hamilton County Cmty. Mental Health Bd.*, 2000). Additional legislation in most states has created public agencies charged with administering child welfare, public health, and other programs offering protection to vulnerable citizens.

All government agencies have a particular administrative burden defined by law, and they carry out this responsibility through the promulgation of rules and regulations governing their internal agency practices. Rules and regulations have the force of law and must be consistent with public policy, also known as authorizing legislation, which creates each agency and empowers it with governmental authority. According to their authorizing legislation, and in a manner consistent with their rules and regulations, government agencies are entrusted to hire qualified public personnel whose ultimate responsibility is the enforcement of each agency's governmental purpose. In the case of agencies that protect specific public interests in the areas of child welfare, public health, mental health, and juvenile probation services, mental health professionals are largely responsible both for providing direct agency services and for directing administrative functions.

In a very real sense, a mental health professional who accepts a position with a public agency assumes the agency's legal obligation to a specific vulnerable population that the agency serves. Put differently, the professional accepts the agency's service population as a primary client and assumes the same legal obligations as owed to any private client with whom a professional relationship is established. Thus, mental health professionals who work with the types of public agencies listed in Table 1 assume as their clients the populations indicated there.

The advantage of understanding the public agency professional's role as a duty owed to a specific class of primary client is that it helps identify the legal obligations owed to that group. As an example pertaining to government-employed social workers, consider the specific legal obligations that child protective service professionals agree to undertake when they provide services to the public. Most important, they agree to represent the interest of the population of children vulnerable to abuse and neglect in the region served by their agency. Included among the responsibilities owed to this client population are the duty to practice reasonably competently and

Table 1: Primary Clients of Public Agencies

AGENCY OR BUREAU	PRIMARY RESPONSIBILITIES	CLIENT POPULATION
Child welfare	Investigation of child abuse, neglect	At-risk and vulnerable children
Health	Maintenance of public health	The public
Mental health	Maintenance of public mental health	The public
	Protection of mentally fragile	Mentally fragile
Adult protective services	Investigation of abuse of physically and mentally fragile adults	Physically and mentally fragile adults
Corrections	Protection of public welfare through deterrence and rehabilitation of inmates	The public
Income Support	Protection of public welfare and provision of assistance to needy	Vulnerable, income-deprived members of the public
Education	Promotion of public education	Schoolchildren

the duty to maintain confidentiality (see chapter 7). In this context, reasonably competent practice means that a child welfare social worker must, among other things, adequately investigate reports of suspected child abuse and neglect and must, in the child's best interests, keep the identity of the presumed victim confidential. Similarly, a psychologist employed by a community mental health center must capably examine severely depressed or psychotic patients for signs that they may be a threat to themselves or others. Finally, as case example 4, "The Welfare Office," demonstrates, a social worker employed by an income-support bureau must obtain informed consent from a client applying for government benefits. The same is asked of a public school guidance counselor offering services to school-aged children.

In many instances, members of the vulnerable client groups that public agencies serve lack legal or mental capacity to provide informed consent for health or human services. This is the case, for example, with children and mentally fragile persons. In these instances, the role of the public agency is in the nature of a guardianship, with the agency obliged to protect the interest of its wards and to consent to services that best meet their needs. Some agencies become the legal guardians of their vulnerable clients, as is the case with child welfare agencies that obtain custody of abused children whose natural parents' continuing custodial rights are being considered by a court. In such instances, agencies have on occasion failed notoriously. In the early 1980s, a number of states' child welfare agencies faced civil rights litigation challenging the management of their foster care systems (see, e.g., *Joseph A. v. N.M. Dep't of Human Servs.*, 1983). Specifically, these public agencies were charged with abandoning their wards—abused and neglected children placed into foster care—by failing to keep track of their whereabouts and further neglecting to provide suitable, permanent home placements. In this respect, the *Joseph A.* case is representative of litigation seeking the reformation of inadequate foster care programs in several states. The *Joseph A.* case was an important factor motivating the creation in New Mexico of a new, cabinet-level government agency—the Children, Youth, and Families Department (CYFD). As with similar statewide bureaus operating in other states, CYFD bears primary responsibility for administering child protective services in New Mexico.

Some social work and other mental health academicians and ethicists raise the question of whether professional values are consistent with public-sector practice. In particular, they raise the argument that a government agency professional representing a public regulatory authority cannot observe important aspirational ideals that the mental health disciplines promote on behalf of vulnerable and oppressed client populations; the ideals usually identified are the advancement of client self-determination, the enhancement of client well-being, and the pursuit of social justice. This argument makes two erroneous assumptions that minimize important legal principles governing mental health practice:

First, it dismisses the doctrine of parens patriae, a societal policy whose enactment into child and adult protective service legislation must be embraced by all mental health professionals, as well as by all participating members of a community protected by the policy. Compliance with this law, as the decision-making framework suggests, is vital to the effective delivery of health and human services to the public. Moreover, it must guide the manner in which professionals interpret their own ethical codes.

Second, it ignores the desirability of encouraging mental health professionals to devote their practices to particularly vulnerable client groups, such as at-risk children who may vitally need their services. With respect to professionals who enter the public sector, commitment to a specific client group is not only mandated by law but also critically necessary for reasonably competent practice. More than that, a legal commitment to a class of under-served clients tends to make professional ethical ideals more realistically attainable. Specifically, it has already been noted that one weakness of ethical codes is generally that they express a laundry list of aspirations that some-times encourage the belief among professionals that they must serve several sectors of society simultaneously. For example, the NASW Code, with its ex-cessively broad definition of *client*, tends especially to promote this diffusive sense of responsibility among social workers. Although the encouragement of social accountability is a noble ideal, it tends to account for the early professional burnout that many providers suffer. Nowhere is this problem more severe than among the ranks of public-sector mental health providers. Indeed, it may be the primary ingredient in the role confusion expressed by many mental health professionals—especially those working at the public agency level—who are unable to reconcile the seemingly conflicting ethi-cal burdens that guide daily practice (Bakker, Schaufeli, Sixma, & Bosveld, 2001; Ben-Zur & Michael, 2007; Lloyd, King, & Chenoweth, 2002; Schaufeli & Enzmann, 1998; Sørgaard, Ryan, Hill, & Dawson, 2007). In contrast to the contradictory messages ethical codes express, the law identifies and limits the nature of the professional relationship between every provider and cli-ent. This fact alone provides a reason for considering all practice decisions in the legal context suggested by the decision-making framework.

Identifying and Performing Duties Owed to the Primary Client

The duty to identify the primary client includes the responsibility to assess all professional obligations owed to that client. Each of these, including the duty to practice reasonably competently, the duty to seek informed consent, the duty to treat clients and coworkers with due process and equal protec-tion (see chapter 6), and the duty to maintain confidentiality (see chapter 7), at times extends not only to the primary client but also to other members of the public who reasonably may be affected by the professional's conduct. Thus, mental health professionals providing services to a primary client who threatens violence have a responsibility to protect the identified victim (*Tara-soff v. Regents of Univ. of Cal.*, 1976). Similarly, public agency administrators have the obligation to enforce constitutional duties, rights, and protections that extend to federal and state employees and clients. Finally, mental health and social researchers have the duty to seek informed consent from and maintain the confidentiality of participants, even though, strictly speaking, such participants may not normally meet the definition of *primary client*.

Despite the fact that some of these basic duties sometimes require mental health professionals to protect members of the general public, they apply most often solely within the unique relationship of professionals and their primary clients. They promote the quality of the professional alliance by requiring the provider to honor its importance above all other social and business entanglements. A key element of this responsibility is the professional's obligation to avoid conflicts of interest, or dual relationships. That avoidance is an inherent part of the commitment owed to the primary client and enhances the provider's ability to honor all other legal obligations.

Avoiding Conflicts of Interest

On occasion, significant factors external to the relationship may compromise a provider's ability to perform the duties the professional relationship imposes. For this reason, avoiding conflicts of interest is an important legal responsibility that applies whenever a mental health provider anticipates forming a professional relationship with a primary client. Conflicts of interest include the following:

- Social or business associations with the primary client
- Social or business associations involving a third party to the professional relationship
- Professional responsibilities imposed by law or by agency regulations
- Proprietary or research interests in services being offered to the primary client
- Business associations with insurance companies, HMOs, and other third-party sources of payment for the primary client's services

Each of these categories of conflict may occur either before or after the professional has entered into a formal relationship with a primary client, and the client may either be aware or lack knowledge of the conflict's existence.

When a primary client is unaware of the existence of a conflict, the professional's failure to discuss its impact interferes with the client's ability to give informed consent because it denies the client information that he or she might reasonably rely on to make a voluntary decision about whether to accept services. For this reason, failure to reveal a known conflict of interest to an unaware client violates a fundamental legal principle—the duty to seek informed consent—applicable to mental health professionals.

Some conflicts are so inherently disruptive to the client's decision-making capacity (e.g., sexual and inappropriate social and business relationships) that, even if the client is a willing participant in the external alliance, its manipulative power undermines the client's ability to consent to professional services voluntarily. Under such circumstances, simply revealing the conflict to the client is not enough to salvage the professional relationship. Maintaining a professional relationship under such circumstances also violates the duty to practice reasonably competently. Therefore, the best overall strategy for avoiding conflicts of interest is to obey the following rule: consider the impact of any conflict of interest on the professional relationship by reviewing the conflict's effect on the duties to practice reasonably competently and to seek informed consent (Moleski & Kiselica, 2005).

Understanding the range of impact that conflicts of interest can have on the creation and maintenance of professional relationships is critical for the decision maker. For this reason, each type of conflict of interest is addressed here individually in light of the previously identified rule.

SOCIAL AND BUSINESS ASSOCIATIONS INVOLVING THE PRIMARY CLIENT

Social and business associations with clients can interfere with the ability of the mental health professional to make independent judgments necessary for reasonably competent practice. When a conflict of interest based on a social or business association threatens to interfere with a professional relationship, the provider involved must make a reasonable evaluation of the extent to which the association may pose a risk of harm to the primary client. Consistent with reasonably competent practice, discerning professionals facing such conflicts must consider and apply regional standards that prevail in the communities where they work, together with treatment alternatives reasonably available to prospective clients. In addition, clients' own psychosocial and cultural backgrounds and expectations must be assessed in an effort to estimate the risk of harm.

When a mental health professional considers entering into a clinical association with a social acquaintance, the impact of the personal connection is a necessary element of the discussion of risks and benefits essential in an informed-consent dialogue. Note that, with the exception of certain types of exploitative social and business associations that are inherently threatening to the client, the law places no absolute restrictions on the provision of professional services either to social acquaintances or to relatives. As noted earlier (see vignette 2, "The Coffee Shop"), professional ethical codes all echo this legal principle. For example, the NASW Code (ethical standard 1.06c) suggests that "dual relationships" with clients are to be avoided to the extent that they threaten a "risk of exploitation or potential harm to the client." Similarly, the NBCC Code (sections A8, A9, and B9) places a burden on professional counselors to avoid the "misuse of their influence" and associations that threaten impartiality and independent judgment. Finally, the APA Code (ethical standard 3.05a) suggests that psychologists avoid business and social associations that "impair the psychologist's objectivity, competence, or effectiveness in performing his or her functions as a psychologist, or otherwise risks exploitation or harm to the person with whom the professional relationship exists." Of these code provisions, only the APA's guidelines (ethical standard 3.05a) state affirmatively that "multiple relationships that would not reasonably be expected to cause impairment or risk exploitation or harm are not unethical." By adding this affirmative provision, it might be argued that the framers of the APA Code recognize, among other things, that the extent of harm or exploitation may depend profoundly on community norms and therefore implicitly grant some leeway to psychologists practicing in rural areas or in cross-cultural situations to include context in their consideration of the extent of harm to the client. With this singular exception, the ethical codes cited simply do not address the impact of cultural and regional norms on professional and personal conflicts.

Summarizing the issues discussed in the preceding sections, the following rule offers the most effective strategy for assessing conflict of interest dilemmas involving social or business associations: consider a decision to enter into a professional relationship where a social or business association with a client already exists by thoroughly reviewing the decision's effect on the duties to practice reasonably competently and to seek informed consent.

As a way of examining the operation of this rule, consider the case of a fifty-five-year-old, lifelong resident of Nome, Alaska. The man knows virtually everyone in town, including the certified alcoholism counselor at a local rehab program. Faced with his own severe drinking problem, the man seeks treatment from the program and its counselor. Strictly speaking, the counselor has a conflict of interest with the man because of their prior social acquaintanceship. However, given the regional community standards, the social association might not reasonably be expected to have an impact on the counselor's ability to provide independent, appropriate services (Moleski & Kiselica, 2005). Moreover, there are no feasible alternatives to providing these services locally at the center. Indeed, denial of services on the basis of a presumed conflict might well prove fatal to this prospective client. At the same time, the duty to seek informed consent requires the counselor to explore the potential impact of the social affiliation on the budding professional relationship.

Entering into social associations with clients after the professional relationship has commenced should invoke the same legal review that has been outlined earlier. In other words, the provider should consider a decision to socialize with a primary client after a professional relationship exists by thoroughly reviewing the decision's impact on the duties to practice reasonably competently and seek informed consent. For example, in vignette 2, "The Coffee Shop," the decision maker performed a conflict-of-interest analysis and ethical review revealing that brief social contact with the client was not inherently dangerous or inappropriate. In completing the analysis, the counselor most likely would receive some assistance from applying the legal rule described previously. The present discussion suggests that the thorough professional would at least want to examine the duty to practice reasonably competently to evaluate the potential impact the coffee-shop encounter could have on the clinical relationship. The professional might find good therapeutic reasons to believe that accepting the cup of coffee supports the client's clinical progress and no reason that suggests the coffee threatens it. As vignette 2 indicates, the professional should evaluate the impact of socialization on the professional relationship with respect to regional and cultural standards. Therefore, with respect to the counselor in Nome, familiarity with the way people behave in this town is likely to lead the prudent professional to conclude that a brief social encounter with the client does not compromise after all the duty to practice reasonably competently, even if the encounter were to occur after the clinical relationship had been established.

In addition to demonstrating the usefulness of a legal conflict of interest analysis, vignette 2 also shows that many ethical standards simply restate pre-existing legal principles. With this in mind, the cautious practitioner can gain much from a thorough survey of the law governing a practice problem.

As noted, some social alliances are so inherently destructive to the professional relationship that they are defined as malpractice, as in the case with sexual associations between psychotherapists and their clients. In some states, this kind of behavior is criminalized. Sexual relationships between other health and human service professionals (e.g., social workers, physicians, nurses, attorneys) are somewhat more complicated to analyze because inappropriate sexual behavior does not immediately and irreparably harm the purposes of these professional relationships as it does the psychotherapeutic bond. Nevertheless, if one performs a thorough conflict-of-interest analysis, any sexual relationship with a client would appear to compromise the professional's ability to deliver services objectively and be so inherently coercive as to substantially interfere with the client's ability to consent voluntarily to the professional relationship. This is the position adopted by the NASW, APA, and NBCC codes. Social workers, for example, are admonished in the NASW Code's ethical standard 1.09a, "under no circumstances to engage in sexual activities or sexual contact with current clients, whether . . .

consensual [or not]." Similarly, the APA Code (ethical standard 10.05) warns psychologists not to engage in "sexual intimacies" with current clients. Finally, the NBCC Code (section A10) flatly advises counselors that "sexual intimacy" with clients, together with physical and romantic intimacy, is unethical. These clear standards may be the most binding and enforceable in all three ethical codes, a fact reflected in data suggesting that sexual misconduct accounts for the most instances nationally of disciplinary actions by licensing boards against mental health professionals (Berkman, Turner, Cooper, Polnerow, & Schwartz, 2000; Moleski & Kiselica, 2005). The treatment of sexual misconduct through license revocation proceedings alone has an important flaw: a mental health professional who has lost a license through sexual misconduct without further consequences can conceivably continue to practice as a therapist in some states simply by using a practice designation that is not regulated by law (i.e., by calling oneself a psychotherapist or lay therapist).

Providing services to clients with whom a past sexual liaison has taken place has strong potential to undermine the professional relationship. The legal conflict-of-interest analysis suggested here should lead the decision maker to conclude that this kind of situation blurs professional boundaries, threatens exploitation of the client, and compromises the ability of the provider to offer reasonably competent mental health services. For this reason, ethical codes take a strong stand against the provision of clinical psychotherapy services to partners of a past sexual relationship (see, e.g., the NASW Code's ethical standard 1.09d and the APA Code's ethical standard 10.07), but only in the case of psychologists does the APA Code plainly require that the professional absolutely rule out the provision of psychotherapy services to such individuals. The NBCC Code imposes no such prohibition on counselors, nor does it seem to apply to social workers not engaged in psychotherapy. Considering the fact that counselors and social workers frequently engage in such diverse fields as school-based counseling, agency administration, program development, community organizing, and other human services not involving direct clinical interaction, this interesting omission leaves the mental health professional without specific ethical guidance covering this practice situation. Here again, the decision maker is urged in such contexts to complete the conflict-of-interest analysis outlined in this section.

Engaging in sexual liaisons with former clients also raises significant conflict-of-interest questions. In this circumstance, the professional relationship technically has terminated before the commencement of the sexual association. Here, however, there exists a profound risk to the former client that the professional may use the lingering impact of the prior professional relationship as a means to manipulate the person into the sexual affiliation. This danger is especially acute when psychotherapy has been provided. In such cases, the intense professional relationship that existed during the formal treatment phase has a permanent effect on the continuing mental health of the client. Therefore, the progress the client has made may be jeopardized if the relationship with the past therapist becomes inappropriately personal. Viewed in this light, a psychotherapist should regard any professional relationship and the duties it imposes as extending beyond the formal termination date of services.

The present conflict of interest discussion might reasonably lead a decision maker who has provided clinical services to a client to conclude that involvement in a sexual relationship with the former client violates the duty to practice reasonably competently because it can be expected to have an impact on the client's continuing health. This is the position of many state legislatures, which have criminalized sexual relationships between psychotherapists and former clients where the professional services have only been terminated for a relatively short time (e.g., one year in New Mexico) (N.M. Stat. Ann. § 30-9-10[A][5], 2008). Even when such conduct is not criminal, it still may be so inherently harmful to the former client as to constitute malpractice. This danger may or may not be present in the case of sexual relationships between other human service professionals, such as social workers and counselors providing solely informational (i.e., nonclinical) services, and their former clients.

Ethical codes in the mental health disciplines (see, e.g., the NASW Code's ethical standard 1.09b, the NBCC Code's section A10, and the APA Code's ethical standard 10.08) suggest that professionals are to avoid sexual relationships with former clients, and the codes place the burden on professionals seeking to engage in such relationships to demonstrate the absence of exploitation. In the case of counselors and psychologists, according to the NBCC and APA codes, respectively, this burden includes the passage of at least two years since the termination of services.

One could certainly conclude reasonably that the ethical codes' treatment of sexual relationships with former clients is too unrestricted. One could argue additionally that the legal standard in place—the duty to practice reasonably competently—probably would never condone the involvement of psychotherapists in sexual relationships with past clients, no matter what the therapist's specific discipline is or the length of passage of time between the professional relationship and sexual association; the danger of harm to the former client is too strong and obvious. With this point considered, is it ever possible for the professional to overcome the presumption that sexual relationships with former clients are inherently harmful? Consider the case of a social worker or counselor serving as a hospital patient advocate. The patient advocate's services during the client's one-day hospital visit consist of communicating the client's grievance concerning the hospital's food to the administrative staff. Ten years pass, and the advocate has been reintroduced to the former client at a social event; she and the client choose to pursue an intimate sexual relationship. Whether the relationship should be avoided depends in large measure on the advocate's assessment of the potential harm to the former client. Applying the test suggested previously, the advocate might reasonably conclude that the prior professional relationship terminated at the time of the hospital discharge and that the professional relationship that previously existed has no continuing impact on the client's present well-being. Indeed, applying the reasonable-competence and informed-consent principles to this analysis, both would seem to be somewhat more forgiving of sexual relationships initiated some time after the termination of nonpsychotherapeutic services.

Acceptance of a gift creates a conflict of interest for the mental health professional if the gift is substantial enough to influence the professional's subjectivity or it threatens to distort the client's expectations regarding services. Thus, if the psychologist Dr. Melfi accepts Tony Soprano's cash gift for her "good work this week," Dr. Melfi can reasonably expect that the acceptance of the gift will encourage Tony to expect more clinical successes in future weeks.

As with other conflict-of-interest dilemmas, it is helpful for decision makers to assess their responsibilities regarding gifts in terms of the duties relating to informed consent and reasonably competent practice. As an example, reconsider the counselor's acceptance of the dream catcher in vignette 3. Taking the gift probably creates no unreasonable client expectations that are likely to harm the professional relationship. Moreover, it is consistent with regional and cultural expectations that help identify standards of reasonably competent practice and informed consent that exist in the rural community identified in the vignette.

Occasionally, state legislation defines the extent to which mental health professionals—especially government employees—can accept gifts, typically defined in terms of a dollar amount. Considering this fact together with the two case scenarios outlined here, the decision maker's best strategy for making a choice concerning the client's gift is to consider it only after thorough review of the duties to practice reasonably competently and to seek informed consent, as well as any applicable local laws or regulations governing the receipt of gifts by public employees.

Gift acceptance should also be considered in the context of ethical standards governing conflict of interest. The general theme of these standards echoes the legal principle cited earlier: avoid risking the harm or

exploitation of a client, and abstain from exploiting the client or taking unfair advantage. Mastering the legal duties related to reasonably competent
practice and informed consent offers the decision maker the best overall
preparation for conflict situations, especially because—unlike the conflicting ethical guidelines mentioned earlier— the legal duties vigorously encourage the consideration of regional and cultural context.

Business associations between mental health providers and their clients
present a comparable threat to the integrity of the professional relationship.
A variety of business affiliations—from formal to informal—can link professionals and their clients, and the more rural or isolated a community is,
the more inevitable is a conflict of interest. For example, a professional may
hold a business meeting at a restaurant owned by an individual who also
is a primary client. Alternatively, a professional may simultaneously buy a
car from and provide services to the lone car salesperson in a small town.
As another example, a professional may exchange services with a physician
using a barter relationship. Another professional may offer treatment to a
community college instructor who teaches an aerobics class the professional
takes. The smaller the town, the likelier are any of these scenarios. The range
of business contexts cited here demonstrates that there can be no reasonable legal or ethical principle barring outright the existence of a business
association between professional and client. However, one should consider
the effect of a business association on the professional relationship through
a thorough review of the duties to practice reasonably competently and to
seek informed consent.

This legal conflict-of-interest strategy requires the professional to consider the business association by reference to its impact on the competent
provision of services to the client, the professional's ability to make impartial clinical choices on the client's behalf, and the client's continuing expectations regarding services (Moleski & Kiselica, 2005). Consistent with
standards governing competent practice and informed consent, these legal principles must be applied with reference to community and cultural
expectations. Thus, in all of the business-conflict situations cited herein, a
professional might reasonably offer services to the client and maintain the
business association where

- It is consistent with community and cultural expectations
- The professional is treated similarly to any other business patron or
  customer
- The business association does not otherwise exploit the client such
  that the benefits of the business association might reasonably alter
  the client's expectations concerning the professional services

- The professional seeks informed consent (i.e., the professional discusses the risks presented by the business association as a condition to providing professional services)

Consider the example of a professional counselor who receives an offer of a personal loan from a bank vice president, also a client, based on the vice president's "vouching for the good reputation and credit worthiness" of the counselor. The counselor's application for and acceptance of the loan exploit the professional relationship with the vice president in a way that is burdensome and unacceptable. Specifically, there is a danger that the vice president may expect quid pro quo from the counselor in the delivery of future clinical services, a belief that clouds understanding of the risks and benefits of the counseling. In this situation, the imposition that the business association places on the professional relationship is so extreme that no amount of open discussion between professional and prospective client can overcome it. In informed-consent terms, the risk created by the banker's offer of loan assistance is not likely to be surmounted simply because both parties discuss it and choose to continue the business relationship.

Compare this situation with the other business and social conflicts described earlier. The difference here is not only in degree but also in the role that the exchange of money has in defining and hampering the professional relationship. Because the professional relationship itself represents a type of business exchange—albeit one that appropriately supports the parties' clinical relationship and trades reasonable payment for services rendered—additional financial entanglements between the provider and client may alter or confuse, at least in the mind of the client, the clear contractual agreement that should form the basis of the parties' essential bond. It is worth noting here that the professional must not allow any disagreement between the parties relating to the business side of the parties' professional relationship—perhaps a quarrel over the exact fee amount owed—to interfere with the professional's delivery of competent services and independent clinical judgment on behalf of the client.

SOCIAL AND BUSINESS ASSOCIATIONS INVOLVING A THIRD PARTY

Social and business associations that involve the provider, a client, and a third party may also interfere with the integrity of the professional relationship. These types of situations arise when the client's or provider's mutual social or business association with another individual threatens to have some impact on the professional relationship. This may occur when the professional and client both share a close friendship with another person, when the professional has a business relationship with a member of the client's family, or even when the professional has a close social or sexual relationship with a member of the client's family. As with other conflicts, this conflict most clearly threatens the bond between professional and client when it interferes with the client's voluntary consideration of the risks and benefits connected with services, and with the professional's ability to exercise independent judgment. With respect to sexual relationships with close relatives of clients, only the APA Code (ethical standard 10.06) places an outright ban on this conduct. The NASW Code (ethical standard 1.09) discourages the behavior to the extent there is a risk of harm or exploitation to the client. The NBCC Code does not address this situation specifically.

With respect to social or business associations with third parties, if, for example, a psychologist provides psychotherapy to the teacher of the psychologist's child, a thorough discussion of the existence of the conflict may be sufficient to allow the client to consider freely the potential impact of the external association on the services; the client may quickly reject its importance and openly consent to treatment. Suppose, on the contrary, that the psychologist's association with the teacher has been a tempestuous and confrontational one, and in the recent past, the two have quarreled publicly during school board meetings over the quality of teaching (including this teacher's skills) at the community elementary school. Perhaps, knowing what an excellent professional reputation the psychologist has, the teacher sees therapy not only as the best way to address long-standing emotional problems but also as a method of mending fences with the psychologist on a social level. In this rather unlikely predicament, the cautious professional might find, after a full discussion of the risks required by the duty to seek informed consent, that the parties' past history is bound to intrude into the clinical dialogue. In this circumstance, a subsidiary issue—the teacher-student-parent triangle—may play an excessive role in the teacher's decision to seek services, and the psychologist realizes this all too clearly. Considered in another light, this turbulent social history compromises the professional's duty to practice reasonably competently.

Other social associations involving the provider and a third party may threaten the professional relationship in a more immediate way. A common example of such a circumstance is sexual contact between the provider and a close friend or relative of the potential client. This situation may impose such a great stress on both parties' comfort level with this arrangement that, even with the provider's full disclosure and discussion with the client of the risks of a professional relationship with this person, the potential for psychological harm to the client is too foreseeable to permit the establishment of a professional relationship.

A legal approach to risk evaluation is also suggested by professional ethical codes, which essentially require the professional to assess the potential for harm to the client when triangular social associations are involved. For example, the NASW Code (ethical standard 1.06) indicates that professionals should avoid such relationships "when there is a risk of exploitation or potential harm to the client." The APA Code (ethical standard 1.17) takes essentially the same position, as does the NBCC Code (section B9). As with conflict situations analyzed here, the decision maker managing dilemmas that involve third-party relationships should consider them by thorough application of the duties to seek informed consent and to practice reasonably competently.

CONFLICTS CREATED BY LEGAL RESPONSIBILITIES AND AGENCY OBLIGATIONS

Services provided to a primary client may be limited by the law or by professional responsibilities that the mental health provider owes by reason of agency policy or other employment obligations. For example, professionals have a legal obligation to report suspected child abuse or to protect the client and other members of the public from the client's threats of violence. Alternatively, an agency may bind a psychotherapist to offer clinical appointments only during regular business hours and not to make exceptions to this policy for particularly needy clients. The professional's duties in these instances may clearly affect the nature of services rendered to the client, and they may supersede other responsibilities ordinarily owed to a client, such as the maintenance of confidentiality. Thus, in these instances, the conflicting obligations of the professional plainly create a conflict of interest. As with any other conflict, the professional must manage it in a manner that satisfies the duties to practice reasonably competently and to seek informed consent. The latter responsibility suggests that the provider should disclose all legal responsibilities and agency obligations as risks associated with any future professional relationship between the provider and the potential client.

Any mental health provider, and particularly one offering direct clinical services, must struggle with the impact that the disclosure of legal responsibilities may have on a professional relationship. To a shy, sensitive, or reticent client entering psychotherapy for the first time, the clinician's recitation of legal responsibilities can have a chilling effect on the client's willingness to disclose information. This is especially true where the provider treats informed consent in an excessively formal and legalistic manner at the commencement of services rather than by encouraging a continuing, open dialogue between professional and client. Therefore, the discussion concerning the professional's legal responsibilities calls for the exercise of good clinical skills and suggests the need for an open, relaxed, informal, and continuing conversation concerning risks associated with the professional relationship. In fact, the competent therapist should discuss the meaning of informed consent itself, so that the client plainly understands the purposes underlying the exploration of risks and benefits.

As already noted, mental health professionals practicing with public agencies frequently have a legal responsibility to protect the interests of a class of vulnerable clients. Often, however, these professionals also provide services to other members of the public who do not fall in the protected class. For example, the legal responsibility imposed on child welfare social workers is to protect the interests of vulnerable children who are at risk for abuse and neglect. These children, in effect, are the primary clients of the agency social worker. In the course of performing this protective function, the social worker may also be called on to provide rehabilitative assistance to the family of a vulnerable child. Indeed, children's courts addressing instances of family violence frequently mandate such assistance. In such cases, a child's custody may hinge on the parents' successful completion of parenting classes, individual therapy, anger management training, or a family preservation service (FPS) program. Family preservation service programs are short-term, intensive interventions that are intended to prevent the removal of children from the homes of families who have experienced abuse or neglect (Kirk & Griffith, 2004; Littell & Tajima, 2000). The FPS programs typically last no more than four months but provide up to fifteen contract hours per week of in-home counseling, parenting skills education, and similar clinical services (Kauffman, 2007; Kirk & Griffith, 2004; Littell & Tajima, 2000). Spurred by federal legislation, including the Adoption Assistance and Child Welfare Act of 1980, and by federal dollars from the Omnibus Budget Reconciliation Act (OBRA) of 1993 and the Adoption and Safe Families Act (ASFA) of 1997, most states have adopted FPS programs (Kirk & Griffith, 2004; Littell & Tajima, 2000).

When the public child welfare agency itself provides clinical services, including counseling, psychotherapy, and FPS programs, the recipients of the services become the agency's secondary clients. Secondary clients are clients to whom services are provided peripherally as part of the agency's satisfaction of its legal responsibilities to a primary client.

In any child welfare case involving a youngster who is threatened by suspected abuse or neglect, the child and parents have interests that are, at least initially, in conflict. Parents usually wish to resolve their problematic behavior and improve their parenting skills. However, these goals in the long run may or may not be realizable. More immediately, parents desire to have their custody rights restored to them. Their children, however, have a state-supported interest in being protected and parented according to minimally acceptable standards. This conflict presents a significant burden for the social worker, who may be forced to alter, limit, or otherwise moderate the services provided to the secondary client on the basis of a primary responsibility to the vulnerable child. For example, the parents' progress in a parenting class the social worker facilitates will help determine whether they maintain custody of the child. A social worker already convinced of the need to remove the child permanently from the parents' custody may allow this fact to affect the services rendered during the family intervention. This might include directing the therapeutic dialogue to include a discussion of how and why the parents' behavior has become irremediable. Moreover, parents' statements during counseling may relate directly to their continuing fitness to be the child's custodians. Consequently, the parents' expectation of confidentiality cannot be enforced to the extent that the social worker's revelation of this conversation is necessary for the protection of the child.

Child welfare agencies that acknowledge the conflict of interest created by the previously described situation may make efforts to contract with independent clinical providers to offer family services to secondary clients. Alternatively, in some child protective service agencies, administrators may attempt to address this problem by separating the delivery of investigative and treatment services between separate internal subagencies. In poor and rural communities, however, neither the funds nor the providers may exist in sufficient numbers to make these independent services routinely available (Landsman, 2002). Consequently, the child welfare agency may offer them directly. Even when independent clinicians are available, they may work frequently in close contact with protective social workers and allow this influence to affect their clinical stance regarding their clients. Despite the fact that a public child welfare agency provides independently contracted clinical services, clinical social workers employed by the agency itself invariably administer FPS programs. How, then, can the public agency social worker or administrator fully resolve this significant conflict of interest? As with any conflict, the most appropriate initial strategy is the legal analysis suggested here. Specifically, the duties to practice reasonably competently and to seek informed consent must govern the resolution of this dilemma.

In any scenario involving FPS or similar programs, the parents may have been court ordered to receive services. Therefore, they may lack legal capacity to consent to the services and are at least in this sense involuntary clients. Nevertheless, the professional treating the parents—an individual best referred to here as the social worker–clinician—should strive to seek the parents' knowledgeable cooperation within the limitations imposed by the court order. This fact suggests that the parents are still entitled to a full disclosure of the risks and benefits of treatment. In addition, the social worker–clinician should facilitate a candid discussion of these risks and benefits—including the fact that the parents' statements may in certain circumstances be shared with child protective social workers in the interest of ensuring the safety of the child. This discussion may help make the parents more willing participants in the clinical relationship. Consistent with the social worker–clinician's duty to the primary client—the vulnerable child—the primary objective of the social worker–clinician must be to remove any threat of danger to the child and to ensure a secure home environment. This responsibility imposes limitations on the social worker–clinician's professional relationship with the parents (including the breach of confidentiality in appropriate circumstances), and these restrictions must be disclosed to the parents as risks of therapy. As part of this responsibility, the social worker–clinician must explain that the child welfare agency's primary legal responsibility is to the child and that family therapy serves essentially as a means to protect the child's best interests. An additional issue raised by the duty to seek informed consent is the social worker–clinician's responsibility to assess fully all relevant clinical issues affecting the parents' relationship with the child and to disclose treatment options available for these issues. Thus, alcoholism, substance abuse, and significant mental illness may have an important role in the underlying parental problem (Rittner & Dozier, 2000), and parents have the right to receive information about responsive interventions.

An intensive service such as FPS often represents a last-ditch effort to reunite the family, and it may ultimately prove unsuccessful. Informed consent suggests that the professional must adequately reveal this reality to the parents. As already noted, the social worker–clinician's legal responsibility to the child includes violating confidentiality with the parents in the event that they reveal matters in therapy that have a bearing on the child's safety, or indeed, if the social worker–clinician arrives at the conclusion that the therapy itself is not proving sufficiently effective to warrant reunification of the family. On the plus side, benefits of intensive therapy may include a healthier family and restored custody, and these potential results are an equally important topic of an informed-consent discussion. Regardless of the outcome of therapy, the social worker–clinician may count on being called on in court to offer an opinion about the parents' progress; this situation ultimately places the social worker–clinician in the position of supporting a particular custodial outcome that runs counter to the parents' legal stance. Planning for this eventuality may at least unconsciously make the so-cial worker–clinician an advocate for a particular result even before therapy begins. Therefore, this risk must be shared with the parents as part of the informed-consent dialogue at the outset of treatment.

The foregoing discussion of informed-consent issues unfortunately does not satisfactorily resolve the conflict of interest facing social worker–clinicians employed by public child protective agencies. Even if the risks and benefits are disclosed candidly and the parents become willing participants in treatment, the social worker–clinician still faces two disturbingly conflict-ing responsibilities. On the one hand, the social worker–clinician provides therapy in an effort to reunify families. On the other hand, the therapy itself may place the child at an even greater risk in the event family reunification is accomplished; abusive parents may reoffend despite treatment and reuni-fication. Still again, the social worker–clinician's recognition of the legal re-sponsibility to protect the child may be so focused as to limit or remove the objective treatment stance necessary for effective clinical practice. Even if the social worker–clinician can focus effectively on clinical responsibilities, the brief, intensive nature of FPS and similar services may be insufficient to treat such long-term problems as parental substance abuse, alcoholism, and mental illness. Even the best social worker–clinician versed in FPS tech-niques may not have the degree of practice specialization to treat extensive mental health conditions in the time permitted; indeed, treatment of such complex problems is simply not susceptible to short-term, intensive therapy. Therefore, regardless of whether the informed consent dilemma is resolved, difficult questions remain about the competence of clinical services offered by social worker–clinicians and their agencies to secondary clients.

This conflict of interest is not one of the social worker's or agency's mak-ing. It is a catch-22 injected into state child welfare legislation by a federal mandate—the Adoption Assistance and Child Welfare Act of 1980—that places manifestly contradictory responsibilities on child welfare social workers and their agencies. Specifically, by this federal decree, state child abuse legislation must require agencies both to protect the interests of chil-dren and to attempt family reunification if possible. In an effort to address both the rights of families and the protection of children, such legislation impedes the accomplishment of both objectives; it effectively creates a di-lemma that cannot be resolved consistently with the agency's obligation to provide reasonably competent services to both the primary and second-ary clients.

As already noted, where clinical services are available and courts direct child welfare agencies to provide them, these agencies should endeavor to contract with independent providers to offer treatment to secondary clients.

To their credit, larger child welfare agencies routinely operate in this fashion. Alternatively, courts should decree in their child welfare case dispositions that parents independently seek such treatment from among a slate of court-approved providers. For the reasons already noted, some parents— primarily rural, poor, and minority—are more likely to receive these services from the child welfare authority itself. This may be part of the reason that there are such racially disproportionate outcomes in child welfare and family reunification, a problem that is national in scope and most severely affects African American families (McRoy, 2008).

Changes in federal law under ASFA have forced states to streamline permanency planning, the process by which child welfare agencies organize the long-term care of children whose families fail to rehabilitate themselves sufficiently to be reunited. In these circumstances, agencies must hasten preparations for adoption by close family members or foster families or, in the alternative, for extended family foster care or guardianship by persons who do not choose to adopt (Wattenberg, Kelley, & Kim, 2001). The ASFA legislation has directed states to hasten the judicial process of terminating parental rights in child abuse, neglect, and abandonment cases. In such instances, the required procedures may result not only in the accelerated transfer of child custody to the state but also in the expedited termination of parental rights and adoption of children placed in the foster care system. The ASFA-mandated system may ultimately be in the best interests of children who have experienced severe abuse and neglect, but it also raises important questions about the capacity of state child welfare authorities to reunify families in an abbreviated time frame. When mental illness, alcoholism, or substance abuse problems have a significant impact on family relationships (Rittner & Dozier, 2000) but cannot reasonably be addressed in a matter of months, the competence of the time-shortened clinical services provided to parents must be questioned.

Ultimately, threats to the sufficiency of services offered to parents and their children affect the rights of both groups. These threats may rise to the level of constitutional violations when fundamental liberties, such as the right to due process and family privacy, are implicated. It remains for future judges to sort out the constitutional problems that child welfare legislation and corresponding agency conduct may raise. In the meantime, however, a conflict-of-interest analysis suggests several immediate responses to the problem.

First, independent contractors not under the administrative management of the child welfare authority must provide ordinary clinical services for secondary clients. The urgency of this point is based on the need not only to provide the most competent clinical services available but also to ensure the confidentiality that is vital to the therapeutic relationship. Ultimately, legislatures should consider the redesign of family preservation services, which should be organized independently and publicly funded under the aegis of an appropriate governmental authority, such as a public health agency, more suited to the care and maintenance of families in crisis. Available services must be expanded to adequately address contributing causes of child abuse and neglect, such as mental illness and substance abuse. Although clinical family services continue to remain under the administrative management of child welfare agencies, more open acknowledgment of persistent conflicts of interest should take place. In the same manner that hospitals provide patient advocates to address specific grievances regarding medical care, child welfare agencies should be prepared to offer secondary clients the services of trained liaisons available to facilitate communication between service providers and recipients.

Children's courts must also bear the responsibility of addressing conflicts of interest. These bodies often make dispositions and approve treatment plans that call for specific family interventions. The burden to design and implement these programs often becomes the obligation of child welfare agencies that are understaffed and ill equipped to provide them. Social workers and children's court attorneys should actively lobby courts to tailor child welfare orders consistent with the informed-consent and reasonable-competence standards discussed here. In addition, courts would do well to consider the implementation of support programs to monitor the progress of parents receiving clinical interventions from child welfare authorities. As with court-appointed special advocates (CASAs) assigned in many state children's courts to observe and report on the progress of children in child welfare proceedings, court-assigned mentors could significantly assist fragile parents, many of whom are more emotionally brittle than their children (Calkins & Murray, 1999). An added benefit of this approach would be to provide courts with an independent, objective assessment of parental response to clinical services.

As noted earlier, some child welfare agencies that acknowledge the important conflict of interest created by the delivery of family preservation and similar clinical and family treatment programs do make an effort to separate the delivery of clinical and investigative services. Thus, "family preservation units" are created to provide expressly clinical services, and agency social workers are typically shunted into either investigative or clinical roles. Overall administrative management typically remains, however, under the leadership of a single child welfare agency, and this perpetuates the delivery of compromised clinical services to secondary clients. In apparent recognition of this problem, no less an authority than the National

Commission on Child Welfare and Family Preservation has made an as-yet-unheeded proposal for the radical reorganization of child welfare service delivery (Schorr, 2000). Nevertheless, in recent years, scholars have written extensively about how organizational service settings and structure may have a significant impact on the effectiveness of child welfare interventions (Yoo, Brooks, & Patti, 2007). This research may yet prompt a renewed discussion of the importance of service settings in the delivery of treatment to families. Clearly, the stress that some child welfare agencies themselves experience in their efforts to deliver child protection and parental treatment services simultaneously is both palpable and ongoing. It may be part of the reason that some states have allowed chronic failures in the protection of children to lead them to privatize child protective services, as has occurred in Florida (Freeman, 2003).

One recent reform in child welfare decision making has been the implementation of team decision making (TDM) in some communities as a means of deciding whether family unification or child removal and adoption is warranted in individual cases (Crampton, Crea, Abramson-Madden, & Usher, 2008). This approach unites families and social workers with community representatives in an attempt to bring consensus to decision making in child welfare interventions. Although this approach does little to address the basic conflict of interest discussed in this section, it nonetheless represents the recognition that making decisions in child welfare cases—including efforts to reunify families—could benefit from increasing the pool of interested stakeholders involved in the consideration of treatment decisions.

The distinction between primary and secondary clients discussed here underscores an important point about many mental health and human services that public agencies offer. For instance, a certified counselor employed by a state-administered prison system to provide clinical and other services to inmates essentially has two sets of clients. First, the counselor represents the public at large (i.e., public citizens benefitting from the prisoner's rehabilitation), to whom the counselor, by assuming employment, owes a primary obligation. Second, the counselor offers treatment to prisoners, who, in truth, are secondary clients. Similarly, a forensic psychologist employed by a state mental health facility may be court appointed to diagnose the mental competency of a violent offender in an effort to assist the court in its determination of the offender's criminal culpability or mental capacity to stand trial. Alternatively, a mental health professional may be court appointed to assess the psychological health and parenting ability of litigants in a child custody case. In effect, the psychologist's primary client in these instances is the state, on whose behalf the psychologist has been appointed to render an opinion about an offender's dangerousness, amenability to rehabilitation, appreciation of the difference between right and wrong, and other related issues. In the case of a child custody proceeding, the court-appointed psychologist's role typically is to give an opinion about the parenting skills and emotional fitness of the parent (*Ghayoumi v. McMillan*, 2006; *Hafner v. Beck*, 1995). At the same time, the diagnostic process is a service being administered to a secondary client, whose future care and rehabilitation by another provider may depend on the accuracy of the court-directed diagnosis.

These conflicts of interest are most serious to the extent they make the reasonably competent delivery of clinical services to the secondary client impossible. As with families involved in child abuse proceedings, severely inadequate treatment may compromise the constitutional rights of other secondary clients, such as prisoners and forensic patients (i.e., persons adjudicated to be incompetent to stand trial or not guilty by reason of insanity) (see, e.g., *Duran v. Apodaca*, 1980). In privatized prisons and forensic treatment centers, the monitoring of service delivery may be even more limited, with an extrabureaucratic layer making oversight of inmate services still cloudier.

With the foregoing discussion in mind, the need is apparent for a set of clear legal principles that summarize the standards discussed in this section governing the provision of services to secondary clients. The following guidelines offer a general strategy for addressing situations involving primary and secondary clients: First, the mental health professional should identify the primary client and the legal responsibility owed to that client. Second, the professional should identify the secondary client(s). The professional should offer services to the secondary client only if they facilitate the professional's duty to the primary client and are peripheral in nature. This is the situation, for example, when case assessment, investigation, and diagnostic services of a secondary client are required to protect the best interests of the vulnerable client(s) whom the professional is required to protect. As illustrations, a social worker's assessment of a family experiencing child abuse, a psychologist conducting a forensic examination of a violent offender, and a county coroner's completion of an autopsy are all peripheral services offered in the interest of satisfying important state interests. Third, the professional should offer all other services to secondary clients only when they can be provided reasonably competently and with informed consent. Ordinarily, this is the case only when the secondary services are provided by a professional administratively separated from the agency responsible for protecting primary clients, such as an independent contractor hired for this express service, and only when confidentiality can be honored.

Thus, a professional serving a primary client must generally avoid simultaneously providing services such as psychotherapy, family preservation services, counseling, and other related services to secondary clients.

THE PROFESSIONAL'S PROPRIETARY INTEREST IN SERVICES

Just like the professional's interest in a research project or the use of advertising in soliciting clients, other proprietary or business factors with which the professional is associated may have a role in influencing the client's entry into a professional relationship. In some instances, the provider may have a personal or financial interest in a treatment modality offered to the client. This type of interest creates a conflict between caregiver and client that may threaten the integrity of the professional relationship. For example, the fact that a physician has staff privileges at a hospital may drive him or her to recommend an ill patient's admission to the hospital. In a series of related federal cases that have alerted the public to the potential abuse of the physician-hospital relationship, a major for-profit hospital system partly settled government allegations that it offered salary bonuses and other direct financial incentives—labeled "kickbacks" by the U.S. Justice Department—to staff physicians based on their referral of Medicaid and Medicare patients (In re *Columbia/HCA Healthcare Corp. Litig.*, 2001). Unsettled questions include the government's remaining allegations that the hospital system used a physician-syndication strategy offering doctors investment opportunities in member hospitals as a means of fostering physician loyalty (Taylor, 2001).

Another major HMO settled a lawsuit instituted by the Texas attorney general challenging the use of financial incentives to physicians who assisted in reducing health-care costs (*State v. Aetna U.S. Healthcare, Inc.*, 2000). Pursuant to the settlement agreement entered into in the *Aetna* case, the HMO was prohibited from using inverse compensation schemes that reward physicians who minimize their patients' consumption of medical services, including doctor visits and referrals for laboratory testing. The effect of financial incentives on the delivery of health-care services continues to pose a major threat to the provision of competent health care and the exercise of independent clinical judgment by providers in the twenty-first century.

Some of the worst abuses by managed care organizations are the target of the Federal False Claim Act (FCA) (2009), which makes unlawful a number of the persistent abuses of payor organizations doing business with the federal government, including the Medicare and Medicaid programs. Chief among the crimes the FCA has identified is the practice of underutilization, or the failure of managed-care organizations to provide needed medical services in the interest of cost reduction. Also included is the practice of filing false claims, referring to the fraudulent bills submitted to government-contracted programs, including state Medicaid agencies. Another example of conduct the FCA makes unlawful is the attempt by managed-care organizations to save costs by simply failing to provide certain categories of care as a result of their costliness or encouraging the use of underqualified health personnel to provide needed services.

As a hypothetical example of a conflict stemming from a professional's proprietary interest in services, consider the example of a psychologist who has written and published extensively on the use of eye movement desensitization and reprocessing (EMDR), a controversial treatment whose proponents claim facilitates the brain's processing of information and painful emotions in sufferers of PTSD (Davidson & Parker, 2001; Hogberg, 2007). Influenced by intense scholarly interest in this field, the professional wishes to attempt this therapy with a new client complaining of persistent memories of a serious car accident. Surely the psychologist wishes to offer services he believes to be effective, but at the same time, his interest in raising public awareness of EMDR and in pursuing publishing opportunities connected with new cases plays at least a part in the psychologist's offer of services. As another example, a mental health facility specializing in the treatment of depression may advertise its program motivated jointly by a desire to increase public awareness of mental health illness issues and by an interest in getting new patients.

As with all of the other conflicts of interest detailed here, the situations described endanger both the voluntariness of the client's choice of services and the professional's ability to exercise free and competent judgment on behalf of each client. As in the resolution of all other conflicts, a provider holding a proprietary or business interest in services offered should assess the impact by considering and applying the duties to practice reasonably competently and to seek informed consent. At the very least, the professional must disclose to the client the existence of the business, research, or proprietary interest. Failure to do so denies the client information that could reasonably play a role in the client's decision to enter into the professional relationship.

In many circumstances, the proprietary interest held by the provider is both a reasonable and necessary part of the professional relationship. As already noted, many professional relationships themselves involve a business exchange and are fee generating. As with most mental health services, the provider has both a right and a need to be paid for rendering the services. Where, however, the business interest eclipses the professional's ability to provide reasonably competent services, the purposes of the professional relationship are fundamentally violated. Consider, for example, the case of a physician paid a salary bonus by a hospital based on the number of patients admitted. Here, the financial motivations both of the hospital and of the physician appear to supersede independent medical judgment in a manner that overtly threatens the patient. The salary incentive in this case represents such a strong potential inducement to the physician that it sabotages the objectivity required to render an accurate assessment of each patient's health and ensure proper treatment. In an era in which managed care, profitability, and cost containment have become operative principles in the health-care industry, these financial factors may continue to tempt hospitals and providers to engage in the kind of practice highlighted in this example. Indeed, the elevation of cost containment to a place of preeminence threatens to undermine the competent provision of health and mental-health-care services to patients and clients.

In the case of the psychologist and PTSD client noted earlier, the psychologist may reasonably be able to assess and treat the client even in the face of strong personal and professional interest in EMDR therapy. Indeed, it is eminently reasonable to expect a mental health professional to pursue scholarly endeavors in a practice specialty and to share the benefits of this scholarship with potential clients. In fact, the duty to seek informed consent requires the disclosure of the full body of professional research relating to clients' presenting problems, together with a discussion of alternative treatment methods that may be of comparable assistance. To the extent, however, that the psychologist allows an interest in EMDR to cause an incomplete assessment of the client's mental health issues or otherwise allows a devotion to EMDR as a treatment modality to avert a discussion of other options, such as cognitive behavioral and medicinal strategies, the provider renders an inadequate service.

Relationships with Third-Party Payors

The duty to identify the primary client requires mental health providers to preserve the integrity of the professional relationship and to protect it from personal, social, and business interests that may compromise it. The steps outlined here present a strategy for defending the professional's relationship with the primary client in a variety of hazardous situations. A key element of this approach requires that the professional first ascertain who the primary client is in settings in which this individual's identity may not always be obvious.

One of the reasons that identifying the primary client may present a challenge is that the busy professional often works in conjunction with third-party payors, including insurance companies, HMOs, government programs (e.g., Medicaid, Medicare), and other payment sources—often close members of the client's own family—that underwrite the client's care and financially support the provider's service. Often, these entities and persons have an important role in financing or otherwise facilitating the client's entry into the professional relationship, and for that reason, their role in making services available to the client may be critical.

The client or the professional may initiate third-party payment relationships. The client initiates them when he or she makes a request for reimbursement from a payor—typically an insurance company—for professional services. In contrast, it is often the provider who agrees to manage the paperwork involved in filing for insurance benefits on the client's behalf, because this service benefits both parties to the professional relationship. On other occasions, a provider who agrees to offer services to clients as a member of an HMO initiates the third-party connection. The professional benefits from associating with the HMO, which provides a financial incentive by ensuring a steady source of clients, but is subject to the policies and guidelines governing the HMO agreement.

In any third-party relationship, the provider's association with the third-party payor is not a professional relationship as defined in this book, nor does the provider owe the payor the duties associated with that relationship. Instead, it is a contractual arrangement in which the professional agrees to perform services on the client's behalf and to receive payment, at least in part, from the payor. The client's association with the third-party payor is also a contractual one, and the parties' rights and responsibilities are defined in the insurance agreement. Despite the existence of a contractual association with a third-party provider, the rights and responsibilities of the client and provider, respectively, continue to consist of all those legal duties previously described, including the provider's duties to practice reasonably competently and seek informed consent. The contractual association created with the third-party payor does not dilute in any way these duties. For this reason, the cautious provider must take steps to ensure that contractual obligations connected to the third-party payor do not interfere with the professional relationship established with each client.

Because they play such an extensive role as gatekeepers in the delivery of health and mental health services to the public, the interests of third-party payors are sometimes elevated inappropriately when assessing the professional responsibilities of behavioral-health-care providers. The conflict of interest thus created may seriously hamper the professional's exercise of independent judgment that serves the best interests of the client. In addition, the contractual pressure that third-party payors exert on professionals and clients may place an inordinate amount of stress on the provider to tailor services in a way that satisfies the third-party payor's requirements and expectations. As with all of the conflict of interest scenarios described here, the decision maker facing conflicts involving third-party payors should assess each conflict by considering the legal duties to practice reasonably competently and seek informed consent from the client.

A classic example of the manipulation of a professional relationship for the benefit of a third-party payor is the service—including hospitalization and medical care—associated with pregnancy and childbirth. In recent years, a cost-savings measure frequently employed by HMO requirements limits hospitalization benefits. Specifically, benefits may be granted for only a limited number of days, irrespective of the professional preference of the attending physician, who may regard more extended hospitalization as in the best medical interests of the patient. In this instance, early release of the patient may well violate the physician's duty to provide reasonably competent medical services. To the extent that the provider deviates one bit from prudent medical judgment to satisfy the HMO's reimbursement limit, he or she violates an essential duty to the patient.

Even more troubling is the link between the historical failure of insurance companies and HMOs to provide adequate, or in some cases, even minimal, coverage for mental health benefits and the inability of patients to access necessary treatment. Indeed, there is overwhelming evidence of a clear connection between the absence of mental health insurance parity and the inadequate use of clinically appropriate mental health services by patients and clients lacking coverage (Trivedi, Swaminathan, & Mor, 2008). A number of states have adopted comprehensive parity laws that require some degree of mental health coverage, but only Connecticut, Maryland, Oregon, and Vermont currently have comprehensive parity laws that require private insurance plans to provide coverage for all mental health and substance abuse disorders (T. Johnson, 2008–2009). As a result, Congress has enacted the Paul Wellstone and Pete Domenici Mental Health Parity and Addiction Equity Act of 2008, which is anticipated to bring enhanced mental health insurance benefits to the approximately 113 million Americans currently lacking such benefits. The law, which became effective for most health plans on January 1, 2010, requires all insurance providers, including self-funded plans under the federal Employee Retirement Income Security Act (1974), to offer mental health insurance coverage for the full continuum of needs—including depression, schizophrenia, substance abuse and alcoholism, and autism, among other conditions (T. Johnson, 2008–2009).

As an example of the way in which health-care and mental-health-care providers can allow the pressure of their contractual relationship with a third-party payor to influence their clinical practice, consider the case of a psychologist who may be persuaded to diagnose a mental health condition in a manner that ensures the client's maximum coverage under available insurance. Some government health programs, such as Medicaid and Medicare, rely on a cost-containment system that employs the use of diagnostic related groups (DRGs) (Gee, 2006; Rosenberg & Browne, 2001). Under this approach, the payor limits insurance coverage to a maximum amount established for a particular medical or psychological condition. The DRGs serve to limit the overall amount the payor spends for health care by requiring providers to anticipate the cost of care through the prospective payment system (PPS). Unfortunately, DRGs also serve as a strong motivation for behavioral-health-care providers to adjust the services rendered on the basis of their knowledge of the maximum covered amount.

The example of a depressed client who seeks the services of a licensed psychotherapist illustrates the problems outlined here. Upon a review of the client's insurance coverage, the therapist discovers that the client is limited to twenty sessions per year of individual counseling. On the basis of this formulation, the therapist engages in a course of time-limited rational-emotive behavioral psychotherapy (Maag, 2008; Yankura & Dryden, 1997). The therapist might choose this approach in part because of the scholarly research suggesting its effectiveness but also because the therapist recognizes that the client will be unable to afford traditional and arguably appropriate long-term care. If this decision is assessed according to the legal conflict of interest analysis presented here, the practice of tailoring services to insurance coverage limits violates the professional's duties to practice reasonably competently and to seek informed consent from the client. Both duties are implicated, because the provider who defines or adjusts services to fit the requirements of an insurance policy fails to apply the independent clinical judgment that is a central part of the professional relationship. Moreover, the provider who depends on an insurance policy to define the extent of the services offered may be tempted to deny full disclosure of this information from the unsuspecting client. Even if the professional candidly discloses that a treatment option has been chosen on the basis of the limits of the client's insurance coverage, and the client freely consents to such treatment, the services may simply be inappropriate for a person who requires a more extensive intervention.

Limitations imposed by insurance coverage may inspire professionals not only to adjust their services but also sometimes to misrepresent them outright. The incidence of Medicaid and insurance fraud among mental health professionals is on the rise, or at least is being increasingly reported, and the government is taking a more active stand in combating it (Paul, 2007; Sparrow, 1998; Stefl, 1999). As noted, FCA is one response to this disturbing trend. Fraudulent reporting of insurance claims is due at least in part to the pressure imposed on therapists to characterize services consistent with coverage limits. In the *Modi* case cited earlier, involving the use of depossession therapy to attempt to rid a patient of his belief that he was possessed by demons, the psychiatrist allegedly reported the treatment to the patient's insurance company as psychotherapy for billing purposes. In a lengthy disciplinary complaint citing billing misrepresentations and informed-consent violations, an appellate court remanded the case to the licensing board to allow it to specify more definitively the licensing standards on which the complaint had been based. In other words, the practice standards specified for psychologists in West Virginia were, according to this court, too vague to accurately capture the essence of the informed consent- and competence-related legal principles that seemed to have been implicated. The case unfortunately suggests the occasional futility of attempting to define the expectations concerning professional conduct through state licensing legislation and broadly stated ethical codes. It also demonstrates that this problem is not unique to social work, counseling, or psychology.

A credible argument can be made that the use of DRGs by government programs and insurance plans violates the duty to provide informed consent because it substantially interferes with the voluntary and unimpeded consideration of treatment alternatives available for client care. Indeed, the prospective payment system itself implies that the consideration of cost is an inherent part of service delivery, a concept that is fundamentally at odds with the free choice that informed consent mandates.

Too often, the pressures imposed by managed care have had tragic consequences for professionals and clients inspired to make important medical decisions on the basis of insurance limits. The most severe consequences of these pressures may well fall on the backs of poor people most dependent on the prospective payment system in effect in government-sponsored health insurance programs. The most bizarre example of this may have occurred at a private hospital emergency room in San Francisco, where a homeless trauma victim with a four-inch knife still protruding from his stomach was apparently discharged without further treatment (Russell, 1996). Under Medi-Cal, California's health insurance program for the poor, the hospital was required only to evaluate and stabilize the man. According to this presumed authority, physicians elected to release the man after determining that his vital signs were stable; his internal organs had not been perforated; and the wound, though bleeding, was not bleeding profusely. The hospital's internal investigation revealed no wrongdoing and no action inconsistent with the terms of the man's insurance coverage (Russell, 1996).

Relationships with third-party payors impose certain constraints on clients and professionals relating to the receipt of payment. The fact that the provider owes a particular legal obligation to the primary client does not nullify the provider's responsibilities to third-party payors; it simply separates them from the scope of the professional relationship with the client. Both clients and providers have contractual commitments to payors. Among other things, these include the prompt reporting of claims and the accurate description of services rendered. Compliance with these obligations on occasion requires some lapse in confidentiality between the client and the professional, and the competent provider obtains the right to share information solely on the consent of the willing client. The fact that confidentiality may be waived to some extent does not allow the payor unbridled access to the client's records; indeed, without an express waiver, these remain confidential. The insurance codes, health legislation, and contract laws of individual states generally define other legal aspects of the relationship among clients, professionals, and third-party payors.

Mental health professionals who write grant applications often design interventions with rigorous attention to the requirements of the granting authority, which may be either a government or a private funding source. Granting authorities are a unique kind of third-party payor that agrees contractually with grant writers to underwrite individual services, professional salaries, and program costs. Professionals who rely on grant money have the same aspirations regarding their relationship with the granting source as do those providers who rely on insurance reimbursement: they are motivated to satisfy the terms of the grant application. In contrast to other kinds of third-party relationships, the associations between grantees and their patrons are subject to far less public scrutiny and regulation. Although a grant may be audited to ensure financial compliance, the consequences to the grantee for fiscal mismanagement may be limited to nonrenewal of the grant or, at worst, recollection of grant money. For this reason, the mental health care of clients being served by a grant may be at greater risk. Consider the example of a community mental health program administrator who, in anticipation of an audit, hurriedly directs program staff members to review client records compiled over the past two years for completeness and asks that "cosmetic changes" be made to "clean up" notes and add demographic information. All of this last-minute work may ultimately provide favorable fiscal and service usage numbers that please the grantor, but haphazard record keeping remains inconsistent with the agency's duty to the primary client to maintain accurate, complete, and timely records of services provided.

The right to custody of client records may confuse the relationship between professionals, clients, and third-party payors. In an effort to obtain easier access to these records, some HMOs have instituted the practice of claiming an ownership interest in the records maintained by providers who affiliate with the HMOs (*Humana Med. Plan, Inc. v. Fischman*, 1999; *Maio v. Aetna, Inc.*, 2000). The intent of this practice appears to be to subvert the duty of confidentiality imposed by law on professional records and client files that a provider maintains. Legally, these records have been recognized as the property solely of the professional and/or the client. Under most states' health and professional codes, clients have the privilege of reasonable access to records and a right to have their confidentiality maintained. The strain that a third-party payor's asserted ownership interest may have on the professional relationship has been the subject of at least several lawsuits challenging the practice (*Humana Med. Plan, Inc. v. Fischman*, 1999; *Maio v. Aetna, Inc.*, 2000). In the *Humana Medical Plan* case, the Florida Court of Appeals specifically rejected Humana's claim of a property interest in patient records under Florida law. Future legal actions may continue to raise questions about the destructive impact this practice may have on the professional relationship between providers and their clients.

Confusion over the ownership of records also sometimes occurs when a client seeks to transfer files from a professional with whom services have been discontinued. As already noted, the law generally recognizes that clients have a property interest in professional records and notes prepared on their behalf (*Sage Realty Corp. v. Proskauer Rose Goetz & Mendelsohn, LLP*, 2002; In re *Application of Castillo*, 1992). At minimum, the law requires that professionals cooperate in the transfer of records when the client switches providers. With respect to some professionals, such as attorneys, the law of some states actually recognizes the client as the absolute owner of his or her files, subject only to a retaining lien, or security interest, held by the professional for any outstanding fees (*Sexton Law Firm v. Milligan*, 1997). Considered in this light, the professional relationships developed by attorneys and their clients give specific proprietary rights to the client in the work product—including documents, case records, and attorney notes—prepared by the attorney. Given the continuing efforts of third-party providers to assert their shadowy presence in client-provider relationships, it would not be surprising for courts in the near future to be forced to reconsider and redefine the respective record ownership rights of all mental health and human service providers, clients, and payors.

Clients' ownership interest in professional records remains one of the unfortunate and unnecessary near secrets complicating the relationship among clients, providers, and third-party payors. As with many aspects of mental health and human services, this little-understood issue may be kept secret by providers interested in containing costs, including, for example, the expense of photocopying on behalf of clients. Regrettably, this practice may have a disproportionate impact on clients who lack the resources to address it. It is an unfortunate reality that some providers attempt to deny or limit access to clients wishing to review their records, sometimes under the protection of professional codes that understate the extent of the client ownership interest. The NASW Code (ethical standard 1.08), for example, admonishes social workers only to "provide clients with reasonable access to their records" and to "limit clients' access . . . only in exceptional circumstances when there is compelling evidence that . . . serious harm [would result]." The NBCC Code (section B5) most closely approximates the law governing ownership of client records when it declares that the "physical records" are "property of the counselors or their employers" but that the information contained in them "belongs to the client." The 1992 version of the APA Code (ethical standard 5.10), which was comprehensively revised in 2002, effectively evaded the question by advising psychologists that ownership "is governed by legal principles" and that the psychologist's responsibility was to make records "available" to clients according to "reasonable and lawful steps" in accord with each client's "best interests." Remarkably, in the 2002 version of the APA Code, all references to psychologists' ownership interest in records were deleted. This important omission seems perilous in light of the continuing significance of this issue to psychologists and their clients.

In reality, the ownership interest that courts recognize clients to hold probably makes their right of access to records more extensive than these ethical codes imply (*Wear v. Walker*, 1990). For example, it would not ordinarily be legally prudent for a social worker to rely on the NASW Code's apparent endorsement of the restriction of a client's access to records when the social worker precipitously concludes that "serious harm" might result. Indeed, despite the permissive language of the NASW Code cited above, any social worker who attempts to "protect" a vulnerable client from access to candid case notes might be surprised to face a lawsuit seeking recovery of the original documents. A client's legal ownership interest in these records simply reflects an important component of the professional relationship: the professional's duty to make competent and complete records of the services provided. The right is also based in part on the business exchange that underlies many a professional relationship: the client pays for services and, therefore, has a proprietary interest in the professional's documentation. As with other important legal protections, this one effectively supports the best interests of all primary clients.

Understanding the client's ownership interest in records reinforces the basic legal reality that, in most circumstances, the client is the primary director of the professional relationship, in accordance with the requirements of informed consent. The client's proprietary right also supports professional accountability. Denying access to records interferes with the client's right to be fully informed about the services the professional renders. In fact, it may frustrate the client's right to terminate the services of one professional and to hire a substitute. If a public health facility denies access to records, it may even violate constitutional standards governing due process and personal privacy (*Huether v. Dist. Court*, 2000).

With the important exception of *Humana Medical Plan, Inc. v. Fischman* (1999), most courts have been reluctant to recognize the mental health client's property interest in records as anything greater than a right to reasonable access. Courts have been more willing to grant a clear ownership interest to legal service recipients (*Cynthia B. v. New Rochelle Hosp.*, 1983). Nevertheless, the mental health professional's recognition of the client's prerogative as a property interest, as opposed to merely a right of inspection subject to the provider's discretion, may inspire more open access. It is important to note that, in circumstances in which the client lacks legal capacity, lacks mental capacity, is emotionally vulnerable, or is the secondary client of a public agency, the right of access to records—especially hospital records—may be starkly limited. State law must be consulted in individual cases to determine the extent of these limitations.

Consequences for Breach of the Duty to Identify the Primary Client

Where a professional's failure to identify the primary client leads to incompetent practice or the neglect of informed consent, the offending practitioner may face the civil, criminal, and disciplinary remedies outlined earlier. The risk that a professional may violate one or more legal principles governing practice is greatest where a third party unduly influences the professional relationship with the primary client.

Identifying the primary client presents a special burden for public-sector mental health professionals who function in child welfare, forensic psychology, mental health services, school-based counseling, and other programs administered by government agencies. In agreeing to assume a public trust on behalf of a vulnerable class of clients, public agency providers essentially represent the government in each professional decision they make. Therefore, mistakes these professionals make are not only personal but also governmental. Such errors represent a threat not only to the individual clients involved but also to the public interest in general.

On occasion, budgetary and administrative exigencies affecting the public sector's delivery of mental health and human services are so severe as to result in the inadequate design or implementation of child welfare systems, public assistance programs, mental health institutions, educational organizations, and other domains that are the ordinary responsibility of government agencies. As noted previously, conflicts of interest involving budgetary and administrative issues can cause a professional to practice incompetently or to violate the duty to seek informed consent. Where this occurs at the level of a government agency, an entire class of service recipients—whose number can range from the hundreds to the millions—may be harmed simultaneously. Sometimes, such harm may become the subject of a class action lawsuit in which a single client, or small group of clients, sues on behalf of a larger class of service recipients to seek judicial relief from the practices of a public agency. The relief granted in a class action suit can include the award of money damages, the issuance of an injunction against agency practices, or an order mandating program changes by the public agency.

Mistakes by public officials can violate important constitutional provisions that protect citizens from excessive government intrusions into personal privacy. This right to individual privacy—a fundamental constitutional cornerstone—has a significant role in framing the professional relationship that each client develops with government mental health and human services agencies. Thus, when public agency employees practice incompetently or fail to seek informed consent from their clientele, those violations may rise to a level of constitutional significance.

Using Identification of the Primary Client to Make Professional Decisions: Case Examples

As with other essential legal responsibilities, recognizing and applying the duty to identify the primary client can assist mental health professionals in evaluating seemingly complex practice scenarios. In contrast to the broad, aspirational, and often-conflicting ideals set forth in professional codes of ethics, the principles underlying the duty to identify the primary client define the basic legal boundaries among professionals, their clients, and third parties. In this respect, the duty to identify the primary client builds on responsibilities at the core of the duty to practice reasonably competently and the duty to seek informed consent. For these reasons, the decision maker should consider all the preceding duties as a first step when encountering practice dilemmas that involve third parties to the professional relationship. Because regional and cultural issues often play a significant role in apparent conflicts of interest between the professional and the client, some of the case examples that follow highlight the usefulness of identifying the primary client in cross-cultural practice. Illustrative examples are drawn from practice with diverse populations in rural and urban settings.

Case Example 9: The Single Psychotherapist

Amy Steinberg, a single mother and licensed clinical social worker in rural Harrison County, Mississippi, works four days per week at a community mental health center. On her day off, she provides services to a cooperative child-care program that requires each participant to supervise the young children of program members one day per week. On the day that Amy is responsible for child care, she receives a call from her supervisor, Sam Dellums, requesting that she make arrangements to come to work. In the aftermath of Hurricane Katrina in 2005, the federal government, through the Substance Abuse and Mental Health Services Administration (SAMHSA), has made millions of dollars available for the provision of crisis counseling to hurricane victims. Now, several years after the disaster, local mental health agencies are continuing to apply these funds to the provision of ongoing follow-up care for the treatment of first responders—those police officers, firefighters, and other emergency workers who initially provided direct rescue efforts to victims. These first responders have in many instances suffered dual trauma as a result of the hurricane, which means that they have been affected not only through occupational exposure to victims suffering through the disaster but also through personal exposure to the event itself (Jordan, 2007). Some years after the hurricane, a good number of first responders are apparently continuing to experience the lingering effects of this trauma. The ongoing, apparent surge in mental health symptoms among first responders has thrown Harrison County off guard; county leaders are blaming a significant amount of employment absenteeism by police officers and firefighters on enduring hurricane-related illness. In addition to missing work, an ever-growing number of first responders seem to be displaying problematic behavioral symptoms in their employment, including agitation, anger, and other work-related personal problems that public safety officials are attributing to long-term hurricane duty. Sam concurs in this opinion, and he is ready to address the ostensible problem by promising county leaders that he would increase the number of therapy hours available for crisis counseling and related services at the mental health center. Luckily, he has the federal dollars to commit to this enhanced intervention. On the basis of this, an increasing number of public safety workers are being referred to the mental health center for follow-up crisis counseling.

Sam explains to Amy that the center has much money remaining from the direct federal grant that must be applied to counseling services. Amy is told that her services are urgently required to provide this counseling, but, Sam tells her, Amy's decision to come to work on her day off would be on a strictly voluntary basis. As Sam puts it to her, "I know you've got other things on your plate." On the particular day in question, Amy could arrange for substitute child care, but it would require her to contact each of the other parents, and Amy would bear the cost of the substitute care.

This dilemma is a variation on a classic example that mental health ethics texts often present. It is sometimes described as a conflict of interest pitting the provider's personal interests against potentially superseding professional obligations. If characterized in this way, the dilemma is misleading and unfairly depicts the professional's choices. Analyzing the dilemma becomes especially confusing if the decision maker seeks guidance first from an ethical code, mainly because of the aspirational nature of many of the standards and values expressed. In contrast, if the duty to identify the primary client is applied to the dilemma, Amy will recognize at first that, at the time of the initiation of the dilemma, she has established no professional relationship with a client and owes no specific legal duty to an identified person. If she has any legal obligation at all, it is in her role as a parent and caretaker for the cooperative child-care program, and she owes that obligation solely to her own child and to the additional children in her temporary custody.

Before one jumps to the conclusion that this is an unfeeling and hypertechnical response to a major public tragedy, consider the benefits of a legal analysis on all those involved. First, if Amy falsely assumes in this scenario that an official duty obliges her to provide a service, she takes on a risk that she simply may be unprepared to accept and unreasonably elevates a presumed responsibility above her personal commitments. If Amy makes this mistake or instead seeks guidance initially from the NASW Code, which, as noted previously, obscures the very meaning of the term *client*, she may easily be overwhelmed by a multitude of considerations. In reality, no legal conflict of interest exists in this dilemma. Amy's obligations here are strictly personal, and as a compassionate professional—but prudent mother and caretaker—she can reasonably decline to offer services immediately.

How insensitive is this decision? Honoring one's personal commitments before making a decision to undertake a professional service may be the surest way to provide competent services once one voluntarily enters into a professional relationship. Put differently, in Amy's situation, a rushed decision to provide services prematurely may do more damage to her own family than it does good for the prospective clients. The risk to the clients includes an incompetent clinical intervention by a therapist preoccupied with personal responsibilities. The lingering mental health issues caused by the hurricane may or may not require the assistance of therapists to the degree proposed by county leaders and the mental health center; indeed, Sam seems as much concerned with spending the mental health center's grant money as with the continuing outbreak of symptoms among first providers. Although the prevalence of mental health problems among first providers might be a serious enough problem to throw Harrison County into a continuing crisis mode, any surge to offer them treatment runs the risk of imposing services on people who have not voluntarily sought them. In fact, an underplanned overresponse is sometimes observed during the human tragedy in the wake of natural disasters. Indeed, research has suggested that the very act of intervening in an excessive or inappropriate manner with first responders may contribute to the behavioral problems themselves. For example, there are numerous reports of first responders simply walking out of debriefing sessions with their superiors because of the fatigue and frustration from seemingly endless discussions of the tragic events (Jordan, 2007). All things considered, one can reasonably question whether the requisite degree of voluntariness on the part of prospective clients is being sought in the mental health center's zeal to provide services.

Clearly, Amy owes the children in her charge her primary attention. At a time when her principal responsibilities to family and youngsters in need of child care have been fully satisfied, Amy may agree to offer crisis intervention services as requested, according to the terms of her employment or, perhaps, during limited overtime hours. In this way, both Amy and her prospective clients will be more likely to have entered into a professional relationship thoughtfully and voluntarily.

Amy's dilemma highlights a general misapprehension about mental health services that may represent the most serious cause of professional burnout among caregivers. Specifically, it underscores the point that a professional's obligations are neither unceasing nor without boundaries in their extent. Ethical codes sometimes add to the professional's role confusion by reciting broad goals that are well intended but at times unattainable, most notably by failing to define adequately *client*. Until a professional relationship is formed and a legal bond between a provider and primary client is established, most ethical aspirations simply cannot be enforced.

Reconsider this case example but with a few factual changes. Specifically, assume that Amy has already established a professional relationship with a client who was rendered homeless by the hurricane and whom Amy has been treating for some weeks for an anxiety disorder. On her day off, Amy learns from the client by telephone that the client's mother—another victim displaced by the flooding—has died. In this situation, Amy's clinical alternatives should be assessed in terms of her duty to practice reasonably competently. Under these circumstances, she may be unable to schedule an office visit with the client immediately but might be able to provide further consultation by phone. If she does so, Amy must not dilute the quality of the clinical services needed to support this client, which most likely should include an office visit at the earliest opportunity. She should be prepared to offer reasonably competent clinical services consistent with her professional relationship with the client. The fact that a phone conversation may temporarily replace more formal services should not inspire Amy to view her role purely as a friendly, informal shoulder to cry on. She must maintain her clinical, objective stance; any more relaxed approach may be both exploitative and countertherapeutic. A friendly, informal stance normally may seem caring, appropriate, and supportive, but consider the danger in some instances of substituting for the clinical relationship a more relaxed approach; its pitfalls are numerous and frequently occur when mental health professionals have the best of intentions.

Child welfare social workers frequently face an example of the danger of providing informal support to a vulnerable client in connection with the services they provide to families involved in abuse and neglect proceedings. Even though their main legal duty extends to primary clients—the vulnerable children of a community whose interests the professionals have voluntarily agreed to protect—parents involved in children's court proceedings sometimes look to social workers for reassurance and counsel, even as the child abuse proceeding presses forward. On occasion, parents contact social workers beyond their normal business hours to address parental crises and to provide consultation and other services the client assumes are part of the social work role. In many circumstances, the social worker may feel obliged to provide this type of assistance to secondary clients in the fulfillment of a sense of ethical and personal obligation. Before this choice is made, however, it is appropriate for the professional to evaluate carefully the extent of the legal obligation owed to the primary client together with the limitation that this places on interactions with secondary clients.

The professional may offer the type of clinical interaction described here in a way that blurs the professional boundaries existing between the parties and misrepresents the professional stance that the social worker must adopt concerning the protection of vulnerable children. Important questions have been raised here about the conflict of interest this kind of situation creates and the competence of a public agency professional to provide clinical services to secondary clients. Moreover, it is questionable whether this type of support is consistent with either the primary or the secondary client's best interests. Aside from the legal conflict of interest it creates, it is bound to tax the provider's own resources. For that reason, if the social worker is not on call and not bound by terms of employment either to offer such services or to be available after hours, then it is not advisable to provide them. The reason is elementary: the availability of a social worker for service that transcends the professional responsibility to the primary client may take an enormous toll on the professional's own mental health. In addition, the legal conflict of the imposition on the professional to provide subsidiary services to secondary clients often plays a significant part in the generally high employee turnover rates in public child welfare agencies nationally (Glisson, Dukes, & Green, 2006; Graef & Hill, 2000).

Case Example 10: The Full-Service Office

Alan Gabriel is a licensed psychologist self-employed in St. Paul, Minnesota. Specializing in the treatment of depression, he is a qualified provider under a group health insurance plan, from which he draws a significant number of referrals. Alan has a receptionist, Alice Contreras, who assists him with greeting and intake of clients. When a new client comes in for services, Alice routinely distributes a client information form that requests personal data, insurance coverage information, and a brief medical history, and also requires the client to provide a brief description of the presenting problem. Pa Yang, a Hmong woman who has recently been laid off from her job as a janitorial worker, schedules an appointment to see Alan for therapy. Pa fills in the information form and includes her group insurance number. Pa has had some high school and has good facility in English but has lived all of her life in the very large Hmong community in St. Paul. She has never sought professional assistance outside this community and therefore has difficulty answering some of the questions. Pa asks for assistance from Alice, who takes the form from Pa and asks her the questions indicated on the form. Listening to Pa's responses, Alice fills these in on the form. In addition, Alice makes a copy of Pa's insurance identification card as Pa explains that the insurance is "still good for six months."

Pa next proceeds to have her initial appointment with Alan. On the way out, she notices a sign in the office that reads: "We will be happy to assist you in the filing of insurance claims, but please remember that the client has the responsibility to pay for all services rendered." Pa asks Alice whether she can receive some assistance with her insurance claim, and in response, Alice cheerfully answers affirmatively and then obtains Pa's signature on an insurance claim form. Pa does not review the claim carefully. After eight weeks of therapy with Alan, Pa receives a computer-generated letter from Alan's office requesting payment in full for the unpaid balance of the office bill. Pa visits Alan's office and asks Alice to investigate the insurance problem. Upon calling the insurance claims office, an insurance representative advises Alice that the wrong form has been filed and that no reimbursement has been sent to Alan's office. Alice repeats this information to Pa, then hands Pa another form and suggests that she "walk it in" herself to the local insurance claims office to save time. As Alice explains this new, more urgent approach: "Dr. Gabriel really needs some payment on the bill."

This scenario depicts an unfortunate runaround involving third-party payment that is all too common in mental health service delivery. At its simplest, it represents a business conflict of interest among Alan, Pa, and the insurance company. Specifically, Alan maintains an ongoing business relationship with the insurance company to the extent that he keeps claim forms on hand, routinely assists in the preparation and submission of these forms, and benefits from the insurer's frequent reimbursement for client services. The business association also, however, requires Alan to complete paperwork and file claims, both of which necessitate that Alan undertake a significant commitment of office time and expense. Alan, like some professionals, seems willing to honor this burden only to a point. He delegates responsibility for claim filing to Alice; uses office signs to advise clients of their independent responsibility for bills; and unfortunately, when the claims process becomes somewhat cumbersome for him, essentially absolves himself—through Alice—from further responsibility for filing claims.

Alan must reassess his responsibilities to Pa using the legal conflict-of-interest analysis presented in this chapter. Specifically, he should identify candidly his legal duties to this primary client and attempt reasonably to fulfill them. This includes accepting some responsibility for following through with his assistance in the claims process. Pa has reasonably anticipated that she would receive some help in this area and has entered into the professional relationship expecting it. Given Pa's personal experience and background, her reliance on this professional assistance is to be expected all the more. In assessing his duty to practice reasonably competently, Alan should recognize that this includes assisting clients with the processing of insurance claims. He undertakes his responsibility both by communicating it at the commencement of services and, along with Alice, by initiating this clerical responsibility to the degree that it becomes part of the professional understanding between provider and client. This is true notwithstanding any disclaimer to the contrary; the office sign disavowing responsibility for filing claims simply does not jibe with the claims process his office routinely initiates.

Courts today have recognized that professionals who agree to assist with clients' paperwork filing have a legal responsibility to do so reasonably competently (*Chew v. Meyer*, 1987; Hall & Schneider, 2008; *Picker v. Castro*, 2003). They have noted additionally that, with the complexity in service delivery that reliance on third-party payors has created, claims assistance and client advocacy in the pursuit of reimbursement often become expected components of the professional relationship and important parts of the services that health-care providers render (*Chew v. Meyer*, 1987; Hall & Schneider, 2008; *Picker v. Castro*, 2003).

Where the client's cultural background, life experience, or language differences make the client more vulnerable to mistakes with third-party claims applications, claims assistance by the professional may become even more vital. Once this advocacy is offered, neither the provider nor a clerical assistant can withdraw it on the empty assertion that it is the client's responsibility. In the present case example, however, this legal conclusion represents only the first part of the picture. Alan should also recognize that it is inappropriate to seek payment immediately from Pa when she has not been responsible for the careless filing of her claim. In this respect, Alan is responsible not only for reasonable competence in his clinical practice but also for ensuring his staff's prudent completion of their administrative responsibilities. When clerical errors cause foreseeable harm to the client, Alan is responsible. This vicarious liability for the conduct of his employees requires Alan to take measures to correct the problem, not the least of which is to modify his payment arrangement with Pa to allow time for the filing of the insurance claim.

The assumption of clerical responsibilities is not always a happy one for the busy professional. However, where the provider benefits as much as the client from the third-party payor, the professional must assume these responsibilities if he or she is to practice competently. Where the client has every reason to expect a communicative and helpful relationship with the provider, the reasonable professional must tailor practice to reflect clients' needs and expectations.

Case Example 11: The Vocational Rehab Counselor

Lucy Chambliss works as a vocational rehabilitation counselor at a residential training center in Miami, Oklahoma. One of her clients, Larry Delgado, is a thirteen-year-old with mild developmental disability and conduct disorder. Larry's parents placed him at the residential program about six months ago, and Larry has received individual counseling from Lucy during that time. Lucy also serves as a house parent at the cottage in which Larry is housed.

During the six months that Lucy has worked with Larry, she has observed substantial improvement both in Larry's behavior and in his attention to his schoolwork. The Delgados visit Larry twice a month, at which time they confer with Lucy concerning their son's progress. As a result of her work with Larry, Lucy has begun to feel that further institutional care is not appropriate and that Larry belongs at home with his family. In conversations with Larry, Lucy has noted that he wants to be home with his parents.

During their most recent meeting with Lucy, the Delgados have expressed their pleasure at the apparent improvement in Larry's conduct. When Lucy suggests that further institutionalization might not be helpful for Larry, the Delgados disagree, noting that Larry has made great strides in the preceding six months. Moreover, they note, Larry has been the primary source of friction in their marriage, and the respite Larry's residency at the center has given them has made home life more bearable for them and their other young children.

Lucy's options in this scenario are most easily addressed if she first considers her duty to identify the primary client. Despite the role of Larry's parents in placing Larry in institutional care, Lucy's primary client is Larry. Consequently, she owes Larry a duty to practice reasonably competently. Although the interests of Larry's parents are peripherally important in the sense that they have the authority to provide informed consent for any treatment on Larry's behalf, it is Larry's well-being that must be of paramount concern to Lucy. If, in her professional judgment, continuing placement at the training center does not serve Larry's best interests, then she must so advise the Delgados. They may have important personal reasons for Larry's continued placement out of the home, but if, in Lucy's independent clinical judgment, placement does not correspond with Larry's health and continued progress, she cannot proceed to provide reasonably competent services; indeed, her services would become unnecessary.

Lucy may well regard her position in this scenario as an uncomfortable one. She may have developed a friendly working relationship with the Delgados and may feel obliged to honor their choices regarding Larry's care. These impressions may be strengthened by cross-cultural considerations that suggest to Lucy, a compassionate counselor who believes in client self-determination, that she must demonstrate respect for the Delgados' right to make autonomous choices on behalf of their family. In honoring her duty to the primary client, however, Lucy must give voice to her central concern with Larry's progress.

In identifying her primary client, Lucy should consider the impact of informed consent. The Delgados have the legal capacity to make decisions on Larry's behalf, and Lucy must discuss with them all reasonable risks and benefits of the care options available for Larry. As the guidelines for informed consent indicate, Lucy has the responsibility to discuss fully her own professional opinions with the client—or those responsible for making decisions on the client's behalf—especially when those views contradict the client's or decision maker's interpretation of the problem. In the present case example, the duty to seek informed consent requires Lucy not to allow her respect for the Delgados' self-guidance to silence her communication of a professional opinion. How effectively and sensitively Lucy expresses this judgment to the Delgados may well determine what decisions they make about Larry's care.

Lucy must recognize from the outset of her conversations with the Delgados that her duty to practice reasonably competently mandates that she identify; assess; and if necessary, report, instances of suspected child abuse and neglect. It may be the case that Lucy regards the Delgados' preference that Larry remain at the center as an abdication of parental authority for Larry's care. In the unfortunate event that the Delgados are unable or unwilling to assume responsibility for Larry's supervision, it is incumbent on Lucy and her supervisors to report the threat posed to Larry's well-being. Cautious communication of this point to the Delgados may help them to reassess their position concerning Larry's institutionalization.

Staff counselors and other mental health providers in the lower echelon of employee responsibility at mental health institutions may feel overwhelmed by the responsibility placed on them to identify and represent the best interests of the primary client. They may be familiar with the administrative routine at their agencies, may contemplate the temptation that third-party funding places on agencies to continue to receive that funding, and therefore may actively participate in their institutions' zealous solicitation of new clients and continued housing of long-standing clients. These issues may place pressure on employees and administrators to maintain amicable relationships with the families of clients. The inducements from funding considerations may be a powerful incentive in the decisions made on their clients' behalf, and cautious agency employees may not be anxious to make waves. Nevertheless, every mental health professional involved in long-term care for institutionalized clients must be prepared to answer the following question: can the provider lawfully maintain a professional relationship with a client for whom no further services are available or who is not likely to benefit from further treatment? The answer, under a strict interpretation of the duty to practice reasonably competently, is plainly no.

The question Lucy is called on to ask in the present case example has been posed in a variety of legal contexts. For instance, in several court cases, an advocate's decision to ask a judge to examine the sufficiency of services in a hospital setting has been at least partly responsible for the deinstitutionalization of many chronically mentally ill patients who had previously been consigned to warehousing in state facilities (see, e.g., *Jackson v. Fort Stanton Hosp. & Training Sch.*, 1990; *Wyatt v. Fetner*, 1996).

Case Example 12: Yucca Mountain

The national organization Cleanspace has decided to take a decisive stand against a proposed deep geological repository for the storage of spent fuel from nuclear reactors and other radioactive waste. As proposed by the U.S. Department of Energy (DOE), the repository is to be located in Yucca Mountain, a ridgeline located in a desert area lying about eighty miles northwest of Las Vegas, Nevada (Moscardelli & Becker, 2007). The DOE will also construct a rail line of approximately two hundred miles, running through Nevada and terminating at Yucca Mountain. The repository will lie in or adjacent to rural Nye County, with the project office to be situated in Pahrump, Nevada. The site has been chosen in part because of the remoteness of the area and the DOE's position that the geologic properties of the area allow for safe transport of nuclear waste with an insubstantial impact on the environment (Moscardelli & Becker, 2007). Some Nye County commissioners and Nevada state political leaders believe that the project will actually benefit Nevada financially and educationally. Specifically, they believe that, through ongoing political negotiations, the DOE will commit to the construction and improvement of regional roads and grant millions of dollars in public health and educational funding in return for construction of the site. The DOE has already announced its intent to build a regional medical center in Nye County. In addition, some area stakeholders have expressed hope that improvement of the regional infrastructure and operation of the facility will result in the creation of employment opportunities and related economic benefits to Nevada.

Cleanspace has retained the services of a community organizer to coordinate an effort against the construction of the repository. The organizer has a master of social work degree and has received additional training at Cleanspace's educational center in Washington, D.C. Cleanspace advocates against the storage of nuclear waste in Nye County because of the environmental hazards associated with the repository and because of the dangers associated with the long-distance transport of nuclear waste material (Thrower & Martinez, 2000). In its training program, Cleanspace teaches social action techniques (Pilisuk, McAllister, & Rothman, 1996), which involve the use of a confrontational approach to mobilize activity against unwanted development projects and to promote public awareness of the health impact of various environmental hazards. Furthermore, Cleanspace's training program emphasizes the use of aggressive lobbying activities at the federal, state, and regional levels. Cleanspace tends to staff its community organization projects with graduates of its training program who receive their salaries from the organization.

Jarrod Heatherton, a recent graduate of Cleanspace's training program, has just arrived in Pahrump, Nye County, Nevada, to open the organization's field office. Jarrod plans to hold an open house to celebrate the opening of the office and to allow an opportunity for meeting the public. Sympathetic legislators from the region, including the Las Vegas area, have been invited to attend. In addition, Jarrod plans to begin his organizational activities with a public demonstration against the Yucca Mountain project. He has sought a municipal permit to allow him to stage a public demonstration against the opening of the site.

This case example demonstrates the usefulness of applying the duty to identify the primary client in the field of community organizing. As in all other mental health and human services, community organizing should be understood to involve the establishment of a professional relationship with one or more primary clients.

The use of terminology associated with the duty to identify the primary client may seem awkward when it is applied outside the traditional realm of health and mental health care. Even so, the duty is no less applicable here than it is to the delivery of psychotherapy and other clinical services. Consider the responsibilities that the duty imposes on Jarrod in this scenario and the impact that they have on his planning of services. First, as noted, Jarrod must establish a professional relationship with one or more identified clients through the pursuit of informed consent. According to this scenario, however, no primary clients have as yet sought Jarrod's assistance or have granted informed consent to the intervention that Jarrod has planned. Indeed, at the moment, the intervention Jarrod has designed is being imposed rather than arrived at through any reasonable assessment of community needs. Moreover, Jarrod appears ready to actively recruit participants in a way that violates not only informed consent but also ethical standards governing the solicitation of potential clients.

In this case example, there are many potential clients whose interests Jarrod ultimately may come to represent, including members of the community who are affected by the proposed Yucca Mountain project and may need a community-based intervention to advance their position. However, the duties to practice reasonably competently and to seek informed consent require that Jarrod ascertain the needs of his potential clients in a way that does not presuppose the outcome and, further, does not simply impose Cleanspace's stated position on his potential clients. To do this, Jarrod may appropriately use any one of several reasonable methods to assess his community; regardless of which community assessment methodology Jarrod chooses, its purpose must be to identify honestly and completely the goals and objectives of a representative sample of the community. This sample must include diverse member of this community, including representatives of regional Native American nations whose vital interests are currently at stake.

If Jarrod plans his assessment thoroughly, he may find that there is actually a wide diversity of opinion in the community about Yucca Mountain. If he surveys opinions among less affluent citizens, he may discover some support for the project and the promised health, educational, and employment benefits it will bring to an economically disenfranchised segment of the community. He may also find significant concern about the health impact of the project but an unwillingness to support a confrontational effort that further isolates this underclass from the economic mainstream of the community. In a sense, Jarrod's uncovering of some hesitation in the minds of some citizens of the community coincides with what any regionally sensitive community organizer might anticipate discovering in a rural environment.

If Jarrod freely discusses the risks and benefits of Cleanspace's approach, he and his potential clients may reasonably conclude that a social action approach will not serve their long-term interests. Informed consent principles suggest that it is appropriate for Jarrod to discuss Cleanspace's preference for the social action approach, but only if he also reveals the risks presented by this strategy. Such risks might include, among other things, jeopardizing the ability of the unemployed to obtain future employment in a community dominated financially by a new industry. After a discussion of these risks, all may conclude that a nonconfrontational, public information campaign that addresses environmental concerns but also supports economic revitalization of the region, job creation, and rebuilding of the community infrastructure may more adequately address the immediate needs of community members. In addition, working to develop a broad, ethnically diverse, and economically based coalition may help interest community members who support the Yucca Mountain project despite the environmental issues Cleanspace has identified.

Even if Jarrod and his potential clients openly discuss the risks and benefits of a social action strategy, and in the event all elect to pursue this approach, Jarrod's social action–inspired methodology still may be inappropriate for a community in which environmental and economic issues should more properly be addressed in a unified manner and with extensive study and long-term planning. Put differently, Jarrod's limited social action approach may offer a strategy that fails to competently tackle the actual needs of the community.

In this scenario, Jarrod's organizational approach thus far has been driven by the organization—Cleanspace—that has trained him and underwritten his effort. If he permits Cleanspace's philosophy to direct the services he ultimately offers community members, he is effectively allowing a third party to predetermine the nature of his professional relationship with his prospective clients. This problem is conceptually similar to the one faced by psychotherapists who feel constrained to diagnose a mental health problem in the manner consistent with their clinical training or in a way that ensures the greatest reimbursement from a third-party payor. Thus, the impact of a conflict of interest may be as far reaching in community organizing as it is in the provision of direct mental health services. In both instances, it may interfere with the professional's ability to practice reasonably competently. In Jarrod's case, competence includes, at a minimum, the design and implementation of a community intervention that appropriately addresses the needs of his clients and is based on their voluntary and knowledgeable consent.

The duty to identify the primary client suggests that an otherwise well-meaning professional can threaten the interests of potential clients by allowing the funding requirements or ideological positions of a financial backer to drive a professional intervention. As in all areas of mental health and human services, failure to observe this duty may fall most heavily on the backs of poor clients for whom assistance a third-party payor, a government agency, or a charitable organization underwrites assistance. One of the important legal premises underlying the duty to identify the primary client is that the rights conferred by the professional relationship apply irrespective of whether payment has changed hands between provider and recipient. Specifically, the privileges of a client receiving free services are no less apparent than those enjoyed by fee-paying clients. Therefore, the fact that services may be charitable does not excuse the provider from the responsibility of carrying them out competently and with informed consent. (Note to the reader: The general factual details concerning the governmental planning of the Yucca Mountain project are true. However, the scenario involving the community organizing intervention is entirely fictional.)

Case Example 13: The Faith-Based Service Revisited

Please reconsider the scenario described in case example 7, "The Faith-Based Service." The counselor in this scenario, Melissa Zak, is struggling with the religious principles that guide service delivery in a church-based counseling program.

As the duty to identify the primary client suggests, a conflict of interest is created between a mental health provider and client when a third party influences their professional relationship. This point has important relevance for Melissa in her effort to provide appropriate assistance to her clients. As in case example 12, "Yucca Mountain," the services that the church offers have in large measure been defined by the strong philosophical principles advocated in its program. The restrictions imposed on Melissa not only limit the nature of the counseling she may provide but also apparently conflict with Melissa's own ideological position regarding counseling. If this is the case, then Melissa's conflict of interest may be irreconcilable, because the limitations forced on her excessively hamper her independent clinical judgment. She cannot presently offer competent services to clients unless her philosophical orientation to counseling is reasonably consistent with the program's ideology. Simply put, if this consistency does not exist, Melissa cannot work for the agency. If she evades this point in the interest of planning a more strategic time for addressing it in the future, she virtually ensures that any service she provides to her clients currently will be deficient. The need to get a job can be a powerful incentive to understate one's professional philosophy to potential employers. It may even inspire a reasonably well-intended job searcher to accept a position in the hope of ultimately reconciling an ideological conflict with the employer. This strategy, however, is plainly inconsistent with competent professional practice, and it subverts the duty to seek informed consent from prospective clients.

Case Example 14: The School Social Worker

Gaspard Fontaine is employed as a school social worker in the Dodge City, Kansas, public school system. Gaspard's school social work position is legally mandated by the Individuals with Disabilities Education Act (IDEA), which promotes the interests of educationally disabled children attending school. Among other things, the law guarantees the right of such children to a free appropriate public education (FAPE) that is uniquely tailored to meet the educational needs of each child.

Through an assessment and planning process, IDEA requires that an individually planned educational program (IEP) be jointly designed by an IEP team to address the special learning needs of each child and provide appropriate support services, such as remedial education and individual counseling. Moreover, IDEA strongly encourages schools to mainstream, that is, to allow a disabled child to be educated with nondisabled peers (*Ala. Coal. for Equity, Inc. v. Hunt*, 1993; *Oberti v. Bd. of Educ.*, 1993; *Robert M. v. State*, 2008). Also, IDEA requires that parents of children entitled to an IEP be included in the plan's design. Finally, IDEA mandates that the school provide children and their parents with adequate support services—including social workers, counselors, and psychologists—to assist them in planning and implementing the IEP. Occasionally, parents disagree with the terms of the IEP that a school establishes for a child. In that case, IDEA grants these parents the right to an administrative appeal before a hearing officer and ultimately the right to challenge a negative result through court proceedings.

One of Gaspard's important roles is to participate with the IEP team in the formulation of appropriate educational plans. Gaspard also provides counseling and other supportive services to children and their families, and in this capacity, he is administratively responsible to his school principal and local school board. According to his job responsibilities, Gaspard also helps parents advocate for themselves throughout the entire IEP design process. Occasionally, he is called on to testify about his recommendations in administrative proceedings concerning the IEP.

Gaspard presently is working with the Ramirez family: Ernesto and Sylvia and their daughter, Amalia, a fifth grader at the school. Amalia is developmentally disabled and has been diagnosed with attention deficit/hyperactivity disorder (ADHD). Her primary spoken language at home is Spanish. Ernesto and Sylvia, both employed in the meatpacking industry, speak little English and can read and write only in Spanish. During the development of Amalia's IEP, Gaspard communicates with both parents in Spanish, of which he has a working knowledge. Gaspard has advised the Ramirez family that the school system's budget is limited and that only one bilingual teacher is available possessing the special education skills necessary to accommodate Amalia's needs.

Gaspard regards himself as a mediator and seeks to reconcile Amalia's best interests with what the school board's budget will reasonably allow. Given Amalia's special needs, Gaspard suggests that Amalia be enrolled in a special education class together with other similarly disabled children, where she can receive more individualized attention. At Gaspard's initial meeting with Amalia's parents, they have consented to the proposed IEP. After discussing it further at home, however, they have more fully realized that the plan means isolating Amalia from her friends at school. Treating Amalia as "different" violates the family's values, and they believe it to be inconsistent with her best interests. They wish to discuss this matter further with Gaspard.

This case example depicts a common conflict of interest that affects school social workers, counselors, and psychologists. In this scenario, Gaspard has established a professional relationship with a primary client—Amalia Ramirez. At the same time, however, his administrative association with the school board and its principal threatens to affect the nature and quality of the services he offers Amalia, as well as his ability to offer independent, objective guidance to the family. This may already be reflected in Gaspard's communication to the parents concerning the school board's limited funds.

Gaspard may face additional pressures from teachers with whom he interacts daily to help them in their quest to keep class sizes reasonable and to avoid taking on additional responsibilities with special needs students who might "detract" from the attention owed to other students. Indeed, Gaspard attends staff meetings with teachers and educational support personnel, at which time these concerns often are voiced openly.

The tasks required as part of the duty to identify the primary client call for Gaspard to honor his commitment to practice reasonably competently and seek informed consent; with respect to the latter responsibility, he owes it to the Ramirez parents. The present case example suggests, however, that these commitments may already have been compromised. Amalia is entitled to mainstreaming, and as IDEA mandates, it is consistent with her best educational interests, which Gaspard is duty bound to represent. In fact, it is probably required under federal and state laws and administrative regulations governing the formulation of IEPs. However, Gaspard appears willing to allow apparent school budgetary issues to influence formulation of Amalia's IEP. If Gaspard is later called on to testify before the school board—and in any subsequent court challenge to the IEP—he may continue to find himself subtly influenced to endorse recommendations that are consistent with the school district's alleged financial constraints. The Ramirez family may ask him to justify his position in terms of Amalia's best interests, a task that may be difficult for him to accomplish under the circumstances.

Gaspard's conflict of interest in this scenario may also threaten his ability to seek informed consent from the Ramirez parents. First, Gaspard owes to the Ramirezes the delicate responsibility of explaining the conflict. The same subtle administrative influences already described may limit Gaspard's free discussion of all available educational alternatives, together with the risks presented by isolating Amalia in a special education environment. These influences notwithstanding, Gaspard must be prepared to discuss the effect that this course of action may have on Amalia's language development and the possible delay it could cause in Amalia's cultivation of English-language skills. Gaspard's limited Spanish-language ability may make it difficult to explain the more intricate aspects of the risks and benefits presented by the proposed IEP. This type of language problem may greatly amplify the existing hazard created by Gaspard's association with his school board and principal. The Ramirez family's hesitance to accept Gaspard's initial recommendations already suggests that his initial communication with them has been flawed.

Even if Gaspard ultimately can obtain informed consent from the Ramirezes, his conflict of interest raises substantial questions about his ability to perform effective client advocacy in his role as a school employee. This role requires the independent development of an educational plan that promotes Amalia's best interests, and it puts him in a position potentially antagonistic to the administrative personnel who supervise him and pay at least part of his salary. Interestingly, a substantial portion of Gaspard's salary is underwritten by an IDEA grant, a fact that further complicates his relationships with the school board and principal. Similarly, his associations with fellow staff members (i.e., teachers) may present comparable influences. These social and economic pressures offer a powerful incentive for Gaspard to temper the assertiveness necessary to represent Amalia adequately. If the most appropriate IEP for Amalia requires her placement in a regular schoolroom, together with individualized attention both from the homeroom teacher and a special education instructor, Gaspard's present suggestion falls far short of it.

To some extent, every professional employed by someone else has an inherent conflict of interest with the client. When one performs services that are salaried or whose provisions are determined by an agency budget, those variables may affect the competence of the services rendered to clients. At one time or another, all diligent agency professionals will raise significant questions with their own employers concerning the constraints that agency budgets or policies place on client services. In most of these ordinary situations, however, professionals find themselves reasonably able to provide competent services to clients, even though these diligent providers have the fervent wish that more could be offered. In such circumstances, the professional's continuing role in the agency is not usually in direct conflict with the agency's interests. Put another way, this kind of everyday conflict does not ordinarily hamper the professional's ability to offer reasonable services consistent with agency policies and the available budget.

What makes Gaspard's conflict unusual is that his role has been designed and largely funded by a federal law—IDEA—that designates Gaspard as an advocate for the best interests of educationally disabled children. This professional role frequently involves the formulation of individualized plans that take a specific toll on a school board's staff requirements. Gaspard is expected as a matter of routine to extend himself on his clients' behalf and, at least in theory, to explore options that may run counter to the school board's fiscal and administrative interests. This conflict not only undermines

Gaspard's individual professional relationships with clients but also reflects an overall problem in the design of school social worker responsibilities that makes the consistent provision of reasonable client services impossible.

Just as the delivery of counseling services to parents by a child welfare agency social worker may not be consistent with the clients' best interests, the offering of school social work services by the employee of a financially strapped school district may also create a serious conflict of interest. Consequently, mental health professionals concerned with public policy governing educational services should be prepared to take extensive action in the protection of client interests. First, a long-range solution would require educational advocacy services offered to clients and their families to be assumed by public agencies equipped to render such services and, more important, not administratively bound to schools. Public health agencies and community mental health centers offer the desired independent judgment necessary to ensure competent representation of client interests regarding educational services. Short of this step, a more immediate alternative is to remove the school-based social worker entirely from administrative responsibility to the school system and to ensure independent funding of this professional's job. Either of these suggested steps would go a long way toward safeguarding the independence of school-based mental health professionals and minimizing the economic and administrative influences on them.

CHAPTER 6

The Duty to Treat Clients and Coworkers with Due Process and Equal Protection

THE U.S. CONSTITUTION CAN BE regarded as a contract between the people and their government. It contains a basic set of general principles that serve as a foundation for all lawmaking at the federal and state levels. One of the Constitution's primary objectives is the protection of individual citizens against oppressive and encroaching legislatures and public officials.

Through the court opinions that have interpreted the Constitution throughout U.S. history, a body of law has developed that describes the rights of citizens and the responsibilities of government servants toward them. Much of this law has come into existence as a result of the actions of mental health professionals, whose constitutional obligations to their clients and coworkers have been defined by many reviewing courts. A thorough review of constitutional law is beyond the scope of this book; indeed, the subject is most aptly addressed in an academic course of a year or more duration. At the same time, however, there are several fundamental constitutional principles that have had such a profound and permanent impact on mental health professionals and their clients that a basic understanding of them is essential for every decision maker.

The constitutional principles that have had the most impact on mental health professionals can be summarized simply as due process and equal protection; both have a critical role in influencing the choices of public- and private-sector professionals on a daily basis. Despite the monumental impact they have on the professional relationship, professional ethics codes do not significantly address these legal principles. For this reason, mental health professionals who understand their meaning and application have a ready tool in addressing practice dilemmas that involve the interaction among health and human service agencies, their employees, and their clients.

A summary of various courts' historical interpretation of due process and equal protection is presented here in a format that emphasizes their use in making professional decisions. Although these principles primarily affect the relationship between publicly employed professionals and their clients, through recent civil rights legislation, their influence has been extended to private agencies as well. Therefore, it is suggested that, along with other fundamental legal principles, the decision maker consider the duty to treat clients and coworkers with due process and equal protection as a first step in the consideration of any practice dilemma.

Introduction to Due Process and Equal Protection

The Fifth Amendment to the U.S. Constitution, ratified in 1791, protects among other things the right of all persons to be free from deprivations of "life, liberty, or property, without due process of law." This so-called due process clause is intended to protect citizens from intrusions on basic rights by the federal government, although the clause does not specifically explain the precise scope of the protection offered.

The Fourteenth Amendment, ratified shortly after the Civil War in 1868, contains a similar due process clause. At the time of its ratification, the Fourteenth Amendment was primarily intended to grant rights to newly freed slaves and to extend a host of protections to citizens against state governments' oppressive practices. The Fourteenth Amendment's due process clause is identical in language to the Fifth Amendment's, except that it applies to the actions of state governments and public officials.

The Fourteenth Amendment adds another layer of protection to state citizens by shielding them from the denial of "equal protection of the laws." The equal protection clause serves to protect individuals from discriminatory acts by state governments based on race, national origin, and other classifications. Note that, although the Fifth Amendment contains no equal protection clause, courts have ruled that its due process clause also extends equal protection to citizens from the discriminatory acts of the federal government (*Rodriguez-Silva v. INS*, 2001).

In addition to granting substantive rights to all persons, the Fourteenth Amendment conveys to Congress the power to enforce those rights through appropriate legislation. Congress has enacted much legislation protecting individuals from unfair and discriminatory practices, although various courts have limited its authority to do so in recent years.

The Fifth and Fourteenth amendments have much in common. They both safeguard persons from unfair and discriminatory government practices, and each grants Congress the authority to enforce its provisions through legislation. However, because state and local governments administer so many of the basic public health, welfare, and safety services provided in the United States, the Fourteenth Amendment's due process and equal protection clauses have become the dominant weapons that citizens rely on to combat government misconduct. For that reason, there is an ever-growing body of common law that interprets the language contained in these provisions.

The Meaning of *Person* and *State Action*

At the heart of the Fourteenth Amendment is the protection afforded to every individual person from state actions. To understand the scope of this protection, each of these terms, as courts interpret them, must be explained individually.

Who is a person for the purpose of the Fourteenth Amendment? The answer to this question is more problematic than it seems. A person, courts have consistently noted, is any individual present in the United States, either native born, legal immigrant, or even someone who is illegally present through violation of immigration laws (*Lozano v. City of Hazleton*, 2007). Because nonhuman entities can own property, it is interesting to note that corporations and other businesses are considered persons under the Fourteenth Amendment (*Ne. Ga. Radiological Assocs. v. Tidwell*, 1982; *Guides, Ltd. v. Yarmouth Group Prop. Mgmt., Inc.*, 2002). Because government action can affect a host of people besides the direct object of the action, the families and survivors of someone injured by the government are also regarded as persons entitled to constitutional protection.

Aside from the more traditional meanings imposed by the term *person*, newer, more controversial interpretations have surfaced in recent years. For example, if an unborn child fails to mature because of the actions of the government—perhaps a police beating resulting in the mother's death or an accident involving the gross negligence of a public bus driver—might the fetus be a person entitled to constitutional protection? Courts have repeatedly answered no to this question (see, e.g., *Lewis v. Thompson*, 2001; *Thornburgh v. Am. Coll. of Obstetricians & Gynecologists*, 1986), although this claim continues to be pressed in a variety of jurisdictions, sometimes with the vocal support of conservative and fundamentalist religious groups. Indeed, more recently, the U.S. Supreme Court has developed the *Casey* standard, which suggests that the government has a legitimate and substantial interest in preserving and promoting fetal life; therefore, the Court upheld a ban on so-called partial-birth abortions (*Gonzales v. Carhart*, 2007). This reinforces the notion that a late-term, or viable, fetus is protected constitutionally. The continued interest of conservative, anti-abortion groups in this issue may be obvious. A court willing to recognize the right of a fetus to constitutional protection in a relatively uncontroversial case might ultimately open the door to a reconsideration of abortion rights recognized in the landmark case *Roe v. Wade* (1973).

For what types of conduct should the government reasonably be answerable? According to the Fourteenth Amendment, the response is conduct that rises to the level of state action. State action is any conduct by the government, its agents, officers, or employees that can be "fairly attributed" to the state and that governs, limits, or affects a person's right to life, liberty, or property (*Lansing v. City of Memphis*, 2000; *Mickle v. Ahmed*, 2006).

The most obvious and formal type of state action is the enactment of a law or promulgation of a regulation by a state legislature or government agency (*Denver Area Educ. Telecomm. Consortium, Inc. v. FCC*, 1996). State action, as the definition implies, also refers to the acts of individual government officers and employees. This has usually been interpreted to mean that an officer or employee is performing a state action only if specific authority granted under the law makes the action possible (*Griffin v. City of Opa-Locka*, 2001). For example, a police officer who places a child in protective custody is performing a state action; a police officer who sexually harasses a coworker while off duty is committing a private action. As another example, a state child welfare worker who investigates suspected abuse and neglect is performing a state action; if the same social worker makes defamatory statements to friends about the family being investigated, he or she is committing a private action. A public employee who takes a state action while performing in an official capacity or exercising responsibilities granted under the law is sometimes described as acting under color of law (*Griffin v. City of Opa-Locka*, 2001).

Note specifically that a state action does not arise unless it intrudes on a person's right to life, liberty, or property. For example, a police officer who places a suspect under arrest clearly restrains the individual's liberty. If the same police officer interviews the suspect about a crime in a noncoercive way and without arresting the person, then no interference with liberty has occurred, and therefore no state action has occurred.

A state-employed psychologist who is fired for insubordination may be losing a property right. If the same psychologist is verbally reprimanded instead of fired, then arguably no state action has occurred. Similarly, a police officer who tells a young African American man involved in a street altercation that he should "stay in his own neighborhood" is probably not committing a state action, despite the toxic implications of the statement.

Local governments, such as county commissions, city councils, and other public bodies, are also included in the definition of *state*. The reason is that these governmental forms are organized under state law, with state legislatures maintaining supervisory authority over the manner in which local governments conduct official business. Therefore, a town constable who rounds up homeless persons and detains them pursuant to the town's anti-vagrancy ordinance is performing a state action. Likewise, a city planning and zoning commission that rejects an applicant's request for a residential group home permit is performing a state action.

In their strict interpretation of state action, courts have limited the power of Congress to enact social welfare legislation controlling the conduct of private parties. A notable example is the U.S. Supreme Court's invalidation of important aspects of the Violence against Women Act (VAWA) of 1994 (*United States v. Morrison*, 2000). The VAWA legislation, which would guarantee the rights of persons to be free from violence motivated by gender, such as rape, sexual harassment, and stalking, includes a provision (42 U.S.C.S. § 13981[c]), allowing victims to sue and collect civil damages from their assailants. In finding this remedy to violate the Fourteenth Amendment, the *Morrison* court noted that VAWA exceeded Congress's power to regulate the behavior of state governments and their employees and agents.

A final word is in order about the terminology used here to describe government behavior: the term *state action* is used most often because of this chapter's primary focus on the Fourteenth Amendment, which is concerned expressly with the conduct of state and local government activities. Indeed, the vast majority of publicly employed mental health professionals work for state and local government agencies and therefore need to be acquainted particularly with state and local agency conduct. Consequently, most of the examples cited hereafter involve actions by state and local government officials. The discussion presented, however, applies equally to the conduct of the federal government and to its agencies and employees, which is regulated under the Fifth Amendment's due process clause. The term *government action*, when used here, refers generically to the behavior of the federal and state governments and their agencies and employees.

Consequences of Performing a State Action

PUBLIC EMPLOYEES

Mental health professionals who work for the government as mental health providers, child protective service workers, public agency administrators, teachers, public hospital employees, prison counselors, and school social workers all need to be aware that their decisions involving clients are often state actions taken under color of law. Thus, placing an abused young-ster in the protective custody of a child welfare agency, conducting a foren-sic interview and assessment, participating in the design of an individual educational plan for an educationally disabled child, and offering mental health services to prison inmates all fall in this category.

Professionals who provide these and numerous other public services plainly represent governmental interests. Therefore, due process and equal protection principles have a special significance for them. Both of these constitutional doctrines govern the manner in which services should be provided and offer important protections to individuals whose rights are affected by them. Failure to honor due process and equal protection can result in civil and even criminal liability for the professional and the agency involved in misconduct. For example, section 1983 of the Civil Rights Act of 1871 offers money damages and injunctive relief—a court order forbidding misconduct from continuing—for the violation of constitutional rights.

PRIVATE EMPLOYEES

Due process and equal protection also have significance for some pri-vately employed professionals whose services are performed for agencies that work closely with the government in the delivery of mental health and human services to the public. For example, when a government agency con-tracts with a private provider to offer certain services (e.g., medical or meal services) in such a manner that both the government and the contractor can be said to be acting in concert to deliver the service, both the private provider and the government assume the constitutional responsibilities or-dinarily reserved solely to the government (*West v. Atkins*, 1988). As an il-lustration, if a state or federal government corrections agency contracts with a private medical provider to perform medical or mental health services, the physician can be considered a state actor whose actions are fairly attribut-able to the government (*West v. Atkins*, 1988). This is true because the ser-vices are compulsory, the inmates have no choice in the agency or individual from whom they receive services, and therefore both the private provider and the government must assume responsibility for the private provider's actions. In this circumstance, both the government and the private agency ordinarily are said to be acting under color of law. As another example, if a public school district contracts with a special education services provider to offer services to an autistic child, and the private provider subjects the child to physical abuse, both the private provider and the school district can be said to be state actors (*Koehler v. Juniata County Sch. Dist.*, 2008). This is true because the governmental body—the school district—is acting in direct concert with the private provider to offer services directly to the client.

In contrast, if an entire agency, such as a correctional facility, is privatized such that solely a private contractor offers services, courts have held that the private facility is not a state actor (*Johnson v. Corrs. Corp. of Am.*, 2008; *McKeighan v. Corrs. Corp. of Am.*, 2008). Note that both the *Johnson* and *Mc-Keighan* courts held specifically that a private facility is exempted from being considered a state actor—and therefore immune from a civil rights lawsuit under section 1983—only if there exists an alternative state procedure for seeking relief from the wrongs committed by the facility. For example, if the victim has a right to sue the facility directly under state law—which is more often the case than not—the private facility is immune from any federal claim arising under section 1983 that it is a state actor or that it has violated the constitution.

In other situations in which the state contracts with private agencies to provide more limited mental health, child care, and other services to the public, and these services are offered completely independently of the state, the actions of these private providers are even less likely to be constitutionally attributable either to the provider or to the state. The present reluctance of courts to extend constitutional protections to the clients and employees of private agencies that provide services under state contracts may leave millions of persons with little or no recourse against the government for agency misconduct except for claims under state law. With the increasing trend toward privatization of essential governmental functions, future courts are certain to revisit this important problem. A more detailed review of the law relating to private agencies and the state action doctrine is therefore timely.

PRIVATIZATION AND THE STATE ACTION DOCTRINE

Privatization of services refers to a management strategy by which the government shifts the delivery of public health, human service, and other functions to the private sector, including both profit and nonprofit agencies, presumably to improve service delivery and save money (Ewoh, 1999; Van Slyke, 2003). Important benefits of privatization claimed by proponents include reduction of government size, expansion of individual freedom, and more efficient and inexpensive service delivery (Ewoh, 1999; Gilmour & Jensen, 1998; Van Slyke, 2003). Privatization is accomplished in two essential ways: First, it occurs when federal, state, and local governments entirely delegate to a private vendor their responsibility for providing an important public service. This is occurring at present most notably in the areas of state corrections and prison support services. It is also taking place in the provision of such diverse public services as air-traffic control, garbage collection, police and fire protection, public landscaping, and vehicle maintenance (Ewoh, 1999; Gilmour & Jensen, 1998). Second, it occurs when governments contract out human services and community health and mental health programs. Thus, governments at all levels use purchase-of-service (POS) contracts with private vendors to provide services in such areas as child welfare, child day care, public assistance, outpatient mental health counseling, substance abuse and alcoholism treatment, nursing care, homeless shelters, group homes for the chronically mentally ill, school psychological and counseling programs, and long-term care for the developmentally disabled (Collins-Camargo, Ensign, & Flaherty, 2008; Gibelman & Demone, 1998; Hacker, 2004; Munger, 2006; Willging, Waitzkin, & Nicdao, 2008). A national political debate has more recently focused on additional proposals to extend government support to religious charitable institutions, or faith-based services, and to offer vouchers to parents who wish to enroll their children in private schools.

Regardless of whether privatization actually accomplishes what its proponents allege it does, it has a very specific impact on the legal relationship between the public and the government, and particularly the constitutional recourse that historically has been available to citizens for inadequate service delivery. In legal terms, contemporary courts regard government vendors as private parties and have disallowed constitutional claims against them (*Blum v. Yaretsky*, 1982; *Estades-Negroni v. CPC Hosp. San Juan Capistrano*, 2005; *Johnson v. Dowd*, 2008; *Lansing v. City of Memphis*, 2000; *Simescu v. Emmet County Dep't of Human Servs.*, 1991; *Wilcher v. City of Akron*, 2007; *Wolotsky v. Huhn*, 1992).

As the previously referenced cases reveal, even when the government subsidizes client costs, provides a substantial part of program funding, regulates vendor practices, is responsible for referring clients, leases space to an agency, or otherwise takes an active role in helping a private provider deliver services to the public, courts have been unwilling to regard conduct by private agencies and their employees as state action. For example, courts have denied constitutional claims arising from the sexual abuse of children by a welfare-to-work participant at a privatized workfare program (*Simescu v. Emmet County Dep't of Human Servs.*, 1991) and the firing of a social worker by a private, nonprofit mental health agency responsible for providing all direct clinical services for an Ohio county (*Wolotsky v. Huhn*, 1992). In explaining their decisions, courts have noted that, unless the government encourages, coerces, or actually conspires with the private actor in the commission of misconduct, there is no state action (*Lansing v. City of Memphis*, 2000; *Simescu v. Emmet County Dep't of Human Servs.*, 1991; *Wolotsky v. Huhn*, 1992). In other words, say the courts, unless the government actively participates in the vendors' misconduct, that misconduct is not fairly attributable to the government (but see contrasting opinions in *Hammons v. Norfolk S. Corp.*, 1998; *Jensen v. Lane County*, 2000). It is to be noted further that, even in those limited circumstances when the courts are willing to recognize that a private vendor or contractor is acting on behalf of the government, the vendor is not to be held liable for its employee's deprivation of civil rights unless an official policy, rule, or institutionalized custom is the root cause of the deprivation (*Warren v. Warden*, 2007).

In more recent years, the federal courts have developed the public function test to determine whether a private individual or agency is acting sufficiently in concert with a governmental body such that the private actor's activities are fairly attributable to the government (*Wilcher v. City of Akron*, 2007), in which case both the private provider and the government may each be liable under section 1983. To satisfy this test, the private party must cooperate with the government in one of three ways: First, the private party must exercise a power normally reserved to the state, as in the maintenance of prison facilities or the holding of elections (*Wilcher v. City of Akron*, 2007). Second, according to the state compulsion test, the private party must exercise coercive authority in the offering of the service such that the activity of the private party is effectively that of the state. Such is the case where a government-run jail permits a private minister to visit the jail and indoctrinate prisoners with religious dogma (*Faulkner v. Johnson County Sheriff's Dep't*, 2001). Third, under the symbiotic relationship and/or nexus test, the private actor must act in a closely cooperative and conspiratorial manner with the government so that the government and private provider are effectively providing the service in unison. An example of this is the provision of medical services to a prison inmate by a private physician with whom the government has contracted to provide medical care to prisoners (*Henry v. Clermont County*, 2005). Another example is described in the *Koehler* case referred to earlier, in which a public school district acted in concert with a private special education provider to offer services to an autistic child.

The practical impact of the courts' present hostility to constitutional claims involving private, government-contracted vendors is profound. It suggests that clients and employees of providers have recourse for professional misconduct only through private civil lawsuits against offending agencies and individuals. The courts have reacted favorably to the ideas that these vendors and their personnel should be responsive primarily to market factors that influence their conduct and that the threat of economic loss arising from their misconduct is one such market factor that should promote appropriate agency practice. Even the U.S. Supreme Court has expressed its approval of the concept that market factors alone should govern the conduct of government-contracted providers (*Richardson v. McKnight*, 1997). According to the Court, therefore, vendors must be required pursuant to their government contracts to carry insurance that protects their clients from agency misconduct, and client recourse against private agencies should be limited to lawsuits founded on traditional liability theories, including tort actions and private contract actions.

Regardless of whether market factors actually promote proper agency practices, the present discussion omits the simple point that the government has become increasingly insulated from any responsibility for its contractors' conduct. For example, a government agency that hires a private contractor to provide services may be immune from responsibility for the contractor's physical and sexual abuse of or racial and gender discrimination against the contractor's clients and employees. If the misconduct referred to is ongoing, systematic, or institutionalized, the broad relief available to victims under section 1983 lawsuits may nevertheless be unavailable from the government. Every public and private mental health professional concerned with the government's ultimate responsibility to its citizens should recognize the policy implications of this disturbing fact. To the extent that voucher systems, faith-based service proposals, and other forms of privatized health and human service delivery remain on the agenda of Congress and state legislatures, policy decision makers must be aware that the use of the Constitution in safeguarding government accountability may become more and more removed from those persons reliant on private providers.

A Constitutional Strategy for Private Professionals

The present constitutional analysis should not dissuade privately employed mental health professionals from understanding and applying the principles discussed here. Even though constitutional protections extend primarily against state actions and acts that public agency professionals commit under color of law, all mental health providers should use the principles.

Two practical reasons compel the use of constitutional standards by private-sector mental health professionals. First, many of the tasks associated with due process and equal protection are enforceable against private agencies and their employees as a result of federal and state legislation such as the Civil Rights Act of 1964. Many states have additional civil rights protections that require equitable procedures and nondiscrimination policies in the delivery of services to the public, and these should be understood and applied as part of the constitutional strategy discussed here. Just as important, this approach ensures compliance with the duty to practice reasonably competently. Second, as noted earlier, private agencies that provide services to the government under contract may in limited circumstances be regarded as government agents, and their activities may be subject to enforcement through the same mechanisms that historically have been used with respect to public agencies, the most notable being the section 1983 action.

Consequently, the duty to treat clients and coworkers with due process and equal protection is a useful tool for all mental health professionals in the consideration of practice dilemmas.

Using Due Process and Equal Protection Cases in Decision Making

A key aim in using due process and equal protection in decision making is to acquire the ability to predict the way courts are likely to interpret the constitutional aspects of practice dilemmas. On occasion, a problem may arise in practice that is comparable to a factual scenario that a court has already assessed. Reference to the summary of court decisions presented here may therefore be helpful to the decision maker for this purpose. Unfortunately, as the cases identified in the next sections demonstrate, courts are not always consistent in the way they interpret due process and equal protection law in individual decisions. Moreover, common law interpretations of due process and equal protection are in a state of constant evolution. For these reasons, it is probably more advantageous for the decision maker to understand the overall reasoning process that courts use in analyzing all due process and equal protection cases rather than to memorize outcomes in individual cases. The streamlined strategies for handling due process and equal protection cases presented later may be especially helpful for the decision maker wishing to apply these principles in the consideration of practice problems.

Due Process

The body of common law defining the principle of due process is rich and extensive. Over the course of centuries of constitutional history, courts have interpreted due process as containing two basic components: procedural due process, which guarantees basic fairness in state and government actions, and substantive due process, which defines a set of fundamental rights specially protected from government invasion. Each of these components is addressed in the section that follows.

Procedural Due Process

When the federal or a state government, county, or municipal council or commission, through its agencies of employees, seeks to interfere with a citizen's right to life, liberty, or property, it must do so with procedural fairness. Procedural fairness generally requires that the affected person have notice of the government's intent to interfere with the right and an opportunity to be heard (*Martin v. Commissioner*, 2000; *Mills v. N.M. Bd. of Psychologist Exam'rs*, 1997; *Tackett v. Vill. of Carey*, 2007). Each of these terms must be addressed individually.

LIFE, LIBERTY, AND PROPERTY RIGHTS

There are numerous instances in which a governmental body can interfere with the right of its citizens to life, liberty, or property. When the government executes a convicted murderer, it is quite literally depriving the convict of continuing life. Similarly, when the government seeks to incarcerate someone accused of a crime, it intrudes on the person's freedom. Courts have extended the definition of liberty to include a variety of situations that the framers of the Constitution probably did not contemplate. An oft-quoted statement by the U.S. Supreme Court describes liberty as follows:

> Not merely freedom from bodily restraint, but also the right of the individual to contract, to engage in any of the common occupations of life, to acquire useful knowledge, to marry, establish a home and bring up children, to worship God according to the dictates of his own conscience, and generally to enjoy those privileges long recognized as essential to the orderly pursuit of happiness by free men. (*Meyer v. Nebraska*, 1923, p. 399)

Under this expansive definition of *liberty*, courts have interpreted its coverage in various ways. Indeed, its meaning depends on regional interpretations and is sometimes defined more liberally under state law (*Wolff v. McDonnell*, 1974). Thus, the right to liberty has been recognized by courts in a variety of contexts of particular concern to mental health professionals. For example, a child welfare agency seeking to obtain custody of an endangered child affects both the child's and the parents' family privacy, a recognized element of liberty in contemporary society (*Tenenbaum v. Williams*, 1999). In developing this family privacy doctrine, courts have made known their intention to protect the right of a family to raise its children in the manner the parents see fit, without fear of governmental intrusion (*Brokaw v. Mercer County*, 2000; Kindred, 2003).

Additional interpretations of the meaning of liberty include the following: A juvenile proceeding that leads to the adjudication of delinquency and detention literally affects the child's continuing liberty (In re *R. G.*, 1996). A disabled child's right to attend class regularly is grounded in the liberty to attend public school (*J. A. v. Seminole County Sch. Bd.*, 2005; *W. B. v. Matula*, 1995). The right of a patient in a long-term-care facility to be free from physical restraints is also an aspect of liberty (*Kansas v. Hendricks*, 1997). A state mental health agency that wishes to confine a mentally ill person exhibiting signs of dangerousness seeks to control the patient's personal liberty (*Kansas v. Hendricks*, 1997). The right of a prison inmate to be free from the forced administration of antipsychotic medication also is a liberty-related right (*Riggins v. Nevada*, 1992), as is the right of a pregnant inmate to have access to an abortion (*Roe v. Crawford*, 2006). Children in foster care have the privilege either to be reunited with their natural parents or placed in permanent adoptive homes (*Joseph A. v. N.M. Dep't of Human Servs.*, 1983). The right of persons to engage in private homosexual relations is a liberty-based privilege that is not to be interfered with by laws banning the practice (*Lawrence v. Texas*, 2003). The right of a government employee or public school student to continue to work at a job or attend classes free from physical or sexual harassment is a freedom inspired by modern notions of everyday liberty and personal privacy (*Doe v. Claiborne County*, 1996; *Griffin v. City of Opa-Locka*, 2001). The right of a school principal to complete the terms of his public employment contract rises to the level of a liberty interest (*Herrera v. Union No. 39 Sch. Dist.*, 2006). Finally, the right to vote is a significant component of liberty in a free society (*Olagues v. Russoniello*, 1986).

Courts have defined the meaning of property as used in the due process clause expansively. In addition to tangible property, such as personal belongings and real estate, a person's rights extend to intangible property, such as a job, a professional practice, a checking account, retirement and medical benefits, public assistance and other welfare privileges, and a public school education (*Bd. of Regents v. Roth*, 1972; *Doe v. Gates*, 1993; *Goss v. Lopez*, 1975). In addition, one has a property right attached to any professional license one holds (*Mills v. N.M. Bd. of Psychologist Exam'rs*, 1997). Courts have even suggested that union members participating in a union election have a property-related right to a fair and impartial election (*United States v. Bellomo*, 1999).

To prove that an intangible property right exists, a person must be able to point to some law, regulation, contract, or other evidence that demonstrates the person's "legitimate claim of entitlement to it" and cannot rely merely on a "unilateral expectation of it" (*Bd. of Regents v. Roth*, 1972, p. 577). For example, a state agency employee on probationary or temporary status has no reasonable expectation this tentative job will continue indefinitely; in contrast, a permanent or tenured state employee does have such an expectation.

Property rights are often at the heart of civil litigation. When one is sued in court for money damages, the outcome affects one's property ownership. When one seeks compensation for the loss of a job or reinstatement to a former position, a property right is similarly at stake.

As with liberty rights, state law may create some property ownership claims, and their definition may therefore vary in different jurisdictions. For example, the New Mexico Constitution (article 7, section 3, and article 12, section 10) protects the right of Spanish speakers to hold public office, to serve on juries, to vote, and to be educated together with their English-speaking neighbors. Because of this explicit definition of the rights of minorities, a compelling argument can be made that the right to speak Spanish while holding a public job, or even while being educated in a public classroom, represents a liberty or property right (*Yniguez v. Arizonans for Official English*, 1994).

NOTICE AND THE OPPORTUNITY TO BE HEARD

As noted, persons facing the government's effort to interfere with a life, liberty, or property right are entitled to notice and an opportunity to be heard. The nature and extent of these protections are defined under federal and state laws, and courts are often called on to evaluate the government's compliance with these laws in individual cases. On occasion, courts are asked to assess the consistency of individual laws and regulations with the Constitution's due process clause.

In general, courts evaluate governmental conduct according to the following rule: the amount of notice that one is entitled to from the government, and the opportunity that one has to be heard, both depend on the importance of the life, liberty, or property right that is being invaded, the significance of the government's authority to invade it, and the risks imposed by the threat of losing the right (*Mills v. N.M. Bd. of Psychologist Exam'rs*, 1997; *Parrish v. Brownlee*, 2004).

Most courts have defined adequate notice as anything that is reasonably calculated to alert a person that the government seeks to interfere with a protected right (*Martin v. Commissioner*, 2000). Under different circumstances, notice can be provided through the publication of a law, the serving of a subpoena requiring attendance in court, or a letter from a government agency advising that it seeks to terminate a person's benefit.

When an individual is sued in court, a liberty or property right is almost invariably threatened. Procedural due process requires that the individual receive notice of the lawsuit's filing; this is commonly accomplished through service of process by a sheriff or a private process server. Most often, this involves personal delivery to the individual affected of a summons, which advises the individual that a lawsuit has been filed requiring a response in a limited number of days, and a copy of the lawsuit. Under some circumstances—most commonly when an individual's whereabouts are unknown—process may be obtained by substituted service, which often involves mailing notice of the lawsuit to the individual's last-known address or publishing it in a newspaper.

Adequate notice also requires that legislation, ordinances, administrative regulations, and other binding expressions of law be made available to the public by publication. In addition, the laws themselves must be tailored to reasonably identify the life, liberty, or property right they purport to affect. When law fails to reasonably identify its purpose because it is overbroad, vague, or otherwise unclear, it violates procedural due process (*United Food & Commercial Worker Union v. Sw. Ohio Reg'l Transit Auth.*, 1998). Courts have stated that a law violates procedural due process "when [people] of common intelligence must necessarily guess at its meaning" (*Connally v. Gen. Constr. Co.*, 1926, p. 391). Put differently, a law is valid when the "ordinary person exercising ordinary common sense can sufficiently understand and comply with [it], without sacrifice to the public interest" (*CSC v. Letter Carriers*, 1973, pp. 578–579).

In light of the preceding definition of procedural due process, consider the case of New Mexico's social work licensing statute, which defines the practice of community organizing as "a conscious process of social interaction and method of social work concerned with the meeting of broad needs and bringing about [*sic*] and maintaining adjustment between needs and resources" (N.M. Stat. Ann. § 61-31-6[B][3], 2008). This law requires social workers practicing as community organizers to be licensed and unlicensed persons to refrain from engaging in this practice. Moreover, the law imposes criminal sanctions for its violation. Despite the apparent authority of New Mexico's Social Work Practice Act (2008), unless social workers reading the foregoing provision have a reasonable understanding of what it is they are expected to do or refrain from doing, the law violates procedural due process. Arguably, this legislative definition of community organizing may fail the procedural due process test.

Some laws are acceptably vague in the protection of an important government interest. For example, legislation defining child abuse and neglect is often intentionally broad with the purpose of covering as many potential instances of child endangerment as possible. For example, Delaware's legislative definition of child maltreatment or mistreatment—two types of child abuse and neglect—refers to "behaviors that inflict unnecessary or unjustifiable pain or suffering on a child without causing physical injury"; the definition goes on to state that "behaviors included will consist of actions and omissions, ones that are intentional and ones that are unintentional"

(Del. Code Ann. tit. 10, § 901[16], 2009). Courts have upheld this type of generally worded legislation as consistent with procedural due process on the basis of the balancing test described earlier (see, e.g., In re J. A., 1991). With respect to child abuse codes, the government's interest in protecting vulnerable youngsters is stronger than the need for specificity. In addition, courts have noted that the consequences for invoking a child abuse statute amount to the potential for loss of custody of a child rather than the more invasive loss of freedom resulting from incarceration, as many criminal statutes call for.

An opportunity to be heard usually refers to a hearing, which can range from an informal administrative proceeding to a formal jury trial. Courts suggest that the nature and time of the hearing depend on the extent of the right interfered with and the importance of the government's interest in invading it. For example, when a state welfare bureau seeks to terminate the public assistance benefits of a client it suspects of defrauding the government, the person is entitled to prior notice of the proposed termination of benefits and a hearing to challenge the factual circumstances underlying the termination (*Goldberg v. Kelly*, 1970). This type of proceeding is often referred to as a predeprivation hearing, so named because the subject faces the loss of a potentially life-sustaining property right. As another example, a predeprivation hearing is called for in the case of a public school teacher facing termination because of a charge that the teacher physically abused a student (*Winegar v. Des Moines Indep. Cmty. Sch. Dist.*, 1994).

In contrast to the preceding examples, if a public child welfare agency wishes to obtain a temporary custody order involving a child whom the authority suspects is presently endangered by abuse or neglect, it may ordinarily do so without prior notice to the child's parents or an opportunity for them to have a hearing (*Tenenbaum v. Williams*, 1999). It is important to note, however, that the failure to grant a predeprivation hearing is authorized only in instances in which there is a reasonable suspicion on the part of child protective workers and/or police that the child is in imminent danger of serious bodily injury and that the intrusion is therefore necessary to avert harm to the child (*Wallis v. Spencer*, 1999) (holding that the protective services workers' and police officers' highly questionable reliance on allegations by a mental patient that the suspect parents were planning to "sacrifice" their child did not give them reasonable suspicion to remove a child without a prior court order). The parents are entitled to a hearing, but it may come some days after the child has already been removed from the parents' physical custody. In the case of the welfare recipient whose benefits are being suspended, the importance of the public assistance in ensuring the person's survival is deemed more significant than the government's interest in terminating benefits. Therefore, the right to a predeprivation hearing is justified. On the contrary, in the case of the parents whose child is removed temporarily from their home, the government's interest in protecting the vulnerable child from harm is greater than the parents' liberty-related right to privacy; consequently, the opportunity for a predeprivation hearing is denied (*Tenenbaum v. Williams*, 1999).

Federal and state laws govern the quality of notice and the nature of the hearing to which an individual facing deprivation of an important right is entitled. As already noted, these laws vary widely in their definition of the nature, scope, and time of the notice and hearing. Generally, however, they have several basic aspects. Notice must be reasonably calculated to advise the person facing a loss of the reason for the government's assertion of its interest (*Livant v. Clifton*, 2004; *N.Y. State Nat'l Org. for Women v. Pataki*, 2001). It must give the person facing a deprivation the chance to request an opportunity to challenge the evidence that the government is relying on to assert its interest (*Livant v. Clifton*, 2004; *Ortez v. Washington County*, 1996).

As examples of instances giving rise to due process rights, consider the following: Parents challenging a proposed individual educational plan (IEP) for their educationally disabled child may request an administrative proceeding presided over by a hearing officer (*Weber v. Cranston Sch. Comm.*, 2000). Although some of the essential elements of procedural due process must be provided in this type of case, the administrative hearing itself lacks the more formal procedural safeguards available in some law courts, such as the right to a jury trial. Similarly, parents facing the removal of a child from their home because of a suspicion of child abuse may discover that the amount of evidence required for the state to justify the child's removal may not be as great as in a criminal case (*K. J. v. Pa. Dep't of Pub. Welfare*, 2001). In contrast, a criminal suspect facing incarceration is entitled to a formal jury trial in which strict procedural safeguards and heightened evidentiary rules serve as a protection against the state's arbitrary interference with the defendant's right to liberty.

Hearings that satisfy procedural due process must include several important elements: First, they must be fundamentally fair under the circumstances. Second, they must allow for the person whose right is implicated to confront adverse witnesses that the state may rely on to support its case. Third, judges or hearing officers charged with deciding the facts and outcome of each hearing must be fair and unbiased (*State v. Kelly*, 2001).

The more important the right that the government wishes to invade, the more formal is the hearing required, for consistency with procedural due process. Next to facing capital punishment, the most significant deprivation that can occur to any individual is the loss of personal freedom; thus, it should not be surprising that the most formal hearings are reserved for criminal defendants facing the death penalty or incarceration. Such individuals are entitled to a trial, the characteristics of which include the rigid collection and presentation of evidence, the examination and cross-examination of witnesses, and the creation of a permanent record of the trial. Basic procedural rules for the conduct of trials have been established over centuries of English and U.S. jurisprudential practice, and these principles vary greatly in the federal and state court systems. All the rules, however, have the same essential purpose of protecting the rights to procedural due process of the criminal defendant, and therefore a number of them are largely universal:

- Direct testimony: Witnesses must appear in court and may testify only as to factual information of which they have firsthand knowledge
- Expert testimony: Specially qualified witnesses may offer opinions when facts require scientific or technical interpretation and when a judge requires their assistance in the assessment of complex factual information
- Hearsay rule: This rule requires that direct testimony avoid the repetition of out-of-court statements that are used in court to prove their truth; such statements are often unreliable and cannot be subjected to cross-examination in court
- Heightened evidentiary standard: This standard requires criminal prosecutors to prove that a crime has occurred beyond a reasonable doubt. This standard has been interpreted as meaning that a judge or jury deciding a criminal case must have "an abiding conviction, to a moral certainty, of the truth of the charge" (*Victor v. Nebraska*, 1994, p. 8). The procedural due process protections recognized in criminal trials have been extended to other types of hearings in which individuals face substantial deprivations of liberty-related rights. For example, many of these safeguards apply in juvenile delinquency adjudications, in which a child's custody may be transferred to a state authority for a lengthy period (In re *Gault*, 1967)

Substantive Due Process

In contrast to procedural due process, as just discussed, an additional and more controversial definition of due process has evolved in a number of court decisions over many years. It provokes debate in that a significant number of jurists believe it extends the meaning of the Constitution's due process clause well beyond the express terminology of the clause and therefore beyond the range of protections that the Constitution's framers intended. According to this definition, some rights involving life, liberty, and property are so important that they must be considered fundamental. Fundamental rights not only must be procedurally safeguarded but also are to be protected from any invasion at all by the government or its employees and agents unless a compelling interest in doing so is demonstrated (*Branch v. Turner*, 1994). Each of the terms associated with substantive due process is best approached individually.

Fundamental Rights

Courts have defined fundamental rights over the years on a case-by-case basis. Although courts have recently become reluctant to expand this list of privileges, they generally agree that it includes, at the least, all the protections contained in the U.S. Constitution's Bill of Rights, which consists of the following basic protections:

- First Amendment: freedom of speech, religion, press, and assembly
- Second Amendment: the right of organized militias to bear arms
- Third Amendment: protection from the forced quartering of soldiers by private citizens
- Fourth Amendment: the right to be free from unreasonable searches and seizures
- Fifth Amendment: the freedom from double jeopardy and self-incrimination in criminal proceedings
- Sixth Amendment: the right to an attorney and a speedy trial in criminal proceedings
- Seventh Amendment: the privilege of a jury trial in criminal proceedings
- Eighth Amendment: the freedom from cruel and unusual punishment
- Ninth Amendment: the protection granted to the people to identify new rights not already established
- Tenth Amendment: the freedom of states from federal interference in local concerns—the so-called states' rights amendment

A variety of additional fundamental rights have been identified in a string of important U.S. Supreme Court decisions. Although nowhere suggested by the express language of the due process clause, the Court has recognized these rights to be implied by the language of the Constitution, most notably by the guarantee of liberty offered in the due process clause and the broad protections offered in the Bill of Rights. Among these penumbral rights, or rights existing within the shadow of the Constitution, are the following defined by the U.S. Supreme Court:

- The right to marry, have a family life, and bring up children (*M. L. B. v. S. L. J.*, 1996), also known as the family privacy doctrine
- The right to share a house with one's extended family (*Moore v. City of E. Cleveland*, 1977)
- The right to bodily privacy, including the freedom from forced medication (*Riggins v. Nevada*, 1992)
- A woman's right to have an abortion (*Roe v. Wade*, 1973)
- The right to have access to contraceptives (*Griswold v. Connecticut*, 1965)
- The right of consenting adults to have sexual, including homosexual, relations (*Lawrence v. Texas*, 2003)
- The right to vote (*Harper v. Va. Bd. of Elections*, 1966)
- The right of a competent person to consent to medical treatment and to enjoy a confidential relationship with a health-care practitioner (*Griswold v. Connecticut*, 1965; *Singleton v. Wulff*, 1976)

In addition to the fundamental rights included in the foregoing list, some states have expanded their own constitutions to create special protections for citizens not recognized under federal law. For example, virtually all states have declared public education for children to be a constitutional right worthy of special protection (*Davis v. Monroe County Bd. of Educ.*, 1999). In the *Davis* case, the U.S. Supreme Court suggested that, where a state constitution protects the right of access to public schools, the right ought to be considered fundamental. This point remains, however, unsettled, and many courts continue to reject the notion that educational access is a fundamental right (*Seal v. Morgan*, 2000). Note also that the right to attend public schools ordinarily is interpreted to extend strictly to primary and secondary education, that is, grade school through high school (see, e.g., *Claremont Sch. Dist. v. Governor*, 1997; *Sheff v. O'Neal*, 1996).

In a major development in the interpretation of substantive due process and fundamental rights, the supreme courts of at least five states—Vermont, Massachusetts, California, Connecticut, and Iowa—have recognized that the family privacy doctrine and the liberty interest associated with marriage include the right to same-gender marriage (*Baker v. State*, 1999; *Goodridge v. Dep't of Pub. Health*, 2003; In re *Marriage Cases*, 2008; *Kerrigan v. Comm'r of Pub. Health*, 2008; *Varnum v. Brien*, 2009). Each of these cases specifically reference the enjoyment of same-gender marital relations as a fundamental right under the federal and all four state constitutions, and in the *Kerrigan* case, the decision also enunciates the impact of the equal protection clause. Several other jurisdictions, including New Hampshire, Maine, and the District of Columbia, have legalized same-gender marriage by legislative action. Public resistance to these court decisions and legislative actions seems to have been most acute in California, where opponents of gay and lesbian marriage rights have spurred a legislative backlash, which resulted in the passage of Proposition 8, banning same-gender marriage. The United States District Court for the Northern District of California has struck down Proposition 8 as unconstitutionally restricting due process and equal protection (*Perry v. Schwarzenegger*, 2010); however, the probability of further appeals within the federal court system leaves this matter as yet unresolved.

COMPELLING INTERESTS

As already noted, neither the government nor its subdivisions or employees may ever interfere with a fundamental right unless a compelling state interest in doing so is demonstrated. What specifically is a compelling interest? Over the years, courts have often described a compelling interest as a reasonable justification related to the government's responsibility to accomplish its constitutional and legislative responsibilities and objectives (*County of Sacramento v. Lewis*, 1998). At the same time, some courts have insisted that the compelling interest test must be more stringent, and therefore, "only the gravest abuses, endangering paramount interests, give occasion for permissible limitation of fundamental rights" (In re *Marriage of Ciesluk*, 2005, p. 144—quoting the U.S. Supreme Court's language in *Sherbert v. Verner*, 1963). At their most basic, legislative responsibilities and objectives constituting a compelling interest include maintaining the public health and safety of citizens and protecting the property rights of individuals and businesses. For example, protecting the safety of vulnerable children is a compelling state interest justifying removal of them from abusive households (In re *LaChapelle*, 2000). It is also helpful to understand compelling interests as reasons grounded in the government's need to provide services reasonably competently and to protect vulnerable members of society. When the government can demonstrate a compelling interest in interfering with a fundamental right, it must do so using the least restrictive means, or the minimum possible invasion of the right (In re *D. W.*, 2001; *Open Door Baptist Church v. Clark County*, 2000).

As an example of the interplay among fundamental citizen rights, compelling government interests, and the rule of least restrictive means, consider the government's important role in protecting the welfare of vulnerable children based on the doctrine of parens patriae (In re *Kendall J.*, 2000; In re *O. R.*, 2002). As noted earlier, when a state official, such as a child protective service social worker, has a reasonable suspicion that a youngster is in danger, the child may be placed in protective custody without the parents' consent (In re O. R., 2002; *Tenenbaum v. Williams*, 1999). Despite the acknowledged concern of the parents in making decisions regarding the child's best interests, the law recognizes a balance between this right and the state's interest in the child's protection. Therefore, the reason for placing the child in protective custody is compelling. Although the child welfare agency is considering and investigating the child's best interests and ultimate custody, the requirement of least restrictive means obligates the agency to take every reasonable step to minimize the necessity to remove the child from home. This requires, for example, that child welfare personnel demonstrate that they have made a good faith effort both to rehabilitate the parents and to reunite the family through the design of an appropriate treatment plan (In re *D. W.*, 2001).

Even while their fundamental right to family privacy is interfered with, parents still have a right to procedural due process. This requires that they be provided with notice—in this case, advisement by the child welfare agency that their child has been placed in custody. It also necessitates that they be granted an opportunity to be heard, meaning here a custody hearing as soon as possible after the child has been placed in protective custody, at which time the parents may respond to allegations that the child has been abused (*Tenenbaum v. Williams*, 1999).

Other examples of compelling circumstances justifying the government's interference with a person's fundamental right involve instances in which the government's authority to maintain health and welfare supersedes individual freedoms. For example, the parens patriae obligation gives the government in some circumstances the right to administer psychotropic medications to a nonconsenting mental patient (*Myers v. Alaska Psychiatric Inst.*, 2006). Governments can regulate the conduct of elections, including the enactment of voting registration and campaign laws, in the interest of maintaining their integrity (*Seymour v. Elections Enforcement Comm'n*, 2000). A city can require demonstrators who wish to stage a parade to obtain a permit so that public safety is protected (*Cox v. New Hampshire*, 1941). A state legislature can regulate lobbying activities for the purpose of combating corruption (*Associated Indus. v. Commonwealth*, 1995). A state prison can deny the request of a death-row inmate to undergo a Native American sweat-lodge ceremony, a religious cleansing ritual involving a domelike structure heated by hot rocks or coals (Colmant & Merta, 1999; McCabe, 2008) because of the potential the practice has for interfering with the prison's maintenance of discipline (*Rich v. Woodford*, 2000). (However, in a scathing dissent by Judges Kozinski and Wardlaw, the *Rich* court's majority position was attacked on the ground that "human decency [does not deny] a condemned man his last rights based on ... implausible security concerns"; *Rich v. Woodford*, 2000, p. 965.) On the issue of the authority of a state penal institution to ban the holding of sweat-lodge ceremonies, see also *Hyde v. Fisher* (2009), which upheld the state's action regarding sweat-lodge ceremonies but also required the penal institution to demonstrate compliance with least restrictive means before regulating related but more contained religious practices in a prison setting.

Additional examples of compelling circumstances include the following: A high school can censor a student newspaper whose printed discussion of sexual activity, pregnancy, and divorce purportedly interferes with the school's educational mission, including the maintenance of classroom discipline (*Hazelwood Sch. Dist. v. Kuhlmeier*, 1988). A county zoning authority can deny a permit to a church because it conflicts with the residential ambiance of a rural neighborhood (*Open Door Baptist Church v. Clark County*, 2000). A court can require a convicted rapist to register as a sex offender (*State v. Kelly*, 2001). A state prison can deny the request of a Native American inmate from the Lakota Nation to grow his hair long in accordance with religious beliefs in the interest of maintaining prison discipline, including the "quick identification" of prisoners and the "removal of a place to hide small contraband" (*Pollack v. Marshall*, 1988, p. 659). More recently, an Orthodox Jewish inmate was found to have a right to kosher meals and Sabbath observance but could not receive clergy visits or have access to musical instruments, as these were held not to be vital to the prisoner's observance of his religion (*Weinberger v. Grimes*, 2009).

The arguments government agencies offer for interfering with fundamental rights are not always successful. For example, a state prison that refuses to honor the religious dietary requests of an inmate improperly interferes with the fundamental First Amendment right to practice religion (*Besh v. Bradley*, 1995; *Fulbright v. Evans*, 2005; *Weinberger v. Grimes*, 2009). Similarly, a prison cannot refuse inmates' requests for religious counseling or, in the case of Native Americans, deny reasonable access to medicine bags and other religious items (*McKinney v. Maynard*, 1991; *Weinberger v. Grimes*, 2009). A public school that refuses to allow students to use a recreation room for after-hours religious club activities similarly interferes with free speech, assembly, and the practice of religion (*Good News Club v. Milford Cent. Sch.*, 2001). In the *Good News Club* case, the U.S. Supreme Court rejected the school's claim that it had a compelling interest based on enforcement of the separation between church and state. Prison officials who require an inmate to complete an Alcoholics Anonymous (AA) program as a condition of parole interfere unjustifiably with the inmate's religious freedom, because AA advocates belief in a "supreme being" (*Rauser v. Horn*, 2001). Parents facing child abuse proceedings cannot be ordered to undergo mandatory psychological testing (In re *T. R.*, 1999). A college professor cannot be fired for the occasional use of profanity and discussion of sexual topics in class (*Vanderhurst v. Colo. Mountain Coll. Dist.*, 2000).

The Immigration and Naturalization Service cannot detain indefinitely an "undesirable" Cuban national on the simple ground that it has been unable to effect deportation because of a lack of cooperation by the detainee's country of origin (*Rosales-Garcia v. Holland*, 2001) (note that, since the creation of the Department of Homeland Security in 2003, the Immigration and Naturalization Service has ceased to exist and its authority has been transferred to Immigration and Customs Enforcement [ICE]). Circumstances surrounding the Iraq War and the indefinite confinement of prisoners at Guantánamo Bay have also led to a statement of principles by the U.S. Supreme Court regarding the rights of detainees; the Court's language eloquently and unmistakably touches on substantive due process and other rights persons within the United States enjoy:

> [Detainees] at Guantanamo Bay and the Government both have a compelling interest in knowing in advance whether [detainees] may be tried by a military commission that arguably is without any basis in law and operates free from many of the procedural rules prescribed by Congress for courts-martial—rules intended to safeguard the accused and ensure the reliability of any conviction. (*Hamdan v. Rumsfeld*, 2006, pp. 589–590)

As noted earlier, the recognition by several state supreme courts of the status of same-gender marriage as a fundamental right has resulted in a number of decisions banning the denial of marital licenses to same-gender couples and stating expressly that such denial therefore does not support a compelling state interest (*Baker v. State*, 1999; *Goodridge v. Dep't of Pub. Health*, 2003; In re *Marriage Cases*, 2008; *Kerrigan v. Comm'r of Pub. Health*, 2008; *Varnum v. Brien*, 2009).

Other practices by public agencies that affect fundamental rights may prove in the near future to violate substantive due process standards. For example, the imposition of dress codes on public school students, a practice often justified on the basis of maintaining school discipline, may limit without compelling justification students' right to privacy and self-expression (see, e.g., *Pyle v. Sch. Comm.*, 1996) Similarly, schools that rely excessively on alternative teaching strategies emphasizing morality training, affective techniques, self-revelation and role-playing, group counseling, and other pseudopsychological methods may violate privacy. In *Altman v. Bedford Central School District* (2001), parents successfully challenged these teaching practices at the trial level, although their victory was overturned on appeal, leaving open the possibility of future substantive due process challenges.

Congress's efforts to respond to terrorist activities that occurred on September 11, 2001, have yielded far-reaching legislation that purports to identify compelling government interests in the pursuit of national safety and security. The Uniting and Strengthening America by Providing Appropriate Tools Required to Intercept and Obstruct Terrorism Act of 2001 (The USA Patriot Act) seeks "to deter and punish terrorist acts in the United States and around the world [and] to enhance law enforcement investigatory tools," among other things. Although a complete discussion of the contents of the act's ten titles is beyond the scope of this book, it is instructive to highlight several aspects that raise significant questions about the government's authority to expand the meaning of compelling interest in the wake of the heightened fear and interest in preventative public safety following 9/11. The most problematic sections of the act in terms of their impact on privacy rights protected by substantive due process include (1) the sanctioning of indefinite detention of immigrants; (2) searches by law enforcement officials of homes and businesses without the knowledge of private citizens and business owners; (3) the authorization of national security letters, a tool used by the Federal Bureau of Investigation to conduct warrantless searches of financial, phone, and e-mail records; and (4) the extension of the federal government's access to information pertaining to the financial records, library usage patterns, and business activities of private individuals. It is interesting to note that the original act, which was to sunset—or terminate—at the end of 2005, was reauthorized by Congress in 2006, a fact that virtually guarantees the ongoing filing and consideration by courts of civil rights litigation testing the constitutionality of the act.

In an unusual case exploring the outer limits of personal privacy and countervailing governmental interests, Wisconsin's highest court upheld a probation order in the prosecution of a man for failing to pay child support; the terms of probation included the condition that the man refrain from having additional children (*State v. Oakley*, 2001). The compelling reason the state offered for the invasion of the fundamental right to procreate is Wisconsin's interest in ensuring that parents support their children (*State v. Oakley*, 2001). It is to be noted that the *Oakley* court clarified its opinion shortly after the initial case was heard and underscored the point that its decision was to be narrowly interpreted and applied solely to extreme situations in which parental neglect is long-standing and severe (*State v. Oakley* [II], 2001). Notwithstanding this caveat, other courts and legal scholars have criticized the *Oakley* decision (see, e.g., Epps, 2005).

Whether the *Oakley* court's decision is consistent with the principle of least restrictive means remains a significant question for future courts. *Oakley* may represent an example of the judiciary's increasing willingness to define parenthood, and particularly fatherhood, in terms of economic and social precepts. Thus, courts have redefined fatherhood as something more than "the mere existence of a biological link," recognizing instead that, from a legal perspective, it comes into existence only when a father agrees to develop a supportive financial and social relationship with his child (*Lehr v. Robertson*, 1983, p. 261). By therefore limiting the characterization of fatherhood as a fundamental right, courts and legislatures have controlled the procedural privileges formerly available to the absent fathers of out-of-wedlock children, such as the right to consent to adoptions (*Lehr v. Robertson*, 1983).

It is clear that the rights of prisoners and other institutionalized persons—and especially Native Americans—to religious freedom has been a prominent theme that courts have addressed in their interpretation of substantive due process law. In New Mexico, a trial court denied a Navajo prisoner the right to participate in a sweat-lodge ceremony after prison officials claimed the ceremony would require hundreds of additional support personnel to oversee and was motivated by the prisoner's intent to disrupt prison functioning (*Chavez v. Lemaster*, 2001). This decision notwithstanding, Native American leaders point to the demonstrable success of sweat lodges in leading convicts to address long-term alcohol abuse and antisocial conduct and in enhancing the spiritual growth and rehabilitation of participants (Colmant & Merta, 1999; McCabe, 2008). According to New Mexico's corrections ceremony, prisoners at high-security facilities are presently "allowed to keep only a minimum number of religious items in their cells," which may include no more than "an eagle feather and a medicine bag" (Terrell, 2001).

Note that, in those instances in which a fundamental right is involved, a government agency seeking to impinge on the right must still satisfy the procedural due process privileges of the person affected. For example, the imposition of long-term discipline on a public school student, the firing of a public employee, the termination of parental rights of an abusive parent, and the promulgation of zoning ordinances in a city all require enforcement measures that guarantee the right of affected persons to notice and an opportunity to be heard before any deprivation is imposed.

Handling Due Process Dilemmas: The Duty to Treat Clients and Coworkers with Due Process

As is revealed in many of the cases cited, the duty to implement due process principles applies not only in relationships with a primary client but also in interactions with other members of the public, including agency coworkers, to whom mental health providers owe professional obligations. Thus, applying the duty not only tends to enhance the best interests of clients but also maximizes broader societal interests, such as the promotion of diversity. Therefore, the prudent professional should identify its application in all practice dilemmas that involve agency responsibilities to clients; employment disputes; disciplinary actions against agency subordinates; professional relationships, including conflicts of interest, with clients and coworkers; and other areas involving individual liberty or property rights.

Consistent with the strategy outlined in the decision-making framework, the duty to treat clients and coworkers with due process should be considered together with other basic legal principles as a first step in the consideration of professional decisions. Remember that this duty is not ordinarily articulated in ethical codes, despite its enormous impact on basic human rights. This point underscores the importance of addressing due process considerations as an initial step in decision making.

Before discussing a suggested approach to handling due process dilemmas, a few words are in order about the complexities presented by constitutional law. The review of cases presented here is intended to provide the decision maker with a general sense of how a variety of courts have interpreted the principles of procedural and substantive due process. The cautious professional should not feel overwhelmed by the broad scope of the factual situations that courts have been called on to consider; these cases are presented mainly as a rough guide to the diverse situations in which due process is relevant. However, under the common law system, courts revisit and reanalyze these examples over time. Therefore, one is better off obtaining a general sense of the letter and spirit of due process, together with a sense of the legal trends contemporary court decisions reveal, rather than attempting to master the names, dates, and holdings of individual judicial opinions.

The procedural and substantive due process rules outlined herein present a strategy for recognizing and addressing due process issues in mental health practice. They can be summarized in the following steps:

1. Identify specifically the life, liberty, or property right affected.
2. Identify whether the right is fundamental.
3. If the right is fundamental, substantive due process requires that the right not be violated unless a compelling government interest is demonstrated.
4. Identify any state action that might interfere with the right:
   • If the actor is a public agency, or an employee of a public agency, the actor's conduct is a state action if it is made possible by

specific authority granted under the law and affects the life, liberty, or property right identified earlier.

- If the actor is a private agency that has contracted with the government to provide services to the public, the actor's conduct may be a state action in limited circumstances (see text).
- If the actor is a private agency providing services independent of the government, there is no state action and the agency alone is responsible for its conduct according to the duty to practice reasonably competently and federal and state civil rights legislation.

5. Identify the person whose life, liberty, or property right is affected.
- If a life, liberty, or property right is affected, procedural due process requires that the person receive reasonable notice and an opportunity to be heard.

6. Identify remedies for violations of due process:
- If the actor is a state agency, section 1983 relief is available.
- If the actor is a state contractor, section 1983 relief is available only in limited circumstances.
- If the actor is a private agency, relief is available under applicable civil rights legislation and through civil lawsuits.

These steps can be demonstrated using two case scenarios previously discussed: vignette 1, "The Angry Client," and case example 14, "The School Social Worker." In "The Angry Client," a Hispanic individual receiving mental health services makes disparaging remarks about Anglo clients and their presumed preferential treatment at a clinic. Using the steps highlighted here, the client's personal privacy and speech, as well as his interest in receiving quality mental health services, can be identified readily as liberty-related rights. He may also have a property-related right to receive government-sponsored health care.

Proceeding to the next step, the client's personal privacy and speech can be identified as fundamental rights. The client's statements, however obnoxious they may be to the therapist, enjoy protection. Unless the therapist can demonstrate a compelling reason, usually defined as some important public safety concern, the therapist should avoid any important treatment decision (i.e., a state action) that hinges on the content of the client's remarks or is either directly or indirectly punitive.

Identifying the state action requires consideration first of the clinic's status as a public or private agency. In the original vignette, the agency is described as public. Assume for the sake of this discussion that state government is directly involved in the administration of the agency. Any action taken by the therapist that might affect the quality of services received by this client or that threatens his right to receive services in the future potentially interferes with the client's liberty and property rights. Should the therapist reassign the client, he or she may perilously make a major treatment decision based on protected speech. If the well-meaning therapist attempts to "correct the client's mistaken impressions" or confronts the client's anger in a way that unduly entangles the client's personal beliefs with the course of his therapy, the provider may mistakenly use the therapeutic relationship in a manner that compromises the client's personal privacy. The client's utterances may inappropriately influence even the therapist's assessment and diagnosis of the client.

Are there any compelling interests that justify the therapist's intervention? In considering this question, it is instructive to review the agency's duties to the client and to the public in general. For this purpose, it is helpful to reconsider the duties to practice reasonably competently and to identify the primary client as they apply in the present case. The agency's essential legal obligation is to provide reasonably competent mental health services. Unless the client's activities interfere with this mission, the client's statements remain protected. Were the client to threaten the therapist, disrupt the agency's functioning, complain about the provider's or agency's services to a clinical supervisor or administrator, or in some other way hinder the agency's ability to meet its obligations to the public, the therapist and the agency would arguably have a compelling reason to respond appropriately. No indication, however, is provided in this vignette that the client has engaged in any such conduct.

What, then, is an appropriate response to the client's statements? Arguably, the best response is to do nothing. Unless the therapist can reasonably identify a relevant mental health issue arising from the client's statements, the therapist's response may do more clinical harm than good. Although this point may not seem terribly pressing in the context of a routine outpatient professional relationship, consider its significance in the case of institutionalized clients. Persons receiving long-term care in public mental health facilities and nursing homes, as well as inmates in penal institutions, often risk differential treatment based on their demeanor and receptivity to services. When the provider allows the client's "attitude," personality, political beliefs, or other expressed opinions to affect the professional relationship, the risk to the client is great. If a psychotherapist allows the client's verbal provocations to compel the treatment delivered, the effect may be not unlike the plot of Ken Kesey's classic novel, *One Flew over the Cuckoo's Nest*.

Reconsider case example 14, "The School Social Worker." If subjected to a due process analysis, Amalia's claim to a free and appropriate public education grants her a property right recognized under federal law and supported by state legislation and administrative regulations governing the design and implementation of IEPs. Even though educational opportunity has not yet been declared to be a fundamental right in Kansas (see *Unified Sch. Dist. No. 229 v. State*, 1994), legislation guarantees the right to a free public school education for educationally disabled children (see Special Education for Exceptional Children Act, Kan. Stat. Ann. §§ 72-961 to 72-999, 2008), a fact that places a special burden on the IEP team to design an appropriate education for Amalia. Construction of the IEP by the school and the professional staff is plainly a state action, and Amalia clearly has a property right in her education, facts that grant Amalia and her family the right to procedural due process in connection with the design and implementation of her IEP.

The social worker plays an intimate role in the IEP's creation and, as the case example notes, may be called on to testify in the event that the parents challenge the plan's contents. The fact that the parents have the authority to challenge an IEP with which they are dissatisfied stems from the property right connected to their daughter's education. The IEP, by its specification of the services to be offered to Amalia, greatly affects her property right. If, for example, the IEP denies her the right to be mainstreamed with her peers, Amalia's parents may object to this deprivation. In this case, the parents have a right to notice, meaning that they must have a chance to see the IEP itself and receive information about the school-created procedures relating to the consideration of parental objections to the plan's contents. In addition, they are entitled to an opportunity to be heard; here, that means the right to request an administrative hearing.

To satisfy the procedural due process obligations presented by this case example, the full and open participation of the school social worker is required. If, for example, the social worker denies parents an opportunity to participate fully in the IEP's preparation, as might occur in this case if they are not provided adequate Spanish translation and an opportunity to take part in an appropriate sequence of IEP planning meetings, the social worker may become an active agent in the denial of procedural due process to the parents. Even the inadequate communication of the IEP's contents, which in this case example has led to the parents' apparent confusion and request for an additional meeting, represents a violation of procedural due process.

Procedural due process also plays an important role in the design of the administrative hearing the parents may request if they disapprove of the IEP. Until fairly recently, such hearings were often conducted with a school board employee serving as hearing officer. Consistent with procedural due process, the Individuals with Disabilities Education Act (IDEA) (§ 1415[b][2])—please review case example 14 for a discussion of IDEA's other main provisions—requires that the hearing officer presiding over an IEP administrative appeal must be independent of the local school district and neither employed by nor affiliated with the school system, in the interest of guaranteeing the officer's impartiality.

Procedural due process also entitles the parents an opportunity to hear specific information concerning the educational assessment and expert opinions of psychologists, counselors, teachers, and other professional members of the IEP team responsible for the plan's construction. Note that, consistent with the purposes of the administrative hearing, the adversarial climate and formal procedural and evidentiary rules associated with complex civil and criminal trials are not employed in an IEP administrative appeal.

Social policy proponents interested in the implementation of IDEA should raise important questions concerning the sufficiency of procedural due process in the creation of IEPs. Specifically, champions of persons with disabilities must be concerned with the quality of the advocacy that parents and children receive in connection with the preparation of IEPs. For example, parents involved in an IEP's design, particularly those for whom language presents a roadblock, may require extensive assistance to participate fully in the process. Aside from the social worker—whose advocacy role is limited, as the case example demonstrates—parents may not receive the aid of an attorney unless they can afford it. Neither state nor federal law grants the right to subsidized legal assistance in the formulation and administrative contest of IEPs, despite the monumental importance of this process in the life of a child with an educational disability.

The right to the assistance of an attorney is an important procedural protection that courts and legislatures have been willing to extend only to those individuals facing an extreme deprivation, such as the loss of liberty that occurs from criminal prosecutions, delinquency proceedings, mental health commitments, and legal guardianship petitions (for the most frequently cited court decisions on the subject of the constitutional right to an attorney in noncriminal proceedings, see In re *Gault*, 1967; *Lassiter v. Dep't of Soc. Servs.*, 1981; *United States v. Deninno*, 1996; see also *Branch v. Franklin*, 2008—holding that there is no constitutional right to counsel in noncriminal, administrative proceedings; for a discussion of the extension by legislation of a right to counsel in noncriminal cases, see Kaufman, 2009). State legislatures have also protected the right of indigent respondents in child abuse and neglect proceedings to obtain the free assistance of counsel (see, e.g., N.M. Stat. Ann. § 32A-4-10[B], 2008), given the impact that a threatened change in child custody has on the fundamental right to parent.

In child welfare, domestic relations cases involving child custody, adult protective service cases, and other types of litigation involving the right of families, minor children, or vulnerable adults, courts may be required or they may voluntarily choose to appoint, a guardian *ad litem*, or legal guardian, to represent the interests of a minor or incapacitated person in court. The need for a guardian *ad litem* often arises when a young person faces a significant threat to a liberty or property right, such as may occur when custody is contested in a child abuse or divorce proceeding. The appointment of the guardian *ad litem* is a means of honoring the child's due process right to be heard in court concerning the issues that are the subject of the litigation.

The failure of legislators and courts to extend due process protections to other types of cases can in part be blamed on the financial cost of providing expanded procedural safeguards. Thus, granting a right to legal assistance and other significant due process protections ordinarily provided in more formal trial settings is a prohibitively expensive and immediate public cost. As already noted, these due process measures are ordinarily reserved only for cases involving the most significant government deprivations. Therefore, the mental health lobbyist who can demonstrate the enormous indirect expenses that result from the failure to provide formal due process protections to IEP contestants and others forced to litigate their right to participate in important government programs, such as Supplemental Security Income (SSI), veteran's benefits, and workers' compensation, may be able to convince future legislatures to reconsider this question.

The foregoing discussion of procedural and substantive due process can provide only a brief overview of the diversity and complexity of these important constitutional principles. However, decision makers who understand the overall role these principles play in the protection of essential human rights have a useful aid in the evaluation of mental health practice dilemmas.

Equal Protection

Equal protection, the second of two fundamental safeguards the Fourteenth Amendment provides, limits the extent to which the government can classify or categorize its citizens. As the equal protection clause reads, no state shall "deny to any person ... the equal protection of the laws." The basic purpose of this provision is to direct state governments "that all persons similarly situated should be treated alike" (*City of Cleburne v. Cleburne Living Ctr.*, 1985, p. 439). Note that this direction also applies to the federal government and its agencies and employees. Courts have explained this by reasoning that equal protection is implied by the Fifth Amendment, which contains a due process clause linked to actions taken by the federal government (*Bolling v. Sharpe*, 1954). This point notwithstanding, most mental health professionals are employed by state government agencies; for this reason, the review of equal protection law presented here focuses on the actions of state and local governments, agencies, and employees.

A review of interpretive court decisions helps define equal protection, explain the extent to which the government can identify and group its citizens, and identify several classifications—such as those based on race, religion, gender, and disability—that the government is especially discouraged from using when it defines the rights of its citizens. Although a complete review of equal protection court decisions is beyond the scope of this book, it is imperative for every mental health professional to acquire a basic knowledge of its boundaries. With this in mind, this section presents a basic historical overview of the parameters of the equal protection clause.

As noted earlier, the Fourteenth Amendment was initially intended to protect newly freed slaves from oppressive and discriminatory practices of state governments, and it therefore targets state action specifically. As with the due process clause, the influence of equal protection as interpreted by a multitude of courts has expanded over the years so that the coverage initially offered solely to African Americans has broadened to include other vulnerable groups.

Governments need to categorize and classify citizens in a variety of ways, and courts have noted that the equal protection clause does not forbid states when necessary from treating "different classes of persons in different ways" (*Reed v. Reed*, 1971, p. 75). In fact, most economic, social, health, and public safety laws and regulations must define the groups that are to benefit from or be burdened by their impact. It is therefore inevitable that, as some groups benefit from government classifications, others may be disadvantaged (*Greenville Women's Clinic v. Bryant*, 2000). For example, states may wish to base eligibility for public assistance on family income or to enforce mandatory retirement ages in certain types of employment. States also need to classify children as "abused" or "delinquent" to establish treatment systems and determine eligibility for services. They must designate some persons as "mentally ill" and others as "incapacitated" to establish standards for protective interventions and to remove some persons from the threat of criminal prosecution for their violent behavior.

Through years of interpretive decisions, courts have developed an analytic system for identifying and restricting certain types of classifications that violate the letter and spirit of the equal protection clause. This three-tiered system examines government classifications by rank ordering them according to the harm they threaten to members of a classified group. Under this system, the more serious the threat of harm the classification presents, the more suspect the classification is. A review of each tier of equal protection analysis clarifies this point.

The first tier of equal protection analysis defines certain types of classifications that courts regard as suspect, which means that they are presumed to have an invidious and harmful impact on the people they categorize. Under this definition, when the government attempts to classify persons on the basis of certain protected characteristics, such as race, religion, national origin, or ethnicity—or if the classification burdens a fundamental constitutional right—the classification is considered suspect, or extremely objectionable (*Ball v. Massanari*, 2001; *Greenville Women's Clinic v. Bryant*, 2003; *Parents Involved in Cmty. Schs. v. Seattle Sch. Dist. No. 1*, 2007).

Perhaps the most notorious historical example of a suspect classification is the de jure, or legalized, segregation of African American citizens through Jim Crow legislation that persisted for years in the United States. One such instance of segregation, involving African American students in the Topeka, Kansas, school system, was successfully challenged in the landmark case *Brown v. Board of Education* (1954).

The denial of a woman's right to an abortion stands as a classic example of a government classification that burdens a fundamental right (*Roe v. Wade*, 1973). Specifically, the *Roe* court found that the absolute denial to women of abortion services discriminates against women because it invades the right to personal privacy, as guaranteed by substantive due process.

Under the analysis used in *Brown*, *Roe*, and other cases in which suspect classifications have been identified, courts have subjected these classifications to strict scrutiny. Strict scrutiny means that courts must examine whether the classification is "narrowly tailored to serve a compelling government interest" (*Adarand Constructors, Inc. v. Pena*, 1995, p. 219). Under this test, the vast majority of state and federal government actions that classify on the basis of suspect criteria or interfere with fundamental rights have been invalidated as discriminatory under the equal protection clause (on discrimination interfering with the fundamental right to have intimate relations, including sexual relations between nonmarried and gay and lesbian persons, see, e.g., *Lawrence v. Texas*, 2003).

Strict scrutiny of state actions that classify on the basis of a suspect grouping has had an important influence in the forging of social policy. For example, some courts have found government affirmative action programs that for years had used racial and gender criteria to enhance the qualification of minority and women applicants for government jobs and public school education to violate the equal protection clause (*Hopwood v. Texas*, 1996). In the *Hopwood* case, a federal appeals court was unimpressed

by the University of Texas Law School's argument that its affirmative action program was intended to heighten the representation of Latino and
African American candidates in the school. Rather, the court found that
the school's state action—the granting of preferential application points to
minority candidates—could not survive the strict scrutiny test. Although
the law school claimed that its program was intended to be ameliorative,
or a helpful effort to correct the historical effects of past discrimination,
the court did not accept the state's claim that this represented a compelling
interest. Remember that a compelling interest has been defined as a reason
motivated by the government's direct public responsibilities. Courts such as
Hopwood have become increasingly hostile to the notion that the correction
of past injustices constitutes an immediate governmental concern.

The *Hopwood* court went on to suggest that the use of race in an ameliorative manner itself tends to stigmatize racial minorities by reinforcing the
view that they are unable to succeed without governmental assistance. The
U.S. Supreme Court, in *Adarand Constructors, Inc. v. Pena* (1995), further
complicated the status of race-based affirmative action by acknowledging
that the government could use the correction of the immediate effects of
past, intentional racial discrimination as a compelling reason to support affirmative action, but only by using a narrowly tailored plan to correct the discrimination. In the *Adarand Constructors* case itself, the Court held that the
government's plan for awarding preferential contracts to minority contractors was not sufficiently and narrowly tailored to uphold equal protection.

Given the inconsistency in court decisions concerning the acceptability of
race-based affirmative action, the U.S. Supreme Court again addressed the
issue directly in 2003 in its consideration of affirmative action programs at
the University of Michigan. Unfortunately, the two resultant decisions do
little either to undo the confusion surrounding race-based affirmative action
or encourage its widespread use. In *Grutter v. Bollinger* (2003), the Court applied the strict scrutiny test to the University of Michigan's law school but
also found that the university could take race into account generally in making admissions decisions, noting that the school had a compelling interest
in creating a racially diverse student body on campus. However, in a companion case, *Gratz v. Bollinger* (2003), the Court struck down the university's
undergraduate affirmative action program because it employed a numeri-
cally based points system—something the Court equated to a quota—and
because the system was not sufficiently tailored to address the university's
diversity-related goals. In a more recent case, *Parents Involved in Community Schools v. Seattle School District No. 1* (2007), the Court struck down
the race-based assignment of students in the Seattle public schools on the
ground that, even though the government might have a compelling interest

in correcting the effects of past, intentional racial discrimination, the mere demonstration of residual racial imbalance in a school system—without a demonstration of intentional discrimination—did not rise to the level of an equal protection violation. Therefore, the Court has demonstrated its inclination to reject affirmative action plans that employ statistical systems and plans used in settings in which no history of invidious discrimination is clearly articulated.

The cumulative effect of the *Grutter, Gratz,* and *Parents Involved in Community Schools* decisions is to raise substantial doubt about the acceptability of broad, race-based affirmative action programs in public employment and education. Indeed, on the basis of these cases, many such programs have been terminated or drastically restructured. In the wake of these court cases, major governmental employers and state-supported educational institutions are considering alternatives to race-based affirmative action.

Notice that equal protection claims such as those raised in the foregoing cases often assert many of the same protections of substantive due process. Thus, if one is classified on the basis of a suspect category or a fundamental right, one may challenge that as a violation either of equal protection or of substantive due process; each claim is subject to essentially the same judicial review (i.e., strict scrutiny).

Another and arguably more constructive impact of strict scrutiny review has been to expand the scope of religious freedom in state-administered institutions. As noted earlier, prisoners have successfully pressed their requests to receive religious counseling and to have religiously based dietary requests honored. Except where state penal institutions have been able to demonstrate compelling reasons for the denial of such requests—usually based on the prison's need to maintain discipline and security, as in the denial of sweat-lodge ceremonies—strict scrutiny review often has upheld prisoners' assertions that limiting religious practices is a discriminatory prohibition that interferes with a fundamental right. In addition, the limitation of certain religious practices represents a suspect classification to the extent that it distinguishes some religious practices—often Native American traditions—from other spiritual pursuits. Consistent with this point, corrective legislation such as the American Indian Religious Freedom Act of 1978 and New Mexico's Native American Counseling Act (2008) have been enacted by Congress and some state legislatures as a means of reinforcing the equal protection and substantive due process rights recognized by courts.

A second tier of equal protection analysis defines some state classifications as quasi suspect. Quasi-suspect classifications include gender and illegitimacy, or the status of having been born out-of-wedlock (*Ball v. Massanari,* 2001; *Bullock v. Sheahan,* 2008; *Kazmier v. Widmann,* 2000). The standard of review that courts are required to apply in gender classification cases is sometimes described as intermediate scrutiny or heightened review, according to which quasi-suspect classifications will be upheld only if they are "substantially related to an important governmental interest" (*Ball v. Massanari*, 2001, p. 823; see also *Bullock v. Sheahan*, 2008; *Kazmier v. Widmann*, 2000). What is the effective difference between strict scrutiny and intermediate scrutiny? The simple answer is "not very much," and in truth, reviewing courts have declared virtually all discrimination on the basis of gender to be unconstitutional. Under intermediate scrutiny, for example, the Supreme Court struck down the Virginia Military Institute's overt discrimination against female applicants to the formerly all-male academy (*United States v. Virginia*, 1996). In its decision, the Court indicated that any gender-based classification would need an "exceedingly persuasive justification," and that, although gender is not an absolutely forbidden classification, categorization by gender "may not be used ... to create or perpetuate the legal, social, and economic inferiority of women" (*United States v. Virginia*, 1996, p. 534).

Because many state constitutions have been amended to include equal rights provisions guaranteeing the equality of the sexes, gender discrimination in state social and welfare legislation is almost always impermissible. The failure of courts to recognize gender as a suspect classification can be based on several factors: First, the nation has failed to adopt a federal equal rights amendment, a step that would settle the question nationally. Second, a factually appropriate case has not yet been appealed to the Supreme Court that would offer an opportunity for the recognition of gender as a fully suspect classification, although the *Virginia* case has come close to accomplishing this task. In view of the deep ideological divisions in the current court, it would be unlikely for a consensus to emerge on the issue of gender classification in the immediate future. Third, the prospect of absolute equality of the sexes may continue to raise the specter in some judicial minds of the "danger" of women fighting alongside men in combat situations, although the performance of women during the Iraq War may have changed this perception. This point notwithstanding, the constitutionality of present federal selective service registration policies that target solely young men who have reached the age of eighteen can be blamed on intermediate scrutiny as applied to gender-based classifications. Fourth, ameliorative legislation, including affirmative action and other protective policies that promote the interests of women in education, health care, business, and other areas may be easier to justify through the use of intermediate rather than strict scrutiny in gender classifications. Court decisions both support and contradict this conclusion. Following an intermediate standard of review, these cases have both affirmed (*Danskine v. Miami Dade Fire Dep't*, 2001; *United States v. N.Y. City Bd. of Educ.*, 2006) and struck down (*Eng'g Contractors Ass'n v. Metro. Dade County*, 1997; *Fla. A. G. C. Council, Inc. v. Florida*, 2004) gender-based affirmative action programs. In the *New York City Board of Education* case, the court noted specifically that the intermediate standard of review means that in justifying a gender-based affirmative action plan, the employer needed to demonstrate only a conspicuous gender imbalance in traditionally segregated job categories and did not need to show purposeful employer or governmental discrimination as a reason for the plan. Thus, the quasi-suspect classification assigned to gender clearly supports the continuation of gender-based affirmative action.

A third tier of classification courts have recognized what is defined as nonsuspect. Classifications that are nonsuspect are regarded, in effect, as presumptively valid (*Johnson v. City of Kankakee*, 2006; *Kaplan v. United States*, 1998). Courts called on to review nonsuspect classifications require the government merely to point to some rational purpose for using a particular categorization. This is ordinarily a fairly easy standard for the government to satisfy because virtually all legislation has at least some logical basis.

The vast majority of classifications that governments are required to make fall into the nonsuspect category. Categorizations based on class, family income, and age are three of the most often used classifications, and in light of the role that governments play in administering public welfare and employment programs, it is fairly easy to understand why these particular groupings of people are considered permissible. Public assistance, Medicare, and Social Security all would be impossible to maintain without means testing or age-based eligibility requirements imposed by law.

The status of class and family income as nonsuspect classifications presents an interesting possibility for the revitalization of affirmative action: government employers and educational institutions that design fair and rational but race-neutral systems for granting reasonable preferences to job applicants and students from lower economic strata may well achieve some of the earlier aims of race-based affirmative action; at the same time, however, they will have avoided dependence on suspect criteria. For this reason, reliance on class, income, and other categories in the design of such programs may have the indirect effect of increasing minority access, given the clear link in U.S. society between income and ethnicity. Therefore, use of socioeconomic status as an eligibility criterion for affirmative action programs may well increase in the near future.

Although the courts' definition of nonsuspect classification makes possible the maintenance of major social welfare programs, it also has effectively limited Congress's power to enact civil rights legislation that protects the interests of population groups that fall within nonsuspect categories. For example, Congress attempted to address age-based discrimination in enacting the Age Discrimination in Employment Act (ADEA) of 1967, the purpose of which was to end the practice of arbitrary age discrimination in hiring and firing in the public and private sectors. In embracing the law, Congress intended to express its position that certain forms of age discrimination have historically been committed on the basis of "inaccurate and stigmatizing stereotypes" (*Hazen Paper Co. v. Biggins*, 1993, p. 610) and that no rational explanation could ever justify this practice. Despite Congress's arguably good intentions, the Supreme Court has found that the requirements ADEA imposes on state and local governments "are disproportionate to any unconstitutional conduct that conceivably could be targeted" (*Kimel v. Fla. Bd. of Regents*, 2000). Thus, according to the Supreme Court, state governments may continue to use age as a measuring stick for other qualifications that are relevant to state interests. For example, mandatory retirement in employment has been upheld on the presumptively rational basis that it maintains the quality of services offered to the public; protects the health of older workers; enforces the state's interest in incorporating new, younger workers into the workforce and tax base; and makes possible the orderly administration of pension plans (*Breck v. Michigan*, 2000). With the constitutionality of ADEA in doubt, the reinstatement of age-related classifications in public employment is a real possibility (see also *Gonzalez v. City of N.Y. Health & Hosps. Corp.*, 2001).

As another example of the limitation that nonsuspect status imposes on the enactment of social welfare legislation, courts continue to consider physical and mental disability to be nonsuspect classifications (*Darvie v. Countryman*, 2009; *Lavia v. Pennsylvania*, 2000). This fact notwithstanding, Congress enacted the Americans with Disabilities Act (ADA) in 1990, which it further amended in the ADA Amendments Act (ADAAA) of 2008, which restores protections of the original 1990 act that several U.S. Supreme Court decisions had restricted. Among other things, the ADA (42 U.S.C.S. § 12112a) prohibits government and private employers from discriminating against qualified disabled individuals in any aspect of employment, including the right to be hired. In addition, the ADA imposes requirements on public and private employers to make "reasonable accommodation" to disabled employees in assisting them to qualify for employment and meet their job responsibilities. In placing this burden on employers, courts have suggested that the ADA unconstitutionally forces on employers greater restrictions than are warranted under the equal protection clause (*Lavia v. Pennsylvania*, 2000). The courts have noted instead that in the case of disability—a nonsuspect classification—equal protection should permit the employer's "rational" consideration of disability in hiring and accommodating persons with disabilities (*Lavia v. Pennsylvania*, 2000).

In light of court decisions restricting Congress's power to enact remedial legislation under the Fourteenth Amendment, the federal government reasonably can be expected in the immediate future to amend some of its civil rights policies, including the laws mentioned herein. The present attitude of conservative judiciary members—including those now comprising a majority of the U.S. Supreme Court's jurists—favoring the strict construction of the Constitution would appear to require legislation to be more narrowly tailored to outlaw specific discriminatory practices proven to have occurred in the recent past and to remedy only their immediate, present-day effects.

It might be anticipated that the limitations placed on legislation benefiting members of nonsuspect groups would inspire an effort to demonstrate that such groups actually should enjoy suspect or quasi-suspect status. Given the historical evidence of human suffering among the aged, the physically and mentally disabled, persons mired in alcohol and substance abuse, the developmentally disabled, and other vulnerable groups, suspect status would appear to have been richly earned. However, courts in recent years have largely refused to include additional classifications within the scope of suspect or quasi-suspect status, despite frequent court challenges seeking this recognition. For example, categorizations based on disability and mental retardation have both been identified recently as nonsuspect, despite the intense and articulate efforts of claimants to demonstrate the "negative attitudes," "fear," and "irrational bases" associated with the treatment of the disabled (*Bd. of Trs. of Univ. of Ala. v. Garrett*, 2001, p. 367). Similar results have been obtained in the case of persons suffering from alcoholism (*Ball v. Massanari*, 2001).

Gay and lesbian persons until recently were unable to persuade courts that homosexuality was anything but a nonsuspect classification (see, e.g., *Equality Found. v. City of Cincinnati*, 1997; *Lofton v. Kearney*, 2001; *Thomasson v. Perry*, 1996). In cases brought by gay servicemen, courts upheld legislation requiring military discharge under the federal government's "don't ask, don't tell" policy, enacted pursuant to the National Defense Authorization Act for Fiscal Year 1994, on the basis that the policy was rationally related to the military's need to maintain troop morale, discipline, and unit cohesion (*Richenberg v. Perry*, 1996; *Thomasson v. Perry*, 1996).

The status of homosexuality as a nonsuspect classification historically has had widespread impact closer to home. Specifically, courts cited this categorization, including the depiction of the gay and lesbian lifestyle as somehow removed from the mainstream of American life, as a decisional factor in child custody determinations. In 1995, the Virginia Supreme Court up-held the award of child custody to the child's grandmother on the basis that the natural mother's "active lesbianism" could burden the child living under "such conditions" by reason of the "'social condemnation' attached to such an arrangement" (*Bottoms v. Bottoms*, 1995, p. 108). The *Bottoms* court's out-rageous assessment was augmented even more recently by a federal court's decision upholding the power of states to enact legislation restricting the right of gays to adopt and provide foster care (*Lofton v. Kearney*, 2001).

In the years since the *Bottoms* and *Lofton* decisions, the civil liberties of gay and lesbian persons have received clear and welcome enhancement by a variety of courts (see, e.g., *Baker v. State*, 1999; *Goodridge v. Dep't of Pub. Health*, 2003; In re *Marriage Cases*, 2008; *Kerrigan v. Comm'r of Pub. Health*, 2008; *Varnum v. Brien*, 2009) and even the U.S. Supreme Court itself (*Lawrence v. Texas*, 2003). As already noted, in the aforementioned cases, the supreme courts of Vermont, Massachusetts, California, Connecticut, and Iowa each recognized the substantive due process rights of gay and lesbian persons. Just as important, these courts also acknowledged under the equal protection clause that the class of gay and lesbian persons must have the status of a suspect or quasi-suspect classification, thus using strict scrutiny analysis to bar discrimination against gay and lesbian persons in their right of access to enjoy legally enforced marital rights. Although the U.S. Supreme Court has yet formally to confer suspect status on the classification of gay and lesbian persons, it did, as already noted, recognize gay and lesbian re-lationships as subject to the right of privacy protected by substantive due process. In addition, in *Romer v. Evans* (1996), the Court ruled that a Colo-rado amendment to the state constitution that effectively repealed all legal protections to homosexuals, failed to satisfy strict scrutiny under the equal protection clause. The Court did not, however, classify gays and lesbians as a suspect class. Rather, the Court ruled that gay and lesbian persons had been denied the fundamental right to participate in the political process; there-fore, the Court enforced protections for gays and lesbians that exist under state and local legislation. Finally, the Court has regarded intimate relations between nonmarried persons, including gay and lesbian persons, as within the fundamental right to privacy; therefore, classifications interfering with this right are considered suspect (*Lawrence v. Texas*, 2003). In light of these facts, it is reasonable to expect that the Supreme Court's full expansion of the equal protection clause to include the protection of gay and lesbian per-sons from discrimination is not far off.

With respect to classifications still regarded as nonsuspect, the Supreme Court has displayed a marked unwillingness to expand the coverage of sus-pect and quasi-suspect status to additional vulnerable groups, suggesting that the presence of "negative attitude" and "fear" concerning these persons "alone does not a constitutional violation make" (*Bd. of Trs. of Univ. of Ala. v. Garrett*, 2001, p. 367). With this philosophy strongly in place in the minds of some of the Court's justices, it is unlikely—with the possible exception of the extension of equal protection standing to gay and lesbian persons—that the years to come will witness any expansion of the definition of suspect and quasi-suspect classifications, at least in the absence of a demonstration that a group has experienced systematic historical discrimination having a discernible, immediate impact.

Defining some classifications as nonsuspect may actually support Congress's authority to enact legislation that benefits historically victimized populations. For example, categorizations associated with legislation that advances Native American interests have been regarded as nonsuspect (*Am. Fed'n of Gov't Employees v. United States*, 2003; *Narragansett Indian Tribe v. Nat'l Indian Gaming Comm'n*, 1998). However, unlike other nonsuspect groupings—such as those defined by age, disability, or income level—Native American classifications are recognized as deserving of special recognition, even though they too are technically classified as nonsuspect. The Supreme Court has suggested that Indian classifications must be considered unique from other suspect racial classifications because of the federal government's regulation of tribes, which is "rooted in the unique status of Indians as a 'separate people' with their own political institutions" (*United States v. Antelope*, 1977, p. 646). This may help explain why some laws aiding nonsuspect groups, such as IDEA and ADA, may be subject to challenge, whereas those seeking to advance Indian interests are generally not.

Examples of legislation specifically intended to promote Native American sovereignty include the Indian Child Welfare Act (ICWA) of 1978. This law guarantees the authority of tribes to decide the custody of American Indian children in child welfare cases. The Indian Civil Rights Act of 1968 extends most Bill of Rights and Fourteenth Amendment principles, including equal protection and due process, to Indian tribes. Finally, the Indian Gaming Regulatory Act (IGRA) of 1988 permits and regulates gambling on Indian reservations for the purpose of promoting tribal economic survival and self-determination.

It must be stressed that the nonsuspect classification imposed on Native American profiling applies only to the government's right to enact ameliorative legislation that benefits its legal responsibility toward Indians. It does not give the government a license to enact prejudicial, racially discriminatory legislation; in fact, such legislation would violate the equal protection clause. However, some would argue that the very maintenance of the trust relationship between the federal government and Native American tribes stigmatizes Native Americans by ensuring federal dominance over Indian people and the perennial dependency of tribes.

The refusal of courts to expand the scope of equal protection to other historically disadvantaged groups may result in an increased role for the states in this area. Numerous state legislatures have enacted legal protections defining the rights of various classes of citizens, including those institutionalized in long-term-care facilities, nursing homes, and mental health centers. Almost every state has adopted legislation guaranteeing the right of access of physically disabled persons to public facilities and government employment (see, e.g., Kansas's Special Education for Exceptional Children Act, 2008). An oft-quoted priority of Congress's legislative agenda is the passage of a bill of rights for health-care patients, a law that would guarantee certain protections to HMO consumers, and, in effect, would recognize medical patients as a discrete class of citizens entitled to government protection. Some regard the comprehensive federal health-care bills that President Obama signed into law in March 2010 (the Patient Protection and Affordable Care Act and the Health Care and Education Reconciliation Act) as a step in this direction.

In addition to enacting civil rights legislation, some states and federal territories have amended their own constitutions in an effort to expand the scope of the equal protection clause. Many states, for example, have ratified an equal rights amendment guaranteeing the equality of both genders. Some states have also amended their constitutions to offer a level of protection to public educational access, a point that makes it especially incumbent on certain state governments to avoid classifications interfering with students' school attendance (*Campbell County Sch. Dist. v. State*, 2008; *D. F. v. Codell*, 2003—the *Campbell County School District* and *D. F.* cases recognized education as a fundamental right under the Wyoming and Kentucky state constitutions, respectively). The Commonwealth of Puerto Rico has taken the additional step of ratifying a territorial equal protection clause that forbids classification on the basis of "social origin or condition"; in doing so, Puerto Ricans have declared their intent to prohibit discrimination on account of poverty (*Nieves v. Univ. of P.R.*, 1993). Whether these innovative state constitutional approaches actually have the intended effect of addressing the targeted social problems remains to be seen.

Handling Equal Protection Dilemmas: The Duty to Treat Clients and Coworkers with Equal Protection

The outline of equal protection principles offered here can be applied practically by mental health professionals in their consideration of practice dilemmas. As noted, constitutional law is always undergoing change. One's success using equal protection principles in making practice decisions depends not so much on having an encyclopedic memory of individual case decisions as on the maintenance of a grounded understanding of the meaning of suspect and nonsuspect classifications. In pragmatic terms, this requires that one acquire the ability to recognize a practice dilemma as presenting an equal protection problem. Whenever one faces a decisional conflict involving the classification of a client, coworker, or some other member of the public with whom the professional comes into contact, an equal protection analysis may be helpful in the assessment of the parties' rights. In such situations, the steps that should be observed can be summarized as follows:

1. Identify the person being classified.
2. Identify the right affected by the classification—life, liberty, or property.
3. Identify the type of classification:
   - Suspect and/or quasi-suspect: race, religion, national origin, ethnicity, gender, and classifications that affect fundamental rights (note that sexual orientation also belongs in this category, even though the U.S. Supreme Court has not expressly acknowledged its status as suspect, because the Court has directed that the right to have intimate, gay relationships be protected as a fundamental right).
   - Nonsuspect: all other classifications, including class, income, age, and the use of Native American categorizations to support tribal interests.
4. Identify any state action that might create a suspect or quasi-suspect classification:
   - If the actor is a public agency or an employee of a public agency, the actor's conduct is a state action if it is made possible by specific authority granted under the law and affects the life, liberty, or property right identified previously.
   - If the actor is a private agency that has contracted with the government to provide services to the public, the actor's conduct may be a state action in limited circumstances (see text).
   - If the actor is a private agency providing services independent of the government, there is no state action and the agency alone is responsible for its conduct according to the duty to practice reasonably competently and applicable federal and state legislation.

5. Determine whether the classification is justified:
   - Suspect and/or quasi-suspect classifications must receive strict or heightened scrutiny, must serve a compelling state interest, and must be narrowly tailored to serve a compelling state interest.
   - Nonsuspect classifications must serve a rational government purpose.
6. Identify remedies for violations of equal protection:
   - If the actor is a state agency, section 1983 relief is available.
   - If the actor is a state contractor, section 1983 relief is available only in limited circumstances.
   - If the actor is a private agency, relief is available under applicable civil rights legislation and through civil lawsuits.

To demonstrate the application of these steps in equal protection cases, consider the following scenario: A school of social work affiliated with a public university is revising its admission standards. The committee in charge of this task has decided to recommend that applicants be rated on, among other things, their "narrative statement of personal history and philosophy." Suggested criteria for rating this statement include an assessment of each applicant's "political activism in the pursuit of social justice," "advocacy on behalf of progressive social policies," and "demonstrable commitment to diversity."

Following the steps suggested here, each candidate assessed under the proposed system can readily be identified as a person classified by the school's selection process. There is a property right involved, because access to education fits this definition. The classification may well be suspect, because it rates students on the basis of written expressions that may involve political ideology and preferences that arguably fall within the individual's zone of privacy protected by the Fourteenth Amendment. This freedom involves a fundamental right, which the government ought not to be using as part of its process of selecting students for admission. Alternatively, it could be argued that the school's methodology for rating students requires classification on the basis of speech-related rights protected by the First Amendment.

There is state action in the school's proposed use of the narrative statement as part of its gatekeeping role in determining admission to the social work program. There is probably no compelling interest that justifies this broad request for a statement of personal philosophy; it does not sufficiently confine its area of questioning to issues reasonably related to the school's legitimate interest in seeking the most academically and experientially qualified applicants for a university social work education. If it were more narrowly tailored to assess the specific academic skill levels of prospective applicants without treading on personal political ideology, it is possible the rating criteria could be revised appropriately. If not, applicants denied admission on the basis of their narrative statements might conceivably have the right to file a civil rights action against the state university and its school of social work.

Consider the following additional example: A mental health agency affiliated with an Indian nation wishes to promote the education of its individual care providers. Toward this end, it will finance scholarships for students who enroll in a master's-level counseling program. Successful applicants must be enrolled members of the tribe.

Equal protection analysis of this scenario focuses on the classification of applicants for a scholarship—a potential property right—based on tribal membership. In effect, non-Indian applicants that hold positions in the agency are excluded from eligibility for the scholarship. The government action (recall that Native American tribes are involved in a legal trust relationship with the federal government) limits the right of access of potential non-Native applicants for the scholarship. Under current law, this classification should be regarded as nonsuspect because it supports an affirmative action program that justifiably promotes the interests of tribal members. It is based arguably on a rational motive, namely to promote the training of qualified Native American professional counselors to provide culturally competent services to tribal members.

Legislative Enforcement of Equal Protection Rights

Congress's power to seek compliance with the Fourteenth Amendment stems from section 5, which authorizes it to "enforce, by appropriate legislation" the amendment's protections. Under this authority, Congress and many state governments throughout history have enacted remedial legislation intended to accomplish two objectives: first, to outlaw discrimination against individuals safeguarded by the equal protection clause; second, to equalize access of protected persons to major social institutions, including education and employment.

Congress has approved much legislation protecting members of suspect and quasi-suspect classes from discrimination in public employment, educational access, public housing, and other areas regulated directly by the federal and state governments. The best-known and most comprehensive law in this category remains the Civil Rights Act of 1964. More recently, Congress has enacted legislation, including the ADA and ADEA, that extends federal protection against discrimination to nonsuspect classes, including persons with disabilities and the aged. As noted earlier, laws offering expansive protections to nonsuspect groups frequently have been the focus of successful court challenges based on the argument that Congress has exceeded its authority under the equal protection clause by providing enhanced benefits to a nonsuspect class of people.

Governmental policies creating race-based affirmative action and other measures intended to equalize access to education, employment, public transportation, and housing have all been grounded in the legislative authority granted by the Fourteenth Amendment. However, some courts often have expressed open hostility to these policies, frequently because they purportedly violate the heightened scrutiny standard imposed on suspect classifications. The same courts have also expressed the view that the equal protection clause authorizes Congress solely to forbid present discrimination, not to enact corrective legislation intended to address the lingering effects of past discrimination. Thus, race-based affirmative action measures in public education and employment, together with the awarding of public contracts, have all been invalidated on the basis of this strict interpretation of equal protection.

CIVIL RIGHTS ACT OF 1964

In light of the inconsistent and restrictive analysis of the equal protection clause many courts have adopted, the Civil Rights Act of 1964 remains the major piece of social legislation that private individuals rely on to enforce Fourteenth Amendment protections. The reason for this lies in the act's sweeping, comprehensive coverage outlawing all instances of discrimination based on race, religion, gender, and national origin. In addition, besides restricting the government from engaging in discriminatory practices, the drafters of the act extended its coverage to private agencies and businesses through the authority of the Constitution's commerce clause (article 1, section 8, clause 3), which empowers Congress to regulate private businesses engaged in activities whose impact extends across state boundaries and therefore affects interstate commerce.

Among other protections, the Civil Rights Act of 1964 and its amendments ensure equal access to voting registration procedures (title I), require desegregation of public schools (title V), and mandate equal access to federal assistance programs (title VI).

Additional provisions of the act prohibit discrimination by private organizations and businesses, including educational institutions, public accommodations, transportation systems, and other employers involved in interstate commerce (titles II and VII). For the purposes of the act, a business is involved in interstate commerce if it employs at least fifteen persons.

At the heart of the act lies title VII's extensive prohibition against discrimination in the public and private sectors based on race, religion, and gender. Title VII additionally creates an enforcement mechanism, the Equal Employment Opportunity Commission (EEOC), through which meritorious claims of discrimination by government and private agencies and employers can be addressed through a civil enforcement process.

The EEOC functions as a civil investigatory agency that, upon the filing of a complaint of discrimination, investigates and responds appropriately. If the EEOC finds evidence of prejudicial conduct, it has the authority to respond by initiating a civil lawsuit seeking cessation of the offending behavior and other forms of relief. If the EEOC rejects the complaint on the basis of insufficient evidence or otherwise chooses against further action, the complainant is free to initiate a private lawsuit seeking damages and other remedies for the civil rights violations committed. Such proceedings are often instituted through the authority of section 1983, whose provisions are addressed next.

A variety of U.S. Supreme Court opinions have made it more difficult for aggrieved employees to sue offending employers by interpreting the 1964 act to require proof of an employer's specific intent to discriminate on the basis of race, religion, or gender. Congress has addressed this issue by enacting the Civil Rights Act of 1991, which, among other things, allows employees to prevail in civil rights cases by demonstrating merely that discrimination has played at least some role in the workplace decisions giving rise to the complaint. Thus, the lowered evidentiary requirement enhances the ability of aggrieved employees to demonstrate discriminatory practices by their employers. In addition, the 1991 act restricts the use of quotas and other race-based measures used by public and private employers in the recruitment and selection of prospective employees.

Remedies for Governmental Violations of Constitutional Rights

Because the Constitution is intended primarily to limit the power of the federal and state governments over the people, virtually all constitutional violations occur when the government itself commits them. Consequently, the ability of citizens to challenge governmental agencies directly when they abuse constitutional principles is a critically important safeguard. Toward that end, Congress has created an important enforcement mechanism for persons who have been deprived of their rights under the due process and equal protection clauses, as well as other basic constitutional protections. The most important of these mechanisms, the Civil Rights Act of 1871, creates a means through which persons who have suffered constitutional losses can seek redress from the responsible government agent. It is the subject of the next section.

Section 1983 of the Civil Rights Act of 1871

In enacting the Civil Rights Act of 1871, Congress intended to create a format for persons aggrieved by governmental misconduct—including violations of due process and equal protection—to challenge the wrongdoing in court and seek redress for its consequences (*Crawford-El v. Britton*, 1998). As with the Fourteenth Amendment itself, the 1871 act was originally intended to address Jim Crow legislation adopted in the post–Civil War South targeting African Americans. Just as courts have expanded their interpretation of the Fourteenth Amendment's coverage to include many other persons and groups besides African Americans, so, too, have judicial interpretations of the 1871 act extended its protections to additional victims of government wrongdoing.

The most significant enforcement mechanism under the 1871 act is section 1983, which has become the most used legal tool for the assertion of constitutional rights against the government. Under section 1983, a person may bring a civil lawsuit against the government requesting relief from its misconduct if the following circumstances exist:

- A constitutional violation has occurred.
- The violation has been caused by a "state actor," that is, a person or agency performing a state action or acting under color of law (*Shrum v. Kluck*, 2001).

Lawsuits filed under section 1983, commonly known as civil rights actions, permit aggrieved parties to seek money damages and other forms of relief from courts. Their usefulness lies in the wide latitude they offer judges to fashion appropriate remedies in individual cases.

Note that section 1983 actions are intended to protect persons mainly from the power of the government, and they target individual persons only to the extent that they enforce or violate some government policy (*Crawford-El v. Britton*, 1998). Consequently, lawsuits filed under section 1983 commonly name as defendants the government agencies accountable for misconduct and the individuals, acting in their official capacities, who have facilitated the wrongdoing.

Under section 1983, actions may be brought against several classes of parties. Most important, they may be instituted against the government itself—including federal, state, and public agencies—whenever a law, ordinance, regulation, or agency policy causes a constitutional violation (*Lanigan v. Vill. of E. Hazel Crest*, 1997). Typically, this occurs when government agencies administer or enforce laws enacted by legislatures in a way that results in harm to a member of the public.

As an example of the strategy section 1983 offers to the victims of an unconstitutional law, consider the following scenario: A state child welfare statute provides that parents suspected of child abuse must undergo a mandatory psychological evaluation, even if they are unwilling to consent to it. The requirement is enforced by a child welfare agency, whose administrator appoints individual social workers to perform investigations and provide services to families in crisis. The administrator also relies on additional staff members, including counselors and psychologists, to assess the family for suspected abuse. Because the legislative requirement pertaining to psychological examinations may violate substantive due process—with specific respect to the parents' right of privacy—families who experience emotional or other harm as a result of the forced implementation of the law can challenge it by instituting a section 1983 suit against those responsible for carrying out the mandatory evaluations, such as the agency administrator and staff members. The lawsuit thereby serves as a vehicle for testing the constitutionality of questionable legislation.

As an additional example of the relief offered by section 1983, consider the case of a county sheriff who forcibly removes children from their home when a protective service social worker requests police assistance, on the basis of reports suggesting that the youngsters are endangered by their surroundings. In this situation, the sheriff's assistance is founded on a customary enforcement process that requires police intervention in the transfer of children to the child welfare agency's custody. Assume further that the practice is not required specifically by law or mandated by agency rule; rather, it is based on a regional tradition that some would argue police have been inadequately trained to carry out. The constitutional sufficiency of this policy and its implementation may be challenged in a section 1983 action naming the county and the sheriff, because they are acting under color of law (*Brokaw v. Mercer County*, 2000).

Section 1983 actions of the type described here often seek court rulings finding a law, regulation, or policy to be unconstitutional, together with an order restraining the responsible government agency from enforcing it. In this respect, section 1983 is often useful in identifying unconstitutional laws and policies while insulating from personal responsibility the individual government officials responsible for their implementation, provided that their behavior is limited to their mistaken enforcement of invalid laws or policies, in situations where the individual officials are not aware of the invalidity of these laws and policies. In other instances, as will be examined later, these government officials may well be liable themselves for misconduct for which a remedy is enforceable under section 1983.

Interestingly, state and local legislators responsible for the enactment of invalid or unconstitutional laws are themselves immune from personal liability and cannot ordinarily be sued under section 1983 (*Bogan v. Scott-Harris*, 1998). The reason for the layer of insulation provided to legislators is that public policy supports the concept that elected officials must enjoy the freedom to consider legislative proposals without the undue pressure that would inevitably result from fear of litigation.

The use of section 1983 actions to protect the public from unconstitutional administrative practices can have a profound effect on the manner in which important public services are administered. For example, if a child welfare agency fails to provide adequate supervision of children in its foster care system, thus resulting in deprivation of the children's liberty rights and the denial of substantive due process, the agency can be sued under section 1983 (*Joseph A. v. N.M. Dep't of Human Servs.*, 1983).

Even when laws, regulations, and government policies are not unconstitutional, section 1983 offers a remedy against the wrongful conduct of government employees if the behavior deprives persons of their constitutional rights. This occurs most often when a public servant violates a federal or state law, regulation, or administrative policy or acts in a manner that a reasonable person would understand to violate established constitutional principles (*Lanigan v. Vill. of E. Hazel Crest*, 1997). As an example, a schoolteacher who sexually abuses a student violates the child's constitutional right to privacy and bodily integrity—both liberty-related, fundamental rights protected by substantive due process (*Maldonado v. Josey*, 1992; *Shrum v. Kluck*, 2001). Consequently, the teacher faces liability under section 1983 for these acts.

For government employees to be vulnerable to a lawsuit under section 1983, their conduct must have directly caused injury to a victim through an act committed under color of law. As an example, unprofessional conduct by child welfare agency employees has prompted section 1983 actions in a variety of situations. Among the most notable of these is the case of a social worker who falsely advised the natural mother of a purportedly neglected child that a child welfare agency had obtained permanent custody of the woman's child (*Holloway v. Brush*, 2000). The act was perpetrated in an apparent effort to discourage the mother from contesting the agency's formal action to terminate her parental rights. In another instance of social worker misconduct, several child welfare agency employees used speculation, conjecture, and other false information to obtain a court order permitting forced entry into a foster home to investigate "suspicions" that children were being abused (*Snell v. Tunnell*, 1990). In this case, section 1983 was found to be an appropriate response to the deliberate manufacture of evidence. Similarly, when a child protective service social worker refused to remove the name of a man suspected of child abuse from a central registry, even after an investigation failed to uncover evidence of any child abuse, section 1983 provided appropriate redress for this unconstitutional conduct (*Achterhof v. Selvaggio*, 1989).

Note that, although individual government employees may be liable for damages under section 1983, their agencies are not responsible for personnel misconduct unless supervisors or administrators knowingly permitted or authorized it to occur or otherwise were indifferent to the conduct in a way that "shocks the conscience" (*Shrum v. Kluck*, 2001, pp. 779–780). As an illustration, an adult protective service agency social worker who failed to investigate suspected elder abuse because of personal incompetence might be liable for damages under section 1983. The worker's agency would not also be liable under section 1983 unless the agency's supervisory staff members were aware of the conduct, encouraged or contributed to it in some fashion, or allowed it to continue after it began to occur. This situation occasionally arises in agencies that have inadequate staff or budgetary resources to meet their legal responsibilities to the public. In an era in which curtailment of resources for social programs, including public assistance, education, and health services, is a fact of life, section 1983 actions may remain virtually the only vehicle for arguing the inadequacy of service provision before the courts. In New Mexico alone, section 1983 actions have successfully challenged the unsatisfactory provision of services to children in foster care (*Joseph A. v. N.M. Dep't of Human Servs.*, 1983), state penitentiary inmates (*Duran v. Apodaca*, 1980), and the developmentally disabled (*Jackson v. Fort Stanton Hosp. & Training Sch.*, 1990).

The foregoing examples demonstrate section 1983's continuing use in protecting the public from misconduct by the government and its agencies. Courts have been most reluctant, however, to extend its coverage to occasional acts of misconduct that can best be addressed through simple malpractice actions. In other words, behavior of public employees that violates the duty to practice reasonably competently but does not rise to the level of constitutional deprivation is most appropriately remedied through civil lawsuits, criminal prosecutions, and other remedies available under state and federal laws.

As already discussed, under the public function test, private vendors or contractors and the government itself may be responsible under section 1983 for their actions when they deprive individuals of constitutional rights and privileges (*Wilcher v. City of Akron*, 2007). This happens particularly when the government assumes responsibility jointly with a private contractor to deliver services in a cooperative enterprise. Thus, when the government contracts with private providers to offer long-term health or mental health services and nursing care in public institutions, section 1983 may impose governmental liability for the misconduct of agency employees (*Conner v. Donnelly*, 1994—private physician providing care in government-run prison; *Faulkner v. Johnson County Sheriff's Dep't*, 2001—private minister indoctrinates prisoners at a public prison; *Henry v. Clermont County*, 2005—private physician providing care in government-run prison; *Richardson v. McKnight*, 1997—guards working for privately managed prison; *West v. Atkins*, 1988—private physician providing care in government-administered prison). The most-often-cited rationale for this liability is that, in the case of persons for whom services are provided under duress, the government cannot escape responsibility for the quality of these mandatory services by offering them jointly with a private contractor (*Conner v. Donnelly*, 1994; *Richardson v. McKnight*, 1997; *West v. Atkins*, 1988). Instead, both the contractor and the government are expected to uphold constitutional standards in service delivery. Note, however, that in the case of a private vendor or contractor, the agency will not be liable for any constitutional deprivations caused by its employee unless the agency's official policy, rule, or custom is responsible for the deprivation (*Warren v. Warden*, 2007). In all other circumstances, private agencies are not vicariously responsible under section 1983 for their employees' actions.

As noted previously, section 1983 provides for two main types of relief to claimants who are able to demonstrate constitutional deprivations. First, money damages are available from individual defendants and the government. Second, a judge may issue injunctions when a public agency or employee threatens to continue a pattern of conduct resulting in a constitutional violation. Temporary restraining orders and preliminary injunctions may enjoin government agencies and individuals from enforcing a law, regulation, or policy that violates due process or equal protection. Temporary restraining orders typically are issued only on a showing that a course of conduct, if not halted at once, endangers a person immediately and irreparably.

In addition to the more common forms of relief, courts on occasion have fashioned extraordinary remedies for alleviating the effects of constitutional deprivations when continuing harm threatens a large segment of the population. In the case of *Joseph A. v. New Mexico Department of Human Services* (1983), a federal court in New Mexico approved a consent decree—a judicial order fashioned by the parties and submitted to the court for its approval—mandating the reorganization of foster care and adoption services conducted by the state's child welfare agency. In a decree unprecedented in its breadth, the New Mexico Human Service Department was directed to put in place a comprehensive system for service provision to the many children in state custody. Among other things, the court ordered the department to plan, supervise, and maintain oversight on a sequential timetable of all of the services provided, from first intake to final discharge.

In agreeing to the unusual relief requested by attorneys representing children in the department's foster care system, the *Joseph A.* court found that the department, which was responsible under state law for the investigation and resolution of child abuse cases, had violated substantive due process and equal protection standards. Specifically, the court noted that the department had failed to honor the children's liberty-related, fundamental right to family privacy by neglecting to promulgate regulations ensuring the quality of services provided to children placed in its custody. Among other problems, youngsters in foster care had often been consigned to an unstable life in multiple foster care settings, with insufficient planning by the department either for the reunification of families or for the placement of children in permanent adoptive homes. So inadequate was the department's supervision of these children that in many cases records identifying their whereabouts could not be located. The department lacked an adequate computer system to assist in maintaining records and had insufficient social work staff—particularly in the area of adoption and permanency planning—to satisfy its constitutional obligations to children in its custody. The novel and expansive relief fashioned by the court pursuant to section 1983 required the department to budget sufficiently for the training, hiring, and retention of social workers, and it further mandated the creation and maintenance of a computer system for the ready identification of children and families served statewide.

A roadblock in the assessment of section 1983 liability against government officials is the concept of sovereign immunity. As granted by the Eleventh Amendment to the U.S. Constitution, sovereign immunity insulates the government, its agencies, and employees from liability in the interest of safeguarding the provision of important public services from the threat of ongoing litigation. Congress and state governments often waive immunity when important public considerations warrant suits by members of the public. This happens most often when government employees commit acts of negligence and engage in other forms of tortious conduct. In such cases, federal and state tort claims legislation governs the extent to which the governmental agency and employees may be answerable to the public in court for misconduct. Mental health professionals serving in child welfare, mental health, and other areas of public-sector practice most often find themselves defendants in civil rights cases when they violate the duty to practice reasonably competently and/or the duty to seek informed consent. Alternatively, in some civil rights cases, conflicts of interest created by an agency's organizational structure or its contracting with private providers may create situations that call into question the agency's duty to identify and remain protective of its primary clients.

Constitutional violations present a special ground for the removal of the immunity shield from public officials. When section 1983 actions are founded on a claim that a law or agency regulation is unconstitutional, in most cases, the government agency responsible for enforcing the policy will waive its own immunity to allow a court to evaluate the legitimacy of the law or rule in question. More routinely, however, section 1983 claims are founded on an accusation of wrongdoing by a public agency and its employees resulting from their failure to comply with constitutional or other legal standards. In such circumstances, the doctrine of qualified immunity often shields agency officials from personal liability for damages under section 1983. With qualified immunity, these individuals will ordinarily be protected from liability if they have reasonably believed that their conduct has been lawful and constitutional according to established standards (*Mabe v. San Bernardino County Dep't of Soc. Servs.*, 2001).

To demonstrate the application of qualified immunity, consider the following dilemma: A child welfare agency in Concord, New Hampshire, receives a phone report from a public school teacher that a child has come to school with several bruises and a badly swollen arm. The agency's follow-up investigation results in the child's placement in protective custody by a social worker and police officer. Assume further that the teacher has failed to advise the social worker and police officer that the child frequently presents disciplinary problems, has been suspended in the past for fighting in the schoolyard, and was disciplined for fighting before school on the morning of the teacher's phone referral.

A brief review of the law governing this scenario lends context to the significant constitutional issues involved. In most if not all states, legislation requires the reporting of suspected child abuse by mental health professionals, medical personnel, teachers, and other providers. (In some states, including New Hampshire, this burden actually is placed additionally on every member of the public; see N.H. Rev. Stat. Ann. § 169-C:29, 2009.) Moreover, laws in every state, including New Hampshire, require that child welfare agencies investigate instances of suspected child abuse. The same legislation usually requires that these agencies place into protective custody— often under the direction of police—children reasonably suspected of being abused or neglected. Note also that due process protects the right of parents to maintain custody of their children unless an emergency—such as the threat of child abuse—justifies immediate action by the state.

If the social worker and police officer in this example place the child in protective custody under a reasonable but mistaken assumption that the youngster may have been abused, they both probably enjoy qualified immunity from any claim of wrongdoing (*Mabe v. San Bernardino County Dep't of Soc. Servs.*, 2001). The teacher most probably would not similarly be protected, because a public employee's failure to share important contextual information violates clear legal responsibilities connected with the reporting of suspected child abuse. For this reason, the teacher might well be subject to section 1983 liability in the event the child's parents seek redress for the violation of their civil rights.

As an alternative example, suppose that a child protective service social worker coerces a parent to allow her to examine a child for signs of physical abuse without any reasonable, prior suspicion that abuse has occurred. This is an extreme but not unheard-of example of the overzealous investigation of suspected child abuse by a state employee. In this scenario, the social worker knowingly violates state law and therefore would not be entitled to immunity for any resulting section 1983 action (*Mabe v. San Bernardino County Dep't of Soc. Servs.*, 2001).

Most elected officials and political appointees enjoy a much greater degree of protection from liability for damages under section 1983 than do other government employees. Under the doctrine of absolute immunity, these individuals provide particularly important public services connected with the creation and enforcement of public policy and therefore are shielded completely from the threat of civil rights lawsuits. As an example, legislators enjoy absolute immunity for their lawmaking activities. In addition, judges, prosecutors, and children's court attorneys acting in a quasi-judicial role enjoy the same immunity. A quasi-judicial role refers to the assistance that judges, prosecutors, and children's court attorneys provide to courts in abuse, neglect, and other child welfare cases. This includes helping in the preparation and filing of petitions requesting court orders, making recommendations to the court on child custody, and presenting testimony in judicial proceedings (*Ernst v. Child and Youth Servs.*, 1997).

Using Due Process and Equal Protection to Make Professional Decisions: Case Examples

The case examples that follow offer an overview of diverse, everyday mental health scenarios that raise significant constitutional problems. They are

offered with the aim of demonstrating the usefulness of applying constitutional analysis in making professional decisions. For this purpose, the
outlines for identifying and addressing due process and equal protection
dilemmas presented earlier in this chapter are helpful in sorting out each of
the constitutional issues presented in the case examples.

Case Example 15: Due Process and the Problem Student

Phillip Shoyo is a freshman at a public high school in Casper, Wyoming.
He and his family, members of the Eastern Shoshone tribe, have relocated
recently from Fort Washakie, on the Wind River Indian Reservation, so that
his mother could find work as a secretary. An average student, Phillip has
found himself in trouble at school repeatedly since the beginning of the academic year. Frequently involved in fights, Phillip's most recent altercation
resulted in another student sustaining a fractured rib. Phillip faces several
alternative disciplinary measures; these are to be considered during a conference involving Elizabeth Ray, the school principal, and Tom Muti, the
school guidance counselor. Elizabeth favors expulsion. Tom favors Phillip's
referral to an in-school suspension (ISS) program, which is a disciplinary
method that ordinarily combines a traditional deterrent intervention with
a preventative approach intended to address the root causes of students'
behavioral problems (Haley & Watson, 2000; Sheets, 1996).

Typically, ISS programs require participating students to be removed
from their regular classes to take part in counseling and remedial courses
that emphasize learning fundamentals, including the improvement of reading and writing skills. The ISS program presently in place at Phillip's school
can be charitably referred to as a work in progress. Neither the funding nor
the staff has been available to provide extensive personal counseling, so
the program functions mainly to remove "problem" students such as Phillip from their classes. Nevertheless, the program does offer students individual attention with their schoolwork, and Tom regards the one-on-one
approach as a means to reach students on a personal level, even if it centers
on academic assistance rather than personal counseling. As far as Tom is
concerned, ISS is a step in the right direction. Phillip's suspension will no
doubt result in a delay in his fulfillment of core academic requirements, and
he is unlikely to graduate with his peers.

Elizabeth's and Tom's consideration of Phillip's discipline benefits from
a thorough review of due process principles. The decision makers must assess the nature of any life, liberty, or property right that may be affected by
their decision and must identify whether any such right is fundamental.
With respect to education, Phillip plainly has a property right. In addition,

as noted earlier, Wyoming is one of the states that has supplemented basic rights recognized in the U.S. Constitution by guaranteeing access to public education in its state constitution (*Campbell County Sch. Dist. v. State*, 2008). The *Campbell County School District* case acknowledged that the effect of guaranteeing the right to public education is to elevate education to a fundamental right in Wyoming, thus placing on state agencies the burden of demonstrating a compelling interest when they undertake to limit educational access in some way (*Davis v. Monroe County Bd. of Educ.*, 1999; *Phillip Leon M. v. Greenbrier County Bd. of Educ.*, 1996).

The fact that Phillip's right to attend school should be considered fundamental in this case has important significance for the decision makers in the scenario. For one thing, it suggests that they cannot deprive Phillip of an education and that they must be prepared to offer him essentially the same services they offer to all other students (*Phillip Leon M. v. Greenbrier County Bd. of Educ.*, 1996). This issue places a special burden on those considering student discipline; specifically, it presents a powerful constitutional argument in favor of an appropriately designed ISS program.

When school administrators contemplate the creation of ISS programs, they often face the sobering reality of a limited budget and insufficient support personnel. This lack of resources may result in an ISS program that serves mainly to remove a troublesome student like Phillip from the class environment he is believed to be disrupting; when this happens, as in the present scenario, the emphasis is more on punishment than on alternative education and counseling or other therapeutic services. The constitutional principles already discussed suggest that this design may well violate Phillip's substantive due process right to an education. Moreover, a hastily structured ISS program that relegates counseling to an afterthought may give insufficient attention to the cultural relevance of the intervention (Morris & Howard, 2003; Sheldon & Epstein, 2002). In Phillip's case, his family's move from the Wind River Reservation may be affecting his behavior in class, and a failure to address this point thus threatens the competence of the intervention. It is interesting to note here that research has revealed that minority students are often overrepresented in the number of students suspended from public schools nationally, which suggests perhaps that they may be targeted as "problem" children more swiftly than others (Eitle & Eitle, 2004).

With the preceding thoughts in mind, Tom may be in a position to advocate for the implementation of an ISS program that offers an alternative educational approach. As an example, Sheldon and Epstein (2002) suggest the usefulness of an ISS model that combines individualized and therapeutic approaches. In their model, the academic component of the ISS program should include personalized education designed in cooperation with the classroom teacher, whereas the therapeutic component requires the ISS teacher to focus on the student's self-image, communication issues, problem-solving skills, and more intensive counseling for students whose life stories suggest the need for it.

Note also the potential problems in this scenario that the Individuals with Disabilities Education Act (IDEA) raises. If Phillip has a diagnosable educational disability connected with his acting out, then his isolation from other students may deprive him of his right to be mainstreamed with his peers. Yet implementation of the ISS approach with Phillip would directly lead to his segregation from other students. This deprivation may rise to constitutional proportions as an interference with liberty rights under the Fourteenth Amendment. Given this reality, it is appropriate to reconsider case example 14, "The School Social Worker," in light of the constitutional analysis presented here.

Phillip's dilemma introduces an important point regarding the usefulness of state constitutions in creating fundamental rights governing areas in which the U.S. Constitution fails to offer clear guidance. It also suggests the need for mental health professionals to be acquainted with state constitutional protections and U.S. constitutional principles. Specifically, to perform completely the due process and equal protection analyses presented in this chapter, decision makers must understand and apply not only fundamental rights created under the U.S. Constitution but also supplemental privileges conferred by the constitutions of states in which they practice.

Case Example 16: "Counseling Out" Wanda Moreno

Dr. Dolores Hickey teaches psychology at a public university in Amherst, Massachusetts. At a monthly faculty meeting with her colleagues, she "staffs" students, which means that she identifies those who appear to be having major academic issues, personal problems interfering with their educational progress, or other difficulties. Dolores, a licensed clinical psychologist, has much experience in the diagnosis and treatment of mental disorders and brings this knowledge to her classroom interactions with students. Her classes tend to be hand-on, with students encouraged to achieve self-awareness by sharing personal issues with the class. She regards this classroom exercise as an important aspect of the use of reflective insight in psychology, a task some professional educators encourage.

At the most recent student staffing, Dolores discusses Wanda Moreno, a second-year master's student and the daughter of Puerto Rican immigrants. Wanda, according to Dolores's description, is a C student and has looked "overwhelmed" in class for the last four weeks. She sits silently, never participating in class discussions, and she looks "withdrawn and depressed." Although her class papers have been submitted on time, they are sparsely written and lack self-disclosure, a specific requirement described in the course syllabus. Wanda has declined all of Dolores's requests for a meeting to discuss these observations, and Dolores seriously questions Wanda's emotional maturity and appropriateness for psychology practice. She seeks her colleagues' advice on whether Wanda should be "counseled out," a process by which university faculty and administrators deliver a strong, personal recommendation to a student to withdraw voluntarily from their degree program.

This scenario represents a classic and unfortunate example of a threatened interference with fundamental constitutional rights by a state actor under color of law. The fundamental rights involved here concern Wanda's personal privacy and self-expression, both liberty-related privileges recognized under the First and Fourteenth amendments. Wanda's personality, her manner of personal expression, and her attitude toward Dolores are her own business until such time as the state actors—university faculty members and administrators—can present a compelling reason for interfering with them. A compelling reason here would need to be grounded in the university's important public responsibilities, which include the training of competent psychologists and the maintenance of an orderly and safe classroom environment in which to perform that task. In the absence of any showing that Wanda's behavior either violates the university's academic standards or interferes with classroom decorum or the rights of other students and faculty members, no compelling reason exists to address Wanda's behavior. Even assuming that Wanda's behavior suggests clinical issues—a conclusion that is as yet highly suspect—the evaluation that Dolores appears to be offering is not reasonably related to her role as a psychology educator. Rather, it threatens to use the power differential between professor and student to impose clinical assessment and "treatment" on an involuntary client. In this respect, the scenario raises clear informed-consent issues. In constitutional terms, Wanda has a liberty-related right to remain free from arbitrary counseling.

This case example can be understood alternatively as an equal protection dilemma. The school's counseling out of Wanda—the state action performed by Dolores and her colleagues—can be regarded as a classification based on Wanda's fundamental right to privacy and self-expression, as discussed earlier.

The foregoing constitutional review of Wanda's case is not intended to suggest that a student's communication can never be interfered with or classified by a public university. The grading of examinations and papers is one such example of a classification. In contrast to the categorization attempted by Dolores in this case example, however, grading is reasonably related to the university's essential purpose and uses uniform standards that keep students more or less on an equal footing. Students' performance in field practicum and clinical training placements may also require faculty evaluations that grade students on the basis of their communications with clients and coworkers. Here again, however, such evaluations must be narrowly tailored to serve the limited purpose of evaluating student competence objectively in specific tasks.

The use of due process and equal protection analysis was described earlier as a means of promoting diversity. The present case example offers a compelling demonstration of this point. In cross-cultural professional relationships, diverse communication styles may sometimes be inappropriately labeled as a failure—often by a minority student—to conform to expectations. By strongly discouraging this type of labeling, the duty to treat clients with due process and equal protection offers specific protections to all recipients of government services, including students. Moreover, recognizing the applicability of due process and equal protection can help discourage the use of speech-based classifications as a proxy for more odious categorizations, such as those based on race and ethnicity.

The present case example also raises interesting procedural due process concerns. In the scenario, Wanda plainly has a property right associated with her education. It cannot be regarded as fundamental, because no constitutional protections—either federal or state—have yet recognized the right to an advanced professional education. Wanda's property right is protected, however, by procedural due process. In her situation, the counseling-out process may be used—either intentionally or not—as an informal, less confrontational form of gatekeeping (i.e., the process of determining the eligibility of entrants into, in this case, the mental health professions). When it is practiced in the manner described in the present case example, it serves to eliminate the procedural rights that a public university student should have, including notice of the reasons justifying formal disciplinary action and an opportunity for a hearing. The faculty's "request" to a student that she withdraw from classes under the circumstances presented is not much different from a police officer's "request" to enter the home of a person having a loud party. Both requests take advantage of a position of authority, and both may be intended to accomplish a specific end without formal process.

Wanda's dilemma offers vital guidance to decision makers considering the impact of constitutional protections on practice problems. As the case example suggests, mastery of the principles underlying due process and equal protection offers decision makers practical assistance in the consideration of critical, cross-cultural practice dilemmas. Moreover, Wanda's case demonstrates that a client's right to life, liberty, and property has concrete implications in all elements of mental health practice.

Case Example 17: The Reprimand

Carlita Maxwell, a social worker at a state adult protective services office in Brownsville, Texas, has a caseload of forty clients. She is required to investigate and assess instances of suspected elder abuse in Cameron County, Texas. As part of her employment responsibilities, she must prepare case notes, maintain client records, perform intakes and assessments, and design treatment plans. A capable verbal communicator, she has good rapport with staff and clients alike. Carlita has worked at the office for three years and has permanent status as a state employee. Permanency in this context means a type of tenure offered after a probationary period in the state employment system. It gives employees such as Carlita a vested interest in continued employment.

Carlita unfortunately is not used to the copious record keeping required in state government. An internal audit has revealed Carlita's failure to use appropriate administrative forms and to include comprehensive case notes in client files. Her supervisor, Abe Chen, has verbally admonished her for this conduct on two previous occasions, and on the basis of the internal audit, Abe has now issued a written reprimand that he has directed be included in Carlita's permanent personnel file. Carlita, upset, has fired off a letter to Abe complaining that the letter is unfair, unfounded, and will surely "have an impact on my ability to get promoted in the future." What is more, she complains, it has been issued without prior warning and without an opportunity for her to address whatever "minor paperwork issues" were the object of the reprimand. As Carlita puts it, "The long-term damage to me will be much worse than the trivial things you're accusing me of." Therefore, Carlita makes it known that she intends to file a grievance in response to the issuance of the reprimand.

Although department policies and procedures must guide Abe in his issuance of a written reprimand, the actions he takes should also be based on a review of due process concepts. If Abe surveys the due process principles discussed here, he should conclude that there are no substantive or even procedural due process issues implicated in this scenario. Carlita does have a property right connected with her job; however, this entitlement is not a fundamental right. Moreover, the reprimand does not directly threaten her right to continued employment. The fact that the reprimand may affect Carlita's future ability to get promoted or hired by another agency is simply too tenuous a connection to suggest any property deprivation. Furthermore, Carlita has no liberty-based right to be free from discipline, including written reprimands (see, e.g., *Haynie v. Bass*, 1990; *Paul v. Davis*, 1976; *Stanton v. City of W. Sacramento*, 1991). Consistent with the deference to agency administrators that is necessary for effective and efficient agency practice, Abe's responsibilities to Carlita in connection with the issuance of the reprimand are minimal and certainly do not rise to the level of providing Carlita with advance notice and an opportunity for a hearing.

An additional note about the property rights of government employees and clients is appropriate here: as has already been demonstrated, a prospective "right" associated with one's employment must attain some threshold level of significance before it will be considered to be a valid property interest subject to procedural due process protections. In the case of government employment, this usually means some deprivation of pay and benefits (*Stanton v. City of W. Sacramento*, 1991). Thus, when a public employee faces demotion, suspension without pay, or dismissal, the impending losses call for the provision of notice and an opportunity for a hearing. As already noted, this right does not extend to all employees but only to personnel whose permanent or tenured status in a public agency allows them to assume a reasonable expectation of continuing employment.

The foregoing analysis of property rights also has application in case example 16, "'Counseling Out' Wanda Moreno." Specifically, consistent with procedural due process principles, Wanda's property interest in graduate education is not affected until such time as the university takes some action to significantly impair it. Were faculty members merely to give Wanda verbal or written expressions of their concerns, these measures would not rise to a level of interference with her property right sufficient to allow her procedural protections. Indeed, anything short of suspension or expulsion would not invoke protections afforded to property rights under due process principles (*Goss v. Lopez*, 1975). It is for this very reason that counseling out could be seen to represent a way to attain an objective—Wanda's dismissal—without any procedural safeguards.

Case Example 18: The Job Announcement

The Brighton Beach section of Brooklyn, New York, has seen waves of Russian Jewish immigration since the 1970s. It is estimated that there are now more than three hundred thousand Russian-speaking Jews residing in New York City. Many of these recent immigrants continue to live at or below the poverty line and remain isolated and in desperate need of health and human services ("Jewish poverty," 2003). In response to this situation, regional social service agencies have attempted to meet the human, health, and mental health needs of this population. The Human Resources Administration of New York City's Department of Social Services has recently opened a new field office in Brighton Beach that offers a gamut of services, including cash assistance, food stamps, and public health insurance, among other programs. The field office is hiring mental health professionals to provide a variety of services to the Brighton Beach community. The posted employment notice for one such position advertises that there will be a hiring preference in favor of applicants who "are bicultural and bilingual and have a special commitment to provide quality service to the Russian immigrant population." The ostensible reason for these requirements is that the successful applicant is to perform intake services to a largely unacculturated client base. Rosalie Shapiro, the agency's deputy administrator, has received a complaint from a job applicant who feels that she has not received an invitation to interview for the position because she is not Russian Jewish, and as her resume indicates, she has only a working knowledge of Russian. On the basis of the complaint, Rosalie has decided to take a fresh look at the job announcement, which apparently had been reviewed and approved by the agency's equal opportunity officer. She is prepared to bring her knowledge of the Fourteenth Amendment, together with state and local laws pertaining to equal employment, to her reexamination of the job notice.

Rosalie's review of the job announcement should include a careful equal protection analysis. First, she must assess whether any persons are being classified improperly and, if so, whether that classification is affecting any constitutional right. Rosalie should quickly decide that a job posting for a state position foresees the agency's intent to classify prospective applicants on the basis of their language skills and ethnicity, among other factors. Moreover, applicants who seek the position should be understood to have a potential property interest in a state job.

In this scenario, the state action—the hiring process that will result in the acceptance of one applicant and the rejection of many others—is in part based on applicants' language and ethnic qualifications. Rosalie can safely decide that at least one of the two criteria under review—bicultural status—appears to point to a preference for persons of Russian Jewish heritage and therefore may represent a suspect classification of applicants. Applying her duty to treat clients with equal protection, Rosalie must identify a compelling reason for this classification. She may point to community need, which she might initially surmise is addressed by the hiring of a person who has familiarity with the ethnic customs of the region.

As to the second criterion Rosalie considers during her equal protection review—applicants' bilingual ability—one could conclude that the agency's performance of its legal responsibilities to the public in part depends on its ability to communicate with clients, a fact that makes this performance-related criterion necessary and appropriate. However, a court is likely to interpret the addressing of this need by rating job applicants on the basis of an additional ethnic preference as an overbroad classification in the sense that it assumes cultural identification is necessary for competent communication. Given the present reluctance of courts to embrace any suspect classification, especially one based on race or ethnicity, this one is unlikely to survive a section 1983 action. In contrast, the second criterion, which bases qualification for the position on bilingual ability, appears to address the same need for communication ability in a manner that is more narrowly tailored to the agency's purposes. Moreover, it is skill based, as opposed to identity based, and does not necessarily suggest a racial or ethnic preference. Viewed in this light, it is a less suspect classification—perhaps a nonsuspect one—and can be rationalized on the basis of client and community need. Indeed, the agency cannot be expected to provide reasonably competent services to its clients and to seek informed consent from them without a sufficient number of bilingual staff members. On the basis of this consideration, Rosalie may wish to rephrase the position announcement in a way that satisfies the letter and spirit of equal protection.

Case Example 19: The Consent Decree

Monica Freeman faces the loss of her children. A member of the small African American community of Berry, a town of fewer than 1,500 people in Fayette County, Alabama, her children attend a local elementary school. On the basis of a school guidance counselor's report to the county office of the child protective service department (CPS) in Fayette County, Monica's two children, eight-year-old Felicity and six-year-old Antonia have been placed in protective custody. Both children had reported to their guidance counselor that Monica's live-in boyfriend, Tony Boyd, had physically abused them. Although Tony is not the children's father, he has resided with Monica for five years, and according to Monica, he has developed a close and loving relationship with the children. Upon receiving the report from the guidance counselor, police officers, with the assistance of Rita Constant, a CPS social worker, brought both children to a "safe house" where a trained clinical specialist interviewed and evaluated the youngsters. On the basis of the safe-house interview, the children were then placed in protective custody, whereupon Rita, in accordance with her legal responsibility, notified Monica immediately.

The CPS has obtained temporary custody of the children, and the agency has begun the process of investigating the case in preparation for an adjudicatory hearing. The adjudicatory hearing is the trial stage of a child abuse proceeding, during which a children's court judge will consider evidence presented by a children's court attorney, representing CPS, demonstrating that the youngsters have been abused and remain in danger because of Monica's relationship with Tony. The evidence presented will also suggest that, because Monica has failed to protect the children from abuse, their best interests warrant a change in custody to CPS. The evidence will include teachers' statements, the safe-house interview, and forensic evidence demonstrating that the children were physically abused. In addition, the judge will review videotaped interviews of the children. The judge's decision will include a factual finding as to whether the abuse actually occurred and a disposition as to the children's custody.

Monica, together with her court-appointed attorney, has taken part in interviews with Rita. During these discussions, Monica has expressed shock and disbelief at the allegations involving Tony. Rita sympathizes with Monica, although the social worker also believes that Monica's position regarding her boyfriend is naive and dangerous to the children's best interests. Aware of the fact that Monica was not directly responsible for the abuse apparently inflicted on the children, Rita, her supervisors, and the children's court attorney would like to devise an outcome that would ensure the children's safety, minimize the trauma to the children of protracted legal proceedings, avoid a costly adjudicatory hearing, and allow an opportunity for the children to remain with their mother. Toward that end, Rita and the children's court attorney propose a consent decree. In the consent decree, Monica would admit that her children have been abused and that they require protection. Supervised custody of the children would remain with Monica under certain strict conditions.

Key conditions that Rita wants in the consent decree are that Monica leave her residence, not reside with Tony, not have contact with Tony, and not allow any interaction between Tony and the children. Should she agree to these terms, the proposed consent decree would be submitted to the children's court judge for approval. During her initial discussions with Rita and the children's court attorney, Monica has expressed some consternation that "Tony's rights" are being ignored in the ongoing negotiations. She is also hesitant to agree to a consent decree because it would remove her opportunity for "a fair day in court."

Rita, the children's court attorney, and the guardian *ad litem* appointed on behalf of the children must make choices with respect to the contents of the proposed consent decree; these are driven largely by constitutional considerations. Indeed, substantive and procedural due process are the operative issues in the analysis of Monica's and Tony's rights. The removal of Monica's children represents a state action that affects her liberty-related right to family privacy. In this case, the protective service department's commencement of a court action has been initiated with the children's court attorney's assertion that Monica has allowed the children to be endangered by permitting Tony to reside with the children. Should she wish to contest the department's petition and refuse the offer of a consent decree, Monica and her attorney might attempt to demonstrate at the adjudicatory hearing that the allegations regarding Tony's violent conduct are untrue and that even if they were true, the incidents of physical abuse were so limited that Monica herself had not been aware of her boyfriend's conduct.

Assume, in contrast, that Monica decides to accept CPS's offer of a consent decree, together with the provision that she terminate her relationship with Tony. If she does so, Monica loses the right to contest any of CPS's allegations in a court hearing and simply concedes that CPS's claims are true. Can the judge approve CPS's request to limit Monica's freedom to have a continuing relationship with Tony? Plainly, CPS has a compelling interest in protecting the children, and this concern supersedes Monica's fundamental right to family privacy. At the same time, however, CPS wishes to impose the consent decree's conditions on Monica without granting her the opportunity to respond to the accusation that the relationship with Tony threatens her children. Is this a denial of procedural due process? Probably not—procedural due process guarantees the right to only an opportunity for a hearing; it does not mean that the hearing must take place if Monica waives her right to it. This would be the case if she agrees to the consent decree, has a good reason for waiving her right to a hearing, and is willing to assert that she agrees with the factual allegations of CPS. In Monica's situation, she would still have the right to be heard at an adjudicatory hearing if she does not consent to CPS's offer to settle the case.

Note that Monica must enter into the consent decree with her informed approval, which means that she must understand the risks and benefits it provides. Her own attorney is the professional primarily charged with explaining this information, although Rita and the children's court attorney also have the responsibility of communicating fully with Monica concerning her expectations surrounding the consent decree. A full explanation of the supportive family services CPS has to offer must supplement this discussion. Unless Monica first attains an informed understanding of the consent decree's potential impact on her, she cannot approve it. Moreover, if Monica were to sign a consent decree without understanding it, the resulting cancellation of the adjudicatory hearing would violate her right to procedural due process.

What about the impact of CPS's proposed consent decree on Monica's relationship with Tony? The decree may be overbroad in the sense that it places a permanent restriction on Monica's personal relationship with Tony rather than being more narrowly limited to measures tailored to ensure the protection of the children. In this respect, it may violate Monica's fundamental right to personal privacy, despite the apparently reasonable grounds that seem to justify it. Moreover, the consent decree may be culturally biased in that it seems to assume the illegitimacy of Monica's relationship with Tony. That is, if Monica and Tony were legally married, Tony's right to maintain a permanent, marital relationship would be apparent. Rather, by denying Tony any role in this "family" proceeding, the department's position in effect signals a preference for the traditional marital relationship. This may well violate the couple's substantive due process rights, which protect the privilege of unmarried couples to enjoy a private relationship free from government interference (*Lawrence v. Texas*, 2003). It would also suggest that the department has completely failed to offer clinical services to Tony that might address his pattern of physical violence and encourage the possibility that this family could ultimately remain intact. Therefore, even if Monica were to voluntarily agree to the consent decree's provisions, a court thoroughly familiar with substantive due process standards might be unwilling to allow Monica to waive these rights.

The importance of recognizing Monica's and Tony's substantive due process rights in this case example is not limited to the protection of unmarried partners and alternative family relationships. Placing restrictions on Monica's relationship with Tony is not far removed from placing other, equally onerous provisions on her. Imagine, for example, that the consent decree were to require Monica to hold a full-time job, get married, avoid extramarital sexual relationships, or refrain from the procreation of children. Here, the imposition of CPS's value system on Monica's personal life would become even more obvious and even less reasonably related to her children's welfare. For this reason, the protections substantive due process offers are real and tangible in this case example.

A few additional words should be shared about Monica's procedural due process rights in the event she declines the offer of a consent decree and elects to contest the child custody case in court. As already suggested, should Monica be unable to reach an agreement with CPS concerning the consent decree, she is entitled to an adjudicatory hearing, a process that bears much resemblance to the more formal trial usually reserved for civil and criminal proceedings. At the adjudicatory hearing, Monica has the right to appear before a judge charged with the responsibility of deciding an important factual issue: whether the children have been abused or neglected as defined by law.

At this hearing, some but not all of the constitutional protections afforded to criminal defendants would be present; according to procedural due process principles, the extent of Monica's due process protection depends on a consideration of the state's interest in the case and the extent of the deprivation Monica faces. For example, Monica would be entitled to hear and respond to evidence suggesting that the children have been abused; this includes an opportunity to confront and cross-examine witnesses who claim that the children have been harmed. A judge would make the factual determination of whether the children have been abused or neglected; Monica does not have the constitutional right to a jury trial. Evidentiary rules would require the omission of hearsay, unless the judge were to find a compelling reason for admitting it. If the children's testimony were to be offered, given the age of the children, this would most likely occur before the trial, at which time safe-house procedures would likely be used to interview and videotape the children's statements; the judge is likely to review any such recording at the time of the adjudicatory hearing. This presents a problem for Monica as her attorney would likely not have the opportunity to question or cross-examine the children.

All of the rules associated with procedural due process in this scenario are consistent with the aim of protecting Monica's right to procedural fairness while protecting the children from being retraumatized by reason of the stress of the court proceeding. Note that these rules are not as extensive as those applied in criminal cases, because Monica's deprivation—the loss of custody of her children—is not considered as severe or as invasive as the loss of her own liberty through incarceration. To the contrary, one could make a reasonable argument that Monica's deprivation is every bit as invasive as her incarceration, yet no court or legislature has formally recognized the merits of this argument.

Finally, it is important to stress that the children's court proceeding initiated by Rita and the children's court attorney is intended solely to determine whether the children are abused and should have their custody transferred to the state. The children's court proceeding, however, is not a criminal case—it is not intended to identify the perpetrator(s) and apply punishment for any misconduct. The behavior giving rise to the child abuse proceeding in this case example might also result in the institution of another court proceeding: the criminal prosecution of Tony and possibly Monica for the physical abuse of the children and Monica's neglect in failing to protect them. If this were to occur, the guilt or innocence of the criminal defendants would be established in a formal trial held separately from the children's court proceeding. During the criminal trial, more extensive procedural protections would be available to the defendants, including the right to a jury and a heightened evidentiary standard (i.e., beyond a reasonable doubt).

Case Example 20: The Forest Fire Revisited

Case example 5, "The Forest Fire," presented the case of Peter Baca, a San Ildefonso Pueblo member suffering the long-term and possibly chronic after effects of the Cerro Grande fire, which devastated lands in several New Mexico counties in 2000. As reported by the national media, the forest fire was the result of a controlled burn started by the staff at Bandelier National Monument as part of a forest management program intended to reduce the possibility of forest fires through the clearance of highly flammable brush on federal lands. The fire became out of control apparently as the result of unpredictably high winds, a problem that incomplete communication about weather conditions between Bandelier and the National Weather Service may have exacerbated. The fire destroyed both public and privately owned property, and displaced hundreds of families and businesses.

Admitting the federal government's responsibility for the fire and its results, Congress enacted legislation, the Cerro Grande Fire Assistance Act (CGFAA) of 2000, to provide compensation for those who suffered damages as the result of the fire. Eligibility for benefits depended on the filing of an application with the Office of Cerro Grande Fire Claims, a bureau organized under the Federal Emergency Management Agency (FEMA). Information concerning eligibility requirements was published in local newspapers and mailed to residents with home addresses in the vicinity. In addition, benefit claim forms were mailed to residents of Los Alamos County, which bore the brunt of the real and personal property losses, including many family residences.

As noted in case example 5, Peter resides at San Ildefonso Pueblo and commutes approximately eighteen miles to his job at the Los Alamos National Laboratory. Peter's symptoms are similar to those reported by other persons who lived through and were evacuated from the fire. Indeed, many of these symptoms related to mental health did not emerge until years after the disaster occurred.

As with all natural disasters, the fire's long-term effects may have been unpredictable at the time of the disaster and might now and in the future be experienced most acutely by the poor, elderly, and those lacking the resources to support themselves without government intervention. However, the government regulations promulgated shortly after the fire in connection with claims administration focused on the documentation of losses relating to land and business. A time limit was imposed on the filing of claims, and documentation requirements were mandated for those filing requests for compensation.

As already noted, Peter's symptoms emerged many years after the fire occurred. Peter currently is bearing part of the burden of the costs for his treatment with his psychotherapist, Noel Patrick. Peter's health insurance benefits cover only some of the expenses of therapy and pay merely for a limited number of sessions. Noel's position as Peter's psychotherapist does not render him qualified to offer legal advice to Peter concerning any right to compensation from the government. However, Noel's understanding of constitutional principles may assist Peter in directing him to a source for funding his continued treatment, thereby allowing the provision of sufficient services to meet Peter's mental health needs. Noel may ultimately advise Peter to seek an attorney's services. Moreover, Noel's awareness of constitutional standards may place him in a unique position to advocate actively on behalf of other clients who find themselves situated similarly to Peter. This type of client advocacy is consistent with the ethical aspirations of the mental health professions.

In light of the preceding discussion concerning the importance of client advocacy, it is important to identify the specific constitutional problems that have contributed to Peter's inability to fully fund his mental health care. In the present case example, Noel's application of due process standards may aid his advocacy on Peter's behalf. Specifically, Noel's due process analysis should lead him to the following conclusions: Although the property interests of home and business owners have been the most immediately affected by the fire, Peter and others who lived through the disaster have suffered health damage. The cost of mental health services has a measureable economic value and is directly attributable to the fire; therefore, Peter has experienced a property loss stemming directly from the blaze. Furthermore, there is a reasonable likelihood that psychotherapy has been made necessary as a result of Bandelier's policy decision to initiate the controlled burn; in this sense, it clearly committed a government action. Also, Congress's enactment of the CGFAA compensation package represents an additional government action because the law defines both the level of compensation and the procedures that must be followed to obtain financial relief. Yet the emergence of Peter's condition has not occurred for three years following the blaze, a fact that surely influences his right to seek compensation from the government. As the legislation offering financial relief has placed a strict time limit on the reporting of claims, Peter most likely has missed the statutory window of opportunity to make a claim. Indeed, the CGFAA provides that claims must have been filed within two years after administrative regulations were adopted for the processing of claims. Because the delayed emergence of mental health symptoms should have been foreseeable, procedural due process suggests that the enforcement of a time limit on claims eligibility is unfair and unreasonable under the circumstances. It is plainly true that, in enacting its compensation legislation, the government has failed to take into consideration the long-term effects of the fire. If Peter is to challenge his ineligibility for damages, he will surely need Noel's assistance to document the characteristics of Peter's condition and their delayed emergence.

Procedural due process also requires that the compensation law carry with it reasonable notice that advises potential claimants of their rights. Most important among these is the claimant's entitlement to a due process hearing in the event that the government disputes a claimed loss.

The strict requirements of procedural due process suggest that the CGFAA may have created a disparity among the different classes of victims affected by the government's actions. In addition to the fact that some losses, such as Peter's, may have occurred after the filing deadline for compensation, other problems are evident. For example, the notice that the government has provided to victims has been delivered through the media and in mailings directed to residential addresses. This suggests the primary targeting of permanent residents of the Los Alamos town site and the government's principal interest in compensating the real estate and business losses. Have the rights of other victims, including those of renters, transients, and workers from surrounding communities been comparably protected? Has the government acknowledged responsibility for all damages, both immediate and long term, that reasonably have occurred as a result of its conduct? Even more to the point, has it designed a comprehensive claims system that adequately allows for long-term and unanticipated costs to be calculated, summarized, and reimbursed? As to all those questions, the answer arguably is no, a fact that may tend to limit the number of claims brought against the government for incidental and chronic health problems that manifested in the years following the Cerro Grande fire. When claims such as Peter's are made and then denied by the government as untimely, the full impact of procedural due process on the CGFAA's reimbursement procedures make it reasonable that one nevertheless pursues these claims against the government through suitable litigation.

Noel's tasks in assisting Peter and other clients should include advocacy and assistance in claims processing. It is likely that many others share the illness Peter manifests. As a mental health professional versed in constitutional principles, Noel may be the first and best-equipped professional available to address fire-related health problems directly. Quite plainly, Noel is not an attorney and should not present himself as one. Nevertheless, he is well suited to identify the health issues presented and assist in the appropriate referral of individual cases to attorneys for further assistance. Moreover, Noel can take other advocacy steps to assist victims: he can create community support groups for persons sharing Peter's symptoms and increase public awareness of the long-term health and mental health effects of the fire.

Note finally how section 1983 might offer a reasonable legal response by the class of victims afflicted by the government's actions as outlined in this case example. At first glance, the government's conduct might seem to fall into the realm of isolated incidents of negligence rather than constitutional violations, and therefore it could be considered inappropriate as the subject of section 1983 actions. Because the behavior of the government and its agents seems initially to have violated no specific law or administrative regulation, the liability of government officials under section 1983 for constitutional deprivations is not immediately apparent. However, a credible argument can be made that the government's policies and customary practices in connection with land management placed the public at unnecessary risk of personal harm and property damage, thus interfering with the fundamental right to personal privacy and bodily integrity. Surely, the manner in which Peter's situation seems to demonstrate the insufficiency of the government's long-term response to the fire makes section 1983 a reasonable option for victims. In view of the government's failure to respond adequately and quickly to other natural disasters, such as Hurricane Katrina, as well as the practical problems that emerge when the government attempts to work with a private corporation to respond to an environmental catastrophe, as has occurred in the 2010 BP Gulf oil spill disaster, understanding the full constitutional implications of governmental action or inaction is critically important for mental health professionals who work with the individual victims of these disasters.

CHAPTER 7

The Duty to Maintain Confidentiality

COMPARABLE TO THE DUTY TO SEEK informed consent, the duty to maintain the confidentiality of clients' statements is one of the essential characteristics of every professional relationship. Even though all ethical codes to some extent impose the requirement of confidentiality on mental health professionals, the duty is a legal responsibility first, and legislation in every state and at the federal level defines its parameters. This point is important to understand, because recognizing the broad significance of confidentiality in advancing public policy encourages its appropriate application, together with other basic legal principles, in the resolution of practice dilemmas.

The decision-making framework encourages the use of law as a first step in the consideration of practice choices in the mental health professions. Considering the duty to maintain confidentiality is an especially useful aid in addressing practice situations that challenge the limits of the professional relationship. Often, these circumstances occur when a client has revealed provocative information that may compromise the rights either of the client or of a third party. The boundaries of confidentiality in these instances are examined in the case examples described later.

The legal doctrine supporting confidentiality in professional relationships promotes an important public interest favoring the encouragement of persons to seek the appropriate professional assistance they may need. As the bank-robber example in chapter 1 indicates, this policy may not be immediately apparent when a provider is forced to consider a difficult practice choice that stretches the professional relationship to the breaking point. Put differently, the need to maintain confidentiality is not always intuitive, nor does it inevitably appear to serve the immediate interests of parties to a professional dilemma. Given this reality, it is all the more important to understand fully the legal considerations favoring confidentiality in professional relationships.

The principle supporting confidentiality in professional relationships is centuries old. Its application, however, has been limited until comparatively recently to only certain established professions, such as law, medicine, and the clergy, to which the public right of access has been deemed an urgent necessity. With the expansion of mental health professions in the past century, legislatures have understood the importance of broadening the duty of confidentiality to cover providers in these fields. As a result, the duty of confidentiality has been extended to psychotherapists, including social workers, counselors, and clinical psychologists. The rule of confidentiality now also applies to licensed social workers engaged in child welfare investigations and other forms of public-sector practice.

Of all the areas in which confidentiality applies, it is perhaps most important—and creates the most problems—in the delivery of mental health services. Given the prevalence of mental illness in contemporary society and the invasive nature of psychotherapy, confidentiality helps ensure the access of clients to mental health professionals. This point was effectively communicated in the U.S. Supreme Court's decision in *Jaffee v. Redmond* (1996), in which the Court expansively reviewed the present state of mental health services in this country and the need to ensure public access to appropriate treatment.

Although all fifty states had already adopted rules protecting confidentiality in clinical psychology and social work at the time the *Jaffee* case was decided (the *Jaffee* decision merely extended the rule of confidentiality to mental health professionals testifying in the federal court system), the *Jaffee* court used the opportunity to review the compelling public policy grounds for confidentiality in psychotherapy. With specific reference to clinical social workers, the *Jaffee* court noted that these professionals have become the most significant providers of mental health services to the poor and that confidentiality has helped equalize the right of access of all economic strata to care. This point has relevance for psychologists and counselors, as well; confidentiality in mental health care promotes equal access of poor people in each of these service areas.

Given the spotty record of community mental health centers in promoting service use by some minority populations (Cook, 2008; Office of the Surgeon General, 2001), heightening public awareness of the right of confidentiality may prove an important part of future public outreach efforts. In addition, with the increasingly prominent role of mental health counseling in contemporary society, the recognition by courts and Congress of new confidentiality-related principles serves as a reminder of its importance in each community.

In 1996, Congress enacted the Health Insurance Portability and Accountability Act (HIPAA), whose provisions took legal effect during the years 2003 through 2006. The HIPAA legislation addresses both the protection of workers' health insurance and—more germane to this chapter—the prevention of health-care fraud and abuse and the assurance of client privacy in health-care settings. Although a comprehensive discussion of HIPAA's policies is beyond the scope of this book, it is fair to note that mental health professionals and their agency administrators cite compliance with HIPAA as a major concern of mental health providers involved in the treatment of clients and the maintenance of confidentiality in client records. For this reason, a general discussion of HIPAA's main points is appropriate here. With that said, however, it is also important to note that compliance with HIPAA is actually most easily ensured if the prudent professional understands the elements of confidentiality and the relevant steps presented in this chapter for the resolution of practice dilemmas involving confidentiality.

The main sections of HIPAA address two main areas of concern: Title I sets forth rules protecting the health insurance coverage of workers who transfer or are laid off from their jobs, and Title II presents rules specifically related to the assurance of privacy and confidentiality in the handling and management of client health information, referred to in the law as protected health information (PHI). Title II's provisions occupy the discussion presented here.

Title II of HIPAA is often referred to as the administrative simplification (AS) section. The AS provisions are presented in three discrete provisions of Title II. These are referred to variously as rules governing privacy, transactions, and security. Each of these is discussed individually.

The HIPAA privacy rule is intended to establish policies for the management of client data that come into the hands of covered entities—including health-care providers, health insurance companies, and other organizations that transfer data through paper or electronic transactions. These covered entities must observe certain practices in their handling of electronic versions and hard copies of PHI, which includes all information related to a client's health status, the nature of services provided, and payment details. Specifically, covered entities must disclose to clients all PHI generated by the entity within thirty days of the client's request. In addition, they must disclose PHI to other agencies—usually for the purpose of seeking payment for services or health consultation with other providers—only upon the prior authorization of clients. Further, covered entities must take all appropriate steps to protect the confidentiality of all verbal and written communications held with clients. Covered entities must also create specific agency privacy policies and procedures consistent with HIPAA. In these policies and procedures, covered entities are to identify the individual agency workers responsible for the handling of client information. They must also appoint a privacy official responsible for the maintenance of these policies and procedures and the receipt of privacy-related complaints. Finally, the privacy rule mandates that clients be notified whenever PHI is shared with outside agencies to collect insurance, seek health consultation with other providers, or for any other purpose; clients have the specific right to challenge the accuracy of information contained in PHI.

The transaction rule presents HIPAA's plan for the management of communications between health-care providers and third-party payors. It establishes certain identifying codes intended to facilitate and expedite the exchange of electronic data information (EDI). These codes are intended to make uniform the computerized coding of EDI, such that providers and payors, to the foremost extent possible, speak the "same language" when sharing EDI.

The HIPAA security rule targets health information contained in electronic form, known as electronic protected health information (EPHI). The rule sets forth protections that require covered entities to adopt uniform policies and procedures relating to the handling of EPHI, to identify those specific employees in each agency who are to use and have access to EPHI, and to hold training programs designed to educate agency personnel in the management of EPHI. The security rule also requires covered entities to establish clear safeguards regarding employee access to computer and other electronic data management systems, and it even requires steps regulating the installation and removal of computer systems and software used in connection with EPHI. These include adopting practices ensuring that transmitted information is protected from viewing by unauthorized parties and the use of procedures that permit each covered entity to accurately identify and authenticate outside agencies with which they communicate.

As a final note about HIPAA's overall effect, mental health researchers performing studies with human subjects have reported that the researchers' procedures have been much affected (Rothstein, 2005; Swartz, 2003). Specifically, researchers indicate that there has already been a HIPAA-related, negative impact on their ability to perform data-based research that reports client and/or patient progress over time in health and mental health studies. Among other issues, researchers observe that HIPAA's privacy rule requires the modification and expansion of informed-consent procedures to better document each researcher's intent to comply with HIPAA in the assurance of participant privacy. The complaints of some researchers notwithstanding, given the risks presented by human subject research to the mental health of participants (refer to the fictional scenario presented in case example 8), one could argue that the added protections introduced by the privacy rule may still have an overall welcome impact on the enhancement of researchers' conduct in human subject research (Setness, 2003).

Elements of Confidentiality

The rules governing professional confidentiality are different in all states, and the reader is cautioned to examine specific licensing and other legislation applicable to the reader's area of practice. For the purposes of the decision-making framework, however, a general discussion of the elements of confidentiality that are common to virtually all jurisdictions helps demonstrate this duty's usefulness in addressing mental health practice dilemmas.

Principles applicable to confidentiality are usually organized by profession; they can ordinarily be found in each state's licensing legislation governing the practice of social work, counseling, psychology, pastoral care, and other mental health services. Sometimes, these standards are also contained in legislation regulating the use of evidence in court proceedings, as well as in other areas, such as law governing the reporting, investigation, and resolution of child abuse cases. As might be expected, this makes for a great number and variety of laws governing confidentiality in each profession. They all have some common elements, however, and these can be summarized in several basic principles.

First, confidentiality is both a duty and a privilege. It is a duty in the sense that it binds each professional to maintain the client's verbal and written confidences in secret, and not to reveal them to anyone else, including other clients, families of the client, additional health providers, insurance companies, attorneys, courts, police, and government officials, without the client's express consent. Adherence to this obligation bears an important relationship to the duty to practice reasonably competently. In many states, the breach of a confidential relationship creates grounds for a civil action against the person who breaches the duty. Therefore, alleged violations of confidentiality and the duty to practice reasonably competently are often raised simultaneously in civil lawsuits seeking compensation. Violating confidences, where no exception permits it, is malpractice (*Doe v. Medlantic Health Care Group, Inc.*, 2003—involving a health-care group's revelation to coworkers that a hospital patient was HIV-positive; *Eckhardt v. Charter Hosp.*, 1997; *Pierce v. Caday*, 1992). It may subject the professional to civil liability and is often defined as a criminal act under professional licensing legislation.

As noted, confidentiality also extends a privilege to the client, which means that the client enjoys the right either to enforce or to waive it. Waiving the right to confidentiality often happens as a matter of course when a client authorizes the filing of an insurance claim, joins a therapy group (thereby allowing the sharing of private information with other group members), or brings a malpractice action against a therapist. When a therapist testifies in a court proceeding about a client's case, the therapist may refuse to testify about areas that are deemed confidential, thereby enforcing the client's privilege that the therapist not discuss these matters without the client's informed consent.

Second, maintaining confidentiality and explaining its limitations to the client are integral aspects of the duty to seek informed consent. The most essential reason for this is that clients' expectation of confidentiality is critical to their commitment to seek professional help. Given this fact, the privilege of confidentiality is coextensive with the client's right to grant informed consent for services, and each right supports the purposes of the other. Thus, the right to enforce confidentiality extends to the person responsible for granting informed consent for a client to enter into a professional relationship with a provider. This may be either the client or someone acting on the client's behalf. Understanding that the privilege belongs to the grantor of informed consent but not necessarily to the client makes it easier to understand why parents are entitled to know details of their child's surgery but may not have as free a right of access to private information their child reveals during psychotherapy.

When clients seek services from a mental health or human service agency, they ordinarily grant informed consent to the agency to perform services that individual agency employees then deliver. This fact helps to explain why the agency has the primary responsibility to maintain the confidentiality of its professional relationship with each client, whereas individual providers in the agency may be allowed legally to discuss aspects of a client's case for proper therapeutic or consultative reasons.

The link between confidentiality and informed consent may be better understood by reconsidering case example 6, "The Guidance Counselor." In this scenario, Clayton Cradle's counseling session may be confidential, and even subject to protection from sharing with Clayton's mother, if Clayton is considered a mature minor (see chapter 4) and is able to provide informed consent for treatment himself. If Clayton is not considered a mature minor and his mother is legally required to provide informed consent for his treatment, then Clayton's mother is entitled to receive information relevant to

Clayton's case. To the extent that Clayton's misconduct raises academic issues, however, his mother has the absolute right to this information because, as Clayton's guardian, she alone has the legal authority to make decisions about his education. In other words, Clayton's mother herself has the authority to grant informed consent for Clayton to attend public school and therefore has a right of access to reports about his educational progress. This information of course remains confidential as to all other individuals and agencies outside the school.

As an alternative example highlighting the association between informed consent and confidentiality, consider the rights of persons experiencing family violence involving young children. In a fairly common situation, a social worker investigating suspected child abuse establishes a professional relationship with a vulnerable child in need of protection. The child lacks legal capacity to provide informed consent in this circumstance, and instead the agency charged with representing the child's best interests provides it. Consequently, statements made by the child concerning the abuse are confidential, but statements made by the child's mother, a focus of the child abuse investigation, are not.

The foregoing example underscores another important issue concerning confidentiality: the right to confidentiality usually extends to primary clients but not to secondary clients of public agencies. This important point is a reminder that services to secondary clients are provided appropriately only under limited circumstances. As an illustration of this issue, consider the responsibilities of a government psychologist assigned to conduct a forensic examination of a criminal suspect for the purpose of evaluating the suspect's propensity for violence. In this situation, the psychologist's primary legal responsibility is to assess the suspect's dangerousness to protect the public. A court provides the consent necessary for the examination, and the suspect enjoys no right to confidentiality with respect to the psychologist's delivery of a clinical report to the court.

Third, confidentiality supports the public policy encouraging the promotion of public access to professional services. This policy is expressed variously in court opinions, legislation, and professional ethics codes, and all may differ somewhat in their technical definitions of confidentiality and its exceptions. These relatively minor differences confuse rather than support the process of resolving practice dilemmas involving client privacy issues. Moreover, they tend to cause the misperception that confidentiality supports different purposes, depending on the special character of each professional relationship. Therefore, although the cautious professional is encouraged to be aware of legislative differences, more assistance in practical decision making is probably gained from understanding the broader context of the public purpose that confidentiality serves. Thus, the prudent decision maker should understand that confidentiality serves essentially the same purpose when a psychologist honors it as when a social worker or counselor upholds it.

Fourth, the duty to maintain confidentiality may apply even when there is no formal professional relationship with a primary client. This is particularly true in the conduct of research involving human subjects. For example, federal policy imposes strict confidentiality standards on educational institutions and hospitals involved in human testing (U.S. Department of Health and Human Service Rules Governing the Protection of Human Subjects, 2009).

Fifth, confidentiality standards frequently require government agencies to maintain the privacy of important public functions, such as child abuse investigations and the storage of adoption records. Children's court proceedings in which child custody, abuse and neglect, and other juvenile issues are litigated are ordinarily sequestered for the protection of the children and families involved. Other legislative policies may affect both public and private providers. For example, HIPAA impacts client and patient record keeping and providers' transmission of health information. Federal law also mandates strict confidentiality in the maintenance of records pertaining to persons who seek treatment for alcoholism and substance abuse (Confidentiality of Alcohol and Drug Abuse Patient Records, 2002). In light of the broad diversity in rules governing confidentiality in the delivery of various mental health services, the provider practicing in a particular specialty area is urged to consult applicable federal and state legislation for more specific guidance.

Sixth, there are some generally recognized exceptions to the rule of confidentiality, and all these are related to important public policy favoring the limited disclosure of information. The exceptions have usually arisen as the result of court opinions, such as *Tarasoff v. Regents of University of California* (1976), and often occur in the context of a court's efforts to define the duties to practice reasonably competently and to seek informed consent. The exceptions found their way into federal and state legislation and professional ethics codes only later. These exceptions ordinarily include the following:

- The client's threat to commit a future act of violence against him- or herself or others
- A reasonable suspicion of child or elder abuse or neglect
- The client's waiver of the right to confidentiality
- The client's charge of malpractice against the professional

Note that the exceptions to confidentiality are risks that should be made known to the client in the course of seeking informed consent. Each of these exceptions is addressed here individually.

Threat of Future Criminal Conduct or Harm

Mental health professionals have the legal duty to practice reasonably competently. Among other things, this includes the obligation to promote their clients' best interests and to avoid conduct that causes foreseeable harm. In psychotherapy and counseling relationships, a client frequently shares information that reflects highly personal and emotional content, together with the client's future plans and aspirations. Because the quality of the professional relationship itself plays an important role in the extent to which the client reveals this information, it is appropriate to impose on the provider a responsibility to manage this material in a competent manner. If, in the course of the professional relationship, a client reveals information or engages in conduct that raises a reasonable possibility that the client might harm him- or herself or others, then the professional has the legal duty to take appropriate steps to forestall injury, including alerting others, such as the police. Here, competent practice reasonably demands that confidentiality give way to protect the health of clients and third parties.

Most mental health professionals have become familiar with the case of *Tarasoff*, which, as it has been interpreted, appears to impose on psychotherapists a duty to take reasonable action to protect not only the client but also other persons to whom harm has been threatened. In reality, as the *Tarasoff* court itself explained, the court did not actually create a new duty but more accurately expanded its interpretation of the common law definition of reasonably competent practice to include the professional's obligation to manage and address information that may cause foreseeable, future harm. Understanding the bridge between the *Tarasoff* rule and the time-honored common law standards governing the mental health professions helps alleviate much of the confusion surrounding *Tarasoff* and subsequent cases that have both embraced and rejected it.

The *Tarasoff* court reasoned that, if a professional knows, or "under applicable professional standards reasonably should have determined," that a client intends to commit a violent act against an identified person, the professional has a duty to take reasonable steps to protect the intended victim (*Tarasoff v. Regents of Univ. of Cal.*, 1976, p. 440). If the duty is violated, the professional and the professional's employer face a negligence lawsuit for civil damages by the victim's family. In effect, the burden that *Tarasoff* imposes on providers specifically authorizes the violation of confidentiality by warning the victim and taking other appropriate steps to prevent foreseeable harm. By suggesting that mental health professionals might incur civil liability for failing to interpret correctly their clients' more ambiguous statements and conduct, the *Tarasoff* decision has created something of a panic among some providers convinced that they now have a duty to diagnose a client's predilection to commit violence, a skill that the training programs of the major mental health professions simply do not address. This is unfortunate to the extent that it may already have had a chilling effect on the willingness of some therapists to enter into professional relationships with clients who have had past episodes of violence, including spouse abusers and sexual offenders, many of whom are most in need of a trusting relationship with a compassionate provider.

Tarasoff has become a household word to mental health professionals, who have incorporated it in their agency policies and continue to rely on it when discussing informed consent and confidentiality issues with their clients. Thus, the NASW Code (ethical standard 1.07c) closely follows the *Tarasoff* theme by authorizing social workers to reveal information when "necessary to prevent serious, foreseeable, and imminent harm to a client or other identifiable person." Similarly, the NBCC Code (section B4) advises counselors to "take reasonable action to inform potential victims and/or inform responsible authorities" when the client "indicates that there is a clear and imminent danger to the client or others." Finally, the APA Code (ethical standard 4.05b) rather vaguely permits psychologists to disclose confidential information when required to "protect the client/patient, psychologist, or others from harm."

Many states have enacted legislation that permits but does not require professionals to reveal confidences if they are concerned over a threat of future violence or criminal conduct. Thus, in many jurisdictions it is flatly wrong to suggest that an affirmative *Tarasoff* duty exists, except to the extent it implies one faces a civil negligence lawsuit for failing to honor it.

Despite the presumed authority that *Tarasoff* continues to have, its application has been limited in many jurisdictions (including California itself) to situations in which the client actually reports a credible threat of immediate harm. This trend may lay to rest any implication that the therapist has any duty that extends to the interpretation or prediction of violent tendencies.

In other jurisdictions, *Tarasoff* has been further limited or even repudiated. Thus, the Tenth Circuit Court of Appeals in *United States v. Glass* (1998) held that disclosure is warranted only when a client's threat is plainly serious when made and when disclosure is the only way to avert harm to the identified victim. In other words, the statement cannot be revealed or testified to for other purposes, such as the subsequent criminal prosecution of the client (*United States v. Glass*, 1998). The Fourth Circuit Court of Appeals has adopted virtually the same rule (*United States v. Hayes*, 2000). The Tenth Circuit has further limited the *Tarasoff* doctrine by suggesting that it has no application unless the therapist has some ability to exert physical control over the threatening patient or client, as is the case with inpatients at a secure mental health facility (*Weitz v. Lovelace Health Sys., Inc.*, 2000; on the point that the therapist's ability to physically control the client is critical, see *Boynton v. Burglass*, 1991; Conner, 2006, n. 182). Moreover, the Tenth Circuit has found that the duty to warn does not apply when the intended victim of threats has independent knowledge of the existence of harm (*Weitz v. Lovelace Health Sys., Inc.*, 2000).

Even more interesting, the Texas Supreme Court has rejected *Tarasoff* entirely, suggesting that imposing liability on mental health professionals would force them to "face a Catch-22," specifically, that "they either disclose a confidential communication that later proves to be an idle threat and incur liability to the patient, or they fail to disclose a confidential communication that later proves to be a truthful threat and incur liability to the victim and the victim's family" (*Thapar v. Zezulka*, 1999, p. 640). Rather, the Texas court suggested, professionals' decisions should lie within their own discretion, based on a reasonable consideration of the provider's own best clinical judgment and the situational context. As the *Boynton* court expressed the issue, "to impose a duty to warn or protect third parties would require the [mental health professional] to foresee a harm which may or may not be foreseeable, depending on the clarity of his [or her] crystal ball" (*Boynton v. Burglass*, 1991, p. 450).

The *Thapar* and *Boynton* decisions have critical implications for any mental health professional who practices under state legislation or an ethical code permitting but not requiring revelation of confidences when a client has made threats of violence. This includes most states' professional licensing legislation governing the practice of social work, counseling, and psychology. The decisions suggest that professionals should base a decision to reveal confidences on individual professional judgment and not simply the fear of a potential lawsuit.

The previously mentioned cases all imply that the public policy favoring confidentiality must prevail over any other consideration except where the professional has a reasonable opportunity to prevent serious future harm by revealing a client's confidence. This interpretation is consistent with many of the common law principles governing mental health practice.

How should mental health professionals interpret the *Thapar* and *Boynton* cases, as well as other recent court definitions of confidentiality and its limitations, in everyday practice? Because these cases are essentially grounded in the duty to practice reasonably competently, providers should make the choice to violate a confidence in a *Tarasoff*-like scenario only when they have a realistic opportunity to interview, assess, counsel, and protect their clients and other members of the public in a prudent manner. *Protection* in this context should be understood to include the ability to cause the physical restraint of the client through commitment or maintenance of in-patient treatment. For example, a provider who prematurely and recklessly reveals information in an attempt to prevent an uncertain harm risks doing more damage than good (*Eckhardt v. Charter Hosp.*, 1997) (reckless release of information about wife's spousal abuse made during her therapy led her spouse to further abuse her). The best interests of clients and third parties are usually better served by a therapist's cautious and complete assessment of the potential risk a client poses. Furthermore, the *Glass, Thapar, Hayes,* and *Boynton* cases reinforce the point that professionals should reveal confidences solely to prevent a future act of violence and only to the extent necessary to avert the harm.

Because no mental health discipline has established a body of practice knowledge that includes the prediction of violent behavior, the reasonable-competence standard does not require any provider to forecast a client's future violence. Rather, it requires solely that a professional act reasonably when a client expresses a credible and immediate threat to commit a specific violent act. The reasonable professional confronted with ambiguous client communications must take appropriate steps to ascertain the meaning of these statements. At the very least, this includes using competent interview and assessment techniques that clarify the intended meaning of client speech.

Revelations of past misconduct, regardless of how horrendous, generally do not create a reason for revelation of this information that supersedes the important public policy favoring the encouragement of clients to seek mental health services (*United States v. Glass*, 1998; *United States v. Hayes*, 2000). The general thinking of courts, as described in the previous bank-robber scenario, is that ensuring confidentiality offers the most effective way to encourage offenders to come forward to relate their past history, offering at least the chance that such conduct ultimately can be addressed appropriately.

Suspicion of Child or Elder Abuse or Neglect

Virtually all states have child and adult protective service legislation requiring medical, school, and mental health professionals to report to an appropriate public welfare or police authority any reasonable suspicion that the abuse, neglect, or exploitation of a child or vulnerable adult is taking place. As noted earlier, this duty is an aspect of reasonably competent practice imposed on mental health professionals. Moreover, if the suspicion of abuse arises in the context of a professional relationship with a client, the duty to report the information supersedes the client's right to confidentiality. Several states have extended the responsibility to report suspected child abuse to all members of the public.

Waiver of Confidentiality

Clients can waive the right to confidentiality in a variety of ways, many of which are defined individually under state and federal laws. In general, however, clients waive their right to confidentiality either expressly (i.e., deliberately and in writing) or by a course of conduct that reflects a specific intent to do so. When they waive confidentiality expressly, clients must do so in a manner consistent with the rules pertaining to informed consent. In other words, only clients who possess the capacity to waive confidentiality, have an understanding of the risks and benefits of confidentiality and its waiver, and act voluntarily may waive the right legally. Unless confidentiality is waived under these circumstances, a client's waiver is invalid, and the professional's disclosure of information violates the duty to practice reasonably competently and any applicable licensure and criminal laws.

The most obvious example highlighting an express waiver of confidentiality occurs when clients sign a written authorization to release medical records for the purpose of making a claim to an insurance or other third-party provider. The fact that an insurer is underwriting services does not give it the right to have medical information absent an express, written waiver from the client. Nor does a provider have the right to release treatment information that is not reasonably necessary for the establishment of a claim for payment. Thus, the release of client data other than a general statement of diagnosis and description of services rendered violates client privacy and is inconsistent with reasonably competent practice.

As discussed earlier, third-party providers are attempting novel ways to circumvent the privacy principles outlined herein. Their continuing efforts to claim an ownership interest in client files and their maintenance of extensive computer database records of client information increasingly threaten well-established principles governing professional relationships. Federal and state policies protecting the privacy of client records, such as HIPAA, the Uniform Health-Care Information Act (1985) (adopted thus far in Washington and Montana), and the Model State Public Health Privacy Act (1999), may offer new assistance in the preservation of client privacy rights.

In view of complex and ever-changing problems involving client privacy, it is necessary to emphasize the importance of reviewing the confidentiality principles outlined earlier before resorting to ethical codes for guidance. As noted, these codes offer guidance that on occasion is aspirational and overbroad in its coverage. This is true particularly in the management of confidentiality issues, as this chapter's case examples demonstrate. For example, the APA Code (ethical standard 4.05b) directs psychologists that they may disclose confidential information without the client's consent "where permitted by law . . . such as to . . . obtain payment for services from a client/ patient." Despite the use of the phrase "where permitted by law," psychologists virtually never have the legal authority to release information without the client's consent merely for the purpose of ensuring payment. Therefore, the ethical statement perhaps unintentionally appears to give license to psychologists to take liberties with confidential records in a manner at odds with basic legal standards governing confidentiality. The NASW Code (ethical standard 1.07h) more accurately directs that social workers "not disclose confidential information to third-party payers unless clients have authorized such disclosure." Note, however, that even this statement merely restates an essential legal principle.

It may be appropriate for a provider to request a client's express waiver of confidentiality in circumstances where doing so facilitates the professional relationship. For example, providers who undertake services with clients who are at risk in the sense that they have a history of depression or self-destructive conduct may contract with the client to allow limited disclosure of information to family members or other professionals whenever there exists a reasonable apprehension that the client may be in trouble. This type of waiver can be designed to suit the needs of the professional relationship. As an illustration, a provider wishing to offer services to a client who has reported a history of sexual misconduct may contract with the client to permit the professional's open communication with other family members to ensure their safety around the client. The same waiver may permit the professional to disclose information under circumstances that fall short of conditions requiring a legal disclosure. For example, the waiver might specify that, if the client manifests depression, fails to maintain employment, or engages in other conduct that in the professional's reasonable judgment creates a risk of harm to the client or others, the professional may share information to the extent necessary to forestall the risk. Used in this fashion, the contractual waiver is an effective way to manage professional relationships with clients who have a prior record of violence or sexual misconduct.

As might be imagined, seeking an express waiver of confidentiality creates problems for clients who lack capacity or are involuntarily receiving professional services. In these instances, the rules of informed consent provide helpful guidance. In the case of clients who lack mental capacity to grant informed consent, their surrogates, including parents, guardians, and courts, exercise informed consent and enforce the right to confidentiality on their behalf. Similarly, clients who lack legal capacity, typically children and adults for whom courts have imposed services, in many instances have their right to confidentiality, together with the right to waive it, enforced by surrogates, most often parents or judges. The same can be said for involuntary clients, whose services are often court ordered. With respect to all clients who lack capacity or are involuntary, although their legal right to confidentiality may be limited, privacy should be honored to the extent reasonably possible, consistent with the aim of respecting human dignity and supporting the principle of client self-determination.

Some waivers of confidentiality are implied by circumstances. For example, a client who joins a psychotherapy group reasonably understands that the group is an open forum for the discussion of confidential matters. Although the group facilitator may contract with group members to maintain confidences outside of formal meetings, these agreements are effectively unenforceable against individual members who choose to share disclosures with the outside world. Maintenance of therapeutically effective group dynamics is therefore the best way for a group facilitator to encourage members to respect one another's privacy. The decision maker should be reminded that, despite the partial waiver of confidentiality that most group settings imply, group facilitators still owe a duty of confidentiality to each group member, at least with respect to maintaining a barrier of privacy that protects the group from external intrusion.

Charge of Malpractice

In all jurisdictions, professional licensing legislation or common law tradition protects the right of all professionals to defend themselves from a client's charge of professional malpractice. Such a charge may often necessitate that a mental health provider share confidential information with licensing officials, attorneys, and judges as a means of demonstrating the nature and scope of the services provided to a client. The waiver recognized by law in these circumstances extends solely to the revelation of information reasonably necessary for the professional to conduct a defense in disciplinary proceedings, civil lawsuits, or criminal prosecutions. It does not, however, grant further license to reveal information to other third parties.

Using Legal and Ethical Principles to Address Technology-Related and Other Problems Involving Privacy

The law generally offers a more effective starting point for professional decision making than do ethical codes. Although they are important in the interpretation of legal standards pertaining to individual disciplines, ethical codes tend to be more general in their discussion of practice parameters and often defer to appertaining law in important professional areas. The treatment of confidentiality in ethical codes bears out this point.

All ethical codes recognize that the confidentiality doctrine is essentially a legal principle that promotes the seeking out of professional services by potential clients. This point is aptly expressed in the APA Code (ethical standard 4.01), which notes that "the extent and limits of confidentiality may be regulated by law or established by institutional rules or professional or scientific relationship." Consequently, psychologists are directed to look to law governing individual situations in the consideration of practice decisions involving confidentiality and privacy. The NASW Code (ethical standard 1.07) and NBCC Code (section B16) contain comparable provisions.

The NASW, NBCC, and APA codes each contain ethical standards requiring professionals to maintain the confidentiality of clients' verbal and written statements. These provisions are intended primarily to explain and enhance basic legal precepts governing client privacy. For example, the NASW Code (ethical standard 1.07c) suggests that confidentiality covers "all information obtained in the course of professional service" and that it may be violated only "for compelling professional reasons." The NBCC Code (section B16) mandates simply that counselors keep "the counseling relationship and information resulting from it . . . confidential." Last, the APA Code (ethical standard 4.01) suggests that confidentiality is a "primary obligation" and that it involves the taking of "reasonable precautions to protect confidential information obtained through or stored in any medium."

The complexities of contemporary mental health practice make the design and enforcement of ethical rules pertaining to confidentiality ever more problematic. With the increasing tendency of public and private agencies and HMOs to maintain copious, computerized databases of client information, and with the consistent use of e-mail, fax, and other electronic transmission methods, access to these data has become increasingly and dangerously easy to obtain. This explains the federal government's direct acknowledgment of this problem in enacting the protections contained in HIPAA. Professionals who offer clinical and consulting services via the Internet face an even greater challenge in ensuring the privacy of their distant clients; given the nature of this medium, however, providing this protection is virtually impossible.

Given the growing use of technological advancements to maintain records and communicate with clients, the ethical codes of the mental health professions have expanded in size and complexity as part of an effort by their framers to keep abreast of scientific progress. Thus, the NASW Code (ethical standard 1.07m) advises social workers to properly use "computers, electronic mail, facsimile machines, telephones and telephone answering machines, and other electronic or computer technology." The NBCC Code (section B14) requires counselors to acquire a "facilitation level of knowledge with any [electronic] system they use including hands-on application, and understanding of the uses of all aspects of the computer-based system." Section B6 asks them to "ensure that data maintained in electronic storage are secure." Similarly, the APA Code (ethical standards 6.01 and 6.02) directs psychologists to maintain confidentiality in the management of client information, both in written form and in computer databases.

Despite the best intentions of ethical codes drafters, lengthier codes do not necessarily make more ethical practitioners with regard to information management, nor do they offer many specific, enforceable standards that guide decisions related to the electronic storage and transmission of client information. This simple fact is a significant reason for Congress's enactment of HIPAA. However, HIPAA notwithstanding, technology-related issues in the immediate future are likely to pose major challenges to the maintenance of confidentiality in professional relationships. Unfortunately, HIPAA itself rarely offers direct, pragmatic advice guiding the professional's everyday management of confidentiality-related practice dilemmas. Indeed, given the convolution of many privacy-related practice dilemmas, professionals can obtain the best initial guidance in addressing them by considering and applying the duties to practice reasonably competently and to seek informed consent.

Consistent with the decision-making framework, the prudent mental health professional is urged to examine all confidentiality and client privacy dilemmas by first reviewing their legal aspects. Specifically, the following steps are encouraged:

1. Identify clearly the participants in the professional relationship, including the agency providing the service, the mental health provider(s) working directly with the primary client, and the primary client. If services are provided in an agency setting, the agency as a whole owes the duty to maintain confidentiality to each client.

2. Identify the confidentiality interest affected.
3. Apply the following general legal principle: maintain confidentiality unless a specific legal reason justifies its violation.
4. Where it is debatable whether any specific legal reason justifies the breach of confidentiality, the following rule helps to resolve any question: manage privacy and confidentiality issues by practicing reasonably competently and with informed consent, with special regard to community standards and characteristics.
5. If technology is involved in the dilemma,
    • Identify the technology used in the communication to or about the client or in the transfer or maintenance of information about the client.
    • Consider whether the technology as used reasonably guarantees the confidentiality and privacy of the client.
    • Consider whether, in light of community standards, the technology employed is used consistently with the duty to practice reasonably competently and the duty to seek informed consent.

As an example of how this decision-making system might be applied in a confidentiality dilemma, consider the following situation: A counselor specializing in the treatment of drug addiction offers an online seminar using Web-based technology. Participants who pay the entry fee will be able to see and hear the live video and audio feed delivered by the counselor during each weekly session. Participants will also be able to participate in an additional biweekly chat session intended to serve as a supportive addition to the main seminar. The counselor will facilitate the chat session.

In this scenario, each of the seminar and chat participants is a primary client, and each enjoys a right of privacy that the use of Internet technology does not lessen. The counselor may take great pains to ensure that the audio feed is encrypted and that only participants who pay a fee receive a password to access the audio and video feeds and chat session. Nevertheless, no participant can actually have a reasonable expectation of privacy because the technology cannot account for the conduct of individual members at various sites who might invite other persons to watch and listen to the feed. The counselor may try to address the confidentiality problem by seeking informed consent from participating members and disclosing the potential invasion of privacy as a risk of participating in the groups. The provider may personally regard the use of Internet technology as the most feasible way to provide group support to members who are isolated, live in rural areas, or lack access to live programs. At the same time, however, the unrestrained access to personal information that this approach risks may influence the mind-set of individual participants so as to hinder their open communication in the groups. Without all participants' open and un-hindered involvement, the whole process—including its therapeutic effec-tiveness and appropriateness—is rendered suspect. Moreover, unless the counselor provides a live, personalized assessment of all participants at the outset of the program, their progress and individual therapeutic responses to group therapy are virtually unknowable.

Consider the following scenario: A nonprofit organization that adminis-ters a counseling and support program to the victims of sexual abuse em-ploys a licensed social worker. A state human services agency partly funds services. Concerned that one of the social worker's clients may be attempt-ing to defraud the government by claiming to be pregnant as the result of rape, the agency director seeks to examine the client's files. The social worker refuses, claiming that ethical standards mandate her maintenance of confidentiality. Specifically, the social worker argues that the promotion of client well-being and self-determination—both aspirational principles the NASW Code advances—preclude revealing this information to anyone, including the agency director.

The foregoing example is inspired by a court case, *Smith-Bozarth v. Co-alition against Rape and Abuse, Inc.* (2000), in which a social worker's as-sertion of confidentiality was examined through legal analysis resembling the decision-making framework presented here. The *Smith-Bozarth* court attempted specifically to define the scope of the professional relationship between client and provider. It also examined both the agency's and the social worker's duties to provide reasonably competent clinical services to the client.

Applying the steps presented earlier, it is reasonable to conclude that the woman seeking services for alleged sexual abuse is the primary client of the agency, not of the social worker individually. Therefore, the agency as a whole, not any one worker, enforces the duty to protect her right to confi-dentiality. In seeking services, the woman likely spoke first with the agency receptionist, was referred to an intake worker, granted informed consent to participate in the program, and was finally assigned to an agency so-cial worker for services. The social worker's denial of information to other agency workers who need access to relevant client data therefore obstructs the overall professional relationship between client and agency, including the multiple providers who jointly fulfill the agency's role. Examined differ-ently, the social worker's duty to practice reasonably competently includes cooperation with agency coworkers in the performance of the agency's mission. In addition, the director's ability to supervise the social worker's performance would be impossible without access to information about the worker's activities. Even though social work ethical principles might broadly support the social worker's claim of confidentiality in this instance, in reality, no agency could perform its essential functions if such a literal interpretation of the right to privacy was allowed to restrict internal communication of client information among agency workers. In this situation, the reasonable fear of welfare fraud would of itself provide an adequate rationale for the agency director's request to review the client's file.

Note that the social worker in this scenario does owe an individual duty to the client to practice reasonably competently; the worker owes this duty both in her role as a provider and in her status as an agency employee. Therefore, the social worker here must cooperate with her agency coworkers in the management of the case to the extent necessary for the agency to provide competent services to the client. However, she must also protect the privacy of client records against access by the outside world, except to the extent that the client waives her right of privacy to allow the sharing of her records with other agencies for the purpose of seeking monetary reimbursement or for some other legitimate purpose.

In this scenario, the social worker's primary reliance on the social work code of ethics arguably leads to an erroneous practice decision. The most important reason for this mistake is the failure of most ethical codes—including the NASW Code—to define the legal parameters of the professional relationship, including the meaning of *client*. The present example demonstrates dramatically that initial reliance on ethical codes in the resolution of confidentiality-related dilemmas may result in errors that compromise both the professional's legal position and the client's right to the receipt of quality services.

Another scenario offers an additional example of the use of legal analysis in addressing client privacy dilemmas. Once again, it is inspired by a court case, *Proenza Sanfiel v. Department of Health* (1999). A man accidentally obtains a computer previously owned but discarded by a large mental health facility. The man, who happens to be a psychiatric nurse, quickly discovers that patient records have not been erased from the computer's hard drive. Aware that the hospital is already under investigation for patient abuse and zealously intending to shed further light on the facility's carelessness, he contacts the media, and allows news reporters to see the computer. He is convinced that the need to protect the great many patients who remain threatened by the facility's recklessness more than offsets the risk of invading the former patients' privacy. Therefore, he permits a television news crew to film the computer screen but also asks that identifying information about patients be blurred through digital video technology. Unfortunately, the television reporters disregard his request and use the data they have viewed to contact one of the patients whose records remain on the computer's hard drive. Understandably, this results in severe emotional distress to the patient after it becomes apparent that information concerning the person's hospitalization has been leaked to the public.

Following the same analytical process suggested earlier, one must conclude that all present and former patients of the psychiatric facility are to be considered primary clients of the facility. Although they have never formed a professional relationship with the nurse, he inadvertently obtained electronically preserved records of their treatment history, together with other confidential information. This information is still privileged, even though it has unintentionally come into the hands of yet another party—the television news team. Therefore, in light of the reckless handling of the computer and its hard drive, it is plain that the mental health facility failed to take reasonable measures in its use of technology to ensure the confidentially of its clients' records.

The nurse's individual responsibilities can also be analyzed by considering the duty to maintain confidentiality. As a licensed mental health professional, he is charged with knowledge of the same essential legal principles that any other provider is expected to understand. Although no specific professional relationship has ever existed between the nurse and the hospital patients whose records remain on the computer hard drive, a fair interpretation of the duty to practice reasonably competently would require the nurse to preserve the confidentiality of other professionals' relationships with their patients and clients. Indeed, this interpretation is consistent with the *Tarasoff*-inspired concept that a mental health provider should avoid any professional conduct that could cause foreseeable harm to a member of the public. The nurse has plainly violated this duty, regardless of his aspiration to acquaint the public with the hospital's wrongdoing. Examined in yet another light, by using confidential information without obtaining the consent of the patients involved, the nurse has made a practice decision without obtaining the informed consent of persons whom his actions might affect.

The discerning reader will note that, had this scenario arisen at a time subsequent to the enactment of HIPAA, the hospital's and nurse's actions would plainly violate HIPAA's privacy rule. With HIPAA's enactment in 1996, however, it applies only to practices implemented after 2003.

Consequences for Breach of the Duty to Maintain Confidentiality

Violating the duty to maintain client confidences can occur through negligence, recklessness, or deliberate conduct. Depending on the severity and

intentionality of the violation, civil, disciplinary, and even criminal consequences may ensue for the unwary mental health professional. Each of these
potential consequences is addressed here individually.

Civil Liability

Violating confidentiality without legal justification is incompetent practice. Whether done negligently or deliberately—the preceding examples
demonstrate that each is possible—it is malpractice and can subject the
violator to civil liability and an award to the client of money damages as
relief for all foreseeable harm the violation caused (*Eckhardt v. Charter
Hosp.*, 1997; *Kennestone Hosp., Inc. v. Hopson*, 2000; *McCormick v. England*,
1997; *Odenthal v. Minn. Conference of Seventh-Day Adventists*, 2002; *Saur v.
Probes*, 1991). Typically, the damages clients claim include emotional suffering and invasion of privacy that occur as the result of the release of privileged information. This may include not only the immediate infliction of
psychological distress caused by the violator's own conduct but also other
incidental harms. For example, in the bank-robber example discussed earlier, the professional's release of information to police authorities might result in the client's in-custodial questioning and further require the client
to hire legal counsel. The costs of these consequential damages could be
compensable.

Violating confidentiality can also cause physical harm. Such was the
unfortunate situation the court described in *Eckhardt v. Charter Hospital*
(1997), when a counseling center's clinical staff member confronted a man
with statements his wife made about him during an individual therapy session. Specifically, the man was told that his wife had stated during therapy
that he was an "abusive alcoholic" whose emotional volatility and physical
abusiveness resulted from his drinking problem. As might be expected, revelation of this information to the husband resulted in his perpetrating additional acts of physical abuse on his wife, and the wife ultimately brought
a civil lawsuit against the counseling center for negligence in the handling
of her confidential statements. The counseling center staff defended their
action on the basis that public policy favoring the protection of an at-risk
client supported the release of the information. This strange argument notwithstanding, the *Eckhardt* court found that a strict interpretation of confidentiality law—not to mention common sense—offered no excuse to reveal
the information the client had shared. The client had never suggested that
her husband posed an immediate threat to her. Rather, her statements made
during counseling had suggested that her husband had been abusive in the
past. Therefore, a *Tarasoff*-like situation arguably did not exist. Even if it had

existed, however, the counseling center's management of the information—specifically its therapist's provocative showdown with the husband—was not performed in a manner consistent with the reasonable protection of the client's best interests. Indeed, the center's actions played a direct role in provoking the violence that followed.

Violating confidentiality can also be understood as a breach of contract, in which the professional's relationship with the client, undertaken by both parties voluntarily, has been wrongfully abandoned (*Eckhardt v. Charter Hosp.*, 1997; *Givens v. Mullikin*, 2002). Moreover, the client or some third party who is the subject of the statement repeated outside of the clinical relationship may regard revealing information that is inaccurate or derogatory as defamatory. The same conduct can subject the offender to civil liability based on the resultant harm to either party. This fact therefore demonstrates another danger to the imprudent professional who listens to client statements made in confidence, accepts them as factual, and then reports the contents to a third party. The bank-robber dilemma should be reconsidered in this light.

Criminal Liability

Licensing legislation governing the practice of each of the mental health professions contains criminal penalties for its violation. Because confidentiality is a duty ordinarily imposed on licensees by state law, its violation can result in criminal prosecution. Prosecution is usually reserved for individuals who have violated confidentiality willfully rather than negligently or unintentionally. Duties under individual state licensing statutes must be consulted to understand the extent of criminal liability.

Policy makers have been increasingly willing in recent years to view new legislative strategies as a valuable way to protect the privacy of certain classes of vulnerable clients, such as persons in drug rehabilitation and HIV/AIDS patients. In addition to federal law guaranteeing the privacy of those in treatment for substance abuse and alcoholism, most states have enacted legislation protecting the confidentiality of records pertaining to HIV/AIDS testing. Criminal penalties often apply to the violation of these statutory duties.

Note that the extension of privacy privileges to HIV/AIDS patients and persons receiving services for substance abuse does not suggest that these rights are limitless. With respect to a client who engages in or reports a credible plan to engage in dangerous health practices that are overtly threatening to the client or others, professionals have a duty to handle the matter with the same degree of competence owed when a client reveals a plan to commit a dangerous criminal act. As noted earlier, this ordinarily involves appropriate warnings and other protective actions that secure the well-being of any intended victim. Recall that at least one court has suggested that a surgeon with AIDS must reveal this fact to a prospective patient; the surgeon's illness presents a possibility that the patient could contract HIV during surgery; therefore, it is a risk that must be discussed during the informed consent dialogue (*Johnson v. Kokemoor*, 1996).

Disciplinary Action

Violation of the duty to maintain confidentiality is unethical in addition to unlawful, and it may result in disciplinary action under the licensing legislation of each mental health profession. Given the significant public policy role that confidentiality plays, violations of client privacy are not easily tolerated, and severe disciplinary penalties are not unheard of in cases in which a violation has been willful. Discipline may result even in instances in which a professional has had a heartfelt belief that revelation of information may provide some benefit, as in the *Eckhardt* case.

As an additional example of the unlawful but possibly well-intentioned revelation of client confidences, the following case is instructive: A psychologist who provided marital counseling to a couple later proceeded to take an active professional role in the couple's eventual divorce (*Miss. Bd. of Psychology Exam'rs v. Hosford*, 1987). Specifically, the psychologist offered the husband's attorney an unflattering opinion about the wife's parental fitness. Not surprisingly, the psychologist had never obtained the wife's consent to reveal this information at trial. Therefore, the psychologist's testimony on the husband's behalf was found to have violated the duty of confidentiality and the psychologist suffered the suspension of his license. This result was mandated despite the psychologist's contention that rendering an opinion was reasonably necessary to promote the best interests of the couple's six-year-old son, the subject of a custody fight. The *Hosford* case underscores the point that confidentiality and loyalty to a client go hand in hand in that they both encourage the client to seek services as appropriate and reveal to the provider all information pertinent to the presenting problem.

The *Eckhardt* and *Hosford* cases both demonstrate the courts' reluctance to deviate from strict enforcement of the client's right to confidentiality. More than anything, these court decisions suggest that a legal analysis of confidentiality issues is the best first step in the consideration of any privacy-related practice choice in the mental health services. Indeed, the *Eckhardt* and *Hosford* courts specifically repudiated some of the broadly worded, aspirational exceptions to confidentiality of the type ethical codes often describe. It is especially helpful to remember this point in the subsequent case examples.

Using Confidentiality to Make Professional Decisions: Case Examples

Professional choices involving confidentiality typically call on the mental health professional to decide the following:

- How to manage and protect a client's privacy
- Whether to reveal a client's confidences to a third party
- Whether to use technology in a way that presents a risk that confidentiality will be violated accidentally

Professional ethical codes sometimes imply—probably without meaning to—that providers have more leeway to violate confidences than is actually authorized under the law. Therefore, addressing confidentiality dilemmas, according to the system offered here, directs the professional's consideration in a way that appropriately emphasizes the public policy encouraging client privacy. Furthermore, it is suggested that the decision maker identify and apply the duty to maintain confidentiality, together with each of the other legal principles addressed in this book, as an initial step in the resolution of all mental health practice dilemmas.

Case Example 21: An AIDS Patient in Northern Idaho

Carlos Fulgenzi has been diagnosed with AIDS. A student at the University of Idaho in Moscow, he resides in this small city of twenty-two thousand people. Feeling somewhat socially isolated, Carlos has used local medical services and the university's counseling center to address his health and mental health needs, but he has not been satisfied in general with the care he has received. From the college town of Moscow, he has decided to travel approximately eighty miles west to Spokane, Washington, a city with approximately ten times the population of Moscow, to seek medical treatment and counseling for his recurrent depression. Carlos seeks out the assistance of Gregory Hartpence, a Spokane psychologist. Gregory advises Carlos that he has a therapy group for AIDS patients, whose members come mostly from Spokane and the surrounding area. Gregory encourages Carlos to join the group on a trial basis, during which time Carlos can determine whether group therapy works for him.

Something of a loose cannon, Carlos, during his first session, advises the group that he is "going out in style." Specifically, he plans "to have as much sex with as many people as possible." Members of the group press him for more information, but Carlos throws up his hands, indicating that he has said all he wants to say. Group members and Gregory alike get the distinct impression that Carlos's language means that he intends to have unprotected sex.

This scenario presents problems for Gregory involving the effective management of client privacy and exceptions to the general rule favoring confidentiality. With respect to the management of confidentiality, Gregory is well advised to consider the duty to practice reasonably competently; he should pay special consideration here to the influence of cultural and regional context. Were Gregory to review scholarly literature pertaining to the experience of AIDS sufferers in different geographic regions, he might familiarize himself with the unique issues patients face in different areas. For example, research suggests that rural AIDS sufferers, wary of the stigma this disease continues to cause, tend to avoid treatment in their own localities, preferring instead to seek support at distant sites or not to seek it at all (Goicoechea-Balbona, 1997; Weiss & McMichael, 2004). Carlos's trek to Spokane may already reflect this intent. Gregory's competent handling of this issue might reasonably lead him to rethink his earlier encouragement of the group setting for Carlos until such time as he has fully explored Carlos's concerns about privacy. Gregory's failure to recognize the special confidentiality-related problems in this scenario, together with culture-specific aspects of privacy—Carlos is a Mexican American residing in a largely Anglo region— may literally drive Carlos from seeking any kind of health care and even hasten his death (Goicoechea-Balbona, 1997; Weiss & McMichael, 2004).

Carlos's outrageous statement during the group session may be less demonstrative of an actual intent to engage in unsafe sex than a reflection of denial, fear, panic, and a need to let off steam. Nevertheless, his outburst during the group session raises questions about whether his right to privacy should be curtailed in the interest of protecting from physical harm Carlos and the people with whom he might have sex. Even though he has not yet formally joined the group, Carlos should be considered one of Gregory's primary clients, and he enjoys confidentiality with respect to his participation in the group. Gregory's competent handling of the situation requires that he explore its meaning privately with Carlos to ascertain, if possible, whether Carlos has any specific intent to engage in a sexual act with an identified person. Unless such an intent is revealed and is credible, the cases cited in this chapter suggest that a *Tarasoff*-like duty to warn others or to protect Carlos—perhaps through an attempt to seek Carlos's commitment for inpatient mental health treatment—has not yet been invoked. Gregory has no reasonable recourse when Carlos's statement made during the group session is as vague and flamboyant as it was. Here, the legal principle mandating the maintenance of confidentiality plainly supports Carlos's best therapeutic interests at the inception of treatment. Gregory must do what he can to ensure he encourages Carlos to stay in treatment rather than drive him away through a premature revelation to others of Carlos's statements.

Case Example 22: The Recovering Sex Offender

Lorenzo Medina is a clinical social worker providing direct mental health services at a community program in Missoula, Montana. His new client, Mike Horn, is a forty-five-year-old member of the Blackfeet Indian Nation who has lived most of his life off-reservation. Indeed, a majority of Blackfeet tribal members live off-reservation, and the remaining members reside on the Blackfeet reservation in northwestern Montana. Mike, who now resides in Missoula, seeks Lorenzo's services for treatment of recurrent depression. Sometime after the institution of weekly counseling sessions, Mike advises Lorenzo that he was convicted in 1984 of the criminal sexual penetration of a ten-year-old girl. For that crime, Mike served two and a half years in prison of a five-year sentence, was released on probation, has stayed gainfully employed since his release, and has had no subsequent criminal record. Mike also advises Lorenzo that he wishes to move to an apartment in a house his brother Max owns. Max is a single parent and has three children younger than the age of twelve living with him. Max is aware of Mike's history but feels capable of managing the situation. Family support, Max believes, is the most important therapy for Mike.

In this scenario, Lorenzo's practice decisions concern the nature of services he should offer Mike and the conditions under which he should offer them. In addition, Lorenzo must examine the limits of confidentiality with specific respect to information about Mike's criminal history and proposed living arrangement.

As with all problems that present client privacy issues, this practice dilemma is best analyzed by strict application of the rules governing confidentiality and its limitations. Furthermore, the principle mandating reasonably competent practice, including its cultural aspects, should determine how the privacy considerations here must be managed.

In the present case, application of the duty to maintain confidentiality extends to the information Mike revealed, despite the admittedly worrisome impact that his past has on his proposed living situation. No specific, *Tarasoff*-driven duty to warn or protect is immediately evident here. Indeed, an early violation of the duty to maintain confidentiality in this instance could render permanent damage to a family that appears mutually supportive and willing to work through a difficult circumstance. Mike is legally entitled to the same scope of protection as any other client, irrespective of his troubled history.

Mike's revelations about his plans should raise sufficient concern in Lorenzo's mind as to suggest the need for a thorough assessment of the potential risk of harm to Mike's family. Reasonably competent practice here would include Lorenzo's comprehensive evaluation of the presenting mental health problem. It is entirely possible that Mike's initial description of the issue masks a reoccurrence of his sexual disorder, which is of a type notoriously resistant to treatment. Lorenzo's interview must screen for this possibility without destroying the confidential bond between client and therapist and compromising the purposes of therapy. Questions concerning Mike's present mental state and future plans must therefore be both specific and candid. Here again, however, Lorenzo's overly aggressive management of these issues may alienate Mike and discourage him from placing full faith in the therapist.

At the completion of the interview and assessment, Lorenzo might feel sufficiently concerned about Mike's home environment to enter into a therapeutic contract with Mike at the commencement of services. Such a contract could ask Mike to waive confidentiality with respect to Lorenzo's authority to share information with Max and seek information about the family's progress. More than that, the situation might call for Max to be intimately involved in the course of Mike's therapy. From the standpoint of Lorenzo's duty to seek informed consent from Mike, Max's potential participation in therapy is a treatment option that might be presented to Mike at an appropriate time in the initial phase of services, together with the anticipated risks and benefits this strategy offers.

An impressive body of research suggests that the use of family therapy with Native American clients facing serious mental health issues reflects culturally competent practice (Brucker & Perry, 1998). This point has a specific impact on Lorenzo's management of confidentiality. Given Native Americans' general underuse of formal mental health services, Lorenzo's appropriate handling of confidentiality may be a critical factor in offering Mike and his family a sufficient incentive to assume the risks involved in therapy. Moreover, it suggests that Lorenzo's supervision of privacy issues must focus not simply on the individual legal duty owed to Mike but also on the maintenance of the family's sense of unity and integrity.

In recent years, the enactment of Megan's Law by state legislatures has authorized the mandatory registration of sex offenders as part of an effort to enhance the protection of persons, primarily young children, most vulnerable to recidivist conduct. In the present scenario, Mike's conviction is too old to invoke the duty to register as a sex offender. Were Mike under such a responsibility, however, Lorenzo might allow this fact to carry over to the professional relationship; specifically, Lorenzo might conclude that his duty to maintain confidentiality in Mike's case simply does not apply. This would be a mistake, because the duty to register as a sex offender serves a public policy need that is quite distinct from the purpose fulfilled by maintaining confidentiality in a clinical relationship. The former policy is justified as an important aspect of the deterrent strategy the criminal justice system embraces, whereas the latter is a technique used to enhance the public's full use of available mental health services. Understanding this distinction may help Lorenzo avoid the unnecessary estrangement of his client in the name of fulfilling a presumably relevant public policy. Lorenzo must recall that it is highly unlikely he would have had the opportunity to intervene in Mike's problem unless Mike's expectation of confidentiality had contributed to his decision to seek therapy.

The preceding discussion notwithstanding, at least one court case has suggested that a professional therapist treating a self-acknowledged pedophile does have a duty to warn potential victims of the client's proclivities, at least where it is reasonably foreseeable that the client intends to place himself in a situation that will give him extraordinary access to children (*Almonte v. N.Y. Med. Coll.*, 1994). In the *Almonte* case, a resident psychiatrist undergoing professional training was in the process of undergoing psychoanalysis with a member of the medical school faculty when the resident disclosed that he was a pedophile and that he planned to specialize in child psychiatry on completion of his residency. The faculty member kept this information confidential. Upon his graduation, the resident began a child psychiatry practice and later molested a ten-year-old patient. The victim's parents sued the medical school and faculty member for failing to disclose the resident's pedophilia and for allowing the resident to graduate. The *Almonte* court agreed with the parents that the duty to disclose had existed.

The *Almonte* case differs from the previous case example in several important respects. First, the court analyzed the case from the standpoint that the pedophiliac patient in this scenario was also a physician in training. This means that the medical school and its faculty member had a responsibility to safeguard the medical profession against incompetent and impaired practitioners; this responsibility created an immediate duty to protect the future patients of a potentially dangerous physician. Second, the *Almonte* court plainly believed that the pedophiliac patient's unusual disclosures to his psychiatrist-instructor represented a specific plan to harm children and that the revelations should have given the psychiatrist-instructor reasonable cause to suspect that his patient intended purposefully to use his future practice as a means to gain access to children.

The *Almonte* opinion bucks the general trend represented by the majority of court decisions that require the disclosure of a specific plan to commit a violent criminal offense against an identified individual before a duty to disclose, warn, or take other protective action is imposed on a professional. As already noted, this policy is based on the courts' reluctance to instill a fear of lawsuit in the minds of clinicians whose professional decisions are best made through a careful, deliberative process.

Case Example 23: Reconsidering the "Counseling Out" of Wanda Moreno

Please reconsider the scenario discussed in case example 16 concerning the "staffing" and "counseling out" of a student in a public university's psychology program. The case example raises interesting questions concerning the extent to which confidentiality should be afforded in general to students. These questions are most appropriately addressed using the legal strategy outlined here.

Wanda Moreno, the student in case example 16, must be regarded as the primary client of the university, not of the individual professor, Dolores Hickey. This situation is evident from the fact that Wanda has contracted with the university to receive educational services, and the university has agreed to provide them through its many educators and staff members. Much like the association between any client and a human service agency, Wanda and her university are the primary participants in the professional relationship.

Identifying the parties to the professional relationship in this dilemma helps explain why it is impossible to impose a duty of confidentiality on Dolores that restricts her sharing of academic and personal information with other members of the university's teaching faculty and administration. Such a burden would make it impossible to grade students, would render Dolores unaccountable for her teaching performance and students' outcomes, and otherwise would leave the university incapable of performing its educational mission. For this reason, it is the university that is primarily responsible for maintaining confidentiality with respect to student records, personal information, and other academic data. This duty means that the university must guarantee the privacy of this information from access by the outside world to the extent necessary to preserve the university's educational objectives; as noted, it does not require that individual instructors and staff members shield student-related information from one another. When universities wish to share student information with external agencies, ordinarily they must seek the prior consent of each student whose information is to be shared.

If university professors are not bound to a confidential relationship with their individual students, what, then, is the extent of professors' legal responsibility to their students? This is not simply an academic question. It is especially important in explaining the duties of professors who teach courses in social work, counseling, psychology, and other mental health disciplines at the university level. Educators, particularly those who teach clinical practice courses, in a sense function simultaneously as mental health professionals and instructors. In recent years, university regents, accreditation organizations, legislators, and professional licensing boards have all struggled with the issue of academic accountability. This concern with educational outcome assessment is part of a broader effort to seek practical ways to make educators more directly answerable to students and the public for their teaching performance.

At least in theory, university professors who teach mental health courses have a duty to practice reasonably competently. In reality, assessing their conformance with this standard has proved most problematic. Courts addressing the issue have described the relationship between teachers and their students to be a special one, whose success largely depends on subjective factors unique to individual educational environments. Put another way, some bad teachers have good students who learn everything they are supposed to, and some good teachers have bad students who fail. Thus, although tempted, most courts have refused to enforce any claim for educational "malpractice" or, indeed, to otherwise define the professional responsibilities of teachers.

What does the foregoing discussion reveal about confidentiality? Most important, it underscores the role of privacy as a defining element of any professional relationship. When confidentiality does not or cannot exist, the professional relationship between provider and client is compromised. This is true in the case of relationships between professors and their students. In the university setting, as in all large agency environments, the development of discreet professional relationships—aided as they are by the creation of a bond of trust between individual provider and client—is sacrificed in the name of promoting the university's efficient delivery of services. The larger the organization, the less likely are individual employees in a position to maintain client confidences. In the most extensive bureaucracies, the ultimate result may be the fundamental alienation of clients from the unique providers who deliver each particular service. This problem is most exacerbated in areas where racial and ethnic differences separate clients from their providers. That being the case, larger mental health and human service agencies should take steps to encourage individual employees to honor the privacy of their clients to the extent consistent with the reasonable functioning of the agency. Thus, even if the strict maintenance of confidentiality between individual agency caregivers and their clients is not possible, workers should endeavor to uphold the dignity, comfort, and solitude of their clients within the larger agency atmosphere.

Case Example 24: Dr. Linda

A certified counselor licensed by the Pennsylvania Board of Social Workers, Marriage and Family Therapists, and Professional Counselors, Dr. Linda Karam has varied experience in marriage and family counseling. A zealous advocate of the exploration of new media in the practice of psychotherapy, Dr. Linda, as she is known in the Orthodox Christian Lebanese American community of Johnstown, Pennsylvania, where she lives and works, also wishes to meet the needs of Arabic-speaking persons in Johnstown and rural areas of the state who lack access to culturally relevant counseling strategies. For these reasons, Dr. Linda has accepted an offer to host an Arabic-language (Lebanese dialect) radio call-in show. During the show, Dr. Linda intends to answer listeners' questions concerning family problems, relationships, dating, and other issues that her audience may raise.

Per the request of the station manager, the show's announcer will offer the following disclaimer in both English and Arabic at the beginning and end of each two-hour program: "While Dr. Linda welcomes her listeners' questions, they should be reminded that her answers are for general information purposes only and that her answers are not a substitute for a thorough evaluation by a licensed therapist." Listeners are reminded by Dr. Linda's switchboard operator not to give their real names on the air, so that "privacy may be ensured."

This case example is indicative of the increasing tendency by mental health professionals, notably counselors, to use mass media for the dissemination of advisory information to the public. Dr. Linda's legal disclaimer notwithstanding, use of mass media certainly does have the effect in some situations of substituting for more formal, in-person professional assistance. So prevalent has counseling through electronic media become that the NBCC Code (section B12) requires counselors who seek to engage in it to "present clients with local sources of care before establishing a continued short or long-term relationship." Nothing in the NBCC Code, however, otherwise restricts the use of long-distance counseling.

Of particular interest in this scenario is the potential confidentiality problem created by Dr. Linda's radio program. Using legal analysis, several points become immediately apparent. Most important, Dr. Linda and her call-in guests voluntarily assume a professional relationship, with the show's participants willfully assuming the role of primary clients. This is plainly true despite the great pains Dr. Linda and her station manager have taken to deny this point through the disclaimer—a clumsy announcement and disclaimer intended to gain informed consent from each caller—offered periodically through the program. Despite all attempts to limit the significance of the information exchanged, the fact remains that callers ask for advice and receive it from Dr. Linda. Given the economic climate of the community in which the show is broadcast, no reasonable counselor in this situation could deny the probability that some listeners are using the show as their only means of access to mental health information. Given the realistic expectations of callers, the NBCC Code's authorization of long-distance counseling through electronic means, and the services the host freely offers, it is indefensible to remove from Dr. Linda the duties to practice reasonably competently, to seek informed consent from her clients, and to maintain confidentiality unless each client knowingly waives it.

Considering the professional relationship created between Dr. Linda and each of her call-in guests, she must honor her duty to maintain confidentiality through the exercise of reasonable competence. Arguably, the show's format fails to meet this standard. In a rural community, where people know one another more readily than in urban areas, any descriptive information is likely to give listeners a fairly good sense of some callers' identities. Moreover, in view of the community and cultural traditions that guide practice, small talk and informal conversation during each discussion between Dr. Linda and her callers are likely to amplify every individual violation of privacy when broadcast over the airways.

How can Dr. Linda minimize the violation of confidentiality that her show's format threatens? She can do so most easily by changing her format drastically to avoid its more exploitative elements. No reasonable clinical purpose justifies the exposure of a professional dialogue on the air. When the main purpose of this device is entertainment, the risk to each client far outweighs the benefits offered either to callers or the listening community as a whole. Providing general information to the public based on Dr. Linda's recapitulations of situations from her private counseling practice—with the anonymity of each client preserved—offers a more competent approach to counseling, more suitable protection of client confidentiality, and the delivery of more usable knowledge for public consumption.

Case Example 25: Gabriel's Problem

Gabriel Tafoya, twelve years old, refuses to attend school. Midway through the fall semester of his middle school in Laton, in rural Fresno County, California, he has complained that he has no friends, is bullied by other children, and hates his teachers. The school guidance counselor has contacted Gabriel's parents regarding his chronic absences. "It's a mental health issue," suggests the guidance counselor, "but it's also a disciplinary problem that has to be dealt with before it gets worse."

Upset by Gabriel's behavior and spurred on by their conference with the guidance counselor, the Tafoyas make an appointment to have Gabriel evaluated at their community mental health center. Cecilia Roanhorse, a clinical social worker at the center, has scheduled an initial meeting with the entire family, during which time she intends to assess the need for an intervention.

This case example presents a typical scenario involving the management of adolescent mental health issues. The seemingly straightforward clinical situation nevertheless raises important questions about appropriate confidentiality oversight and the public policy guiding it. The initial decisions Cecilia makes about client privacy will affect her future interactions with the Tafoya family and Gabriel's success in treatment.

As chapter 4 outlined, minors in some states under certain circumstances have the right to grant informed consent for a variety of mental health interventions. In California, children may grant informed consent for counseling and therapy at the age of twelve. As chapter 12 also noted, however, it is unclear how the child's right to grant informed consent is affected if parents initiate the intervention. In other words, courts have been most unclear about whether minors have the right to refuse mental health treatment when a parent or guardian has sought it. In California, a court has recognized the right of a child under detention for juvenile delinquency to refuse psychotropic medication under state administrative regulations (In re *Manuel L.*, 2002). With this point in mind, it is fair to suggest that Manuel may also have the privacy based right to decline participating in mental health treatment. Because this is an unsettled question, however, Cecilia must develop a practice strategy that addresses Gabriel's possible rights in this scenario.

On the basis of the foregoing, it is suggested that Cecilia assume the posture that Gabriel has the right to grant informed consent for mental health services. Consequently, Cecilia should also assume that Gabriel has at least an initial right to confidentiality at the moment Cecilia agrees to provide services. Considering the factual scenario presented, Cecilia should assume that Gabriel is her primary client, at least at the inception of services, which should include an initial interview with Gabriel alone. In taking this approach, Cecilia would seem to be enforcing a plausible legal position—one that recognizes Gabriel's fundamental right to personal privacy and therefore arguably is more catered to protect his best interests.

These points compel that Cecilia begin the family intervention by seeking Gabriel's permission to interview him concerning the presenting issues the guidance counselor identified. The holding of a private meeting with Gabriel also accomplishes the aim of questioning him in a manner that allows him to speak openly about his relationship with his parents and also permits Cecilia an opportunity to explore whether family abuse or neglect may have affected Gabriel in this case. Clearly, Cecilia's explanation of Gabriel's right to confidentiality—together with its limitations—will enhance the likelihood that Gabriel will be willing to participate freely in this interview.

This dialogue must include the therapist's reasonably competent—including age-appropriate—psychosocial assessment. At such time that Cecilia obtains Gabriel's informed consent and his permission to include Mr. and Mrs. Tafoya in a therapeutic group, it is appropriate for Cecilia to engage the entire family in a suitable intervention. Obviously, if Gabriel wishes to participate with his parents in an intervention, both parents must also provide informed consent to allow Cecilia to continue. If Gabriel refuses to participate, Cecilia should honor that position. She may continue to work with the Tafoya parents, however, if they so choose, and in the process, seek to identify ways the Tafoyas can assist Gabriel. It may well be that the Tafoyas' involvement with Cecilia in a therapeutic setting will have a beneficial effect on Gabriel. At the least, they may leave their therapeutic sessions with new ideas about how to make changes in their own parenting that will assist Gabriel as he faces his challenges.

The foregoing analysis may unnerve any therapist familiar with the experience of observing parents drag a reticent adolescent to the "shrink's office" for the purpose of a mental health consultation. When parents take such a step, they often become the willing providers of information about their child concerning the child's presumed psychological state and behavioral problems. The all-too-typical result of such behavior is for such parents to inspire their child to remain entirely silent. In this case scenario, however, the strict recognition of Gabriel's status as the primary client, the person empowered to grant informed consent for therapy and the holder of the right to confidentiality, is consistent with the clinical objective of isolating individual factors—such as Gabriel's impression of his home environment and family relationships—that may help Cecilia to assess Gabriel's condition. In interviewing Gabriel, Cecilia must be especially careful to evaluate Gabriel's risk for child abuse or neglect in his present family environment.

Cecilia's professional training as a clinical social worker may have emphasized a family-systems approach to certain clinical issues. Indeed, some research suggests that this is a culturally appropriate stance for work with Hispanic, and particularly Mexican American, families (Bean, Perry, & Bedell, 2001). Nevertheless, if Cecilia's predisposition to this treatment approach causes her prematurely to treat the whole family as a singular primary client and ignores Gabriel's right to be a voluntary participant in his treatment, then she undermines not only Gabriel's right to privacy but also his receptivity to success in therapy. Without first speaking to Gabriel in a confidential interview before assessing the rest of the family, Cecilia risks harming Gabriel's chance for a positive clinical outcome. Assessing Gabriel's level of acculturation, which may be different from that of his parents and a major contributing cause of his problem, should be an important part of his initial, private assessment. The results of this individual dialogue may affect future interviews with Gabriel's parents and ultimately direct the nature of the chosen intervention (Bean, Perry, & Bedell, 2001).

CHAPTER 8

Incorporating Law, Ethics, Context, and Pragmatism in Decision Making

UNDERSTANDING THE SCOPE OF EACH of the essential legal principles governing the mental health professions is a necessary first step in considering practice dilemmas. It is not, however, the final step. The mental health decision maker must be prepared to understand how these principles interrelate and are interpreted in a particular community. For these purposes, learning to assess the applicability of law in individual practice situations provides an invaluable tool in the resolution of dilemmas. In addition, understanding the manner in which local policies, as well as ethical standards and regional and cultural practices, interpret legal principles is the best way to ensure that professional decisions correspond with the expectations imposed on mental health providers in a specific region. Moreover, these steps advance the communitarian purpose of promoting both the client's best interests and the shared social goals of the decision maker's community.

Completing a Legal Inventory

In responding to any practice dilemma, the decision maker needs to consider the potential application of each legal principle outlined in the framework. These include the following:

- The duty to practice reasonably competently
- The duty to seek informed consent
- The duty to identify the primary client

- The duty to treat clients and coworkers with due process and equal protection
- The duty to maintain confidentiality

In assessing whether particular principles apply in any dilemma, the decision maker is urged to follow the order maintained in the framework. The legal principles are presented in sequence from general to specific, and each successive rule builds on preceding ones. Consequently, the decision maker should evaluate any important practice decision by assessing the applicability of each of the aforementioned principles individually, in the order presented. This inventory approach ensures efficiency in the framework's use.

As an example of the legal inventory's application in resolving a practice dilemma, consider the following scenario: The director of patient services at a public, in-patient mental health treatment program receives a call from a board member of one of the clinic's supportive foundations. The call concerns the board member's brother, who is suffering from major depression. The board member states that he would be deeply appreciative if his brother could be admitted to the facility as soon as possible. The board member also asks the director to "see what he can do" to facilitate his brother's admission. The program has an extensive waiting list, and the director suspects that he may enhance the program's ability to receive additional funding by boosting the board member's brother to the top of the list. He can do so by subtly manipulating the criteria on which urgent care admissions are based. In his own mind, the director is prepared to rationalize that the ends justify the means; specifically, the potential for increased funding will ultimately serve the greater good of persons served in the program's catchment area. He withholds his decision, however, pending the completion of a legal inventory.

This rather obvious scenario offers nonetheless an opportunity to demonstrate the usefulness of the legal inventory. Applying the framework's first two principles, the duty to practice reasonably competently and the duty to seek informed consent, the director finds that neither relates specifically to the situation at hand. Proceeding further, the director discovers that more immediately helpful guidance comes from the duty to identify the primary client and the duty to treat clients and coworkers with due process and equal protection. Both of these are useful to the director in arriving at an ultimate decision: the conflict of interest created by aiding the board member's cause undermines the quality of care provided to other patients and arguably denies due process and possibly equal protection to patients on the waiting list seeking admission.

Seeking the assistance of professionals familiar with law and policy always aids in the completion of a legal inventory. In this regard, mental health providers sometimes have access to agency or personal counsel, whom decision makers are urged to consult first as a reference for explanation of regional legal standards governing practice.

The intimidation this type of deliberation may cause the hesitant decision maker often thwarts the act of seeking legal consultation. To the mental health professional who might never think of using the law in everyday decision making, consulting an attorney often does not become an option until a practice dilemma becomes so overwhelming or out of control as to mandate legal assistance. The result all too frequently is that the professional presents a general—often rushed—description of a case scenario to an attorney and then defers to that person for an "opinion." This is an ineffective method of seeking legal advice and usually results in a complete abdication of responsibility for decision making in favor of the attorney. Moreover, it defies the principle that decision making founded on legal reasoning is within reach of every mental health professional.

An alternative approach to using legal counsel allows the provider to maintain a preeminent role in decision making. In this system, consultation with a lawyer occurs earlier in the decision-making process and is aided by the provider's specification of the subject area in which guidance is sought. Thus, the decision maker should be prepared to ask for guidance with respect to each of the framework's legal principles. Examples of appropriate questions to ask an attorney include the following:

- In the present scenario, under this state's laws, what are my responsibilities with regard to reasonably competent practice?
- How much information must I share to satisfy informed consent?
- Does my agency's admission process comply with due process and equal protection standards?
- What are the limits of confidentiality?
- Who is my primary client in this scenario?

By obtaining an answer to these specific questions from the lawyer and bringing prior understanding of these principles to the legal consultation, the decision maker and attorney can arrive at a resolution to a problem in a collaborative and fully informed manner. Moreover, using the attorney interview to address specific questions elevates the role of the mental health professional from deferential advice seeker to primary issue framer.

The foregoing discussion assumes the luxury of ready access to legal counsel. The harsh reality of contemporary mental health practice—particularly in rural areas—is that formal legal assistance may be neither readily available nor affordable. Lack of such access should not dissuade the decision maker from incorporating the framework in daily professional problem analysis. Indeed, the framework presumes that legal counsel may not be immediately available to respond to practice questions pertaining to professional responsibilities. Instead, the framework's usefulness in resolving practice dilemmas depends on the decision maker's creative ability to recognize and apply legal principles in everyday situations. These skills are best developed through an understanding of important public policies driving the law, as well as by practice in applying the framework.

Regardless of the availability of legal support services, a general familiarity with regional interpretations of basic legal principles by courts, legislatures, and even county and municipal governmental bodies aids the decision maker's success in using the framework immeasurably. This familiarity is best obtained through an awareness of the protections one's state constitution, local legislation, and regional appellate courts afford.

Acquiring the ability to perform basic legal research is a skill to be expected of contemporary mental health professionals. Although a full review of legal research techniques is beyond the scope of this book, several essential elements need to be established here.

First, court decisions interpreting legal principles may be found in books—commonly referred to as digests—that compile U.S. judicial decisions in individual cases and organize them by subject matter. The most famous of these digests are those compiled by the West Publishing Company (now affiliated with Thomson/Reuters), which over the course of years has developed an expansive key number system that organizes decisions in individual court cases and then assigns them key numbers according to each legal topic area. Because West publishes individual digests for the state and federal court systems, and uses the same uniform numbering system in each, it is possible to trace the interpretation of a particular legal principle by numerous state and federal courts. For assistance in the use of digests as well as the key number system the reader is referred to the many treatises available for mental health professionals that present a general review of basic legal research strategies.

Second, the wide availability through the Internet of state and federal legislation and administrative policies has given even the most geographically isolated mental health professional immediate access to the regional standards that govern professional practice. Because this material is ordinarily presented in the form of a keyword-searchable database, the availability of basic legislative and administrative information pertaining to the mental health professions has become markedly enhanced in the past several years. For help in accessing this material, the reader is again referred to one of the many treatises available on the market that offer guidance in Internet-research techniques.

In addition to a basic familiarity with local legislation, administrative policies, and court decisions, the agency-affiliated professional is aided in applying the framework by his or her conscious awareness of agency policies and procedures that guide problem analysis in the professional's own practice environment. Thus, agency policies defining the services offered to clients and governing their intake and assessment may be of invaluable assistance in considering standards defining competent practice and informed consent.

The agency based decision maker's thorough familiarity with personnel rules and hiring contracts that define the terms and conditions of employment also aids the legal inventory. Such documents typically contain important guidance concerning the professional's contractual obligations to an agency, including job performance expectations. These standards may in turn help clarify the parameters of competent practice expected of the professional. Moreover, they may impose obligations above and beyond basic duties defined in law. For example, rules governing the maintenance of client confidentiality may define specific procedures an agency develops in compliance with HIPAA; these procedures may relate to the handling of client records and databases and the maintenance of privacy with respect to communications with outside agencies, including third-party providers.

The decision maker's consideration of law beyond the elemental principles addressed in the framework assists the finalization of the legal inventory. For example, all practice decisions benefit from the professional's general familiarity with regional criminal and civil law; indeed, such familiarity should be considered an important aspect of reasonably competent practice. The decision maker should therefore be prepared to assess whether any practice choice is consistent with relevant federal, state, or tribal law. This awareness of certain legal principles does not suggest familiarity with the law comparable to that of a licensed attorney. Rather, it implies knowledge sufficient to give the professional awareness that a problem has legal implications requiring further consultation with an attorney. Plainly, if an agency or client seeks to involve the professional in activities that may be criminal or subject multiple parties to civil liability, this possibility is an important consideration in arriving at a practice decision.

The foregoing strategy can be summarized in a series of steps that require the decision maker to complete a legal inventory by reviewing each of the following:

- The application of the framework's legal principles, from general to specific (i.e., principles 1 through 5; see the appendix)

- Regional legislative and judicial interpretations of each of the basic principles
- The impact of other relevant federal, state, or tribal laws and administrative rules and regulations
- Any internal agency policies and procedures that define client services or the professional's job responsibilities or contract obligations

As an example of how these steps support completion of a legal inventory, consider the following situation: A social worker employed by the income support division of a state welfare bureau has learned during an interview with a client that the client's ownership interest in a real estate parcel renders him ineligible for continuing public assistance. The client has received this assistance for several months, including payments under the Temporary Aid to Needy Families (TANF) program, a welfare reform initiative inaugurated under the Personal Responsibility and Work Opportunity Reconciliation Act (PRWORA) of 1996, and food stamps. The client remains impoverished and malnourished, yet the failure to reveal the existence of the real estate during the first three months of his receipt of benefits likely will result in liability for overpayment of benefits. The social worker must make a practice decision concerning the appropriate use of the information the client reveals.

Following the legal inventory's steps, the social worker might reasonably conclude that the duties to practice reasonably competently and to identify the primary client generally support a commitment to serve the client's best interests, but they do not immediately appear to offer more specific guidance concerning the client's plight. The duty to maintain confidentiality clearly does not mandate the social worker's personal protection of the client's secret, because sharing of information with other agency personnel is required so that the agency meets its obligation to provide appropriate services to the public.

Proceeding further through the inventory's steps, the social worker would likely conclude that both law and agency policies require identification and reporting of factors that render a client ineligible for benefits. Given this reality, the social worker is obliged to follow the law. In this context, if the social worker reconsiders the duty to practice reasonably competently, the social worker may well conclude that this duty mandates that the agency do more for this client than simply terminating services. Rather, practicing reasonably competently should be interpreted to require that further client assistance should be offered. Specifically, this aid should include the taking of steps that might help in the reestablishment of eligibility and securing of emergency aid pending resolution of the client's problem. Stated differently, the duty to provide reasonably competent services does not end simply because additional legal obligations limit the range of services the professional can render. This point is sometimes forgotten in agency settings in which a bureaucratic atmosphere stifles the full consideration of legal obligations to clients.

Using Ethics in Making Professional Decisions

Much has been stated previously regarding the difficulties posed by the use of ethical codes in specific professional situations. When the decision maker relies on a profession-specific ethical code as an initial step in the resolution of a practice problem, the decision maker is often forced to observe that the broad, aspirational, and occasionally conflicting ideals presented raise more questions than they answer. The idealistic, goal-oriented tone that some professional codes adopt frequently leaves the decision maker with insufficient practical guidance for everyday practice situations. Often the most usable and enforceable standards included in ethical codes, such as those governing competent practice, informed consent, and conflicts of interest, merely restate duties that already exist under the law.

In view of the foregoing discussion, what role should ethical codes play in the resolution of practice dilemmas? As noted earlier, ethical codes offer practice goals—unique to each of the mental health professions—that can help the decision maker interpret basic legal principles, most notably the duty to practice reasonably competently. With this point in mind, ethical codes are best reviewed only as a second step supplementing the legal inventory. In addition, it is important to remember that the law should represent the paramount consideration in any practice decision and that conflicting or ambiguous ethical standards should be considered and applied in a light that gives support to each of the legal principles outlined in the framework.

The framework's emphasis on the legal inventory should not be read to imply that ethical principles are either irrelevant or unnecessary in making practice choices. Rather, as part of a strategic plan for efficient decision making, they are best considered only after the legal inventory is completed. In some practice situations, the decision maker may be satisfied that the legal inventory yields no helpful guidance. In this event, the decision maker is encouraged to undertake a thorough review of ethical standards that offer assistance in the resolution of a dilemma.

Another practical reason to perform a thorough review of ethical standards is that they may jog the decision maker's reasoning process in a manner that prompts a reconsideration of the law. Thus, for example, reviewing a variety of ethical principles may inspire the decision maker to invoke again the duties to practice reasonably competently, to seek informed consent, or to identify the primary client that were not immediately apparent on initial consideration of the problem. For this reason, the maximum benefit is obtained from the decision-making framework if the decision maker first performs the legal inventory, then reviews relevant ethical standards, and finally returns to the legal inventory once more. In noting that reconsideration of practice dilemmas is a welcome strategy to ensure thoroughness in decision making, it should also be stressed that the need for promptness in addressing certain problems should not lead the decision maker to avoid the thoughtful review of all available sources of guidance for resolving mental health predicaments. Stated differently, the desire for a quick answer in practice may be a cause of much stress for the decision maker. Rather than giving in to the immediate gut instinct, the decision maker will gain much from the thoughtful reconsideration of dilemmas in a way that recognizes that ambiguity may sometimes creep into practice situations; in such circumstances, tolerance of this sense of ambiguity, careful reflection, use of the legal inventory, and reconsideration of potentially helpful ethical standards are the best means of ensuring a fully considered response.

The decision-making framework as outlined in the appendix presents a summary of ethical standards from the NASW, NBCC, and APA codes that outline professional expectations for social workers, counselors, and psychologists, respectively. There is much overlap in the subject areas covered, which suggests that the formal goals of the mental health professions are similar. Because the framework offers only an outline of each code's salient points, the decision maker is urged to consult the full text of a relevant code when considering any practice choice.

As an example of how ethical standards can supplement the legal inventory, consider the following practice situation: A community mental health agency on the outskirts of Dearborn, Michigan, serving a geographical area that contains the largest Arab American community in the United States, decides to embark on a public outreach campaign to address the underuse of services by Arab American persons. It elects to do so through a community open house and festival featuring live music, health exhibits, and public speakers. The agency's director, a clinical psychologist, has received an offer from a regional alcohol distributor to donate a substantial portion of the funding for the festival. The director must consider the implications of accepting funding in light of the potential good it may do for the community.

The director's decision must begin with a legal inventory. In this scenario, the director on initial review receives no clear guidance from the framework's legal principles. Turning to relevant APA Code standards, the director is impressed by ethical standard 3.06, which outlines principles governing conflicts of interest, and by ethical standard 5.01, which governs advertising and exhorts psychologists to refrain from false and deceptive statements.

Summarizing the applicable ethical standards, the director concludes that it would advance the interests of potential clients, including the community at large, if funding from the distributor is accepted. As the director reasons, taking the money would not be inherently different from the government's funding of smoking prevention programs and drunk-driving victims' funds through so-called vice taxes on cigarettes, alcohol, and traffic violations. The director also, however, interprets the same ethical standards to mandate that acceptance of funding be conditioned on the stipulation that advertising or other public acknowledgment of the distributor's involvement be restricted. The director's aim in taking this position is to minimize the possibility that alcohol consumption be promoted; that the agency's objectivity might be interfered with by the acceptance of funding; and that the agency could be understood to endorse the distributor's business practices, which some claim involves advertising specifically targeting underage populations.

Having completed an ethical review, the director realizes that it has prompted him to revisit several principles contained in the legal inventory. Specifically, the ethical standards already examined inspire the director to revisit in a new light the duties to practice reasonably competently, to seek informed consent, and to identify the primary client; they may indeed have application in this scenario after all. As the director now sees it, competent practice should include prudent administrative and fiscal management, a point that might argue in favor of the solicitation and acceptance of all legally available funding. At the same time, however, protecting the needs of the agency's primary clients mandates the agency's avoidance of financial entanglements that compromise the independent delivery of competent mental health services. Therefore, the requirements of informed consent suggest that, if the funding is accepted, details concerning it and other gifts should be disclosed to potential clients, together with an explanation of the agency's philosophy in making the decision to accept this funding.

As another example of the use of ethical standards in supplementing a legal inventory, examine the following scenario: A social worker employed by an adult day-care service is assigned the task of visiting, interviewing, and assessing the agency's new client, an elderly woman whose family has reported her to be neglecting herself physically and not eating regularly, although she is mentally alert in every other respect. Fearing for her safety, members of her family report that they would "like her in a nursing home in the neighborhood" but will consider the agency's services as a first option.

One of the social worker's tasks is to provide a report to the agency administrator on the woman's suitability for the agency's services, which include supportive assisted-living care. If the social worker's assessment indicates that the woman requires around-the-clock supervision, long-term institutional nursing home care will be recommended to the family.

Applying the framework, the social worker's legal inventory at once suggests the applicability of the duties to practice reasonably competently, to seek informed consent, and to identify the primary client. These responsibilities indicate that the social worker should conduct an interview and assessment of the woman independent of the family's influence. These duties also require that the social worker perform the client evaluation immune from subtle agency pressure that might inspire a presupposed need for the agency's services. Further, the social worker must explain to the woman in plain language the risks and benefits of any proposed intervention, including those presented by the agency (i.e., assisted living) and long-term nursing care, respectively.

Moving on to the NASW Code of Ethics, the social worker notes the applicability of ethical standard 1.02, which supports the social worker's duty to promote client self-determination. The social worker interprets this standard to further buttress the legal responsibilities to competently assess and provide appropriate services to the woman; these duties mandate that the social worker engage in reasonable efforts to maintain her independent living arrangement.

Incorporating Context in Decision Making

Cultural and regional characteristics play a role in the definition of legal standards governing the mental health professions. As noted previously, reasonably competent practice is in part defined by reference to the expectations imposed on providers in the communities where they work. Similarly, the cultural and language traditions of clients can have a significant impact on the interpretation of legal responsibilities governing informed consent and confidentiality.

Apart from their role in assisting the decision maker to interpret legal principles, cultural and regional factors stand alone as criteria that may aid in the resolution of practice dilemmas where law and ethics fail to offer sufficient guidance, or where such guidance is inconsistent. As an example, the earlier scenario involving an agency director's consideration of a grant from an alcohol distributor may have a somewhat different resolution if the example takes place in an area in which there is a high proliferation of alcoholism. For example Gallup, McKinley County, New Mexico is often identified as an impoverished community with a long-standing history of alcohol abuse in the Navajo population (Robert Wood Johnson Foundation, 2010). In fact, McKinley County has been singled out as the county with the highest rate of alcohol-related problems, including criminal activity, in the United States (Robert Wood Johnson Foundation, 2010). Considering the abundance in that community of persons with dual diagnoses (i.e., individuals with joint diagnoses of alcoholism and mental illness), the symbolic gesture of accepting money from an alcohol distributor may compromise the agency's ability to solicit funding from other regional sources. More than that, if the agency's acceptance of the gift becomes widely known, it may provoke distrust of the agency's agenda in its catchment area and therefore discourage the outreach effort that the gift is intended to promote.

The acceptance of funding from the alcohol industry has been an issue hotly debated in recent years by concerned members of various Indian nations, which have at times declined such funding on the basis of the preceding considerations. Thus, despite the stark need for the financing of major public health initiatives, Indian nations have sometimes estimated the potential, negative long-term consequence of promoting alcohol consumption to overshadow the short-term good that may result from the funding. This discussion must be understood in light of the devastating social effects of chronic alcoholism in Indian territory of many regions of the United States. In addition to the chronic health issues associated with alcoholism, it continues to be linked to violent crime, child abuse, and family decay, among other problems (Kunitz & Levy, 2000; Valdez, Kaplan, & Curtis, 2007). Consequently, the legitimization—however indirect or unintended—of alcohol consumption in a community suffering from a high rate of alcoholism may not be consistent with appropriate social planning in the region. This regional context plays an important role in considering the legal duties associated with the issue of agency funding; thus, this context may strongly affect the duty to practice reasonably appropriate fiscal management of a mental health agency.

Raising Pragmatic Concerns in Decision Making

Recognizing cultural and regional context in decision making has a practical side. Enhancing diversity through the culturally competent design and implementation of mental health and human services is the best way to ensure that all members of a community will use them. Moreover, understanding the culturally based expectations that clients place on their mental health providers enhances every professional relationship to the extent that it encourages competent practice. In the case of the agency director considering whether to accept funding from an alcohol distributor, reasonably competent fiscal management must include the practical consideration that the long-term costs of taking the money may be severe; the indirect encouragement of drinking, together with the agency's diminished public credibility, might have a profound economic cost.

Despite the overall effectiveness of including legal, ethical, and cultural considerations in the resolution of mental health practice dilemmas, reference to the exigencies of life in the community where the problem is experienced may best determine the solution to a problem. The practical consequences of any choice therefore must be a part of any decisional approach in which legal and ethical principles do not provide an immediate, consistent answer. When law and ethics do suggest a general outcome, pragmatic concerns help shape how to carry out that outcome.

The idea that pragmatic concerns should be a part of a decision-making framework is not so obvious a point as it would seem at first glance. Indeed, the mental health professions—particularly in their ethical codes—often exhort licensees to attain lofty goals, including social justice, the advancement of the general welfare of society, and the improvement of global living conditions (see, e.g., NASW Code, ethical standard 6.01), without providing a mechanism for doing so that satisfies the practice and time constraints of the average provider. To the typical agency-based social worker, counselor, or psychologist, the most common limitation involves budgetary restrictions. Despite the exhortations of ethical codes, the average professional trying to meet daily obligations cannot persistently be asked to do what is simply not possible, for budgetary, administrative, personnel, or other practical reasons.

In view of the foregoing, how and when should pragmatic considerations be introduced in decision making? Put simply, they should be a final step in the decision-making process such that each professional considers the practical consequences of any decision, whether they are immediate budgetary repercussions or long-term, communitywide effects unique to a region. Consistent with the framework, it is not appropriate to consider these pragmatic concerns first, because every decision maker should always respect and advance the primacy of the law—to the extent that it presumptively advances the best interests of individual clients and their communities. Moreover, a premature reliance on pragmatic factors may lead the decision maker to shy away from certain problems, including those with potentially costly outcomes or those that involve significant social dilemmas whose resolution may not be simple. Instead, along with a thorough review of the cultural and regional context of any decision, practical considerations should be introduced in the evaluation of any problem to which the legal inventory and ethical review provide no clear-cut solution. Even in situations in which the decision maker has identified the applicability of relevant legal principles, a further review of the practical consequences of applying them may reinforce a decision or inspire a reconsideration of the law, both of which occurred in the examples cited earlier.

The fact that pragmatic concerns may reinforce legal principles demonstrates that the law itself is often a reflection of practicality in everyday life. Indeed, legislation and judicial decisions are often based on a functional analysis of the immediate consequences of problematic issues. Even the landmark decision in the *Tarasoff* case in part rested on the California Supreme Court's mundane consideration that liability for a murder should be imposed on the defendants because they had insurance available to pay for its consequences (*Tarasoff v. Regents of Univ. of Cal.*, 1976). In view of this reality, incorporating a review of pragmatic considerations serves to complete the cycle of decision making that begins with the legal inventory.

As an example of the consideration of pragmatism in the resolution of a practice dilemma, consider the following scenario: A partially disabled student at a regional community college has a muscular disorder that causes his arms to fatigue after prolonged writing. He has requested assistance from his state's vocation and rehabilitation office, but the application has been denied. He now seeks through the university counselor in charge of disability services a new laptop computer on which he can complete papers, type class notes, and take examinations. The disability counselor is aware of a serious funding shortfall that has curtailed the college's budget. In light of these facts, the counselor must make a recommendation to the dean of students concerning the student's case.

If guided by the framework, the counselor's decision will include a legal inventory that recognizes the importance of basic laws protecting the access of persons with disabilities to an education. The counselor should specifically recognize the applicability of the ADA. Knowing that the law requires the college to take feasible steps to equalize the student's access to education—the reasonable accommodation rule—the counselor must translate this principle into specific action.

Considering the framework's pragmatism step, the counselor assesses the college's reasonable response to the student's disability in light of the budgetary issue. The counselor concludes that the student's problem can appropriately be addressed in a more affordable manner than by providing an expensive laptop for the student's exclusive use. Specifically, the college can provide the student with assistance in the form of student note takers and can grant him special, enhanced access to computer-lab facilities in the library. This more modest response conserves valuable resources for the immediate use of needier students with more profound disabilities.

The legal principles initially reviewed virtually mandate the measured, fiscally appropriate response of the counselor. This example therefore serves as an illustration of the manner in which pragmatism may ultimately support the legal resolution of a dilemma.

Compare the present scenario with case example 14, "The School Social Worker," which concerned the Ramirez family and their educationally disabled child. In that situation, the guidance counselor prematurely applied pragmatic concerns in apparent violation of applicable law. Specifically, the counselor was prepared to propose an individualized education plan that removed the child from her primary classroom, in breach of the principle requiring mainstreaming for the educationally disabled.

Another way to analyze the school social worker dilemma is to recognize the long-term practicality of mainstreaming. Even if the guidance counselor failed initially to recognize his responsibilities under the law, he might still have reached the conclusion that the child's removal from her social environment could cause substantially greater immediate harm to the child, as well as higher financial costs to the school, than the reasonable and simple alternative—providing available services to her in her regular classroom. Despite the counselor's instinctive reluctance to break his school district's budget, he could have found through careful research and economic analysis that the overall administrative costs resulting from segregated special education might ultimately be greater than the costs of bringing these services to the child's own natural environment.

As a final example of the use of pragmatism to address practice dilemmas, consider the following scenario: A community-based agency in a rural town targets the needs of minority latchkey children and their families. Funded by public grants and by research subsidies from a local college, the agency offers several discrete services to clients. Among these are a series of after-school activities for elementary school children, a counseling program for children and their families, and a fathering support group. An executive director who has a doctorate in social work, a clinical director who is a psychiatrist, and several staff therapists administer the agency. The executive director has recently learned that funding from one of the grants has been slashed significantly, thus resulting in near-certain service cutbacks.

Applying the framework, the executive director realizes that the funding problem must not compromise the duty to provide reasonably competent services. However, the cutbacks create a budgetary shortfall requiring the practical consideration of program changes. If the executive director recommends scaling down in individual programs, such as elimination of one-on-one therapy sessions, a critical component of the agency's therapeutic services, the basic integrity of the clinical services offered to clients may be significantly affected. Similarly, if the executive director eliminates staff positions in the after-school program, the agency's ability to provide adequate supervision to children may be endangered.

A review of practical considerations suggests that the executive director's best choices lie in the entire removal or restructuring of one or more of the individual programs the agency offers. This requires the executive director to identify the agency's most critically important services and to protect them outright from cutbacks. At the same time, he should target—as difficult as this task may seem—the agency's less vital services and find ways to eliminate or combine them in a cost-saving manner. Thus, elimination of the fathering group and a folding over of fathering-related issues into the counseling program may be the most effective choice and may eliminate some repetition of services. More than anything, pragmatism requires that the executive director strive to reduce administrative costs in a way that avoids hindering the agency's essential clinical purposes.

Integrating Law, Ethics, Context, and Pragmatism in Professional Dilemmas: Case Examples

The decision-making framework combines a legal inventory with a review of interpretive factors; these include professional ethical standards, cultural and regional context, and individual pragmatic concerns that may influence unique practice situations. The utility of this system is that it integrates objective and subjective factors in a unified process that advances communitarian ideals yet also recognizes the individuality of clients, mental health professionals, and the practice situations that bind them. It therefore promotes the goal that, in every practice decision, mental health professionals should strive to advance the values shared in each community while respecting the principle that all clients and practice situations are distinct.

The final case examples offer the reader an opportunity to put it all together. They present scenarios whose resolution depends on the consideration of all the framework's steps. For this reason, they each serve as a paradigm for decision making in the mental health professions.

Case Example 26: Suspected Neglect in Lumberton

Gussie Shirley is a forty-three-year-old single mother living in Lumberton, Robeson County, North Carolina, a diverse community of Anglo, African

American, Native American, and Hispanic people. Lumberton, a city of about twenty thousand people, has been beset over the past few years by the closing of multiple local industries, which has resulted in an unemployment rate among the highest in the U.S. for cities of its size. Not unexpectedly, Robeson County has one of the highest poverty rates in the United States (Gutiérrez, 2007). Gussie, a Lumbee Indian, has recently suffered a badly broken leg. After her treatment at a regional health clinic, an infection has set in. Following a brief hospital stay, Gussie has been released to her home with a discharge plan calling for a series of ten nurse visits. Gussie is confined to bed rest and required to take a regimen of antibiotics.

Lambert Urbano is the visiting nurse assigned to the Shirley family's case. During Lambert's initial home visit, he surveys the rustic cabin in which Gussie lives with her ten-year-old daughter, Alice. Lambert notices that the Shirleys have no running water but draw their supply from a nearby well. Having no plumbing facilities, they rely on an outhouse and an old tub that they fill with heated water for bathing. Several of the cabin's windows are broken, with glass shards surrounding the outside areas. Hastily prepared cardboard covers are taped to the inside of two windows to protect the cabin from the elements. The family has a woodstove on which Gussie cooks and that provides heat during the winter months.

Lambert, a recent transplant from Chicago, is not used to the living conditions he witnesses. Observing Alice, Lambert notes that she is very thin, wears a dress she probably has worn for some time, and that her arms and legs are dirty.

During his examination of Gussie, her leg shows no signs of healing. To make matters worse, Lambert receives hesitant and conflicting reports from Gussie regarding her attention to the discharge plan. In particular, Lambert suspects that Gussie might not be taking her prescribed medications. When asked about this, Gussie responds that she "tries to."

Lambert has concerns about the family's living conditions and more specifically believes that the environment might be sufficiently unhealthy for Alice as to constitute child neglect. Moreover, he has fears about Gussie's ability and/or willingness to care for herself. In view of these concerns, Lambert elects to consult with his agency supervisor, Clara Tobarn, a licensed social worker and Lumberton native, regarding the possibility of making a referral to the county's child protective services unit, a step that would then require a formal investigation of the Shirley family by that agency.

In beginning their legal inventory, Lambert and Clara will probably at once recognize and apply the duties to practice reasonably competently and identify the primary client. In the present scenario, the professional relationship Lambert has established with Gussie exists for the sole purpose of providing home health care and related services. It is not, therefore, Lambert's duty to diagnose or treat any condition that does not fall within the scope of this professional relationship. The duty to practice reasonably competently, however, also entails the responsibility to recognize and report suspected child abuse and neglect to appropriate authorities. In addition, it requires the protection of vulnerable adults who may be self-neglectful to the degree that they pose a reasonable threat of harm to themselves.

Legal duties that are specific to Clara include the responsibility to give reasonably competent supervision to Lambert. In the exercise of this duty, Clara must draw on her understanding of community expectations in Robeson County regarding the daily lifestyles of local people.

Understanding the legal duties applicable to both, Clara and Lambert initially agree that in the present case they are required to report suspected child neglect or adult self-neglect only in the event that there is a reasonable suspicion that either harm is occurring. This standard is intended as a precaution to ensure investigation of marginal cases. Consequently, as a relative newcomer unaccustomed to the lifestyles of some Robeson County residents, Lambert's initial assessment is that his observations of the Shirleys' home life are enough to satisfy the reasonable suspicion standard. Lambert thinks this is true with respect to both Gussie and Alice, meaning that he believes Gussie is neglecting both Alice and herself; therefore, he believes that the agency should err on the side of caution and refer the family for investigation. At the least, Lambert believes that making the report will provide the family with needed support services.

In consultation with Clara, Lambert shares his opinion but finds that Clara regards the situation to be more ambiguous. If Clara brings her understanding of community lifestyles to her assessment of the Shirley family, she is likely to conclude that the family's living arrangements are not unusual for Robeson County, which, as noted, ranks among the poorest in North Carolina and the United States. In consultation with her agency counsel, Clara may well conclude that poverty in itself must never give rise to the presumption of child neglect.

As to the possibility of Gussie's self-neglect, Clara's interpretation of the conduct Lambert has described to her should also be based on a consideration of community norms. Specifically, Clara might note that Gussie's apparent reticence in describing her self-care is as likely the result of fear and suspicion than subterfuge. Moreover, Clara might note, in a community in which homemade, culturally based remedies are a common form of treatment and antibiotics are not deemed the only acceptable response to infection, Lambert's hypothesis that neglect is occurring is not necessarily accurate or helpful.

Summarizing the foregoing considerations, a regionally and culturally based interpretation of applicable law argues against a premature referral for suspected neglect in this case. Consistent with reasonably competent practice, further assessment—with the assurance of cultural and regional consistency—should follow to clarify some of the medical issues that have identified themselves with respect to Gussie's self-care. This assessment should include attention to the duty to seek informed consent, which in this scenario requires an open and appropriate discussion of health issues specifically related to the treatment of Gussie's leg. Although Gussie's living arrangements may distress Lambert, they are not unusual for this community, and therefore should not fall within the scope of his assessment, at least to the extent that they do not directly affect the healing of Gussie's leg. Moreover, Lambert cannot allow his initial impression of the family to dictate his future course of services. In this instance, his attention to his primary role as a medical provider with limited, agency-defined duties advances his patient's best interests.

A review of pragmatic considerations supports the legal and cultural assessments. Specifically, it underscores the consequences of an overly hasty referral for an investigation of neglect. The imposition of a government intervention on a family that is marginal economically but apparently functional in other respects may upset the family's equilibrium and drive it into social isolation, perhaps hastening the very health problems that the agency wishes to prevent. Indeed, although good intentions here may support the early reporting of suspected neglect, thoughtful consideration of the consequences does not.

Case Example 27: The Telethon

In response to Hurricane Katrina's devastating impact on the Gulf Coast in 2005, a private consortium of citizens, community organizers, and celebrities in Branson, Missouri, embarked on a fund-raising initiative for storm victims. As part of this enterprise, they created an agency, the Branson Heart Club, which opened a bank account under the name Katrina Fund. In addition to collecting and distributing funds, the Branson Heart Club has attempted through several agency-sponsored social events to raise public awareness about the plight of survivors of the disaster. In the immediate aftermath of Hurricane Katrina, the agency distributed the funds it collected to a variety of programs for hurricane survivors, including food banks, homeless shelters, and even programs for the victims of family violence, a problem that has spiraled in the wake of the Katrina disaster.

In the months and years following the hurricane, the Heart Club and its staff members have dedicated themselves tirelessly to collecting funds through the acceptance of individual and corporate contributions, as well as small grants from several private foundations. This fund-raising has been carried out despite the fact that, at the time of its creation, the Heart Club's organizers lacked formal fund-raising experience. Nevertheless, the agency has attempted to carry on its work with the additional benefit of the do-nated services of a small group of committed volunteers. Now, five years after the catastrophe, the Heart Club finds that its small group of devoted backers lacks the time and energy to continue its earnest commitment to ongoing fund-raising activities. It now seems evident that an organized, full-time fund-raising effort is simply beyond the means of the relatively modest number of Branson locals who first organized it.

At the same time, as they realize that Katrina's impact promises to cause long-term, newly emerging social problems, the organizers of the Heart Club are interested in ensuring that their efforts to provide for victims continue. They are also driven by their concern that the environmental damage result-ing from the BP oil-spill disaster in the Gulf of Mexico will have a significant effect on tourism and the fishing industry in the region, with an ensuing ex-pansion of the social problems that area residents have already been experi-encing in Katrina's aftermath. Knowing that they can no longer individually commit themselves to ongoing fund-raising, they are determined to seek assistance from other experienced fund-raisers who, the organizers believe, can create the infrastructure and organize the participants necessary to keep the Heart Club's efforts ongoing. Toward this end, the organizers have en-gaged the assistance of a regional telemarketing organization experienced with large-scale charitable collection activities. Through the efforts of the telemarketer and with the donated support of a network of area television stations, the Heart Club has planned a three-hour telethon whose proceeds are to be earmarked for the agency's relief efforts. Consistent with charitable telemarketing practices, a small percentage of the funds collected are to go to administrative costs and the telemarketer's fees.

Disagreement among the Heart Club's organizers has occurred as to ex-actly how much of the funds collected from the telethon should be applied specifically to the needs of fund victims and deposited in the Katrina Fund. Several of the organizers are concerned that the federal government and private sources have addressed the immediate needs of Katrina survivors in the years following the disaster and that it is therefore wrong to collect money for this specific purpose when doing so will only divert necessary attention away from other important regional purposes, such as combating poverty, hunger, and homelessness throughout the southern United States. The group also believes that a solitary emphasis on aiding Katrina victims is no longer timely and serves only to distract potential contributors from these other vital purposes, such as responding adequately to the social needs that can be expected to emerge as a result of the oil spill. Indeed, other charitable organizations have reported that, in the first years following Katrina, a decrease in contributions occurred, presumably as a result of the attention focused on Katrina and its consequences. The idea that the long-term needs of hurricane victims have been satisfied is both naive and plainly disputed by research (Lamberg, 2008). Indeed, the long-term mental health impact of the disaster is just now becoming evident, and the ongoing problems of victims—including homelessness and family decay as a result of relocation— are likely to continue indefinitely.

In light of the present scenario, the Branson Heart Club's organizers must make important decisions concerning their agency's mission; their responsibilities to the clients targeted by that mission; and their duty, if any, to prospective recipients of funding resulting from the telethon. The decision-making framework provides a tool for analysis of the Heart Club's dilemma. If organizers conduct a thorough legal inventory, they will likely note the applicability of the duties to practice reasonably competently, to seek informed consent, and to identify the agency's primary clients.

In the present case example, reasonably competent practice provides the general standard by which the agency must conduct its fund-raising. This includes management of the fiduciary responsibility connected with solicitation of funds from the public. The Heart Club's organizers have taken an appropriate first step in fulfilling this obligation by affiliating with an experienced fund-raising organization that can compensate for the organizers' lack of expertise in this area. Fund-raising is a discrete responsibility requiring competent methodology, attention to detail, and fiscal responsibility both to donors and to recipients of donations.

From whom must the organizers seek informed consent in this situation? The answer depends on the organizers' creation of a professional relationship with one or more primary clients. The most critical professional relationship in this scenario is the one that the Heart Club has sought to create with the survivors of Hurricane Katrina. After all, at the time of the Heart Club's creation, money to be collected ostensibly was to be directed to their benefit, and that point has been plainly revealed to the public. It is important to remember that the duty to identify a primary client is as important a legal responsibility in community organizing as it is in clinical mental health practice. This point suggests that the Heart Club should not engage in funding efforts without the voluntary support of the families and the seeking of informed consent from them. The Heart Club's duties to seek the voluntary support of survivors and gain their informed consent may be more difficult to accomplish than in one-on-one therapeutic relationships, but they can be satisfied just the same. This requires the concerted effort of the Heart Club to reveal fully its fund-raising strategy and to obtain clear permission from the families to collect funds and to contribute these funds to programs that have been organized on their behalf. This can be accomplished, at least in spirit, through the holding of public meetings with families themselves or with the leaders of hurricane victim associations that have come into existence since the disaster occurred. The use of mass media may be instrumental in fostering communication between the Heart Club and its beneficiaries, given the scope of the fund-raising effort undertaken by the agency.

Without first identifying the families' immediate needs regarding support services, the collection of funds arguably was not carried out with adequate attention paid to this point. Moreover, at the initiation of the fund-raising effort, organizers had no experience in fund-raising and did not seek out the assistance of persons with expertise. Given these facts, it is fair to conclude that the Heart Club's efforts for the first three and a half years of its existence were not carried out with due regard for the legal responsibilities mentioned here. However, the agency's current determination to regroup and organize its future fund-raising strategy with the assistance of a firm experienced in this area provide it with the opportunity to satisfy its duties regarding the identification of its primary clients and the solicitation of informed consent.

If Hurricane Katrina victims are the Heart Club's primary clients, then what association exists between the agency and the donating public? Although not strictly in the nature of a professional relationship, as that term has been used in this book, it is nonetheless a fiduciary association, akin to the contractual bond that exists between a service provider and a third-party payor or insurance company. Viewed in this light, the Heart Club has a responsibility to use fair solicitation techniques that include openness and clarity in identifying the purposes to which it will apply donated funds.

In acknowledging hurricane victims as the Heart Club's primary clients, organizers should carefully consider whether broadening the agency's mission to include other needy persons and groups is a wise decision. Clearly, the agency's efforts have historically targeted solely hurricane victims, and it is certain that its public association with the Katrina tragedy and its aftermath has increased its ability to raise funds.

In completing the legal inventory, Heart Club organizers should evaluate the impact of federal and state policies governing trade practices and funds solicitation. This evaluation is likely to support the result mandated by informed consent and competent practice standards: money solicited for Katrina survivors must be earmarked expressly for those persons and programs that directly support them.

A supplemental review of ethical, regional, and cultural factors enriches the legal inventory in this case scenario. It reveals that persons touched by human tragedy are sometimes motivated to help alleviate its effects regardless of the cost. Therefore, it is not unusual in such circumstances to find individuals of modest means pledging donations out of a sense of emotional attachment to victims. The use of mass media to solicit donations increases this phenomenon. Therefore, the use of a telethon to seek donations must be planned sufficiently competently to ensure that the information shared with the public is accurate and that prospective donors are not exhorted to donate money to an extent that is inconsistent with their own family budgets. In this regard, telethon viewers are particularly vulnerable. Indeed, they are particularly vulnerable to any television fund-raiser in which organizers use a newsworthy event to inspire donations from the public. In less populated areas, people tend to rely particularly on the media to obtain news and public information and to choose charities they wish to support. These considerations make it clear that the fund-raisers in the present example have a special responsibility to their community to be honest and fair in their efforts.

Finally, pragmatic considerations compel the conclusion that fund solicitation planned for a particular purpose—in this case, to aid hurricane survivors—must be dedicated to that purpose. It is patently unreasonable for organizers to plan a telethon to aid Hurricane Katrina victims and even consider diverting funds from the telethon to other purposes. Although it is true that there is a multitude of social problems that persons experience in the South and elsewhere, this fact alone cannot justify the diversion of funds and the resultant violation of immediate professional duties owed to primary clients—in this case, hurricane survivors. To do otherwise would be to mislead the public. In practical terms, mismanagement of the telethon and the diversion of monies from its intended recipients compromise the Heart Club's public credibility and may hamper its future ability to raise funds.

This final case example, inspired as it is by a recent national event, is intended to alert the professional decision maker to the utility of a law-based framework in the resolution of dilemmas both small and large. The scenario stands as a model for the maintenance of a community focus in all daily practice decisions. With respect to each important choice that every mental health professional makes, this approach surely is the most effective way to champion both the client's best interests and the community's shared values.

Decision-Making Framework: Legal Principles to Apply in Any Practice Dilemma

Principle 1: The Duty to Practice Reasonably Competently

When to Consider the Duty

The duty should be considered in all practice situations.

Elements of the Duty

The definition of reasonably competent practice varies depending on the profession and the jurisdiction. In general, however, a professional owes a legal duty to the client to practice reasonably competently according to the nature and scope of his or her professional training. This duty extends to the client and to members of the public who can reasonably be expected to suffer if the professional fails to honor this duty (see, e.g., *Tarasoff v. Regents of Univ. of Cal.*). It also includes the duty to protect vulnerable individuals, primarily children and frail elderly, at risk of physical or emotional abuse, neglect, or exploitation. This duty may include warning appropriate authorities about the existence of suspected abuse or neglect.

Reasonably competent practice includes the following:

- Conforming to the standards expected of professionals in a discipline, including social work, counseling, psychology, and other mental health professions
- Conforming to the standards expected of professionals in a particular specialty area, such as psychotherapy, counseling, child welfare investigations, research, teaching, and community organizing

- Recognizing the extent and limits of one's training and understand-ing the scope of any physical or mental limitations affecting the ability to practice
- Understanding the need to seek consultation or refer a client to an-other professional when appropriate
- Engaging in culturally and regionally competent practice
- Adhering to the duty to make appropriate documentation and to maintain adequate records concerning services

Reasonably competent administration and supervision include the following:

- The duty to administer programs and services and to supervise employees appropriately, as well as to provide consultation to su-pervisees whose level of training and terms of employment should reasonably be expected to require it

Finding Local Information about the Duty

The duty is governed by individual licensing standards in each mental health profession, and also by state law, including court-made and legislative standards.

Principle 2: The Duty to Seek Informed Consent

When to Consider the Duty

The duty should be considered especially in the following situations:

- When working with children, mentally ill, frail elderly, and other vulnerable clients
- When clients have been directly and indirectly solicited by means of professional seminars and advertising
- Whenever there are cross-cultural or language differences between the professional and the client
- When conducting research

Elements of the Duty

It is incumbent on professionals to obtain informed consent from their clients before the commencement of services. In a legal sense, informed consent refers not so much to the document that the client signs agreeing to the services but more to the quality and completeness of the provider-client dialogue that forms the basis of the agreement for professional services. This dialogue must address the following points:

- The client must have an understanding of the benefits and risks of various services, together with the capacity to understand this information.
- *Capacity* means both legal capacity and mental capacity.
- Informed consent also requires that the client consent to services voluntarily.

The law may modify the legal capacity to consent by either augmenting it or diminishing it; thus, underage minors in some states have the legal capacity to consent to limited mental health treatment and the receipt of contraceptive information. Courts that mandate that a client receive mental health services can be thought of as assuming on the client's behalf the right to consent to services.

Finding Local Information about the Duty

State law, including court-made and legislative standards, governs the duty.

Principle 3: The Duty to Identify the Primary Client

When to Consider the Duty

The duty should be considered especially in the following situations:

- Whenever one is employed as a public agency professional
- When asked as a public agency professional to provide multiple behavioral or human services to individuals and families
- When working with children, frail elderly, mentally disabled, and other vulnerable persons
- When a client has an insurance company or other third-party reimburser responsible for the client's bills or otherwise interested in the client's progress
- When conducting research
- When a court has ordered a client to receive services

- When an attorney or other professional has referred the client for services
- When retained to offer an expert opinion concerning a client's condition and/or the services a client has received from another professional

Application to Public-Sector Mental Health Professionals

Public agencies, including child welfare bureaus, state hospitals, and mental health bureaus, probation service departments, and educational systems, among others, have legal responsibilities defined in state and federal laws. Their public responsibilities often include the protection of certain classes of vulnerable citizens and create specific professional-client relationships between the agency and the vulnerable group.

Mental health professionals employed by public agencies agree to accept the agency's legal responsibilities as their own. For example, in the case of a social worker employed by a child protective service agency, a psychologist, clinical social worker, or counselor employed by a government mental health facility, a public school counselor, or a probation service worker, the professional's primary clients are the vulnerable members of the public whom the provider agency is required to protect, such as abused or neglected children and the elderly. This duty ordinarily supersedes any other professional obligation.

Application to Mental Health Professionals in Private Practice

A mental health professional in private practice must evaluate who the primary client is and what legal obligations he or she owes to the client according to state, federal, or tribal law. The mental health professional must carefully consider this issue when providing services primarily to one person, but the interests of family members or others may be peripherally involved and may threaten to interfere with the duty owed to the primary client.

A professional must also avoid conflicts of interest with the primary client. Conflicts of interest may include social or business relationships with the primary client or a close relation of the primary client's, professional responsibilities imposed by the provider's position that control or limit the nature of services provided to the primary client, and the professional's proprietary or research interest in services that are offered to the primary client.

Finding Local Information about the Duty

State, federal, and tribal law, including court-made and legislative standards, govern the duty.

Principle 4: The Duty to Treat Clients and Coworkers with Due Process and Equal Protection

When to Consider the Duty

The duty should be considered especially in the following situations:

- When making decisions as a public agency administrator or employee that may affect clients' rights to benefits or services
- When considering disciplinary action against a public employee
- When making decisions as a private mental health or human service agency administrator or employee that may affect clients' rights to services
- When considering transfer of or disciplinary action against the student or resident of a public or private educational or rehabilitative institution
- When considering the hiring of a public or private agency employee

Elements of the Duty: Procedural Due Process

When the federal government or a state, county, or municipality, through its public agencies and employees, threatens to interfere with a client's or employee's right to life, liberty, or property, the client or employee has a right to procedural due process. *Procedural due process* means "fairness" and generally requires that the affected client or employee must have notice of the government's intent to interfere with an interest and an opportunity to be heard (e.g., hearing, trial).

Examples of property and liberty rights that require notice and a hearing or trial include the following situations:

- A state employee or federal employee faces disciplinary proceedings.
- A state welfare client has benefits suspended.
- A veterans' administration mental hospital recommends transfer of a patient.
- A public school student is suspended or expelled.

- A child welfare authority seeks to change the custody of a child.
- A person is arrested and charged with a crime punishable by imprisonment.

Elements of the Duty: Substantive Due Process

Some rights are so important that they are considered fundamental. These include all of the privileges guaranteed by the Bill of Rights (e.g., freedom of speech, religion, assembly, and press; protection from unlawful searches and seizures) and the right to individual and family privacy (consisting of, among other things, the right to make medical decisions, the right to marry, the right to raise a family, and the freedom from bodily restraint). The government and its agents and employees must never interfere with these fundamental rights unless they can demonstrate a compelling interest. A compelling interest ordinarily means an interest related to the government's responsibility to maintain the health and safety of the public or to perform some important government function.

Examples of the relationship between fundamental rights and compelling government interests include the following:

- A state psychologist usually cannot seek commitment of a patient without demonstrating the patient's violence.
- A public school counselor cannot be required to live in the town where the counselor is employed.
- A state welfare authority can seek custody of a child it believes is threatened by abuse or neglect.
- A city can require protest marchers to register in advance of a demonstration.

Elements of the Duty: Equal Protection

Equal protection requires that diverse clients and employees must not be classified on the basis of suspect categories, including race, religion, ethnicity, and national origin. Some classifications, including family income and socioeconomic status, are not considered suspect.

Examples of suspect and nonsuspect classifications include the following:

- A state child welfare authority may not deny licensure to foster parents on the basis of their race.
- A state welfare authority may deny welfare benefits to a family whose income rises above the maximum qualifying amount.

Elements of the Duty: Civil Rights Legislation

Various laws, including the Civil Rights Act of 1964 and other federal and state legislation, extend some of the constitutional obligations and protections of the Fourteenth Amendment to public and private agencies and their clients.

Finding Local Information about the Duty

The U.S. Constitution (Fifth and Fourteenth amendments), as well as interpretive state and federal court decisions and legislation, mainly govern the duty. State and federal agencies often define additional rules and regulations regarding due process and equal protection, and in some instances, these extend to private parties providing services under government contract.

Principle 5: The Duty to Maintain Confidentiality

When to Consider the Duty

The duty should be considered especially in the following situations:

- At the time the professional seeks informed consent from clients
- Before any practice decisions that may interfere with clients' privacy
- Before any practice decisions that may test the limits of confidentiality
- When working with clients who have insurance companies or other third-party reimbursers responsible for bills or otherwise professionally interested in client progress
- When providing services to a primary client that may also affect the interests of family members or others peripherally involved
- When providing services to children, mentally disabled, or frail elderly for whom a parent, guardian, or other third party has consented to services

Elements of the Duty

The duty to maintain confidentiality generally requires mental health professionals, and especially psychotherapists (social workers, counselors, and psychologists), to keep their clients' statements confidential unless

- The statements concern the intent to commit a violent, criminal, or other harmful and preventable act against an identified person
- The statements invoke the professional's legal duty to report child abuse or neglect
- Clients have waived the right in writing
- Clients have brought malpractice charges or disciplinary complaints

In general, the right to confidentiality is expressed in terms of a privilege belonging to the client and a duty imposed on the professional. The right affects the extent to which professionals can communicate with courts, police, insurance companies, and other parties concerning the services provided to the client and the information the client reveals.

The public policy behind confidentiality is to encourage those in need of mental health and human services to seek them out. Conversely, the public policy behind the limitations on the duty of confidentiality is that professionals who are in a position to help prevent a foreseeable harmful act should have the legal responsibility to take reasonable action to prevent it from occurring.

The client's right to confidentiality assumes the client's capacity to grant informed consent (i.e., the legal and mental capacity to engage in a professional relationship with the provider). For that reason, the duties to seek informed consent and to maintain confidentiality are interdependent.

Finding Local Information about the Duty

State, federal, and tribal law, including court-made and legislative standards, governs the duty. The law of the jurisdiction one practices in defines the limits of confidentiality. Fifty states have legislation governing confidentiality as it applies to social workers, counselors, psychologists, other licensed psychotherapists, medical doctors, clergy, attorneys, and additional mental health and human service professionals. This legislation generally appears either in professional licensing acts or in evidentiary codes.

Principle 6: Completing a Legal Inventory

When to Complete a Legal Inventory

A mental health professional should complete a legal inventory after he or she considers the potential application of each of the preceding legal principles. The professional should be versed in the state and local court and legislative interpretations of each of these principles, including understanding the protections offered by state constitutions and other regional legislation that may address a problem. Access to legal advice, including agency or personal counsel, concerning all potential legal aspects of a practice decision is especially helpful for this purpose. In completing an inventory, the professional should be prepared to ask several key questions concerning the legal impact of a practice decision. These include the following:

- Will the professional's decision be consistent with all relevant federal, state, and/or tribal law, as well as administrative rules and regulations?
- If the professional is employed by an agency, what are the legal obligations of the professional to the agency and of the agency to the professional?
- Which, if any, agency rules, regulations, or policies govern the situation or the agency's delivery of client services?
- Which, if any, agency rules, regulations, or policies define the professional's job responsibilities or employment contract obligations?
- Is an employee or client of an agency seeking to involve the professional in potentially unlawful behavior?
- Which, if any, state constitutional provisions create fundamental rights? (See the preceding section "Principle 4: The Duty to Treat Clients and Coworkers with Due Process and Equal Protection")

Codes of Ethics

Using Codes of Ethics to Supplement the Legal Inventory

Following completion of the legal inventory, the mental health professional should examine applicable standards from a relevant ethical code. This review may enhance the legal inventory by helping explain or interpret individual legal duties, particularly with respect to profession-specific practice guidelines. It may also prompt a consideration of additional legal principles that govern a practice situation. For these purposes, a summary of ethical standards from the social work, counseling, and psychology professions follows in Tables A1–A3.

TABLE A1: SUMMARY OF NASW CODE'S ETHICAL STANDARDS

NASW CODE STANDARD	SUMMARY OF STANDARD (SOCIAL WORKERS SHOULD . . .)
1.01 Commitment to clients	Promote client well-being
	Obey legal obligations that supersede loyalty to clients
1.02 Client self-determination	Promote client independence
1.03 Informed consent	Seek informed consent
	Use clear and understandable language with clients
1.06 Conflicts of interest	Avoid social and business contacts that risk harm to or exploitation of clients
1.07 Confidentiality	Maintain confidentiality except for compelling professional reasons
	Use technology—including electronic mail and fax machines—properly to safeguard confidentiality
1.08 Access to records	Provide clients with reasonable access to records
1.09 Sexual relationships	Refrain completely from sexual relationships with current clients
	Refrain from sexual relationships with clients' relatives and friends when there is a risk of exploitation or harm
2.07 Sexual relationships with colleagues	Avoid sexual relationships with colleagues when there is potential for a conflict of interest
	Refrain from sexual relationships with supervisees, students, and others over whom professional authority is exercised
3.01 Colleague relationships supervision/consultation	Provide competent supervision
	Avoid conflicts of interest that risk harm to or exploitation of supervisees
3.02 Education and training	Practice competently
3.07 Administration	Be competent and fair administrators

TABLE A1 (CONTINUED)

NASW CODE STANDARD	SUMMARY OF STANDARD (SOCIAL WORKERS SHOULD . . .)
3.09 Duties to employers	Honor commitments to employers
4.02 Discrimination	Refrain from all forms of discrimination
4.07 Solicitations	Refrain from advertising services to vulnerable persons
6.01 Duty to society	Promote the general welfare of society
	Promote social justice
	Promote development of people, communities, and environments
6.04 Social and political action	Engage in social and political action that ensures equal access to resources
	Work to prevent exploitation of individuals and groups

TABLE A2: SUMMARY OF NBCC CODE'S ETHICAL STANDARDS

NBCC CODE SECTION	SUMMARY OF STANDARD (CERTIFIED COUNSELORS SHOULD . . .)
A1, A6, A7	Practice competently
	Refrain from diagnosing, assessing, or treating clients unless prior training or supervision has been obtained
	Be guided in their work by prior research
A2	Honor commitments to clients and agency employers
A8, A9, B9	Avoid dual relationships that may harm clients or impair professional judgment
	Avoid personal, social, organizational, financial, or political activities that might lead to a misuse of influence
A10	Refrain from sexual relationships with present clients entirely and with past clients for a minimum of two years after the counseling relationship has been terminated

TABLE A2 (CONTINUED)

NBCC CODE SECTION	SUMMARY OF STANDARD (CERTIFIED COUNSELORS SHOULD ...)
A12	Be aware of the impact of stereotyping and discrimination on their clients
	Safeguard the personal dignity of the client
A13	Obey moral and legal standards
	Promote public confidence in the counseling profession
	Be accountable at all times for their behavior
A15	Withdraw from practice in the event of unethical conduct or mental disability
B1	Promote client welfare as a primary interest
	Protect the integrity of the client
B8	Seek informed consent
B4, B6, B14, B16	Maintain confidentiality except where there is a clear and imminent danger to the client or others
	Ensure that electronic data are secure
	Use electronic systems and data appropriately
	Ensure clients are emotionally compatible with computer applications
B5	Recognize the client's property interest in information contained in the counselor's records
B9	Refrain from dual relationships that might impair objectivity and judgment
B12	Avoid electronic means of counseling unless clients are told first of local sources of care
F1	Abide by NBCC Standards for Web Counseling
	Use accurate advertising

TABLE A3: SUMMARY OF APA CODE'S ETHICAL PRINCIPLES AND STANDARDS

APA CODE PRINCIPLE/ STANDARD	SUMMARY OF PRINCIPLE/ STANDARD	SUMMARY OF STANDARD (PSYCHOLOGISTS SHOULD . . .)
Principle A	Beneficence and non-maleficence	Benefit clients and do no harm
Principle B	Fidelity and responsibility	Establish relationships of trust
Principle C	Integrity	Promote honesty and accuracy
Principle D	Justice	Promote fairness and equal access to services
Principle E	Respect for people's rights and dignity	Promote client self-determination
1.02	Conflicts between ethics and law	Take reasonable steps to resolve conflicts
2.01	Boundaries of competence	Practice competently according to training
3.04	Avoiding harm	Avoid harming clients, students and colleagues
3.05	Multiple relationships	Avoid conflicts that risk harm to clients or impaired objectivity or judgment
3.10	Informed consent	Seek informed consent from clients
		With clients who lack capacity to consent, seek assent
4.01–4.05	Maintaining confidentiality	Honor their primary obligation to maintain confidentiality
		Where limits are defined by law, disclose confidences with client's consent

TABLE A3 (CONTINUED)

APA CODE PRINCIPLE/ STANDARD	SUMMARY OF PRINCIPLE/ STANDARD	SUMMARY OF STANDARD (PSYCHOLOGISTS SHOULD . . .)
		Disclose confidences where permitted by law, such as to protect client or others from harm, or to obtain compensation for services from a client
		Maintain client information databases properly
		Minimize intrusions on client privacy
5.01a	Avoidance of false and deceptive statements	Avoid false, fraudulent statements in advertising
5.01b	Avoidance of false and deceptive statements	Avoid false, fraudulent statements in describing training, experience and research
5.06	In-person solicitation	Avoid uninvited, in-person solicitation of clients
7.07	Sexual relationships with students and supervisees	Do not engage in such relationships
8.01–8.07	Research	Conduct research competently and lawfully
9.01–9.03	Assessments	Design and use competent assessments
10.05	Sexual intimacies with current therapy clients/ patients	Avoid entirely
10.06	Sexual intimacies with relatives or significant others of current therapy clients/patients	Avoid entirely
10.07	Therapy with former sexual partners	Avoid entirely
10.08	Sexual intimacies with former therapy clients/ patients	Avoid for at least two years after termination of therapy

Incorporating Cultural and Regional Context

Using Cultural and Regional Context to Supplement the Legal Inventory

The mental health professional should consider cultural and regional issues both during and after the legal inventory and ethical review. They may aid considerably in the interpretation of legal and ethical principles or help resolve an issue for which no clear legal or ethical answer has emerged. With this in mind, the mental health professional should

- Apply community standards to interpret legal and ethical duties
- Apply personal ideological or moral standards

Using Pragmatism to Supplement the Legal Inventory

Practical considerations may aid in the interpretation of legal and ethical standards. The professional should apply them only after completion of the legal inventory and ethical review. Pragmatic concerns include the following:

- The practical consequences of any decision, including but not limited to budgetary issues and unforeseen costs to an agency, its administration, personnel, and clients
- Whether any internal agency policies and procedures are already in existence to govern the situation
- Past methods of handling a particular problem

References

Books, Journals, and Other Sources

Alabama to investigate 112 uncertified programs. (2008). *Alcoholism and Drug Abuse Weekly, 20*(33), 3–5.

Alan Guttmacher Institute. (2009, April 1). An overview of minors' consent law. *State Policies in Brief.* Retrieved April 15, 2009, from http://www.agi-usa.org/pubs/spib.html.

Albee, G. W. (1999). Prevention, not treatment, is the only hope. *Counseling Psychology Quarterly, 12*(2), 133–146.

Albright, J. (2006). Comment: Free your mind: The rights of minors in New York to choose whether or not to be treated with psychotropic drugs. *Albany Law Journal of Science and Technology, 16*, 169–194.

American Psychiatric Association. (2000). *Diagnostic and statistical manual of mental disorders-DSM-TR* (4th ed.). Washington, DC: Author.

Appelbaum, P. (2005). Law and psychiatry: Assessing Kendra's Law: Five years of outpatient commitment in New York. *Psychiatric Services, 56*(7), 791–793.

Applewhite, S. L. (1995). *Curanderismo*: Demystifying the health beliefs and practices of elderly Mexican Americans. *Health and Social Work, 20*(4), 247–253.

Baert, P. (2005). *Philosophy of the social sciences: Towards pragmatism.* Cambridge, UK: Polity.

Bakker, A. B., Schaufeli, W. B., Sixma, H. J., & Bosveld, W. (2001). Burnout contagion among general practitioners. *Journal of Social and Clinical Psychology, 20*(1), 82–98.

Bean, R. A., Perry, B. J., & Bedell, T. M. (2001). Developing culturally competent marriage and family therapists: Guidelines for working with Hispanic families. *Journal of Marriage and Family Therapy, 27*(1), 43–54.

Ben-Zur, H., & Michael, K. (2007). Burnout, social support, and coping at work among social workers, psychologists, and nurses: The role of challenge/control appraisals. *Social Work in Health Care, 45*(4), 63–82.

Berkman, C. S., Turner, S. G., Cooper, M., Polnerow, D., & Schwartz, M. (2000). Sexual contact with clients: Assessment of social workers' attitudes and educational preparation. *Social Work, 45*(3), 223–235.

Brucker, P. S., & Perry, B. J. (1998). American Indians: Presenting concerns and considerations for family therapists. *American Journal of Family Therapy, 26*(4), 307–319.

Bureau of the Census Staff. (2001). *Statistical abstract of the United States: The national data book 2000* (120th ed.). Springfield, VA: U.S. Department of Commerce, National Technical Information Service.

Calkins, C. A., & Murray, M. (1999). The effectiveness of court appointed special advocates to assist in permanency planning. *Child and Adolescent Social Work Journal, 16*(1), 37–45.

Callan, E. (2005). The ethics of assimilation. *Ethics, 115*(3), 471–500.

Chandler, S., & Bell, S. (1995). Wai'anae, Hawai'i, United States: A culturally sensitive mental health care innovation. In R. Schulz & J. Greenley (Eds.), *Innovating in community mental health: International perspectives* (pp. 151–165). Westport, CT: Praeger.

Christensen, S. L. (2008). The role of law in models of ethical behavior. *Journal of Business Ethics, 77*(4), 451–462.

Collins-Camargo, C., Ensign, K., & Flaherty, C. (2008). The National Quality Improvements Center on the privatization of child welfare services: A program description. *Research on Social Work Practice, 18*(1), 72–81.

Colmant, S. A., & Merta, R. J. (1999). Using the sweat lodge ceremony as group therapy for Navajo youth. *Journal for Specialists in Group Work, 24*(1), 55–73.

Conner, D. (2006, Fall). Article: To protect or to serve: Confidentiality, client protection, and domestic violence. *Temple Law Review, 79,* 877–938.

Conry, E. J., & Beck-Dudley, C. L. (1996). Meta-jurisprudence: A paradigm for legal studies. *American Business Law Journal, 33*(4), 691–754.

Cook, A. (2008). Integrative medicine for the poor and underserved: A win-win situation. *Journal of Health Care for the Poor and Underserved, 19*(4), 1023–1028.

Corcoran, J. (2001). Multi-systemic influences on the family functioning of teens attending pregnancy programs. *Child and Adolescent Social Work Journal, 18*(1), 37–49.

Crampton, D., Crea, T., Abramson-Madden, A., & Usher, C. (2008). Challenges of street-level child welfare reform and technology transfer: The case for team decisionmaking. *Families in Society, 89*(4), 512–520.

Daniels, B. (1996, July 24). Social worker pleads not guilty in foster case. *Albuquerque Journal,* p. C1.

Daniels, B. (1997, January 1). Outgoing D.A. agrees to drop charges. *Albuquerque Journal,* p. A1.

Davidson, P. R., & Parker, K. C. (2001). Eye movement desensitization and reprocessing (EMDR): A meta-analysis. *Journal of Consulting and Clinical Psychology, 69*(2), 305–316.

Davis, G., & Stevenson, H. (2006). Racial socialization experiences and symptoms of depression among black youth. *Journal of Child and Family Studies, 15*(3), 303–317.

Echevarria-Doan, S., & Marquez, M. (2006). Counseling Cuban Americans using the framework for embracing cultural diversity. In C. C. Lee (Ed.), *New approaches to diversity* (3rd ed., pp. 195–205). Alexandria, VA: American Counseling Association.

Eitle, T., & Eitle, J. (2004). Inequality, segregation, and the overrepresentation of African Americans in school suspensions. *Sociological Perspectives, 47*(3), 269–287.

Emanuel, E., Wood, A., Fleischman, A., & Bowen, A. (2004). Oversight of human participants research: Identifying problems to evaluate reform proposals. *Annals of Internal Medicine, 141*(4), 282–291.

Epps, A. (2005, April). Article: Unacceptable collateral damage: The danger of probation conditions restricting the right to have children. *Creighton Law Review, 38*, 611–656.

Etzioni, A. (1998). *The new golden rule: Community and morality in a democratic society.* New York: Basic Books.

Ewoh, A. I. (1999). An inquiry into the role of public employees and managers in privatization. *Review of Public Personnel Administration, 19*(1), 8–27.

Freeman, M. (2003). Privatization of child protective services: Getting the lion back in the cage? *Family Court Review, 41*(4), 449–456.

Garner, B.A., & Black, H.C. (1999). *Black's law dictionary* (7th ed.). St. Paul, MN: West.

Gee, P. (2006). DRG do-over: The need for a service-line strategy. *Healthcare Financial Management, 60*(8), 52–55.

Gibelman, M., & Demone, H. W. (1998). *The privatization of human services: Policy and practice issues* (Vol. 1). New York: Springer.

Gilmour, R., & Jensen, L. (1998). Reinventing government accountability: Public functions, privatization, and the meaning of "state" action. *Public Administrative Review, 58*(3), 247–257.

Glisson, C., Dukes, D., & Green, P. (2006). The effects of the ARC organizational intervention on caseworker turnover, climate, and culture in children's service systems. *Child Abuse and Neglect, 30*(8), 855–880.

Goicoechea-Balbona, A. (1997). Culturally specific health care model for ensuring health care use by rural, ethnically diverse families affected by HIV/AIDS. *Health and Social Work, 22*(3), 172–180.

Graef, M. I., & Hill, E. L. (2000). Costing child protective services staff turnover. *Child Welfare, 79*(5), 517–533.

Green, T., McIntosh, A., Cook-Morales, V., & Robinson-Zañarto, C. (2005). From old schools to tomorrow's schools: Psychoeducational assessment of African American students. *Remedial and Special Education, 26*(2), 82–92.

Gutiérrez, C. M. (2007). *Statistical abstract of the United States, 2008* (127th ed.) Washington, DC: U.S. Census Bureau.

Hacker, J. (2004). Privatizing risk without privatizing the welfare state: The hidden politics of social policy retrenchment in the United States. *American Political Science Review, 98*(2), 243–260.

Haley, A. N., & Watson, D. C. (2000). In-school literary extension: Beyond in-school suspension. *Journal of Adolescent and Adult Literacy, 43*(7), 654–661.

Hall, M., & Schneider, C. (2008, February). Article: Patients as consumers: Courts, contracts, and the new medical marketplace. *Michigan Law Review, 106,* 643–695.

Harris, M. L. (1998, September). Curanderismo *and the* DSM-IV: *Diagnostic and treatment implications for the Mexican American client* (Occasional Paper No. 45). East Lansing: Michigan State University, Julian Samora Research Institute.

Haugaard, J., & Hazan, C. (2004). Recognizing and treating uncommon behavioral and emotional disorders in children and adolescents who have been severely maltreated: Reactive attachment disorder. *Child Maltreatment, 9*(2), 154–160.

Hellwage, J. (2000). Law of informed consent poised for revolution, experts say. *Trial, 36*(7), 128–130.

Hewlett, S. (1996). Consent to clinical research—adequately voluntary or substantially influenced? *Journal of Medical Ethics, 22*(4), 232–237.

Hogberg, G. (2007, May 4). Post-traumatic stress disorders therapy: Findings from Karolinska Institut, Department of Clinical Neuroscience provide new insights into post-traumatic stress disorders. *Drug Week,* 962–963.

Ishii-Kuntz, M. (1997). Intergenerational relationships among Chinese, Japanese, and Korean Americans. *Family Relations, 46*(1), 23–32.

Jewish poverty soars in New York. (2003). *Society, 41*(1), 3–4.

Joas, H. (1993). *Pragmatism and social theory.* Chicago: University of Chicago Press.

Johnson, D. (1979). Court rulings unleash health care advertising. *Advertising Age, 50*(15), S12.

Johnson, T. (2008–2009). Mental health advocates laud new federal parity law. *Nation's Health, 38*(10), 1–2.

Jordan, K. (2007). A case study: Factors to consider when doing 1:1 crisis counseling with local first responders with dual trauma after hurricane Katrina. *Brief Treatment and Crisis Intervention, 7*(2), 91–101.

Kauffman, F. (2007, September). Intensive family preservation services: The perceptions of client families. *Child and Adolescent Social Work Journal, 24,* 553–563.

Kaufman, D. A. (2009). The tipping point on the scales of civil justice. *Touro Law Review, 25,* 347–397.

Keegan, L. (1996). Use of alternative therapies among Mexican Americans in the Texas Rio Grande Valley. *Journal of Holistic Nursing, 14*(4), 277–294.

Kindred, K. (2003, Spring). Of child welfare and welfare reform: The implications for children when contradictory policies collide. *William and Mary Journal of Women and Law, 9,* 413–478.

Kirk, R., & Griffith, D. (2004). Intensive family preservation services: Demonstrating placement prevention using event history analysis. *Social Work Research*, *28*(1), 5–16.

Kunitz, S. J., & Levy, J. E. (2000). *Drinking, conduct disorder, and social change: The Navajo experience.* New York: Oxford University Press.

Lamberg, L. (2008). Katrina's mental health impact lingers. *Journal of the American Medical Association*, *300*(9), 1011–1013.

Landsman, M. (2002). Rural child welfare practice from an organization-in-environment perspective. *Child Welfare*, *81*(5), 791–819.

Lehrman, N. S., & Sharav, V. H. (1997). Ethical problems in psychiatric research. *Journal of Mental Health Administration*, *24*(2), 227–250.

Littell, J. H., & Tajima, E. A. (2000). A multi-level model of client participation in intensive family preservation services. *Social Service Review*, *74*(3), 405–437.

Lloyd, C., King, R., & Chenoweth, L. (2002). Social work, stress and burnout: A review. *Journal of Mental Health*, *11*(3), 255–265.

Long, A. (2003). Afterword. *Health Law Journal* [Special issue], 263–265 (expressing concern about the direct media promotion of mental health drugs and services).

Lorenzo, O. (2005). Nostalgia, shame and the transplanted Cuban: "La cubana arrepentida." *Portal Journal of Multidisciplinary International Studies*, *2*(1), 1–25.

Luna, E. (2003). Nurse-*curanderas*: *Las Que Curan* at the heart of Hispanic culture. *Journal of Holistic Nursing*, *21*(4), 326–342.

Lunstroth, J. (2007). Regulating the research enterprise: International norms and the right to bodily integrity in human experiment litigation. *Issues in Law and Medicine*, *23*(2), 141–199.

Maag, J. (2008). Rational-emotive therapy to help teachers control their emotions and behavior when dealing with disagreeable students. *Intervention in School and Clinic*, *44*(1), 52–57.

Matsuoka, J., & Benson, M. (1996). Economic change, family cohesion, and mental health in a rural Hawai'i community. *Families in Society*, *77*(2), 108–117.

McCabe, G. (2008). Mind, body, emotions and spirit: Reaching to the ancestors for healing. *Counseling Psychology Quarterly*, *21*(2), 143–152.

McGrath, E. Z. (1994). *The art of ethics: A psychology of ethical beliefs.* Chicago: Loyola University Press.

McMichael, A. J., & Beaglehole, R. (2000). The changing global context of public health. *Lancet*, *356*(9228), 495–499.

McRoy, R. (2008). Acknowledging disproportionate outcomes and changing service delivery. *Child Welfare*, *87*(2), 205–210.

Mercer, J. (2001). Attachment therapy using deliberate restraint: An object lesson on the identification of unvalidated treatments. *Journal of Child and Adolescent Psychiatric Nursing*, *14*(3), 105–114.

Moleski, S., & Kiselica, M. (2005). Dual relationships: A continuum ranging from the destructive to the therapeutic. *Journal of Counseling and Development*, *83*(1), 3–11.

Moore, S. (2009). Cognitive abnormalities in posttraumatic stress disorder. *Current Opinion in Psychiatry, 22*(1), 19–24.

Morris, R., & Howard, A. (2003). Designing an effective in-school suspension program. *Clearing House, 76*(3), 156–159.

Moscardelli, V., & Becker, L. (2007). Not on your (half) life: The partisan geography of nuclear waste disposal. *Congress and the Presidency, 34*(1), 55–78.

Munger, F. (2006). Dependency by law: Poverty, identity and welfare privatization. *Indiana Journal of Global Legal Studies, 13*(2), 391–415.

Murphy, L. (2001). Beneficence, law, and liberty: The case of required rescue. *Georgetown Law Journal, 89*(3), 605–665.

Nakashima, D. Y. (2004, Winter). Comment: Your body, your choice: How mandatory advance health-care directives are necessary to protect your fundamental right to accept or refuse medical treatment. *Hawai'i Law Review, 27,* 201–232.

Nicholson, K. (2001, June 19). "Rebirth therapists" get 16 years. *Denver Post,* p. A1.

Office of the Surgeon General. (2001). *Mental Health: Culture, race and ethnicity* (SAMHSA Report). Washington, DC: U.S. Department of Health and Human Services.

Olson, T., & Anders, R. (2000). Ethnicity, marginalisation and mental illness in Hawai'i. *Disability and Society, 15*(3), 463–473.

Paul, R. (2007). On guard: The auditor cometh. *Drug Topics, 151*(1), 34–37.

Peebles, I. E. (1999). Therapeutic jurisprudence and the sentencing of sexual offenders in Canada. *International Journal of Offender Therapy and Comparative Criminology, 43*(3), 275–290.

Pestello, F., & Davis-Berman, J. (2008). Taking anti-depressant medication: A qualitative examination of internet postings. *Journal of Mental Health, 17*(4), 349–360.

Pilisuk, M., McAllister, J., & Rothman, J. (1996). Coming together for action: The challenge of contemporary grassroots community organizing. *Journal of Social Issues, 52*(1), 15–37.

Quigley, W. (2001, August 11). Health-care ads due for an exam. *Albuquerque Journal,* p. A1.

Redman, B., & Caplan, A. (2005). Off with their heads: The need to criminalize some forms of scientific misconduct. *Journal of Law, Medicine and Ethics, 33*(2), 345–348.

Regehr, C., & Antle, B. (1997). Coercive influences: Informed consent in court-mandated social work practice. *Social Work, 42*(3), 300–306.

Rittner, B., & Dozier, C. D. (2000). Effects of court-ordered substance abuse treatment in child protective services cases. *Social Work, 45*(2), 131–140.

Robert Wood Johnson Foundation. (2003, July). Group fights back against alcohol abuse in Native American community in New Mexico. Retrieved April 1, 2010, from http://www.rwjf.org/reports/grr/031824.htm.

Roberts, M. J., & Reich, M. R. (2002). Ethical analysis in public health. *Lancet, 359*(9311), 1055–1059.

Rosenberg, M. A., & Browne, M. J. (2001, October). The impact of the inpatient prospective payment system and diagnosis-related groups: A survey of the literature. *North American Actuarial Journal, 5,* 84–94.

Rothstein, M. (2005). Research privacy under HIPAA and the common rule. *Journal of Law, Medicine and Ethics, 33*(1), 154–159.

Rouse, K. (2001, April 22). Rebirthing verdict may curb restraint therapy. *Denver Post,* p. A3.

Rousey, A., & Longie, E. (2001). The tribal college as family support system. *American Behavioral Scientist, 44*(9), 1492–1504.

Rubin, R., Billingsley, A., & Caldwell, C. (1994). The role of the black church in working with adolescents. *Adolescence, 29*(114), 251–266.

Russell, S. (1996, September 13). Hospital released patient with knife in belly—"I'll pick the deck when I'm out back." *San Francisco Chronicle,* p. A1.

Sacks, D. (2008, December). International sex torts. *Fordham Law Review, 77,* 1051–1093.

Santa Clara University. (2010, February 24). A framework for thinking ethically. Retrieved March 23, 2010, from http://www.scu.edu/ethics/practicing/decision/framework.html.

Schaufeli, W., & Enzmann, D. (1998). *The burnout companion to study and practice: A critical analysis.* London: Taylor and Francis.

Schorr, A. L. (2000). The bleak prospect for public child welfare. *Social Service Review, 74*(1), 124–136.

Setness, P. (2003). When privacy and the public good collide: Does the collection of health data for research harm individual patients? *Postgraduate Medicine, 113*(5), 15–6, 19.

Shalin, D. N. (1986). Pragmatism and social interactionism. *American Sociological Review, 51*(1), 9–29.

Shaw, W. H. (1998). *Contemporary ethics: Taking account of utilitarianism* (Contemporary Philosophy Series). Malden, MA: Blackwell.

Sheets, J. (1996). Designing an effective in-school suspension program to change student behavior. *National Association of Secondary School Principals Bulletin, 80*(579), 86–90.

Sheldon, S., & Epstein, J. (2002). Improving student behavior and school discipline with family and community involvement. *Education and Urban Society, 35*(1), 4–26.

Smolar, A. I. (2002). Reflections on gifts in the therapeutic setting: The gift from patient to therapist. *American Journal of Psychotherapy, 56*(1), 27–45.

Sørgaard, K., Ryan, P. Hill, R., & Dawson, I. (2007, August). Sources of stress and burnout in acute psychiatric care: Inpatient vs. community staff. *Social Psychiatry and Psychiatric Epidemiology, 42,* 794–802.

Sparrow, M. K. (1998). *License to steal: Why fraud plagues America's healthcare system.* Boulder, CO: Westview Press.

Stanford University. (2010, March 4). Stanford encyclopedia of philosophy. *The natural law tradition in ethics.* Retrieved March 23, 2010, from http://plato.stanford.edu/entries/natural-law-ethics/.

Stauffer, J. (2007). The rule of law and its shadow: Ambivalence, procedure, and the justice beyond legality. *Law, Culture and the Humanities, 3*(2), 225–243.

Stefl, M. E. (1999). Editorial. *Frontiers of Health Services Management, 16*(2), 1–2.

Stephens, J. (2007). Pfizer faces criminal charges in Nigeria. *Washington Post*, May 30, p. A10.

Swartz, N. (2003). Could HIPAA hamper research? *Information Management Journal, 37*(5), 16.

Takeuchi, D., Kuo, H., Kim, K., & Leaf, P. (1989). Psychiatric symptom dimensions among Asian Americans and Native Hawai'ians: An analysis of the symptom checklist. *Journal of Community Psychology, 17*(4), 319–329.

Tam, H. (1998). *Communitarianism: A new agenda for politics and citizenship.* New York: New York University Press.

Tamanaha, B. Z. (1999). *Realistic socio-legal theory: Pragmatism and a social theory of law* (Oxford Socio-Legal Studies). New York: Oxford University Press.

Taylor, M. (2001). A costly strategy. *Modern Healthcare, 31*(14), 34–35.

Terrell, S. (2001, July 13). Judge denies inmate more access to religious items, rituals. *Santa Fe New Mexican*, p. B5.

Thrower, A. W., & Martinez, J. M. (2000). Reconciling anthropocentrism and biocentrism through adaptive management: The case of the waste isolation pilot plant and public risk perception. *Journal of Environment and Development, 9*(1), 68–97.

Topper, K. (2000). In defense of dignity: Pragmatism, hermeneutics, and the social sciences. *Political Theory, 28*(4), 509–539.

Trivedi, A., Swaminathan, S., & Mor, V. (2008). Insurance parity and the use of outpatient mental health care following a psychiatric hospitalization. *Journal of the American Medical Association, 300*(24), 2879–2885.

Turner, D. C. (1996). The role of culture in chronic illness. *American Behavioral Scientist, 39*(6), 717–728.

Valdez, A., Kaplan, C., & Curtis, R. (2007). Aggressive crime, alcohol and drug use, and concentrated poverty in 24 U.S. urban areas. *American Journal of Drug and Alcohol Abuse, 33*(4), 595–603.

van Seters, P. V. (2006). *Communitarianism in law and society.* Lanham, MD: Rowman and Littlefield.

Van Slyke, D. (2003). The mythology of privatization in contracting for social services. *Public Administrative Review, 63*(3), 296–315.

Villa, R. F. (2001). *Program evaluation and community assessment: Project Recovery of northern New Mexico* (Cerro Grande Fire Disaster, FEMA-1329-DR-NM). Las Vegas: New Mexico Highlands University.

Vukadinovich, D. M. (2004). Minors' rights to consent to treatment: Navigating the complexity of state laws. *Journal of Health Law, 37*(4), 667–683.

Walker, D., & Irvine, N. (1997). Lokomika'i (inner health) in a remarkable hospital. *Nursing Management, 28*(6), 33–36.

Watson, B. C. (1999). Liberal communitarianism as political theory. *Perspectives on Political Science, 28*(4), 211–217.

Wattenberg, E., Kelley, M., & Kim, H. (2001). When the rehabilitation fails: A study of parental rights termination. *Child Welfare, 80*(4), 405–431.

Watts, C. (2005, Summer). Asking adolescents: Does a mature minor have a right to participate in health care decisions? *Hastings Women's Law Journal, 16,* 221–249.

Weiss, R., & McMichael, A. (2004). Social and environmental risk factors in the emergence of infectious diseases. *Nature Medicine, 10*(12), S70–S76.

Werth, J. L., Jr. (2001). U.S. involuntary mental health commitment statutes: Requirements for persons perceived to be a potential harm to self. *Suicide and Life-Threatening Behavior, 31*(3), 348–357.

Willging, K., Waitzkin, H., & Nicdao, E. (2008). Medicaid managed care for mental health services: The survival of safety net institutions in rural settings. *Qualitative Health Research, 18*(9), 1231–1246.

Woodcock, R. (2008). Preamble, purpose and ethical principles sections of the NASW Code of Ethics. *Families in Society, 89*(4), 578–586.

Yankura, J., & Dryden, W. (1997). *Using REBT with common psychological problems: A therapist's casebook.* New York: Springer.

Yoo, J., Brooks, D., & Patti, R. (2007). Organizational constructs as predictors of effectiveness in child welfare interventions. *Child Welfare, 86*(1), 53–78.

Court Decisions*

Abdullahi v. Pfizer, Inc., 562 F.3d 163 (2d Cir. 2009).

Achterhof v. Selvaggio, 886 F.2d 826 (6th Cir. 1989).

Adams v. Bd. of Clinical Soc. Workers, 119 P.3d 260 (Or. Ct. App. 2005).

---

* Sometimes the process of reading and identifying court decisions is difficult for readers who do not have experience with the way decisions are published in the legal field. Therefore, a brief word is in order concerning the conventional style of referencing court decisions that appears in this book. In general, cases are identified by reference to the names of the parties, often separated by *v.*, for *versus*, which indicates that the parties are in conflict (e.g., *Smith v. Jones*). It is also conventional in legal citation style to abbreviate words, titles, and organizations whenever possible. It is often easy to identify the meaning of these terms simply by reading the citation (e.g., *Adams v. Bd. of Clinical Soc. Workers = Adams v. Board of Clinical Social Workers*).

By reading the citation to a court decision, it is often possible to identify whether the decision arises from a state court, federal court, or the U.S. Supreme Court. In a state court decision, the abbreviated state name is often found in the citation (e.g., Vt. 1999, for Vermont), typically at the end. In a federal court decision, the abbreviated name of the reporter that published the decision appears in the citation. For example, a federal district court decision is reported in the Federal Supplement, abbreviated *F. Supp.* in the citation. A federal court of appeals decision is reported in the Federal Reporter, abbreviated as *F., F.2d,* or *F.3d* (referring to the Federal Reporter or its second or third edition, respectively). Finally, a U.S. Supreme Court decision is reported in the U.S. Reports, abbreviated as *U.S.* in the citation.

Adarand Constructors, Inc. v. Pena, 515 U.S. 200 (1995).

Ala. Coal. for Equity, Inc. v. Hunt, Nos. CV-90-883R, CV 91-0117-R (Ala. Cir. Ct. Apr. 27, 1993) (consolidated civil actions).

Alejo v. City of Alhambra, 89 Cal. Rptr. 2d 768 (1999).

Almonte v. N.Y. Med. College, 851 F. Supp. 34 (D. Conn. 1994).

Altman v. Bedford Cent. Sch. Dist., 45 F. Supp. 2d 368 (S.D.N.Y. 1999), rev'd in part, 245 F.3d 49 (2d Cir. 2001).

Am. Acad. of Pediatrics v. Lundgren, 940 P.2d 797 (Cal. 1997).

Am. Fed'n of Gov't Employees v. United States, 330 F.3d 513 (D.C. Cir. 2003).

Am. Home Assurance Co. v. Pope, 487 F.3d 590 (8th Cir. 2007).

Andrews v. Bd. of Soc. Worker Licensure, 2005 Me. Super. LEXIS 117 (Super. Ct. Cumberland County 2005).

Ashe v. Radiation Oncology Assocs., 9 S.W.3d 119 (Tenn. 1999).

Associated Indus. v. Commonwealth, 912 S.W.2d 947 (Ky. 1995).

Aufrichtig v. Lowell, 650 N.E.2d 40 (N.Y. 1995).

Baker v. State, 744 A.2d 864 (Vt. 1999).

Ball v. Massanari, 254 F.3d 817 (9th Cir. 2001).

Bates v. State Bar, 429 U.S. 1059 (1977).

Bd. of Regents v. Roth, 408 U.S. 564 (1972).

Bd. of Trs. of Univ. of Ala. v. Garrett, 531 U.S. 356 (2001).

Bee v. Greaves, 744 F.2d 1387 (10th Cir. 1984).

Besh v. Bradley, 47 F.2d 1167 (6th Cir. 1995).

Bielaska v. Orley, Nos. 215286, 215287 (Mich. Ct. App. Feb. 9, 2001).

Bienz v. Cent. Suffolk Hosp., 557 N.Y.S.2d 139 (App. Div. 1990).

Blum v. Yaretsky, 47 U.S. 991 (1982).

Bogan v. Scott-Harris, 523 U.S. 44 (1998).

Bolling v. Sharpe, 347 U.S. 497 (1954).

Bottoms v. Bottoms, 457 S.E.2d 102 (Va. 1995) (quoting Roe v. Roe, 324 S.E.2d 691, 694 (1985)).

Boynton v. Burglass, 590 So. 2d 446 (Ct. App. Fla. 1991).

Branch v. Franklin, 285 Fed. Appx. 573, 2008 U.S. App. LEXIS 162 (11th Cir. 2008).

Branch v. Turner, 27 F.3d 1334 (8th Cir. 1994).

Breck v. Michigan, 203 F.3d 392 (6th Cir. 2000).

Briscoe v. Prince George's County Health Dep't, 593 A.2d 1109 (Md. 1991).

Brokaw v. Mercer County, 235 F.3d 1000 (7th Cir. 2000).

Brown v. Bd. of Educ., 347 U.S. 483 (1954).

Buckey v. County of Los Angeles, 968 F.2d 791 (9th Cir. 1992).

Bullock v. Sheahan, 568 F. Supp. 2d 965 (N.D. Ill. 2008).

Campbell County Sch. Dist. v. State, 181 P.3d 43 (Wyo. 2008).

Cardwell v. Bechtol, 724 S.W.2d 739 (Tenn. 1987).

Chavez v. Lemaster, No. D-101-CR-9900896 (N.M. Dist. Ct. Santa Fe County Oct. 2, 2001) (consolidated cases).

Chew v. Meyer, 527 A.2d 828 (Md. Ct. Spec. App. 1987).

City of Cleburne v. Cleburne Living Ctr., 473 U.S. 432 (1985).

Claremont Sch. Dist. v. Governor, 703 A.2d 1353 (N.H. 1997).

Commonwealth v. Bruno, 735 N.E.2d 1222 (Mass. 2000).

Connally v. Gen. Constr. Co., 269 U.S. 385 (1926).

Conner v. Donnelly, 42 F.3d 220 (4th Cir. 1994).

Corgan v. Muehling, 574 N.E.2d 602 (Ill. 1991).

County of Sacramento v. Lewis, 523 U.S. 833 (1998).

Cox v. New Hampshire, 312 U.S. 569 (1941).

Crawford-El v. Britton, 93 F.3d 813, 829 (D.C. Cir. 1996) (Silberman, J., concurring), *vacated on other grounds*, 523 U.S. 574 (1998).

CSC v. Letter Carriers, 413 U.S. 548 (1973).

Cynthia B. v. New Rochelle Hosp., 470 N.Y.S.2d 122 (1983).

Danskine v. Miami Dade Fire Dep't, 253 F.3d 1288 (11th Cir. 2001).

Darvie v. Countryman, 2008 U.S. Dist. LEXIS 107565 (N.D.N.Y. 2009).

Davis v. Monroe County Bd. of Educ., 526 U.S. 629 (1999).

Deatherage v. Examining Bd. of Psychology, 948 P.2d 828 (Wash. 1997).

Denver Area Educ. Telecomms. Consortium, Inc. v. FCC, 518 U.S. 727, 782 (Kennedy, J., concurring and dissenting) (finding that "state action lies in the enactment of a statute altering legal relations between persons").

Dep't of Health and Mental Hygiene v. Kelly, 918 A.2d 470 (Md. Ct. App. 2007).

DeShaney v. Winnebago Dep't of Soc. Servs., 489 U.S. 189 (1989).

Desnick v. Dep't of Prof'l Regulation, 665 N.E.2d 1346 (Ill. 1996).

Dezen v. Bureau of Prof'l & Occupational Affairs, 722 A.2d 1135 (Pa. Commw. Ct. 1999).

D. F. v. Codell, 127 S.W.3d 571 (Ky. 2003).

Doe v. Claiborne County, 103 F.3d 495 (6th Cir. 1996).

Doe v. Finch, 942 P.2d 359 (Wash. 1997).

Doe v. Gates, 981 F.2d 1316 (D.C. Cir. 1993).

Doe v. Harbor Schs. Inc., 843 N.E.2d 1058 (Mass. 2006).

Doe v. Medlantic Health Care Group, Inc., 814 A.2d 939 (D.C. Ct. App. 2003).

Dunn v. Catholic Home Bureau for Dependent Children, 537 N.Y.S.2d 742 (Sup. Ct. 1989).

Duran v. Apodaca, No. Civ-77-721-C (D.N.M. July 14, 1980).

Duttry v. Patterson, 771 A.2d 1255 (Pa. 2001).

Eckhardt v. Charter Hosp., 953 P.2d 722 (N.M. Ct. App. 1997).

Elliott v. N.C. Psychology Bd., 485 S.E.2d 882 (N.C. Ct. App. 1997), *rev'd in part*, 498 S.E.2d 616 (N.C. 1998).

Eng'g Contractors Ass'n v. Metro. Dade County, 122 F.3d 895 (11th Cir. 1997).

Equality Found. v. City of Cincinnati, 128 F.3d 289 (6th Cir. 1997).

Ernst v. Child and Youth Servs., 108 F.3d 486 (3d Cir. 1997).

Estades-Negroni v. CPC Hosp. San Juan Capistrano, 412 F.3d 1 (1st Cir. 2005).

F. G. v. MacDonell, 696 A.2d 697 (N.J. 1997).

Faulkner v. Johnson County Sheriff's Dep't, 2001 U.S. Dist. LEXIS 4156 (N.D. Tex. 2001).

Faya v. Almaraz, 620 A.2d 327 (Md. Ct. App. 1993).

Feldman v. Tenn. Bd. of Med. Exam'rs, 2003 Tenn. App. LEXIS 797 (Ct. App. 2003).

Figueiredo-Torres v. Nickel, 584 A.2d 69 (Md. 1991).

Fla. A. G. C. Council, Inc. v. State, 303 F. Supp. 2d 1307 (N.D. Fla. 2004).

Franet v. County of Alameda Soc. Servs. Agency, 291 Fed. Appx. 32 (9th Cir. 2008).

Fulbright v. Evans, 2005 U.S. Dist. LEXIS 40240 (W.D. Okla. 2005).

Ghayoumi v. McMillan, 2006 Tenn. App. LEXIS 472 (Tenn. Ct. App. 2006).

Gibbs v. Ernst, 647 A.2d 882 (Pa. 1994).

Gillespie v. Univ. of Chicago Hosps., 2008 Ill. App. LEXIS 1329 (Ill. App. Ct. 2008).

Givens v. Mulliken, 75 S.W.3d 383 (Tenn. 2002).

Goldberg v. Boone, 912 A.2d 698 (Md. Ct. App. 2006).

Goldberg v. Kelly, 397 U.S. 254 (1970).

Gonzales v. Carhart, 550 U.S. 124 (2007).

Gonzalez v. City of New York Health & Hosps. Corp., 135 F. Supp. 2d 385 (E.D.N.Y. 2001).

Good News Club v. Milford Cent. Sch., 533 U.S. 98 (2001).

Goodridge v. Dep't of Pub. Health, 798 N.E.2d 941 (Mass. 2003).

Goss v. Lopez, 419 U.S. 565 (1975).

Gratz v. Bollinger, 539 U.S. 244 (2003).

Greenville Women's Clinic v. Bryant, 222 F.3d 157 (4th Cir. 2000).

Grey v. Allstate Ins. Co., No. 81 (Md. Apr. 9, 2001).

Griffin v. City of Opa-Locka, 261 F.3d 1295 (11th Cir. 2001).

Grimes v. Kennedy Krieger Inst., Inc., 782 A.2d 807 (Md. Ct. App. 2001).

Griswold v. Connecticut, 381 U.S. 479 (1965).

Gruenke v. Seip, 225 F.3d 290 (3d Cir. 2000).

Grutter v. Bollinger, 539 U.S. 306 (2003).

Guides, Ltd. v. Yarmouth Group Prop. Mgmt., Inc., 295 F.3d 1065 (10th Cir. 2002).

Hafner v. Beck, 916 P.2d 1105 (Ariz. Ct. App. 1995).

Hamdan v. Rumsfeld, 548 U.S. 557 (2006).

Hammons v. Norfolk S. Corp., 156 F.3d 701 (6th Cir. 1998).

Harper v. Va. Bd. of Elections, 383 U.S. 663 (1966).

Hart v. Bennet, 672 N.W.2d 306 (Wis. Ct. App. 2003).

Haupt v. Kumar, 288 S.W.3d 704 (Ark. Ct. App. 2008).

Haynie v. Bass, 902 F.2d 33 (6th Cir. 1990).

Hazelwood Sch. Dist. v. Kuhlmeier, 484 U.S. 260 (1988).

Hazen Paper Co. v. Biggins, 507 U.S. 604 (1993).

Heinmiller v. Dep't of Health, 903 P.2d 433 (Wash. 1995).

Henry v. Clermont County, 2005 U.S. Dist. LEXIS 9334 (S.D. Ohio 2005).

Herrera v. Union No. 39 Sch. Dist., 917 A.2d 923 (Vt. 2006).

Hertog v. City of Seattle, 979 P.2d 400 (Wash. 1999).

Hertzel v. Palmyra Sch. Dist., 733 N.W.2d 578 (Neb. Ct. App. 2007).

Holloway v. Brush, 220 F.3d 767 (6th Cir. 2000).

Hopwood v. Texas, 78 F.3d (5th Cir. 1996).

Horak v. Biris, 474 N.E.2d 13 (Ill. App. Ct. 1985).

Huether v. Dist. Court, 4 P.3d 1193, 1197 (Mont. 2000) (Trieweiler, J., dissenting or concurring [sic]).

Hull v. So. Ill. Hosp. Servs., 826 N.E.2d 930 (Ill. App. Ct. 2005).

Humana Med. Plan, Inc. v. Fischman, 750 So. 2d 677 (Ct. App. Fla. 1999).

Hyde v. Fisher, 2009 Idaho App. LEXIS 7 (Idaho Ct. App. 2009).

In re Application of Castillo, 580 N.Y.S.2d 992 (Sup. Ct. Suffolk County 1992).

In re Columbia/HCA Healthcare Corp. Litig., Civ. A. No. 01-MS-50 (RCL) (D.D.C. Aug. 7, 2001).

In re D. W., No. 2D00-3845 (Fla. Dist. Ct. App. May 23, 2001).

In re Disciplinary Proceeding against Marshall, 157 P.3d 859 (Wash. 2007).

In re E. G., 549 N.E.2d 322 (Ill. 1989).

In re Gault, 387 U.S. 1 (1967).

In re Investigation of Underwager, No. C0-97-55 (Minn. Ct. App. July 8, 1997).

In re J. A., 601 A.2d 69 (D.C. Ct. App. 1991).

In re K. L., 774 N.Y.S.2d 472 (2004).

In re Kendall J., 616 N.W.2d 525 (Wis. 2000).

In re LaChapelle, 607 N.W.2d 151 (Minn. Ct. App. 2000).

In re McKnight, 550 N.E.2d 856 (Mass. 1990).

In re Manuel L., 2002 Cal. App. Unpub. LEXIS 6306 (Ct. App. 2002).

In re Marie H., 811 N.Y.S.2d 708 (App. Div. 2006).

In re Marriage Cases, 183 P.3d 384 (Cal. 2008).

In re Marriage of Ciesluk, 113 P.3d 135 (Colo. 2005).

In re Mental Illness of Thomas, 671 N.E.2d 616 (Ohio Ct. App. 1996).

In re O. R., 767 N.E.2d 872 (Ill. App. Ct. 2002).

In re Rebekah R., 33 Cal. Rptr. 2d 265 (Ct. App. 1994).

In re R. G., 669 N.E.2d 1225 (Ill. App. Ct. 1996).

In re R. M. J., 455 U.S. 191 (1982).

In re T. R., 731 A.2d 1276 (Pa. 1999).

J. A. v. Seminole County Sch. Bd., 2005 U.S. Dist. LEXIS 29993 (M.D. Fla. 2005).

Jackson v. Fort Stanton Hosp. & Training Sch., 757 F. Supp. 1243 (D.N.M. 1990), *rev'd in part*, 964 F.2d 980 (10th Cir. 1992).

Jackson v. State, 956 P.2d 35 (Mont. 1998).

Jacqueline T. v. Alameda County Child Protective Servs., 66 Cal. Rptr. 3d 157 (Ct. App. 2007).

Jaffee v. Redmond, 518 U.S. 1 (1996).

Jarzynka v. St. Thomas Univ. Sch. of Law, 310 F. Supp. 2d 1256 (S.D. Fla. 2004).

Jensen v. Lane County, 222 F.3d 570 (9th Cir. 2000).

Johnson v. City of Kankakee, 2006 U.S. Dist. LEXIS 62136 (C.D. Ill. 2006).

Johnson v. Corrs. Corp. of Am., 2008 U.S. Dist. LEXIS 85861 (D. Kan. 2008).

Johnson v. Dowd, 2008 U.S. App. LEXIS 25325 (5th Cir. 2008).

Johnson v. Kokemoor, 545 N.W.2d 495 (Wis. 1996).

Jones v. Lurie, 32 S.W.3d 737 (Tex. App. 2000).

Joseph A. v. N.M. Dep't of Human Servs., 575 F. Supp. 346 (D.N.M. 1983).

Kansas v. Hendricks, 521 U.S. 346 (1997).

Kaplan v. United States, 133 F.3d 469 (7th Cir. 1998).

Karen L. v. Dep't of Health & Human Servs., 953 P.2d 871 (Alaska 1998).

Karlin v. IVF Am., Inc., 712 N.E.2d 662 (N.Y. 1999).

Kazmier v. Widmann, 225 F.3d 519 (5th Cir. 2000).

Kelm v. Kelm, 749 N.E.2d 299 (Ohio 2001).

Kennestone Hosp. v. Hopson, 538 S.E.2d 742 (Ga. 2000).

Kerrigan v. Comm'r of Pub. Health, 957 A.2d 407 (Conn. 2008).

Kimel v. Fla. Bd. of Regents, 528 U.S. 62 (2000).

King v. Conant, 20 Mass. L. Rep. (Super. Ct. 2005).

K. J. v. Pa. Dep't of Pub. Welfare, 767 A.2d 609 (Pa. 2001).

Koehler v. Juniata County Sch. Dist., 2008 U.S. Dist. LEXIS 32079 (M.D. Pa. 2008).

Kovacs v. Freeman, 957 S.W.2d 251 (Ky. 1997).

Kus v. Sherman Hosp., 644 N.E.2d 1214 (Ill. App. Ct. 1995).

Lanigan v. Vill. of E. Hazel Crest, 110 F.3d 467 (7th Cir. 1997).

Lansing v. City of Memphis, 202 F.3d 821 (6th Cir. 2000).

Laskowitz v. Ciba Vision Corp., 215 A.D.2d 25 (N.Y. App. Div. 1995).

Lassiter v. Dep't of Soc. Servs., 452 U.S. 18 (1981).

Lavia v. Pennsylvania, 224 F.3d 190 (3d Cir. 2000).

Lawrence v. Texas, 539 U.S. 558 (2003).

Lehr v. Roberston, 463 U.S. 248 (1983).

Lewis v. Thompson, 252 F.3d 567 (2d Cir. 2001).

Livant v. Clifton, 334 F. Supp. 2d 321 (E.D.N.Y. 2004).

Lofton v. Kearney, No. 99-10058-CIV-KING (S.D. Fla. Aug. 30, 2001).

Logan v. Greenwich Hosp. Assoc., 465 A.2d 294 (Conn. 1983).

Lozano v. City of Hazleton, 496 F. Supp. 2d 477 (M.D. Pa. 2007).

M. L. B. v. S. L. J., 519 U.S. 102 (1996).

Mabe v. San Bernardino County Dep't of Soc. Servs., 237 F.3d 1101 (9th Cir. 2001).

Maio v. Aetna, Inc., 221 F.3d 472 (3d Cir. 2000).

Maldonado v. Josey, 975 F.2d 727 (10th Cir. 1992).

Martin v. Commissioner, 232 F.2d 901 (10th Cir. 2000).

Martino v. Family Serv. Agency, 445 N.E.2d 6 (Ill. App. Ct. 1982).

McCormick v. England, 494 S.E.2d 431 (S.C. Ct. App. 1997).

McKeighan v. Corrs. Corp. of Am., 2008 U.S. Dist. LEXIS 72512 (D. Kan. 2008).

McKinney v. Maynard, 952 F.2d 350 (10th Cir. 1991).

Meyer v. Nebraska, 262 U.S. 390 (1923).

Mickle v. Ahmed, 444 F. Supp. 2d 601 (D.S.C 2006).

Miller v. Ratner, 688 A.2d 976 (Md. Ct. Sp. App. 1997).

Mills v. N.M. Bd. of Psychologist Exam'rs, 941 P.2d 502 (N.M. 1997).

Miss. Bd. of Psychological Exam'rs v. Hosford, 508 So. 2d 1049 (Miss. 1987).

Modi v. W. Va. Bd. of Med., 465 S.E.2d 230, 244 (W. Va. 1995) (Workman, J., concurring).

Mohr v. Commonwealth, 653 N.E.2d 1104 (Mass. 1995).

Moore v. City of E. Cleveland, 431 U.S. 494 (1977).

Moore v. Regents of Univ. of Cal., 793 P.2d 479 (Cal. 1990).

Myers v. Alaska Psychiatric Inst., 138 P.2d 238 (Alaska 2006).

Naidu v. Laird, 539 A.2d 1064 (Del. 1988).

Narragansett Indian Tribe v. Nat'l Indian Gaming Comm'n, 158 F.3d 1335 (D.C. Cir. 1998).

Ne. Ga. Radiological Assocs. v. Tidwell, 670 F.2d 507 (5th Cir. 1982).

New Hampshire v. City of Dover, 891 A.2d 524 (N.H. 2006).

Nieves v. Univ. of P.R., 7 F.3d 270 (1st Cir. 1993).

N.Y. State Nat'l Org. for Women v. Pataki, 261 F.3d 156 (2d Cir. 2001).

Oberti v. Bd. of Educ., 995 F.2d 1204 (3d Cir. 1993).

Odenthal v. Minn. Conference of Seventh-Day Adventists, 649 N.W.2d 426 (Minn. 2002).

Olagues v. Russoniello, 797 F.2d 1511 (9th Cir. 1986).

Open Door Baptist Church v. Clark County, 995 P.2d 33 (Wash. 2000).

Ortega v. Sacramento County Dep't of Health & Human Servs., 74 Cal. Rptr. 3d 390 (Ct. App. 2008).

Ortez v. Washington County, 88 F.3d 804 (9th Cir. 1996).

Overton v. Bd. of Exam'rs in Psychology, No. 01-A-01-9603-CH-00098 (Tenn. Ct. App. Nov. 14, 1996).

Parents Involved in Cmty. Schs. v. Seattle Sch. Dist. No. 1, 551 U.S. 701 (2007).

Parrish v. Brownlee, 335 F. Supp. 2d 661 (E.D.N.C. 2004).

Paul v. Davis, 424 U.S. 693 (1976).

People v. R. R., 807 N.Y.S.2d 516 (Sup. Ct. N.Y. County 2005).

People v. Simms, 736 N.E.2d 1092 (Ill. 2000).

People v. Watkins, 83 P.3d 1182 (Ct. App. Colo. 2003).

Perreira v. State, 768 P.2d 1198 (Colo. 1989).

Perry v. Schwarzenegger, 2010 U.S. Dist. LEXIS 78815 (N.D. Cal. 2010).

Petrillo v. Syntex Labs., Inc., 499 N.E.2d 952 (Ill. App. Ct. 1986).

Phillip Leon M. v. Greenbrier County Bd. of Educ., 484 N.E.2d 909 (W. Va. 1996).

Picker v. Castro, 776 N.Y.S.2d 433 (N.Y. App. Term 2003).

Pierce v. Caday, 422 N.E.2d 371 (Va. 1992).

Planned Parenthood v. Farmer, 762 A.2d 620 (N.J. 2000).

Pollack v. Marshall, 845 F.2d 656 (6th Cir. 1988).

Proenza Sanfiel v. Dep't of Health, 749 So. 2d 525 (Fla. Dist. Ct. App. 1999).

Protection & Advocacy Sys. v. City of Albuquerque, 195 P.3d 1 (N.M. Ct. App. 2008).

Pyle v. Sch. Comm., 667 N.E.2d 869 (Mass. 1996).

Rasmussen v. Fleming, 741 P.2d 674 (Ariz. 1987).

Rauser v. Horn, 241 F.3d 330 (3d Cir. 2001).

Reed v. Reed, 404 U.S. 71 (1971).

Reiff v. Ne. Fla. State Hosp., 710 So. 2d 1030 (Fla. Dist. Ct. App. 1998).

Reynolds v. Giuliani, No. 98cv08877 (S.D.N.Y. Jan. 19, 1999).

Rich v. Woodford, 210 F.3d 961 (9th Cir. 2000).

Richardson v. McKnight, 521 U.S. 399 (1997).

Richenberg v. Perry, 97 F.3d 256 (8th Cir. 1996).

Riggins v. Nevada, 504 U.S. 127 (1992).

Robert M. v. State, 2008 U.S. Dist. LEXIS 103104 (D. Haw. 2008).

Rodriguez-Silva v. INS, 242 F.3d 243 (5th Cir. 2001).

Roe v. Catholic Charities, 588 N.E.2d 354, 363 (Ill. App. Ct. 1992).

Roe v. Crawford, 439 F. Supp. 2d 942 (W.D. Mo. 2006).

Roe v. Jewish Children's Bureau of Chicago, 790 N.E.2d 882 (Ill. App. Ct. 2003).

Roe v. Wade, 410 U.S. 113 (1973).

Rogers v. County of San Joaquin Human Servs. Agency, 487 F.3d 1288 (9th Cir. 2007).

Romer v. Evans, 517 U.S. 620 (1996).

Rosales-Garcia v. Holland, 238 F.3d 704 (6th Cir. 2001).

Roska v. Sneddon, 437 F.3d 964 (10th Cir. 2006).

Sage Realty Corp. v. Proskauer Rose Goetz & Mendelsohn, LLP, 743 N.Y.S.2d 72 (App. Div. 2002).

Sain v. Cedar Rapids Cmty. Sch. Dist., No. 155/98-2273 (Iowa Apr. 25, 2001) (en banc).

Sakler v. Anesthesiologist Assoc., 50 S.W.3d 210 (Ky. Ct. App. 2001).

Saur v. Probes, 476 N.W.2d 496 (Mich. Ct. App. 1991).

Schneckloth v. Bustamonte, 412 U.S. 218 (1973).

Schreiber v. Physicians Ins. Co. of Wis., 588 N.W.2d 26 (Wis. 1999).

Seal v. Morgan, 229 F.3d 567 (6th Cir. 2000).

Sexton Law Firm v. Milligan, 948 S.W.2d 388 (Ark. 1997).

Seymour v. Elections Enforcement Comm'n, 762 A.2d 880 (Conn. 2000).

Sheff v. O'Neill, 678 A.2d 1267 (Conn. 1996).

Sherbert v. Verner, 374 U.S. 398 (1963).

Shrum v. Kluck, 249 F.3d 773 (8th Cir. 2001).

Simescu v. Emmet County Dep't of Human Servs., 942 F.2d 372 (6th Cir. 1991).

Simmons v. United States, 805 F.2d 1363 (9th Cir. 1986).

Singleton v. Wulff, 428 U.S. 106 (1976).

Smith-Bozarth v. Coal. against Rape & Abuse, Inc., 747 A.2d 322 (N.J. Super. Ct. App. Div. 2000).

Smothers v. Gresham Transfer, Inc., 23 P.3d 333 (Or. 2001).

Snell v. Tunnell, 920 F.2d 673 (10th Cir. 1990).

Stanley v. Swinson, 47 F.3d 1176 (9th Cir. 1995).

Stanton v. City of W. Sacramento, 277 Cal. Rptr. 478 (Ct. App. 1991).

State v. Aetna U.S. Healthcare, Inc., No. GV-000584 (Tex. Dist. Ct. Travis County Apr. 11, 2000).

State v. Kelly, 770 A.2d 908 (Conn. 2001).

State v. Lattimer, 624 N.W.2d 284 (Minn. Ct. App. 2001).

State v. Louis, 614 N.Y.S.2d 888 (Sup. Ct. N.Y. County 1994).

State v. Oakley, 629 N.W.2d 200 (Wis. 2001).

State v. Oakley (II), 635 N.W.2d 760 (Wis. 2001).

State ex rel. Dean v. Cunningham, 182 S.W.3d 561 (Mo. 2006).

State *ex rel.* Taylor v. Johnson, 961 P.2d 768 (N.M. 1998).

Stebbings v. Univ. of Chicago, 726 N.E.2d 1136 (Ill. App. Ct. 2000).

Steele v. Hamilton County Cmty. Mental Health Bd., 736 N.E.2d 10 (Ohio 2000).

T. D. v. N.Y. State Office of Mental Health, 626 N.Y.S.2d 1015 (Sup. Ct. N.Y. County 1995), *aff'd and modified in part*, 228 A.D.2d 95 (N.Y. App. Div. 1996).

T. M. v. Executive Risk Indem., Inc., 59 P.3d 721 (Wyo. 2002).

Tackett v. Vill. of Carey, 2007 U.S. Dist. LEXIS 39775 (N.D. Ohio 2007).

Tarasoff v. Regents of Univ. of Cal., 551 P.2d 334 (Cal. 1976).

Tenenbaum v. Williams, 193 F.3d 581 (2d Cir. 1999).

Terrell C. v. Dep't of Soc. & Health Servs., 84 P.3d 899 (Wash. Ct. App. 2004).

Tex. Bd. of Med. Exam'rs v. Burzynski, 917 S.W.2d 365 (Tex. Ct. App. 1996).

Thapar v. Zezulka, 994 S.W.2d 635 (Tex. 1999).

Thomasson v. Perry, 80 F.3d 915 (4th Cir. 1996).

Thornburgh v. Am. Coll. of Obstetricians & Gynecologists, 476 U.S. 747 (1986).

Unified Sch. Dist. No. 229 v. State, 885 P.2d 1170 (Kan. 1994).

United Food & Commercial Worker Union v. Sw. Ohio Reg'l Transit Auth., 163 F.3d 341 (6th Cir. 1998).

United States v. Antelope, 430 U.S. 641 (1977).

United States v. Bellomo, 176 F.3d 580 (2d Cir. 1999).

United States v. Brown, 441 F.3d 1330 (11th Cir. 2006).

United States v. Deninno, 103 F.3d 82 (10th Cir. 1996).

United States v. Glass, 133 F.3d 1356 (10th Cir. 1998).

United States v. Hayes, 227 F.3d 578 (6th Cir. 2000).

United States v. Morrison, 529 U.S. 598 (2000).

United States v. N.Y. City Bd. of Educ., 448 F. Supp. 2d 397 (E.D.N.Y. 2006).

United States v. Virginia, 518 U.S. 515 (1996).

Valcin v. Pub. Health Trust, 473 So. 2d 1297 (Fla. Dist. Ct. App. 1984), *modified sub nom.*, Pub. Health Trust v. Valcin, 507 So. 2d 596 (1987).

Vanderhurst v. Colo. Mountain Coll. Dist., 208 F.3d 908 (10th Cir. 2000).

Varnum v. Brien, No. 07-1499 (Iowa Apr. 3, 2009).

Vernon v. Rollins-Threats, 2005 U.S. Dist. LEXIS 41789 (N.D. Tex. 2005).

Victor v. Nebraska, 511 U.S. 1 (1994) (quoting Commonwealth v. Webster, 59 Mass. 295, 320 (1850)).

W. B. v. Matula, 67 F.3d 484 (3d Cir. 1995).

Wallis v. Spencer, 202 F.3d 1126 (9th Cir. 1999).

Ward v. Most Health Servs., Inc., 2008 U.S. Dist. LEXIS 61573 (E.D. Pa. 2008).

Warren v. Warden, 2007 U.S. Dist. LEXIS 97952 (W.D. La. 2007).

Wear v. Walker, 800 S.W.2d 99 (Mo. Ct. App. 1990).

Weaver v. Dep't of Soc. & Health Servs., No. 25366-6-II (Wash. Ct. App. Aug. 10, 2001).

Weber v. Cranston Sch. Comm., 212 F.3d 41 (1st Cir. 2000).

Weinberger v. Grimes, 2009 U.S. App. LEXIS 2693 (6th Cir. 2009).

Weitz v. Lovelace Health Sys., Inc., 214 F.3d 1175 (10th Cir 2000).

West v. Atkins, 487 U.S. 42 (1988).

White v. N.C. Bd. of Exam'rs of Practicing Psychologists, 388 S.E.2d 148 (N.C. Ct. App. 1990).

Wicks v. Vanderbilt Univ., 2007 Tenn. App. LEXIS 146 (Ct. App. 2007).

Wilcher v. City of Akron, 498 F.3d 516 (6th Cir. 2007).

Williams v. Coleman, 488 N.W.2d 464 (Mich. Ct. App. 1992).

Winegar v. Des Moines Indep. Cmty. Sch. Dist., 20 F.3d 895 (8th Cir. 1994).

Wolff v. McDonnell, 418 U.S. 539 (1974).

Wolotsky v. Huhn, 960 F.2d 1331 (6th Cir. 1992).

Wyatt v. Fetner, 92 F.3d 1074 (11th Cir. 1996).

Yniguez v. Arizonans for Official English, 69 F.3d 920 (9th Cir. 1994), *vacated sub nom.*, Arizonans for Official English v. Arizona, 520 U.S. 43 (1997).

Zagaros v. Erickson, 558 N.W.2d 516 (Minn. Ct. App. 1997) (dictum).

Zinermon v. Burch, 494 U.S. 113 (1990).

Ethical Codes

American Bar Association. (2004). *Model rules of professional conduct.* Chicago: Author.

American Psychological Association. (2003). *Ethical principles of psychologists and code of conduct* (2003). Washington, DC: Author.

National Association of Social Workers. (2009). *Code of ethics* (1996 & Supp. 2008). Washington, DC: Author.

National Board for Certified Counselors. (2005). *2006 code of ethics.* Greensboro, NC: Author.

Legislation and Administrative Rules

10 Guam Code Ann. § 12827 (2008).

225 Ill. Comp. Stat. § 15/2 (Bender 2009).

405 Ill. Comp. Stat. Ann. § 5/3-501 (Bender 2009).

ADA Amendments Act of 2008, Pub. L. No. 110-325 (2008).

Adoption Assistance and Child Welfare Act of 1980, 42 U.S.C.. §§ 670–676.

Adoption and Safe Families Act of 1997, Pub. L. No. 105-89, 111 Stat. 2115 (1997).

Age Discrimination in Employment Act of 1967, 29 U.S.C.S. §§ 621–634.

Ala. Code §§ 22-8-4 to 22-8-6 (Michie 2009).

American Indian Religious Freedom Act of 1978, 42 U.S.C. § 1996.

Americans with Disabilities Act of 1990, 42 U.S.C. §§ 12101–12213.

Cal. Bus. & Prof. Code § 4996.9 (Deering 2008).

Cal. Fam. Code §§ 6924–6925, 6926(a), 6929 (Deering 2008).

Cal. Health & Safety Code § 121020 (Deering 2008).

Cerro Grande Fire Assistance Act, Pub. L. No. 106-246, 114 Stat. 584 (2000).

Civil Rights Act of 1964, 42 U.S.C. Chapter 21.

Civil Rights Act of 1871, 42 U.S.C. § 1983.

Civil Rights Act of 1991, Pub. L. No. 102-166, 105 Stat. 1071 (1991).

Confidentiality of Alcohol and Drug Abuse Patient Records, 42 C.F.R. Chapter 1 (2002).

Del. Code Ann. tit. 10, § 901(16) (2009).

Employee Retirement Income Security Act, Pub. L. No. 93-406, 88 Stat. 829 (1974).

Federal False Claims Act, 31 U.S.C. 3729-3733 (2009).

Ga. Code Ann. § 16-5-90(d) (2009).

Health Care and Education Reconciliation Act of 2010, Pub. L. No. 111-152.

Health Insurance Portability and Accountability Act, Pub. L. No. 104-191, 110 Stat. 1998 (1996).

Indian Child Welfare Act of 1978, 25 U.S.C. §§ 1901–1963.

Indian Civil Rights Act of 1968, 25 U.S.C. §§ 1301–1303.

Indian Gaming Regulatory Act, 25 U.S.C. §§ 2701–2721 (1988).

Individuals with Disabilities Education Act, 20 U.S.C. §§ 1400–1482 (1990/2004) (formerly known as the Education for All Handicapped Children Act).

La. Rev. Stat. Ann. § 37:2372 (Bender 2008).

Md. Code Ann., Health-Gen. §§ 20-102 to 20-103 (Bender 2008).

Mich. Comp. Laws Serv. § 750.520a–b (Bender 2009).

Minn. Stat. Ann. §§ 609.341–342 (LexisNexis 2008).

Model State Public Health Privacy Act (Georgetown University Law Center, Model State Public Health Privacy Project, 1999).

National Defense Authorization Act for Fiscal Year 1994, Pub. L. No. 103-160 (1993).

Native American Counseling Act, N.M. Stat. Ann. §§ 33-10-1 *et seq.* (Michie 2008).

N.H. Rev. State. Ann. § 169-C:29 (Bender 2009).

N.M. Stat. Ann. §§ 30-9-10, 32A-4-3, 32A-4-10[B], 32A-6A-14, 43-1-6, 61-9-17, 61-9A-4, 61-31-6(B)(3) (Michie 2008).

N.Y. Mental Hyg. §§ 9.60, 33.21 (Consol. 2009).

Omnibus Budget Reconciliation Act of 1993, Pub. L. No. 103-66, 107 Stat. 312 (1993).

Patient Protection and Affordable Care Act, Pub. L. No. 111-148 (2010).

Paul Wellstone and Pete Domenici Mental Health Parity and Addiction Equity Act of 2008, Pub. L. No. 110-343, div. C, tit. V, 112 Stat. 3881.

Personal Responsibility and Work Opportunity Reconciliation Act of 1996, Pub. L. 104-193, tit. I, § 103(a)(1), 110 Stat. 2112 (1996).

Restatement of Bill of Rights for Mental Health Patients, 42 U.S.C. § 10841 (2008).

S.C. Code Ann. § 20-7-280 (LexisNexis 2007).

Social Work Practice Act, N.M. Stat. Ann. §§ 61-31-1 *et seq.* (Michie 2008).

Special Education for Exceptional Children Act, Kan. Stat. Ann. §§ 72-961 to 72-999 (LexisNexis 2008).

Tex. Fam. Code Ann. § 32.004 (Bender 2009).

Tex. Occ. Code Ann. § 503.003 (West 2007).

Uniform Health-Care Decisions Act (1993) (proposed act drafted by the National
     Conference of Commissioners on Uniform State Law).

Uniform Health-Care Information Act (1985) (proposed act drafted by the National
     Conference of Commissioners on Uniform State Law).

Uniform Probate Code §§ 5-301 to 5-318 (2004/2006) (proposed act drafted by the
     National Conference on Uniform State Law).

Uniting and Strengthening American by Providing Appropriate Tools Required
     to Intercept and Obstruct Terrorism Act (USA Patriot Act) of 2001, Pub. L.
     No. 107-56, 115 Stat. 272.

U.S. Const. amends. I–X, XIV.

U.S. Const. art I, § 8, cl. 3.

U.S. Department of Health and Human Services Rules Governing the Protection of
     Human Subjects, 45 C.F.R. §§ 46.101 to 46.505 (2009).

Violence against Women Act of 1994, Pub. L. No. 103-322, 108 Stat. 1796, 1902–
     1955.

Wis. Stat. Ann. § 940.22 (LexisNexis 2008).

Wyoming Health Care Decisions Act, Wyo. Stat. Ann. § 35-22-406(C) (2008).

Index

About the Author

ANDREW B. ISRAEL received his J.D. from Syracuse University College of Law, where he served as lead articles editor of the *Syracuse Law Review*. He is associate professor of social work at New Mexico Highlands University's School of Social Work and served as associate dean of the university from 2004 to 2010. Before his teaching career, Professor Israel practiced law in New Mexico, mainly in the areas of civil rights, child welfare, and domestic relations. He is a past director of the State Bar of New Mexico's Section on Public Law. He is the author of *Applied Law in the Behavioral Health Professions: A Textbook for Social Workers, Counselors, and Psychologists* (2002). Professor Israel is both a licensed attorney and a social worker, and he is active as a researcher, lecturer, and consultant in the areas of forensic mental health issues and law-based decision making in the mental health professions.